INTERNATIONAL RESEARCH HANDBOOK ON SUCCESSFUL WOMEN ENTREPRENEURS

To Moira, Roy and Bryson

International Research Handbook on Successful Women Entrepreneurs

Edited by

Sandra L. Fielden

Senior Lecturer in Organisational Psychology and Co-Director, Centre for Equality and Diversity at Work, Manchester Business School, University of Manchester, UK

Marilyn J. Davidson

Professor of Work Psychology and Co-Director, Centre for Equality and Diversity at Work, Manchester Business School, University of Manchester, UK

Edward Elgar

Cheltenham, UK • Northampton, MA, USA

Published by
Edward Elgar Publishing Limited
The Lypiatts
15 Lansdown Road
Cheltenham
Glos GL50 2JA
UK

Edward Elgar Publishing, Inc.
William Pratt House
9 Dewey Court
Northampton
Massachusetts 01060
USA

A catalogue record for this book
is available from the British Library

Library of Congress Control Number: 2009942852

Mixed Sources
Product group from well-managed
forests and other controlled sources
www.fsc.org Cert no. SA-COC-1565
© 1996 Forest Stewardship Council

ISBN 978 1 84720 918 4 (cased)

Printed and bound by MPG Books Group, UK

Contents

List of contributors   vi

1   Introduction   1
    Sandra L. Fielden and Marilyn J. Davidson
2   Australia   10
    Glenice Wood
3   Brazil   26
    Andrea E. Smith-Hunter
4   Canada   37
    Karen D. Hughes
5   China   49
    Jonathan M. Scott, Javed Hussain, Richard T. Harrison and Cindy Millman
6   Denmark   60
    Suna Løwe Nielsen, Kim Klyver and Majbritt Rostgaard Evald
7   Fiji   73
    Gurmeet Singh, Raghuvar Dutt Pathak and Rafia Naz
8   India   84
    Tanuja Agarwala
9   Lebanon   98
    Dima Jamali and Yusuf Sidani
10 New Zealand   106
    Marianne Tremaine and Kate Lewis
11 Pakistan   117
    Jawad Syed
12 Portugal   132
    Christina Reis
13 Russia   147
    Anna Shuvalova
14 South Africa   163
    Babita Mathur-Helm
15 Turkey   175
    Mine Karataş-Özkan, Gözde İnal and Mustafa F. Özbilgin
16 United Arab Emirates   189
    Nnamdi O. Madichie
17 United Kingdom   204
    Susan Marlow and Maura McAdam
18 United States of America   216
    Mary C. Mattis and Leslie Levin

Index   231

Contributors

Tanuja Agarwala is Associate Professor in the Department of Human Resource Management and Organizational Behaviour at the Faculty of Management Studies, University of Delhi, India from where she received her PhD. She has Postgraduate and Master of Philosophy degrees in Psychology with specialization in Organizational Behaviour from the University of Delhi. With over 20 years of teaching and research experience, she has received national and international awards for her research, notably the ASTD (American Society for Training and Development) Research-to-Practice Citation in 2004. Her research interests focus on organizational commitment, human resource innovations, career management, work–life integration, performance and reward management, gender issues, corporate social responsibility, HR across cultures and in organizational transformations. She has authored one book and has published several book chapters, journal articles and conference papers in journals such as the *International Journal of Human Resource Management, Career Development International, Indian Journal of Industrial Relations, Indian Journal of Training and Development*, among others. She is currently on the Editorial Advisory Board of *Equal Opportunities International*, and on the Editorial Review Board of *Gender in Management*. She is also an Associate Member, Centre for Equality and Diversity at Work (Manchester Business School), and DECERe (Diversity and Equality in Careers and Employment Research – Norwich Business School, University of East Anglia). She is a life member of National HRD Network and Indian Society for Training and Development. She is also presently the International Students Advisor of the University of Delhi.

Marilyn J. Davidson is Professor of Work Psychology and Co-Director of the Centre for Equality and Diversity at Work in the Manchester Business School at the University of Manchester, UK. Her research and teaching interests are in the fields of occupational stress, the management of diversity, equal opportunities, women in management and female entrepreneurs. She has published over 150 academic articles and 20 books, including: *Shattering The Glass Ceiling – The Woman Manager* (with C.L. Cooper); *Women in Management – Current Research Issues* (Vol. and Vol. 2) (both edited with R. Burke); *The Black and Ethnic Minority Woman Manager – Shattering the Concrete Ceiling* (shortlisted for the Best Management Book of the Year); *Individual Diversity and Psychology in Organizations* and *The International Handbook of Women and Small Business Entrepreneurship* (both edited with Sandra L. Fielden). She is a Fellow of the British Psychological Society (BPS); a Chartered Occupational Psychologist; and a member of the Division of Psychology Woman's Section (BPS). She has acted as a consultant and advisor for numerous public, private and government bodies including The Council of Europe and the Equality and Human Rights Commission. Recently she was awarded the 2008 British Psychological Society Award for Promoting Equality of Opportunity.

Majbritt Rostgaard Evald received her PhD in 2005. Since 2006, she has been Assistant Professor at the Department of Entrepreneurship and Relationship Management,

University of Southern Denmark. Her research is mainly focused on corporate entrepreneurship with particular interest in entrepreneurs' networks, private incubator systems and spin-offs. She has written more than 50 publications and has published some peer-reviewed articles in journals such as the *Journal of Enterprising Culture* and *International Entrepreneurship and Management Journal*. Moreover, she has written several peer-reviewed articles for Nordic and Danish journals such as *Nordiske Organisasjonsstudier* and *Danish Journal on Management and Business Administration* and won an award for one of these articles. Furthermore, she has written and co-edited several books. Currently, she is co-editing a textbook about entrepreneurship, corporate entrepreneurship and social entrepreneurship in a Danish and English version.

Sandra L. Fielden is a Senior Lecturer in Organisational Psychology in the Manchester Business School, University of Manchester. She is Co-Director of the Centre for Equality and Diversity at Work and her research interests are diversity, female small business owners, ethnic small business owners, entrepreneurial coaching, women in management, coaching and mentoring, the psychological contract and sexual harassment. Sandra is a Chartered Occupational Psychologist and Editor of the Emerald journal *Gender in Management: An International Journal* for which she was awarded Editor of the Year 2002 and 2004. She is well published with numerous journal papers and book chapters and is Co-Editor of the recently published books (with M.J. Davidson) *Individual Diversity and Psychology in Organizations* and *International Handbook of Women and Small Business Entrepreneurship*.

Professor Richard T. Harrison is Director of Queen's University Management School, Belfast, UK, and has worked previously at the Universities of Edinburgh, Aberdeen and Ulster. He has almost 30 years' academic and applied research experience in entrepreneurship, business development, regional economic policy and company strategy development and implementation. This research experience has been gained in academic environments in the UK, with international research experience in the EU, Pacific Rim (particularly China and Malaysia) and North America (particularly Canada). His research experience has included projects on regional economic development policies, entrepreneurship and business development, university spin-outs and commercialization strategies, early-stage venture capital and business angel markets, financing innovation, developing commercialization strategies for major university research institutes, attracting and retaining talent in regional economies, gender and finance, and the development of technology clusters. He is a leading authority internationally on business angel finance and early-stage venture capital, and has worked with the Department of Trade and Industry/Small Business Service, HM Treasury, British Business Angels Association, Scottish Enterprise, European Business Angel Network, LINC Scotland and agencies in Sweden, Finland, EU, OECD and Canada (inter alia) on research and policy in the early-stage capital market. He is a member of the Conference and Editorial Board, e-Business Research Centre Annual Research Forum: Frontiers of e-Business Research, Tampere University of Technology/University of Tampere/University of Jyväskylä; Member, NORFACE Research Group on Venture Capital in Europe; Member, International Advisory Board, Centre for Innovation, Research and Competence in the Learning Economy (CIRCLE), University of Lund.

Karen D. Hughes is a Professor at the University of Alberta in the Department of Strategic Management and Organization (School of Business) and the Department of Sociology (Faculty of Arts). She holds a PhD from the University of Cambridge. Her research and teaching addresses women's changing economic and family roles, with a special interest in women's entrepreneurship and employment. She has published extensively on issues of gender, organizations and economic change, and is the author of *Female Enterprise in the New Economy* (University of Toronto Press).

Dr Javed Hussain is a Reader in Finance and leads the Finance Research Group at Birmingham City University (Birmingham City Business School), UK. He has a PhD and M. Soc. Sci in Money, Banking and Finance from the University of Birmingham, a first degree in Economics, BA (Hons) and a Postgraduate Diploma in Education. He has held posts in finance in public and private sector organizations and provides consultancy services to businesses. Before joining the staff at Birmingham City University, Dr Hussain was a financial analyst with the Forward Trust Group (a subsidiary of HSBC bank) and prior to that he has worked for Birmingham City Council. He has collaborated on a number of research projects funded by public sector clients. He has published extensively on issues of bank finance for SMEs with a particular focus on ethnic firms and has co-authored papers in a number of journals.

Gözde İnal is a lecturer in the Department of Business at Cyprus International University (North Cyprus). She completed her PhD degree at Queen Mary University of London. Her research project involved a comparative study on the reasons for and means of setting up Turkish Cypriot restaurants and law offices in North Cyprus and Britain. Her research interests include mainstream and minority ethnic small business ownership.

Dima Jamali (PhD) is an Associate Professor in the Suliman S. Olayan School of Business, American University of Beirut (AUB). She holds a PhD in Social Policy and Administration, from the University of Kent at Canterbury, UK. Her research revolves primarily around corporate social responsibility (CSR), and gender, diversity and careers. She is the author of over 30 articles in international peer-reviewed journals, focusing on different aspects of CSR and gender issues in developing countries, including *Corporate Governance: An International Review*, *Journal of Business Ethics*, *Business Process Management Journal* and *Gender in Management: An International Journal*. She worked as an expert consultant for the United Nations on Social Policy and CSR as well as various projects funded by the World Bank, the US Agency for International Development, NGOs and other local public and private firms.

Mine Karataş-Özkan is a Lecturer in Entrepreneurship at the School of Management, University of Southampton (UK). Her research interests include nascent entrepreneurship from a learning perspective, social and science entrepreneurship, and diversity aspects of entrepreneurship and knowledge work, and gender studies. She has published a number of research papers and reports in these areas. She has co-authored a book with Elizabeth Chell entitled *Nascent Entrepreneurship and Learning* (2010, Edward Elgar). She completed a PhD in Entrepreneurship at the University of Southampton in 2006. She has previously worked at the University of Derby (UK) as a researcher.

Kim Klyver received his PhD in 2005. Since then, he has worked as a Postdoctoral Research Fellow at the Australian Graduate School of Entrepreneurship at Swinburne

University of Technology and as an Assistant Professor at the University of Southern Denmark. Since the beginning of 2009, he has been working as a Postdoctoral Research Fellow at Stanford University after been awarding the Scancor Postdoctoral Fellowship Award 2009. Kim has been member of the Global Entrepreneurship Monitor (GEM) project since 2000, and has been part of both the Australian national team and the Danish national team. He has more than 80 publications and has published several peer-reviewed articles in journals such as *International Entrepreneurship and Management Journal, International Journal of Entrepreneurial Behaviour & Research, International Journal of Entrepreneurship and Small Business* and *Journal of Small Business and Enterprise Development*. Currently, he is co-editing a handbook on new venture creation research for Edward Elgar. He has won several awards for his research. Kim's main research interests are women's entrepreneurship, entrepreneurial networks, nascent entrepreneurship, entrepreneurship policy and advisory for entrepreneurs.

Leslie Levin, PhD, is Associate Professor in the Division of Accounting and Business Management at Marymount Manhattan College. Currently she heads the Marketing Department and teaches marketing, advertising and consumer behavior as well as teaching part-time at Columbia University. She has authored several articles on management women in Fortune 500 companies and diversity in corporate America. She is the author of *Metaphors of Conversion in 17th-century Spanish Drama* (Tamesis, 1999). Her current research focuses on religious imagery in US advertising. Prior to teaching, she worked for more than 20 years in marketing and communications at the former Bristol-Myers, Lever Brothers, Burson-Marsteller Public Relations and Catalyst.

Kate Lewis, PhD, is a Senior Lecturer in the School of Management and a Research Associate of the New Zealand Centre for Small and Medium Enterprise Research – both at the Wellington campus of Massey University. She teaches papers in the Enterprise Development programme at both undergraduate and postgraduate level. Her research is focused on entrepreneurship and small firms, and she has a particular interest in youth entrepreneurship. She has also done research in the areas of ecopreneurship, business assistance, women and self-employment, enterprise education, and human resource practices and small firms.

Nnamdi O. Madichie, PhD, is Professor of Marketing at the College of Business Administration, University of Sharjah, UAE. Prior to this he was Senior Lecturer at the Business School, University of East London (UK). His research interests are in the fields of consumer behaviour, small business and entrepreneurship (corporate, ethnic, social and women) especially in the context of emerging markets – areas in which he is well published. Notable amongst these include papers in the *Journal of African Business* and the *International Journal of Entrepreneurship and Small Business*. He has also recently presented a paper entitled 'Women's entrepreneurship in the UAE: in search of a theoretical framework' at the recently concluded Academy of Marketing Conference at Leeds Metropolitan University, UK. He is currently working on the above theme with SEED grant funding from the University of Sharjah. In addition to being on the editorial boards of leading business and management journals such as *Management Decision*, Dr Madichie is also recipient of the Emerald Highly Commended Paper Award 2009 for a paper on entrepreneurship in the *Journal of Enterprising Communities: People and Places in the Global Economy*.

Susan Marlow is Professor of Entrepreneurship within the Department of HRM at De Montfort University, Leicester. She has researched and published in the fields of managing labour in small firms and the influence of gender upon entrepreneurship; has been invited to the United States on a number of occasions as Visiting Professor; has been a key contributor to European Union initiatives on gender and entrepreneurship and is a regular commentator for the BBC on gender issues. Susan Marlow is Vice-President of Research for the Institute for Small Business and Entrepreneurship (ISBE), programme manager of ISBE's RAKE fund initiative, track leader of the gender track for the annual ISBE conference; a member of the Association of Certified Chartered Accountants Small Business Committee and Consulting Editor for the *International Small Business Journal*.

Babita Mathur-Helm is a Senior Lecturer at the University of Stellenbosch Business School (USB), University of Stellenbosch, Cape Town, South Africa. She is the recipient holder of the position in Transformation at the USB sponsored by diversified mining company Kumba Resources. Her area of specialization is Leadership, Gender Studies, Organizational Change and Development; Diversity Management and Broad-based Black Economic Empowerment (BBBEE). Babita has researched and taught on the USB's MBA programme in the field of Leadership, Organizational Change and Development, Gender Empowerment and Personal Leadership Development courses. Her current focus of research is on 'women and leadership roles, exploring various models and implementation of black empowerment within Southern Africa, transformation of South African organizations and ways forward for South African leadership, and managing diversity in South African organizations'. She has developed and facilitated the following training programmes: Women in Leadership and Management; Transformational Leadership; Organizational Change and Renewal and Gender Sensitivity for the Private and Public Sector Organizations, National, Provincial and Local Government Departments in the Southern African Region.

Mary C. Mattis, PhD, is Director of Evaluation and Research at the New York City Department of Education's Research and Policy Support Group where she chairs the Institutional Review Board and responds to external and internal requests involving research and evaluation in NYC schools. She has authored numerous publications on the status of women in business and the professions, best practices for advancing women in management, women on corporate boards and women entrepreneurs. During her 14 years at Catalyst, she provided leadership for research and advisory services in Fortune 500 companies. Prior to joining the NYC Department of Education, she was the Senior Officer for Evaluation and Research at the Wallace Foundation.

Dr Maura McAdam is a Lecturer in Management at Queen's University Belfast. Her research explores three complementary themes: female entrepreneurship, high-technology-based enterprises and support mechanisms such as incubators and science parks. In particular, she is interested in the intersection of these domains, namely the growth patterns of female-owned high-technology firms and the role of incubators in supporting growth. She has published in *R&D Management, International Journal of Entrepreneurial Behaviour and Research, International Journal of Small Business*, and *Journal of Technology Analysis & Strategic Management*. She has a broad practical foundation from her work in industry prior to entering academia.

Cindy Millman (nee Liu) holds an MSc in International Business and Management and is a PhD candidate and Senior Lecturer at Birmingham City Business School. Cindy teaches in the areas of international business, international marketing and management at both undergraduate and postgraduate level. Her research interests lie in three main areas: international entrepreneurship, entrepreneurship education and SME internationalization. Cindy has worked on various funded research projects, for example, the EU-funded large EU Asia Link programme, and the UK national-funded projects in entrepreneurship and innovation, with a specific focus on small and medium-sized enterprises (SMEs). This is also an area in which she has published some journal papers and book chapters. Prior to her academic career, Cindy worked for more than ten years in industry and commerce in international trade in China.

Rafia Naz is a faculty tutor, School of Management & Public Administration, The University of the South Pacific, Suva, Fiji. She was awarded her Master of Arts in Management from The University of the South Pacific in 2007 and is currently working on her Doctoral thesis.

Suna Løwe Nielsen holds an MSc in International Business Economics, a PhD in Knowledge-intensive Student Entrepreneurship from Aalborg University (Denmark), and is currently Assistant Professor at the Department of Entrepreneurship and Relationship Management, University of Southern Denmark. In 2001, she won The Tuborg Fund award for her research, and she worked as a research fellow at The Arthur M. Spiro Center for Entrepreneurial Leadership, Clemson University (US) along with conducting her PhD thesis. She has published several articles, and she is a member of the Global Entrepreneurship Monitor (GEM) project. At present, she is co-editing a Danish teaching book in entrepreneurship. Her main research area is the entrepreneurial process, and she has special expertise in studying this process from the point of view of women, students and creative designers.

Mustafa F. Özbilgin is Professor of Human Resource Management at the Norwich Business School and the Co-Director of DECERe, (Diversity and Equality in Careers and Employment Research), a multidisciplinary centre for research at the University of East Anglia, UK. Having obtained a PhD in Sex Equality in the Financial Services Sector in Britain and Turkey from the University of Bristol in 1998, he has previously worked at the University of Hertfordshire and University of Surrey and Queen Mary, University of London as a lecturer/senior lecturer, and at CEPS-INSTEAD (Differdange, Luxembourg), Cornell University, School of Industrial and Labor Relations (New York), Japan Institute of Labour Policy and Training (Tokyo) and St Gallen University (Switzerland) as a Visiting Fellow.

Raghuvar Dutt Pathak is Professor in Management and Acting Head, Graduate School of Business, Faculty of Business and Economics, The University of the South Pacific, Suva, Fiji Islands. Dr Pathak has taught in various universities for 30 years and also worked as a Commonwealth Academic Staff Fellow at the Manchester Business School in the UK and as Visiting Fellow in the Department of Management, The University of Melbourne, Australia during the last three years. He has published three books and many papers in refereed international journals. He was awarded a PhD in 1982 from Himachal Pradesh University, Shimla, India.

Christina Reis is currently Assistant Professor at the University of New Haven, in the United States. She has collaborated and has taught at different institutions, namely University of Innsbruck in Austria, Swedish School of Economics in Finland, University Nova-Lisbon in Portugal, among others. Her present research focuses on gender in management and careers of expatriates. She earned her PhD in 2002 from the University of London and in 2005 was anonymously elected among the best reviewers from the careers division of the American Academy of Management.

Dr Jonathan M. Scott is a Senior Lecturer at Teesside University Business School and was a Visiting Research Fellow at TSE Entre, Turku School of Economics, Finland in summer 2009 and again in 2010. He has collaborated on over 20 research projects funded by public sector clients. His research interests are in SME finance, strategy, policy and entrepreneurial learning. He has co-authored papers in journals such as *International Small Business Journal* and *Environment and Planning C*, and he is a member of the editorial review board of *Gender in Management: An International Journal*.

Anna Shuvalova was born in Moscow in 1981. She studied economics at the Moscow Lomonosov State University (MGU), earning a Bachelors (2002) and then a Masters degree in economics (2004). She also matriculated from the Franco-Russian Magistratura of International Management – a joint programme of Moscow Lomonosov State University and the Chamber of Commerce of Paris – receiving her MBA degree in 2005. Having completed her studies in Moscow, Anna applied for a PhD fellowship at Buckinghamshire New University and was accepted for the three-year course with a bursary. The topic of her thesis was Russian women entrepreneurs. This comprised qualitative research based on 30 in-depth interviews with women who founded their own businesses in the Moscow metropolitan area between 1989 and 2004. During her study Anna participated in several international conferences (Entrepreneurship Colloquium at the International School of Commerce in Paris, British Academy of Management Conference, International Small Business and Entrepreneurship Conference), where she presented the papers on Russian women entrepreneurs, entrepreneurial intuition and sense-making approach in entrepreneurship research. In September 2009, she completed her thesis and was awarded a PhD degree. At the present time, Anna is preparing a course of lectures on the Theory and Practice of Entrepreneurship.

Yusuf Sidani (PhD) is a faculty member at the Suliman S. Olayan School of Business, American University of Beirut (AUB) where he chairs the management, marketing and entrepreneurship track. His main teaching areas include organizational behaviour and business ethics, and he also taught graduate courses in gender and diversity in the Middle East. His research interests include gender issues, entrepreneurship and entrepreneurial behaviour, business ethics and ethics education, corporate social responsibility and cross-cultural management behaviour. His publications have appeared in *Journal of Business Ethics*, *Gender in Management: An International Journal*, *Business and Society Review*, and *The Journal of Social Psychology*.

Gurmeet Singh is Associate Professor in Marketing and International Business and Associate Dean (Research and Graduate Affairs), Faculty of Business and Economics, The University of the South Pacific, Suva, Fiji. He was previously working as Assistant Professor in the Department of Management, Addis Ababa University, Ethiopia. Dr

Singh has taught in various universities for more than 15 years. He has published a number of papers in refereed international journals. He was awarded a PhD in commerce and management from the University of Jammu, India in 1995.

Andrea E. Smith-Hunter is a Professor at Siena College in Loudonville, New York. She holds a PhD in Organizational Studies from the University at Albany – State University of New York. Her research interests include entrepreneurship across racial, ethnic, gender and economic lines. Dr Smith-Hunter has published journal articles in the *Journal of Business and Entrepreneurship*, the *Journal of International Business and Entrepreneurship, Women in Management Review* and the *Journal of Business and Economic Research*, among others. Her first book, *Diversity and Entrepreneurship: Analyzing Successful Women Entrepreneurs*, was published in 2003 and her second book, *Women Entrepreneurship Across Racial Lines: Issues of Human Capital, Financial Capital and Network Structures* was published in 2006. Her third book, *Women Entrepreneurs in the Global Marketplace* is scheduled for publication in December 2010. She is the current holder of the Hickey Chair at her college, an endowed faculty position.

Jawad Syed is a lecturer in industrial relations and human resource management at Kent Business School, University of Kent, UK. His research interests include gender and diversity in organizations, emotional labour, organizational learning and international human resource management. His articles on these topics have appeared in scholarly journals such as *International Journal of Human Resource Management, Gender, Work and Organization, Asia Pacific Journal of Management, Equal Opportunities International* and *Human Resource Management Review*. In the gender and diversity stream, Jawad's research interests relate to developing diversity management models in less developed and emerging societies.

Marianne Tremaine is a senior lecturer in Massey University's Department of Communication, Journalism and Marketing (Palmerston North, New Zealand) teaching papers on organizational communication, gender and communication and cross-cultural communication. Her own university study has been in English and Philosophy, Local Government and Education and in Management with a PhD on women mayors titled, 'Her Worship the Mayor: women's leadership in New Zealand local government'. She was a founding member of the executive of the NZ Centre for Women and Leadership at Massey University, which has the mission of advancing women as leaders and is now a co-director of the Centre. Her current research is on women's leadership of government departments and shared leadership at CEO level.

Glenice Wood is an Associate Professor and the Deputy Head of the School of Business, Learning and Teaching portfolio at the University of Ballarat. Her background is in psychology, and she received undergraduate and Masters degrees from LaTrobe University, Australia. She worked in the area of psychology and management consultancy for ten years prior to joining the University of Ballarat, Australia where her main teaching responsibilities have been in the delivery of management units. She completed her PhD at Monash University, Australia in the area of Women in Management, particularly focussing on alternative explanations for the glass ceiling (i.e., the so-called barrier that keeps women from entering senior management positions in greater numbers). She has published widely in this field, and has written a book on the results of a ten-year follow-up of a portion of the sample in the PhD study. Her current research interests include writing a book (with M.J. Davidson and S.L. Fielden) entitled *Minorities in Entrepreneurship: An International Review*. She is also actively involved in the supervision of graduate students across a range of human resources and organizational behaviour topics, an activity she enjoys immensely.

1 Introduction

Sandra L. Fielden and Marilyn J. Davidson

This book is the second in a series dedicated to the exploration of women's global small business ownership. The first book in the series, *International Handbook of Women and Small Business Entrepreneurship* (Fielden and Davidson, 2005, Edward Elgar) focused on the personal, situational and contextual factors surrounding women's small business ownership around the world. This second book builds on that knowledge and, rather than being a retrospective account of the area, it takes a more positive forward-thinking approach. It also explores many of the countries that were not included in the first book, specifically those from emerging markets. Markets and economies are classified based on their gross domestic product (GDP) per capita (i.e., GDP divided by the level of population) and are referred to in terms of either level of market development (Financial Times Stock Exchange, 2009) or economy income level (World Bank, 2009). The term 'developed markets' refers to countries that are thought to be the most developed and therefore less risky in terms of investment. These are also referred to as upper-income economies (i.e., an annual income of more than US$11 906 per capita). The term 'emerging markets' is commonly used to describe business and market activity in industrializing or emerging regions of the world and signifies a business phenomenon that is not fully described by or constrained to geography or economic strength. These are classified as middle-income economies (differentiated by upper- and lower-middle-income economies, i.e., an annual income of US$3856–11 905 and US$976–3855 per capita respectively). Finally, the term 'developing markets' is generally used to describe nations with a low level of material well-being, which are classified as low-income economies (i.e., an annual income of less than US$975 per capita). This book covers a range of countries from developed and emerging markets and their income classifications are detailed in Table 1.1.

On a regional level, industrialized countries had the highest enterprise entry rates between 2003–05 (Klapper et al., 2007), although they recommend that when considering entry rates, total business density should be taken into account. Total business density is calculated as the number of registered businesses as a percentage of the active population (aged 15–64) and the differences among regions are pronounced. For example, business density ranges from 23 per 1000 in Australia to less than 1 per 1000 in many low-income African countries. The highest density is found in the developed world with an average of 64 businesses for every 1000 active individuals, whereas all the other regions have a density lower than 40 businesses for every 1000 active individuals.

BACKGROUND

The number of women entering small business ownership has increased significantly across the world and these women make a crucial contribution to the economic growth and development of local, national and global economies, especially in middle-income

Table 1.1   Economic classification of countries

Chapter	Country	Region	Market	Income
2	Australia	Australasia	Developed	High
4	Canada	North America	Developed	High
6	Denmark	Europe	Developed	High
10	New Zealand	Australasia	Developed	High
12	Portugal	Europe	Developed	High
16	United Arab Emirates	Middle East	Emerging	Upper-middle
17	United Kingdom	Europe	Developed	High
18	United States	North America	Developed	High
3	Brazil	South America	Emerging	Upper-middle
7	Fiji	East Asia	Emerging	Upper-middle
9	Lebanon	Middle East	Emerging	Upper-middle
13	Russian Federation	Central Asia	Emerging	Upper-middle
14	South Africa	Africa	Emerging	Upper-middle
15	Turkey	Eurasia	Emerging	Upper-middle
5	China	East Asia	Emerging	Lower-middle
8	India	South Asia	Emerging	Lower-middle
11	Pakistan	South Asia	Emerging	Lower-middle

economies (Allen et al., 2008). Indeed, the global recession appears to be accounting for the growth of a new generation of women entrepreneurs in many countries. For example, a recent 2009 report by the Future Laboratory for Avon emphasized that the number of self-employed women in Britain has risen by 17 per cent to more than 1 million since 2000, and predicts that this number could double over the next decade. Furthermore, the report suggests that job redundancies (especially those affecting male partners) have particularly spurred women into self-employment, with the Internet enabling women to set up micro-enterprises working from home (Groom, 2009). Even so, women are still only half as likely to be involved in entrepreneurial activity as their male counterparts (Allen et al., 2008) but the picture varies greatly between countries. For example, as can be seen from Table 1.2 (which shows the most recent statistics on the prevalence rates of women's business ownership for the countries covered in this book), women business owners range from 0.39 per cent of the working population in the United Arab Emirates to 21.77 per cent in New Zealand. Taking account of the complexities surrounding the international comparison of women-owned businesses (Crompton and Lyonette, 2006), the GEM (2009) report found that women are less likely than men to be expecting to start a business, know an entrepreneur, see good business opportunities, or think that they have the necessary skills to start a business. Barriers to female entrepreneurship are wide-ranging and cover the whole spectrum of business development, from pre-start-up to maturity. These barriers have all too often been the focus of previous work in this area, with the emphasis on inhibition rather than on progress (e.g., Mitchell and Weller, 2001; Chell, 2002; Prowess, 2004).

Despite the increasing numbers of women business owners around the globe, as an international community they have received little attention from the academic commu-

Table 1.2 *Prevalence rates of business ownership across countries by gender*

Chapter	Country	Women (%)	Men (%)	Difference (%)
2	Australia*	14.65	23.70	−9.05
4	Canada*	10.65	23.93	−3.89
6	Denmark***	8.00	14.75	−6.75
10	New Zealand*	21.77	25.96	−4.19
12	Portugal***	10.36	21.49	−11.13
16	United Arab Emirates**	0.39	8.06	−7.67
17	United Kingdom***	6.15	15.00	−8.85
18	United States***	10.73	18.45	−7.72
3	Brazil***	19.95	25.43	−5.48
7	Fiji[a]	3.10	4.00	−0.90
9	Lebanon[c]	11.60	29.60	−18.00
13	Russian Federation***	3.37	5.41	−2.04
14	South Africa*	5.49	15.54	−10.05
15	Turkey ***	3.73	18.12	−14.39
5	China***	20.47	28.93	−8.46
8	India***	9.66	18.21	−8.22
11	Pakistan[b]	0.68	27.82	−27.14

Sources: *Minniti et al. (2006 [GEM 2005]), **Preiss and McCrohan (2007 [GEM UAE 2006]), ***Allen et al. (2008 [GEM 2007]), a. FIBS (2009), b. FBS (2005), c. ESCWA (2004).

nity and research into the experiences of small business owners is confined to a relatively small number of established markets. The motivations for any individual to enter into business ownership are varied (Walker and Brown, 2004) and this issue, along with the subsequent barriers encountered by women in their pursuit of business ownership, is explored at length in the first book in this series, *International Handbook of Women and Small Business Entrepreneurship*. Yet, despite the barriers faced by women entering and operating small businesses, their stories are frequently ones of success. Thus, this second book, rather than solely focusing on the disadvantages women business owners encounter from the gender systems in society, is concerned with how they overcome such disadvantages to operate successful businesses.

When looking at women small business owners we need to take account of the different factors influencing women's experiences, such as ethnicity, culture, age, class and educational background (Tillmar, 2007). Yet, while recognizing that women are not a heterogeneous group, research that has focussed on small business ownership among women has noted that their businesses do share similar characteristics. For example, they tend to be concentrated in service sector industries, be part-time and operate from home (Harding, 2005); they attract lower levels of inward investment, have poorer access to business support and have smaller business networks (Fielden et al., 2006). Women's businesses also tend to remain small in terms of employment, sales, profitability and market share (Carter and Marlow, 2007). According to OECD (1999) statistics, women business owners tend to favour less ambitious projects, smaller investments and smaller loans. In France 6 per cent of women entrepreneurs consider hiring employees against

11 per cent of men and three years after starting a business the majority of micro-firms still did not have employees. Nevertheless, in France the average activity of firms with no employees after three years is 49 per cent, although for women the average is much higher at 71 per cent. This situation has meant that, as measures of small business performance are still heavily reliant on financial gender-neutral models, women's businesses have often been judged as underperforming (Ahl, 2006), and hence unsuccessful.

SUCCESS IN SMALL BUSINESS OWNERSHIP

The focus of this book is on how women, despite the barriers they have encountered, have become successful small business owners. Yet in order to determine whether women have in fact been successful we must consider what success actually is and take account of the contexts in which definitions of business success are applied. The dictionary definition of success (noun) is 'the accomplishment of an aim or purpose' (*Concise Oxford English Dictionary*, 2008). Yet, measurements of 'success' in business terms are often far more orientated around financial achievements than any other goals that the business owner may have had for entering into business ownership. This is illustrated by a definition given by Gadenne (1998), which suggests that success is 'arrived at by comparing profits generated from business with the amount of assets invested in the business (i.e., return on investment) . . . it is argued that this measure most accurately reflects the efficiency (or effectiveness) with which resources have been allocated'. It is believed that the performance by small firms is influenced by a range of factors including: entrepreneurial activity, task motivation, control of environmental influences and behavioural and cognitive strategies (Keats and Bracker, 1988). Interestingly in Gadenne's inter-industry comparison, it is only in the service sector where 'employee relations' are considered as a factor related to small business success.

It has been argued that it is inappropriate to judge the performance of women-owned small businesses on the basis of these measures alone. The apparent inability of women to attain the same levels of financial success as men has been termed the 'female underperformance hypothesis' (Watson, 2002). This has contributed to the debate around whether women underperform in comparison to men and brings into question the factors, measures and criteria used to determine small business success. Watson argues that starting capital is the critical factor when measuring performance and, when controlling for extraneous variables such as working hours, a comparison of input and outputs resulted in no performance differences between women and men. Thus, it is the starting point that differs and not the relative business performance. However, this measurement of success is still built around financial criteria and the pursuit of active business growth, and does not take account of the other motivational goals that drive small business ownership.

In contrast to financial measures, non-financial measures of success are often much more difficult to quantify because of their subjective and personal nature. Although 'all business must be financially viable on some level in order to continue' (Marlow and Strange, 1994, p. 180) making a fortune is not always the primary driving factor in business creation, particularly for women. Jennings and Beaver (1997) proposed that the economic benefits of small business ownership were not as significant as the desire for independence, personal involvement, responsibility and quality of life. This was supported further by Fielden et al. (2000) who found that while 88 per cent of women small business owners cited making money as a motivator, 71 per cent stated that job satisfaction, greater independence, creating opportunities, encountering new challenges and pursuing one's own interests were important criteria. These soft measures are often referred to as lifestyle choices and include factors such as job satisfaction, autonomy and the flexibility to balance work and family responsibilities (Parasuraman et al., 1996; Buttner and Moore, 1997). Walker and Brown (2004) also found support for the importance of lifestyle factors in judging business success by individual small business owners, although the specific factors used to make such judgements vary between individuals depending on their personal goals and factors such as age, class, ethnicity, family circumstances and so on (Essars and Benschop, 2007).

Although women are not a homogeneous group, gender does appear to be an important factor in determining how small business ownerships themselves define and perceive success (Walker and Brown, 2004). The way women entrepreneurs perceive their own chances of success in business is often different from the way men perceive their potential as entrepreneurs. US studies by the MS Foundation concluded that women were less confident about their entrepreneurial abilities, less interested in starting a business and also more negatively disposed towards market mechanisms. However, while this has always been assumed to be detrimental to the creation and successful operation of a small business, not all research supports this view. There is evidence to suggest that high levels of optimism and confidence can negatively affect decision-making and judgement, thereby adversely affecting business performance (Aspinwall et al., 2005). Further, highly optimistic business owners learn less from past experiences and take more risks; this means that although they tend to be more financially successful, they are also more susceptible to failure (Hmieleski and Baron, 2009). In contrast, less optimistic individuals are more realistic and have a better chance of long-term survival, but less opportunity for impressive gains. As women tend to fall into the less optimistic category, they may be expected to make less money but have more sustainable businesses. Therefore, as business failure is the one criterion that is universally deemed to characterize a lack of success, women may indeed be overall more successful than men.

WOMEN'S SUCCESS IN THE GLOBAL CONTEXT

It has been suggested that, in order to fully understand the complexities in measuring performance in small businesses, it is essential to examine variables operating at different levels of analysis (e.g., individual, group, community and societal) (Hitt et al., 2007). Thus, this book is aimed at identifying the success of women small business owners around the globe, taking into account the cultural, religious and legal barriers to women's small business ownership that are inherent in each country, as well as acknowledging that success in economic terms is not valued to the same degree around the world (Walker and Brown, 2004). In recognizing such factors, it provides a platform from which the degree of success achieved by women from different backgrounds can be demonstrated. It presents an up-to-date review of the position of women small business owners in developed (high-income) and emerging (upper- and lower-income) markets across five continents. In doing so it demonstrates that women business owners around the globe face many similar barriers to success, even though the contexts in which they live and work differ.

These contexts are sometimes related to the economic classification of the country (see Table 1.1). For example, there are generally higher numbers of opportunity-driven women business owners in high-income countries (with Denmark ranked highest) and more needs-based women's business ownership in middle-income countries (this is the case for almost all of women business owners in Fiji). However, these trends bear little resemblance to factors that may be expected to underpin women's decision to enter into business ownership, for example, the degree of business support available to women. This is demonstrated in China (low-middle income), where women's entry into business ownership is ranked as one of the highest in the world, yet the level of formal business support that is available to women is extremely limited. In contrast, the United Arab Emirates (high income) has one of the lowest participation rates for women in business ownership, yet it has one of the best funded programmes of formal business support. The relationship between economic classification and rates of women's business ownership is also complicated by the relationship between factors such as socio-cultural traditions that serve to restrict women's progression and legislation that supports women's progression. This can be clearly seen when looking at China (lower-middle income) and Denmark (high income) who have '*Guanxi*' and 'Jante Law' respectively (see Chapters 5 and 6 for full explanations). These social rules may be considered as serious barriers to business ownership, especially in China where the legislation supporting women into business ownership is weak compared with Demark. However, as can be seen from Table 1.2, the level of women's business ownership in China is two-and-a-half times that of Denmark. Thus, it appears that factors such as equality legislation and government support for women's business ownership do not necessarily have a direct relationship with the level of business ownership.

Although a country's economic, political and legislative context does appear to have some impact on the degree to which women participate in business ownership, as previously discussed the greatest influences are more often driven by deeply rooted socio-cultural traditions and values. Patriarchal societies, which dominate in all high-, upper-middle- and lower-middle-income economies, mean that traditional gender roles lead to restricted access to labour markets, feminized occupations, glass ceilings, discrimination and stereotypes – all of which are consistently referred to by authors throughout the book. The degree to which these barriers are experienced does differ between countries, with women in Pakistan and the United Arab Emirates experiencing some of the greatest restrictions. It could be argued that religion is responsible for the situation of women in these countries, yet in countries with fewer religious constraints, such as Russia, the United Kingdom and Denmark, we do not see significantly higher rates of business take up by women. On the contrary, some of the highest rates are seen in highly religious countries, such as Brazil and Portugal, again demonstrating the complexity of women's experiences.

In terms of business ownership there appears to be a great deal of consensus around the barriers that women face around the globe. Poor access to finance, home/work conflict, role overload, lack of business experience, lack of relevant skills and exclusion from men's business networks are consistently cited throughout the book as barriers to participation in business ownership. In addition, poverty (Fiji, Brazil and South Africa in particular), geographical constraints, government corruption (especially Russia), lack of information, the need for flexibility, a lack of support, discrimination by clients and suppliers, a lack of confidence and self-esteem, are also referred to as inhibiting factors. This high degree of similarity between women business owners is in some way surprising given the vastly different context (legal, cultural, religious, economic etc.) within which women operate their businesses. However, what is evident is that these barriers have a psychological impact on the establishment, operation and growth of women-owned businesses. Despite this, women continue to be successful perhaps because for many, women's business ownership is viewed as a survival strategy that provides them with a personal and economic freedom they cannot gain through traditional forms of work.

As well as examining the complexities around the barriers to women's business ownership and providing cases studies of success, the book also provides strategies relating to the further development of women's business ownership. Chapters explore the practical initiatives within their own country that have worldwide transferability, approaching the area from the perspective of how success is achieved rather than simply recommending the removal of barriers. There are a wide range of government and private initiatives outlined in each chapter of the book, although the level of investment in such schemes varies considerably between different countries. For example, countries such as New Zealand (high income), Turkey (upper-middle income), Fiji (upper-middle income), and India (lower-middle income), rank highly in terms of the business support available, whereas Denmark (high income), Lebanon (upper-middle income), Brazil (upper-middle income), and Pakistan (lower-middle income), rank poorly. This book demonstrates that the relationship between support and levels of women's business ownership is not a linear one, highlighting that there is no simple formula for the promotion and development of women's business ownership. Therefore, each chapter provides a balance between theory and practice: as Essars and Benschop (2007) point out, there is value in studying the 'lived practices' of gender and entrepreneurship. In order to make this information as accessible as possible each chapter follows the same format and presents two cases studies of successful women business owners. Furthermore, in line with Nicolson's (1996) belief that women should be given space to 'voice' their contextual experiences, taking account of all of the variables involved, 'success' is defined within the context of each environment within which women operate.

REFERENCES

Ahl, H. (2006) 'Why research on women entrepreneurs needs new directions?'. *Entrepreneurship Theory and Practice* **30**(5), 595–622.

Allen, I.E., Elam, A., Langowitz, N. and Dean, M. (2008) *Global Entrepreneurship Monitor 2007 – Report on Women and Entrepreneurship*. Global Entrepreneurship Research Association, available at: http://www.gemconsortium.org/about.aspx?page=special_topic_women; accessed 2 February 2010.

Aspinwall, L.G., Sechrist, G.B. and Jones, P.R. (2005) 'Expect the best and prepare for the worst: anticipatory coping and preparations for Y2K'. *Motivation and Emotions* **29**(4), 357–88.

Bosma, N. and Levie, J. (2009) *Global Entrepreneurship Monitor (GEM) 2009 Global Report*. Global Entrepreneurship Research Association, available at: http://www3.babson.edu/ESHIP/research-publications/upload/GEM_2009_Global_Report.pdf; accessed 13 February 2010.

Buttner, E.H. and Moore, D.P. (1997) *Women Entrepreneurs: Moving beyond the Glass Ceiling*. Thousand Oaks, CA: Sage Publications Inc.

Carter, S. and Marlow, S. (2007) 'Female entrepreneurship: theoretical perspectives and empirical evidence'. In N. Carter, C. Henry, B. O'Cinneide and K. Johnson (eds) *Female Entrepreneurship: Implications for Education, Training and Policy*. London: Routledge, pp. 11–37.

Chell, E. (2002) 'Women in science enterprise: an exploration of the issues, some policy implications and research agenda'. Paper presented at the Gender Research Forum, 8 November, Women and Equality Unit, London.

Concise Oxford English Dictionary (2008). Oxford: Oxford University Press.

Crompton, R. and Lyonette, C. (2006) 'Some issues in cross-national comparative research methods: a comparison of attitudes to promotion and women's employment in Britain and Portugal'. *Work, Employment and Society* **20**(22), 403–14.

Economic and Social Commission for Western Asia (ESCWA) (2004) *Where do Arab Women Stand in the Development Process: A Gender-based Statistical Analysis.* New York: United Nations.

Essars, C. and Benschop, Y. (2007) 'Muslim business women doing boundary work: the negotiation of Islam, gender and ethnicity within entrepreneurial contexts'. *Human Relations* **62**(3), 403–23.

Federal Bureau of Statistics (FBS) (2005) *Economic Census of Pakistan*, available at: http://www.statpak.gov.pk/depts/fbs/publications/ec_2005/ec_2005.html; accessed 2 February 2010.

Fielden, S.L. and Davidson, M.J. (eds) (2005) *International Handbook of Women and Small Business Entrepreneurship*. Cheltenham, UK and Northampton, MA, USA: Edward Elgar.

Fielden, S.L., Davidson, M.J. and Makin, P.J. (2000) 'Barriers encountered during micro and small business start-up in North-West England'. *Journal of Small Business and Enterprise Development* **7**(4), 295–304.

Fielden, S.L., Dawe, A.J. and Woolnough, H.M. (2006) 'Government small business finance initiatives: social inclusion or discrimination'. *Equal Opportunities International* **25**(1), 25–37.

Fiji Island Bureau of Statistics (FIBS) (2009) *2007 Census of Population and Housing*, available at: http://www.statsfiji.gov.fj/Census2007/Release%202%20-%20Labour%20Force.pdf; accessed 2 February 2010.

Financial Times Stock Exchange (2009) available at: http://www.ftse.com/; accessed 5 February 2010.

Gadenne, D. (1998) 'Critical success factors for small business: an inter-industry comparison'. *International Small Business Journal* **17**(1), 36–56.

Groom, B. (2009) 'Recession spurs rise of "lipstick entrepreneurs"'. *The Financial Times*, 3 November.

Harding, R. (2005) *Global Entrepreneurship Monitor (GEM) 2004: UK Report*. London Business School/Babson College, available at: http://www.gemconsortium.org/files.aspx?Ca_ID=107; accessed 2 February 2010.

Hitt, M.A, Beamish, P.W., Jackson, S.E. and Mathieu, J.E. (2007) 'Building theoretical and empirical bridges across all levels: multilevel research in management'. *Academy of Management Journal* **50**(6), 1385–99.

Hmieleski, K.M. and Baron, R.A. (2009) 'Entrepreneurs' optimism and new venture performance: a social cognitive perspective'. *Academy of Management Journal* **52**(3), 473–88.

Jennings, P. and Beaver, G. (1997) 'The performance and competitive advantage of small firms: a management perspective'. *International Small Business Journal* **15**(2), 63–75.

Keats, B.W. and Bracker, J.S. (1988) 'Towards a small firm performance: a conceptual model'. *American Journal of Small Business* **12**(4), 41–58.

Klapper, L., Ami, R., Guillén, M.F. and Quesada, J.M. (2007) 'Entrepreneurship and firm formation across countries'. World Bank Policy Research Working Paper No. 4313.

Marlow, S. and Strange, A. (1994) 'Female entrepreneurs: success by whose standards?'. In M. Tanton (ed.) *Women in Management: A Developing Presence*. London: Routledge, pp. 172–84.

Marlow, S., Henry, C. and Carter, S. (2009) 'Exploring the impact of gender upon women's business ownership'. *International Small Business Journal* **27**(2), 139–48.

Minniti, M., Allen, I.E. and Langowitz, N. (2006) *Global Entrepreneurship Monitor 2005 – Report on Women and Entrepreneurship*. Global Entrepreneurship Research Association, available at: http://www.gemconsortium.org/about.aspx?page=special_topic_women; accessed 2 February 2010.

Mitchell, J. and Weller P. (2001) 'The Small Business Service's research agenda on female entrepreneurship'. London: SBS Research and Evaluation Unit.

Nicolson, P. (1996) *Gender, Power and Organizations: A Psychological Perspective*. London: Routledge.

OECD (1999) *Women Entrepreneurship: Exchanging Experiences between OECD and Transition Economy Countries.* Paris: OECD.

Parasuraman, S.P., Ourohit, Y.S., Godshalk, V.M. and Beutell, N.J. (1996) 'Work and family variables, entrepreneurial career success and psychological well-being'. *Journal of Vocational Behavior* **48**(3), 275–300.

Preiss, K.J. and McCrohan, D. (2007) *Global Entrepreneurship Monitor 2006 – A Study of Entrepreneurship in the United Arab Emirates 2006*. Global Entrepreneurship Research Association, available at: http://www3.babson.edu/ESHIP/upload/GEM_2006_Global_Report.pdf; accessed 2 February 2010.

Prowess (2004) *Bridging the Enterprise Gap*. UK: Phoenix Development Fund/European Social Fund.

Tillmar, M. (2007) 'Gendered small-business assistance: lessons from a Swedish project'. *Journal of European Industrial Training*, **31**(2), 84–99.

Walker, A. and Brown, A. (2004) 'What success factors are important to small business owners?'. *International Small Business Journal* **22**(6), 577–91.

Watson, J. (2002) 'Comparing the performance of male and female controlled businesses: relating to outputs and inputs'. *Entrepreneurship Theory and Practice* **26**(3), 91–100.

World Bank (2009) available at: http://go.worldbank.org/D7SN0B8YU0; accessed 2 February 2010.

2   Australia
Glenice Wood

INTRODUCTION

The early colonization of Australia was characterized by hardship and isolation, together with antagonistic relationships with Aborigines, and between the classes of the early settlement (military authorities, convicts and free settlers). Most women were of convict origins and were dependent and marginalized in society. These early beginnings exerted a strong impact on people to be individualistic, to hold firm beliefs in relation to survival and to believe in themselves. It also bred a deep desire to be independent, and a dislike of class and authority figures. The early history of the nation would have forged a resourceful character in both women and men to survive both economically and physically, and to be strongly independent.

Contemporary Australia has been categorized as an individualist society, characterized by low power distance (i.e., a low tolerance of power being unequally shared), low uncertainty avoidance (i.e., a low reliance on norms and procedures to deal with unpredictability) and a strong tendency and desire for independence, which may lead to a willingness to take risks (Hofstede and Hofstede, 2005). Such qualities as a positive attitude to risk and a desire for independence are strongly linked to the intention to engage in an entrepreneurial activity (Douglas and Shepherd, 2002). Individual expression is very dominant and highly valued. These characteristics have forged a national identity that influences the way women and men behave, particularly where roles of authority and power are evident, such as in management or leadership positions.

Culture clearly exerts an influence on management roles. An example of this is found in research by Still (2006), who concluded that there is a strong Australian 'macho' culture that underpins the progress of more men than women into important roles in management, and roles of power and authority have traditionally been seen as a male domain in the workforce (Sinclair, 1998). As a consequence, leadership roles have been stereotyped as occupations more suitable for men than women (Still, 2006), with Australian women being perceived as not a 'fit' in senior executive roles in the workplace (Wood, 2006).

This pervasive attitude has been instrumental in the inequitable career advancement of women in management roles. According to Sinclair (1998) negative stereotypes held toward women are capable of expanding into all aspects of senior appointments in powerful positions across organizations in the nation. Therefore, it is likely that women are disadvantaged through systematic discrimination and a double standard widely practised in organizations (Sinclair, 1998; Still, 2004, 2006). This phenomenon appears to be incongruous in a country where social policies and legislations relating to equal employment and affirmative action practices have been in operation for more than 20 years (Wood, 2006). Such pervasive gender-stereotypical attitudes appear to permeate the workplace environment, and are evident in data illustrating the unequal numbers of men and women in the upper echelons of power, in senior or executive roles in government and non-government organizations in Australia (EOWA, 2006).

This chapter explores the impact of those cultural influences on women's participation in the Australian workforce, and the underlying factors that have inhibited or facilitated their move into small business ownership.

THE POSITION OF WOMEN IN EMPLOYMENT

Recent statistics on Australia's workforce participation (that is, the measure of the proportion of economically active individuals within an economy) indicate that over 10 million working-age Australians were engaged in the workforce (defined as the ratio of the employed and unemployed to the working age population, aged 15 years and over) in 2005 (Abhayaratna and Lattimore, 2006). Of this number, 5.8 million (55 per cent) were male and 4.7 million (45 per cent) were female. Australians of prime working age (25–54 years) made up the majority (67 per cent) of the workforce in 2005 (ibid.).

Male participation in the workforce has declined over the last 25 years, while the reverse is true for female participation. For example, between 1980 and 2005, male workplace participation declined from 78.3 per cent to 72.1 per cent, whereas the female participation rate reached 57.0 per cent, an increase of 12.3 percentage points during the same period (ibid.).

One of the major areas of growth has been the participation of females in managerial roles. Currently, 26 per cent of managers are female, compared with 74 per cent of managers who are male. This is a dramatic increase over one decade; in 1998, only 17.5 per cent of managers were females, compared with 82.5 per cent of managers who were male (Australian Bureau of Statistics, 2008).

It is interesting to note that there has also been a growth in the proportion of female professionals, while there has been a decline in the numbers of men in this occupational classification. Currently, 46 per cent of females, and 54 per cent of males are classified as 'professionals'. For women, this is an increase from 42 per cent in 1998; however for men, the figure represents a decline from the 58 per cent reported in 1998 (ibid.).

The growth in female participation in the workforce is mainly attributed to married women, whose participation has increased from approximately 42 per cent in 1980, to almost 60 per cent in 2005. This figure has now overtaken the rate of participation by non-married women in Australia. The largest increase in female participation is reported in the 45–54 age group; an increase of 28 percentage points (Abhayaratna and Lattimore, 2006).

The changes in the rise in female workforce participation in Australia are attributed in part to the following trends:

• increased involvement in education by women;
• increased social acceptance of the need for mothers to work;
• improved access to child care services and part-time work; and
• working arrangements becoming more flexible (ibid., p. 11).

In addition, the increasing economic pressures experienced by families often necessitates that both partners work. Furthermore, the traditional 'dip' in female participation between the ages of 25 and 44 years (in other words during the 'childbearing years') had reduced significantly in 2005. This may relate to the decrease in child birth (1.94 children per family in 1981 to 1.75 births per woman in 2001; Wood and Newton, 2006) and the propensity for some women to put off the birth of children until they are well established in their careers. For example, some women in management are reported to have a perception that motherhood would put an end to current management careers (Liff and Ward, 2001), and that 'childlessness is a precondition of a successful management career' (Wajcman, 1999, p. 143).

Recent Australian data from the Equal Opportunity for Women in the Workplace Agency (EOWA) suggest that women fill a reasonably high proportion (44.2 per cent) of managerial and professional positions, although this figure includes all managerial levels, which tends to create a more positive picture than when figures of senior management and leadership roles are analysed. For example, although 9 per cent of Australian Stock Exchange (ASX200) Board Directors are women, only 3 per cent of CEOs, and 2 per cent of ASX200 chairs are women (EOWA, 2006).

Nearly one-third of the Australian workforce is categorized as part-time workers, with the majority of this group being female (72 per cent). Of the total females in the workforce, 46 per cent are employed on a part-time basis (Abhayaratna and Lattimore, 2006). This figure represents the disproportionate influence of family commitments on the participation of many females in the workforce, and reflects a desire to achieve a balance of paid work and family or caring commitments. Such attempts to balance family and work, and to create a more flexible working environment, have been seen as a motivating factor in the phenomenal rise in women starting small business ventures.

THE CURRENT POSITION OF WOMEN AND SMALL BUSINESS OWNERSHIP

A Question of Definition of Terms

To address the topic of small business ownership in Australia, it is necessary to clarify what this category of enterprise encompasses. Researchers in this area have often drawn on data from a variety of sources including small business enterprises set up as commercial operations, small and medium enterprises (SMEs), home-based businesses and individual entrepreneurial activities. A brief comment on each of these areas will serve to clarify these overlapping categories.

In Australia, SMEs are businesses with less than 20 employees; with micro-businesses being defined as those with less than five employees (Still and Walker, 2006). Large businesses are those with more than 200 employees, and medium-sized enterprises fall in between these parameters (Watson, 2003).

Many small business ventures are located within the home, with home-based businesses (HBBs) being classified as the fastest-growing business sector (Walker, 2003), constituting 67 per cent of all small business enterprises (Australian Bureau of Statistics, 2002). Approximately 250000 Australian women now operate a business from a home base, which is an increase of more than 20 per cent over the past five years. There is a strong motivation and significant advantages for women to operate their businesses in this manner, including being able to meet the demands of family, flexible working hours and some degree of autonomy. The contribution of women in small business is significant as it is estimated to generate an economic benefit to the country in excess of tens of billions of dollars (Frederick et al., 2007).

Some researchers have made a link between small business and entrepreneurial activity. For example, Legge and Hindle (1997) defined entrepreneurship as 'the creative application of change' (p. xii) and recognized the possibility that this definition encompassed the operation of small business enterprises. Other authors in the field of entrepreneurship give emphasis to the importance of recognizing potential opportunities and innovatively addressing a need. For example, Shane and Venkataraman (2000) see entrepreneurs as having the ability to seek out new ways of creating future goods and services, evaluating the risk and exploiting the opportunity. Drucker (1985) underscored the importance of innovation, considering it to be the specific function of entrepreneurship: 'It is the means by which the entrepreneur either creates new wealth-producing resources or endows existing resources with enhanced potential for creating wealth' (p. 20).

In general, entrepreneurs have been traditionally seen as risk-takers who have the ability to recognize opportunities and start their own businesses (Leibenstein, 1968). They are believed to have high levels of commitment, and are motivated by achievement (McClelland, 1961). In addition, they are comfortable with high levels of uncertainty (Deakins, 1996), and exhibit the necessary cognitive characteristics to exploit opportunities when they arise (Shane and Venkataraman, 2000). There is a belief that entrepreneurs focus on profit maximization, being in control of their own lives and taking business opportunities that allow growth through exploiting market opportunities in an innovative way (McKay, 2001).

Previous research has reported that enterprises run by women are not really 'entrepreneurial', but rather come about through necessity, a desire to support themselves, and bring a degree of balance and flexibility to their lives that has not been possible in the corporate world. The 'glass ceiling', which is widely proposed as an explanation for women's lack of career advancement to senior and executive positions of management, is believed to have provided an impetus for women embarking on entrepreneurial business ventures (Still and Walker, 2006). That is, women have sought to find another way of working that they believe will bring them more satisfaction (Still, 1990). Therefore, women have not been seen as true entrepreneurs as they have been viewed as lacking the necessary innovation, ability to sell their ideas and networking capabilities required of the entrepreneur (e.g., Goffee and Scase, 1985; Symons, 1986).

However, recent research (e.g., Collins, 2003; Foley, 2003; Kupferberg, 2003; Bruni et al., 2004; Menzies et al., 2004; Minniti et al., 2005) reports that there has been an unprecedented growth in the entrepreneurial *activity* of women in general, and in minority groups and immigrant and indigenous populations over the past few years. From this spread of research, it can be seen that there is a wide diversity in the groups who are entrepreneurial in their activity. However, much research needs to be done to explore possible gender differences in these areas. For example, the role of women *within minority groups*, women in *immigrant populations* and women in *indigenous populations*, suggests an interesting and important area of future research. Possibly, women within these groups may operate with a double disadvantage. For example, indigenous Australians are reported to be three times less likely to be self-employed when compared with non-indigenous Australians (Australian Bureau of Statistics, 2004b). Certainly, not all groups operate on a level playing field. According to the Global Entrepreneurship Monitor (GEM) there is a gender gap particularly in early-stage entrepreneurship. Despite this, women entrepreneurs operate in all countries and under a wide variety of circumstances (Allen et al., 2007).

Australian Small Business Enterprises

In Australia, small business has been seen as 'the engine room of the Australian economy' and the trend is shifting from businesses set up as firms, to home-based businesses (HBBs). Since 1996, Australia government policies have been introduced with the express purpose of developing the small business sector. In particular, the policies that have been developed have been designed to provide women with the opportunities to participate in this sector. While these initiatives have been beneficial (a third of all small businesses were owned and operated by women in 2004) (Australian Bureau of Statistics, 2004a), the early-stage business participation of females has dropped from 11 per cent in 2003 to just 7.6 per cent in 2005 (Frederick et al., 2007).

In 2005, Australia had a start-up rate of new business ventures (defined as the percentage of adults between 18–64 who were currently engaged in early-stage entrepreneurial activities) of 10.5 per cent, compared with 12.4 per cent in the United States, 2.2 per cent in Japan and 20.7 per cent in Thailand (Minniti et al., 2006). In addition, 9.3 per cent of entrepreneurs in Australia are classified as 'high growth' in comparison to Singapore (20.5 per cent), China (12 per cent) and the United States (11.4 per cent) (Allen et al., 2007). These ventures are defined as businesses that anticipate creating 19 or more jobs within five years of the commencement of the business (Frederick et al., 2007).

There are currently 1 660 000 small business (non-agricultural) operators in Australia; sole operators were found in 73 per cent of small business enterprises (up from 69 per cent in 2003), and 25 per cent of small businesses had two operators (down from 29 per cent). Most small business operators are male (68 per cent) with a third of all small businesses being owned and operated by women (Weaven et al., 2007). By 2002, the growth in businesses owned by women had exceeded the rates of growth in enterprises owned and operated by males (Australian Bureau of Statistics, 2003); however, recent figures indicate a drop of 3 per cent (to 17 per cent) in the number of businesses operated solely by females (Australian Bureau of Statistics, 2004a). The incidence of Australian women sole-owners in franchises is much lower, with only 11 per cent of women choosing this business model (Frazer and Weaven, 2004).

The age of the majority of small business operators (59 per cent) is between 30 and 50 years, with the proportion of operators over 50 years of age falling by 2 percentage points. However, there has been an increase in the proportion of male operators under 30 years of age; in 2003, 65 per cent of operators fell in this category whereas in 2004, the figure was 73 per cent. In contrast, female operators in the same age group decreased by –1.7 per cent (Australian Bureau of Statistics, 2004a).

Small business operators in Australia appear to work longer hours than the average working week with 65 per cent of this group working between 35 and 50 hours, 30 per cent working between 51 and 75 hours, and 5 per cent working in excess of 75 hours per week (ibid.). The majority of the male small business operators (80 per cent) worked full-time, whereas 40 per cent of the female small business operators did likewise. Almost a third of the small business operators in Australia were born overseas, and this figure is rising (ibid.).

In terms of the financial performance of small businesses, a large study into Australian SMEs between 1995 and 1998 concluded that there were no significant differences 'between male and female owner-managed business' (Johnsen and McMahon, 2005, p. 133), nor were significant differences found in the business growth of SMEs owned and managed by men or women. However, businesses controlled solely by females tended to be smaller and exhibited less growth than those headed solely by men. This seeming paradox offers a fruitful area for further research. The authors concluded that women may make a deliberate choice not to grow their business because of a desire to pursue other goals, which may include the interests of their immediate family at a given time (ibid.). Of interest, however, is that while desire for growth has been reported to be stronger amongst male-controlled businesses, ventures owned by women are equally likely to survive (Kalleberg and Leicht, 1991).

A profile of the self-employed female business owner and her business in contemporary Australia has been compiled in recent research by Still and Walker (2006). The benchmark profile is a woman who is well-educated, married with children and is aged 30 years and over. She is an Australian-born/naturalized citizen who works full-time in the business, which is the only one in which she is involved. In addition, the business provides the majority of support for the household. The business is a micro-business or a sole-trader operation that employs few full-time or part-time staff (typically five employees or less). Usually, the business operates in the service sector and the majority of the businesses have been operating for more than one year, confirming earlier UK research findings (e.g., Rosa et al., 1996).

The fastest-growing sector of small business operations are home-based businesses (HBBs) with an annual growth rate of 16 per cent in 2001, compared with 11 per cent for small business generally (Australian Bureau of Statistics, 2002). HBBs make up more than half (58 per cent) of all businesses (ibid.), and therefore make a very valuable contribution to the national economy (Walker, 2003). In terms of size, 69 per cent of HBBs were classified as non-employing businesses, with 28 per cent employing between one and four people, and 3 per cent employing 5 to 19 people (Australian Bureau of Statistics, 2004a). The length of operation of HBBs follows closely the distribution patterns of all small business in this country:

- 17 per cent have been in operation for less than one year.
- 36 per cent have been in operation for one year to less than five years.
- 18 per cent have been in operation for five years to less than ten years.
- 29 per cent have been in operation for ten years or more. (ibid.)

According to the Australian Bureau of Statistics, as at June 2004, almost three-quarters of all HBB operators were male (71 per cent; cf. 29 per cent female). The majority of HBBs (66 per cent) are operated by males predominantly, with 21 per cent being operated solely by females, and the proportion of HBB operators born overseas (30 per cent) was similar to that of small business operators overall. In addition, a high proportion of HBBs (94 per cent) were involved in one business, which is a similar figure to that of all small business (93 per cent) (ibid.).

These statistics suggest that high turnover occurs in HBBs, with over half of the businesses being in operation for less than five years. Further research in this area is required to ascertain the proportions of men and women who start, and sustain, small businesses of this kind. In addition, if businesses fail, is there a gender difference in the likelihood of further ventures? Serial entrepreneurship is reported to be widespread in other countries such as the United Kingdom and Germany (Hyytinen and Ilmakunnas, 2007), however, little information is available in Australia. Another interesting area of research is an examination of gender differences in the likelihood of further ventures *after an initial failure*. It may be that the reason for entry into the entrepreneurial venture may impact on how likely it is for an entrepreneur to become a serial entrepreneur by setting up a new venture.

STRUCTURAL AND CONTEXTUAL BARRIERS

The unequal proportions of male and female small business owners and operators suggest that different barriers may be experienced by men and women. Despite the growth in women's participation in entrepreneurial activities worldwide, it is still much less than the male rate. In Australia, there is an entrepreneurial 'gender gap' (defined as a lower rate of women's entrepreneurship), which illustrates that men are more strongly represented in early-stage entrepreneurial activity, with Australian women only achieving 53.3 per cent of the male entrepreneurship rate. This is lower than the world gender gap, which is estimated to be 60.5 per cent of that of the entrepreneurial activity of men (Frederick et al., 2007).

Although both women and men can experience challenges when setting up their own businesses, research suggests that some of the challenges are unique to women. Such differences in experiences may be influential in the barriers experienced by men and women in small business entrepreneurial activities. According to Frederick et al. (ibid.), the following general factors are barriers to women setting up, or continuing in a successful small business operation:

- Women are more risk-averse than men, and tend to choose a path that is more likely to bring about success, even if this is at a lower rate of return.
- Work–home conflict: 'entrepreneurial women frequently bear the major responsibility for domestic work and, where applicable, child care' (p. 572).
- Child care: there is often a lack of adequate and affordable child care. Difficulties also arise in the care of older children after school hours.
- Many women feel that they are not a part of the power networks that are often dominated by men. As such, 'women entrepreneurs tend to be isolated in marginal economic areas such as micro and informal enterprises' (ibid.).
- Lack of training is also perceived as a problem by women entrepreneurs.
- Cultural prejudice can play a part in holding women back from taking a more dominant role in economic life.

- In terms of finances, female entrepreneurs may obtain bank credit, but few are successful in acquiring venture capital, and those that do, receive a very small proportion of the available funds. In general, men rely on investors, bank loans, personal loans and personal funds to finance a start-up in a small business venture while women rely on personal assets, savings and credit cards.
- Some additional research has suggested that although 'women are contributing to new business development in every sector, their ability to acquire equity capital remains limited, in part, due to the persistence of myths' (Brush et al., 2001, cited by Frederick et al., 2007, p. 573).

In relation to barriers to success in Australian small businesses, Still and Timms (2000) concluded that the following issues were likely to be more inhibiting for women in terms of business expansion, as opposed to men. First, a lack of 'entrepreneurial culture' in Australia was felt to be particularly restricting, which had far-reaching repercussions. This extended to how the business was run, and included a reluctance to obtain the best possible advice regarding business information and training, to hire staff, to delegate responsibility, to take risks, and a desire to remain small in order to operate within a known 'comfort zone' (p. 276).

Second, there was a view that women in general exhibit lower levels of self-confidence, and this impacted directly on their entrepreneurial activities. Women appear to believe that they lacked knowledge about economic matters, which in turn created a more cautious and risk-averse attitude along with lower expectations about their potential within the business. Women's lack of confidence was also believed to be evident in their reticence to take on the role of employer, and in particular to manage staff. In addition, there was a reluctance to deal with issues of an industrial relations nature. Lower confidence in these areas was considered to be caused by lack of information and opportunities for training.

Third, the authors believe there is a skills gap for women in small business, with women exhibiting fewer educational qualifications in business as well as less work experience compared with male small business operators. In particular, women had more difficulties accessing debt and equity finance through the appropriate networks. In the past, financial institutions operated with barely concealed discriminatory attitudes toward women, resulting in a lack of equity. This impacted on access to potential business partners through appropriate business networks exacerbating the isolation of many small business women.

Fourth, women have a propensity to by-pass government assistance training programmes. Barriers in relation to training were believed to include cultural issues, where a male orientation dominated; criteria-based barriers, where prior experience was considered essential; or structure-based barriers, where difficulties were experienced by women when courses were offered at times they were not able to attend.

Other issues were felt to be gender-specific barriers, which impacted directly and uniquely on women in terms of expanding their businesses. First and foremost was the issue of domestic division of labour and the resultant time poverty for women who fulfil numerous social roles such as primary caregiver of dependent children, or domestic responsibilities (Still and Timms, 2000).

In addition, women were believed to be 'invisible' in the context of Australian business culture, with very few female role models having a high profile. Women did not have equal representation 'with men in business associations, economic development organizations, or in local, state or federal government policy and planning groups' (ibid., p. 277). Thus, exclusion from decision-making bodies at all levels culminated in a lack of representation at government and bureaucratic levels, and fostered a societal view that business is a male domain.

In essence, the authors concluded that a 'culture of advantage' operates against women when gender stereotypes are applied to women and their skills, competencies and capacities when they operate in the world of business (ibid., p. 278). Such gender issues have also been reported in numerous Australian research studies (e.g., Yellow Pages Australia, 1996; Still and Timms, 1997; Newton et al., 2001). According to Still and Timms (2000), such exclusion from the 'culture of advantage' has a very negative effect on the way women operated in business. Consequently, women have additional burdens placed on them when they set up small business ventures, simply because they are women.

More recent Australian research has provided a contemporary picture of the barriers to women in small to medium-sized business ventures. At the point of start-up, one-fifth of women (n = 517) in a sample drawn from all Australian states had experienced barriers in obtaining finance, with almost 25 per cent stating they had difficulty in locating advice regarding business start-up. Women in this phase of their business cited lack of confidence and ability to sell their ideas as impediments. During the operational phase of the business, a lack of a formal business plan was seen as a barrier by half of the sample and no government support was being accessed (Still and Walker, 2006).

Despite these issues for female entrepreneurs, most women engaged in entrepreneurial activities in Australia are seen as 'opportunity entrepreneurs' (i.e., exploiting a new market niche) rather than 'necessity entrepreneurs' (i.e., being forced to start a business due to job loss or redundancy) (Frederick et al., 2007, p. 567) and some remarkable success stories are evident.

STORIES OF SUCCESS

Notwithstanding the numerous barriers experienced by female small business owners, the business performance of women overall is similar to that of males when appropriate measures of performance are adopted:

> the Australian evidence suggests that differences in the relative performances of male- and female-controlled enterprises reported by previous international studies may have been due to methodological issues, such as small samples, limited data which is often financial in nature, or restricted geographical locations, rather than an inability of female SME operators to put resources to effective use. (Watson, 2003, p. 5)

In the past, purely economic measures have been used to consider the performance of SMEs (Watson, 2003), however, other measures have been proposed, such as 'employee satisfaction, social contributions, goal achievement and effectiveness' (Brush, 1992, p. 22).

Australian research (Newton et al., 2001) attempted to isolate the features of female small business operators that were associated with success, through applying an objective measure of success, which included profit, length of time in business and reports of growth by the operator (ibid.). When these criteria were applied, one-third of the sample (n = 359) met the criteria of 'success'. To explore further the question of success in small business operations, the subjective perceptions of the operator were sought. In follow-up interviews and focus groups, respondents were asked to elaborate on 'What does business success mean to you?' The themes that emerged were market dominance and respect, better income, profit and comfortable lifestyle (ibid.).

Other factors that influenced success for female entrepreneurs include effective people and communication skills, with an ability to build good relationships with others. Business is often conducted on the basis of consensus, and effective negotiating practices are often evident. Women are believed to bring a degree of imaginative thinking to their business ventures, and to embrace web technology to further their businesses. They exhibit the ability to multitask, and have a higher than average tolerance for ambiguity (Frederick et al., 2007).

The following case studies are used to illustrate two highly successful business ventures in Australia, which started out as small business enterprises. The factors that may have been instrumental in ensuring the success of the company are considered, along with how barriers were overcome.

BOX 2.1   SECOND SKIN AT THE CUTTING EDGE

In 1988, Jenni Ballantyne set up a small manufacturing business with three employees in a suburb of Perth, Western Australia. The business – Second Skin – produced pressure garments for burns victims. These garments had previously been manufactured and imported, often with considerable delays, from the United States. Jenni, who worked as an occupational therapist in a hospital, heard surgeons complaining about this and questioned why no one was producing the garments locally.

Jenni's business is based on two primary product ranges. First, pressure suits that promote healing and reduce scarring worn by people with severe burns. Second, lycra-based rigid splints that re-educate the limbs. These are designed for patients whose movements have been restricted because of stroke or head injuries, neurological disorders or multiple sclerosis. Her innovative designs have been incorporated into a range of 'world first' products that have significantly improved the quality of life and the medical management of clients and patients who wear them.

Many of the innovations have been simple but ingenious and have their origins in Jenni's ability to accurately observe what is required, and then change the design to suit specific requirements. For example, many children who wear pressure socks over long periods (sometimes several years) had problems with the traditional design, which tended to restrict growth. Jenni designed a toe gusset into a sock that would allow for growing feet.

She combines commitment to the care of her clients with a dedication to finding the most appropriate clinical solution possible, and believes this underpins the culture at Second Skin. Jenni has a passionate commitment to her work and a desire to live life to the full, rather than 'saving things for tomorrow'. Her philosophy can be summed up as 'do it well today'. She was always confident of success, but admits that her confidence was tested at various times. Her view is that as long as people have the ability to cope with the little rejections and frustrations and not see them as signs of personal failure, they are then able to withstand the setbacks and eventually succeed.

It sounds like good advice. Her business has grown to the extent that it supplies Australia and New Zealand with her products. She has offices in Sydney, Brisbane and the United Kingdom, and has been exporting to South-East Asia since 2005.

BOX 2.2   BOOST JUICE

The founder of Boost Juice, Janine Allis left school before she was 17. She worked in numerous areas including a period working overseas and she came across a concept in California in the late 1990s that she felt was worthy of trial in Australia. After returning from an overseas working holiday as a single mother with a two-year-old child, her mother loaned her $5000, which helped her acquire a home unit, but finances were very tight necessitating a strict budgeting regime – a skill that remains important to her. Janine met and married her husband, and they had two more children.

In 2000, she started her business from 'absolute scratch' and opened her first juice and smoothie bar after testing the recipes in her kitchen at home; she describes this period as 'learning on the run'. Her products were created free from preservatives and artificial colours and she took advice from a naturopath and nutritionist.

This first venture in small business was not initially successful, with a loss of $30000 being recorded in the first year of operation. In part, this may have been due to the fact that her healthy 'fast food' was competing in a sector that was at the opposite end of the spectrum, with a range of foods such as pizzas, fries and burgers. However, the following year a profit was made, which has been the pattern ever since.

Janine, who recently turned 40, has high levels of energy, which she brings to her business venture. Her attitude toward business is that it is the journey that is important, and being interested in what you are able to create, and then moving this concept forward until it is highly successful. Janine and her husband made a decision to move into franchising because of their desire to expand the business as quickly as possible. They obviously made the right choice. The franchising group of over 200 outlets currently turns over more than $90 million a year, and employs approximately 3000 staff. In addition to Australia, she operates in Singapore and Kuwait, with new franchises planned for Indonesia, Chile and the United Kingdom. Janine has an estimated wealth of $36 million and has won the prestigious Telstra Business Woman of the Year award.

FACTORS INSTRUMENTAL IN THE SUCCESS

Both of the case studies illustrate similar indicators of success. Jenni Ballantyne and Janine Allis have displayed an ability to identify a gap in the market and to seize the opportunity to innovatively address this with a new business venture. In addition, they have communicated their goal, their passion and their business ideas to others, convincing them of the potential success of their business, and both women have had an ability to conduct their businesses on the basis of consensus, and to use effective negotiating practices when necessary.

The conceptual ideas for both companies display a high degree of imaginative thinking, and their websites highlight their ability to embrace and utilize the best technology available to them. In addition, both women have displayed an impressive ability to multitask during the early development and launch of their business ventures; one as a fully employed occupational therapist and the other as a mother of three young children. They also exhibited a higher than average tolerance for ambiguity, riding out the early setbacks and continuing on with confidence that their goal would be achieved.

Other aspects of these two case studies do not appear to correlate with the extant literature, suggesting that further research on the profile of highly successful female entrepreneurs would be beneficial. First, in the example of the two women showcased in the above case studies, a lack of 'entrepreneurial culture' in Australia (Still and Timms, 2000) has not appeared to have hindered the floating of their business ventures, their initial growth, or their eventual success. Likewise, such a cultural paradigm has not influenced them to remain small and to operate within what could be called a 'comfort zone'. Both women grew their businesses quite dramatically, and both have taken their original ideas and sold them successfully into overseas locations. However, it is possible that these experiences may be atypical given the low proportion of women in small business who consider accessing venture capital and the relatively high proportion who 'had never heard of these sources of finance' (Still and Walker, 2006, p. 304).

Second, the belief that women exhibit lower levels of confidence is not borne out in either of these cases. In fact, the reverse appears to be the case. Both women have displayed exceptional confidence in their ideas and their ability to create a success of their entrepreneurial activities. It is possible that either Jenni or Janine may have experienced reservations about economic matters or their own abilities in this regard, however, this has not stopped them taking risks to achieve the full potential of their business ventures. It appears that both women have embraced the role of employer, and are successfully managing large staff numbers, even though many of the personnel involved in the businesses may be based interstate in Australia, or overseas.

Finally, for both women, prior experience was not necessary for the success of either business venture. The author has no knowledge of any training programmes that were undertaken in the early stages of these business ventures. Neither Jenni nor Janine had specific experience or indeed knowledge, of the type of small business they pioneered and turned into the highly successful large businesses they have become.

Therefore, in terms of the barriers to success outlined by Still and Timms (2000), these do not appear to have hampered either Jenni Ballantyne or Janine Allis in setting up, negotiating the growth phase, or the expansion into overseas markets of their highly successful businesses. These cases highlight the enormous diversity in the entrepreneurial experience; they also illustrate the complexities in researching in this area. While all of the success factors were evident throughout the journey of both of these entrepreneurial women, very few of the barriers experienced by many small business operators appear to have hindered these women in achieving their notable successes. However, these conclusions are drawn from limited information relating to the two case studies presented above. Much more research is required to ascertain in what way the characteristics of the highly successful female entrepreneur differ or are similar to less successful women endeavouring to sustain their small business ventures.

SUMMARY AND RECOMMENDATIONS

From the above data on the incidence of women in small business operations in Australia, as well as the information contained in the two case studies, the following recommendations can be made in an attempt to ensure best practice for female entrepreneurs.

Given the ability for women to be innovative in their ideas, and to be able to multitask, more women need to have roles in decision-making bodies. It is highly likely that women, when given the scope, authority and resources, are able to introduce very innovative solutions to business problems that could be of great benefit to any community group or committee.

In terms of women entering small businesses ventures on their own, it would seem that capability is unquestioned. Low confidence levels of the two highly successful entrepreneurs outlined in the case studies has not been a factor in holding them back in achieving the success of their companies. However, as many women do appear to have problems in this regard, it would seem that communities as a whole would benefit from setting up schemes where women starting out in small business operations could be paired with successful entrepreneurs. Mentoring could provide advice, support and networking opportunities into the future.

Policy-makers within government may wish to design training programmes that are accessible to women only. Reflecting on the enormous success of another Australian entrepreneurial venture, Fernwood gymnasium for women only, it may be of great benefit for women to have access to training where they would not feel intimidated by their perceived lack of knowledge in relation to financial expertise. The government could subsidize accounting firms, bank advisors and so on to be aligned with these programmes, and hence the appropriate business information could be made available to women, when it was required.

Finally, recent research has highlighted that there is a gap between what is experienced by nascent entrepreneurs and what is taught in traditional University Business School courses in entrepreneurship (Edelman et al., 2008). Therefore, universities could consider incorporating male and female guest speakers who are actively involved in entrepreneurial ventures into their course designs. Case studies could be utilized that present data relating to women in small business ventures – both successful and unsuccessful stories – but with an equal representation with information relating to male entrepreneurs presented throughout the course. In this way, both men and women would challenge any stereotypes about the suitability of women in small business, and significant role models would be introduced. Care would need to be taken in the curriculum design of the units studied to ensure opportunity was given for assignments to be carried out on entrepreneurs of choice, either male or female.

Although previous research has highlighted a lack of confidence and role models to be among the most important causes of the relatively low involvement of women in entrepreneurship compared with men, the two case studies highlighted in this chapter do not illustrate this phenomenon. When women have access to resources, this often allows them to create an entrepreneurial venture that not only provides for themselves and their families, but their entire communities.

It is obvious that women entrepreneurs and small business owners are becoming an increasingly important component of the world economy. The under-utilized potential of women provides opportunities for communities and governments to tap into this rich resource and benefit from the entrepreneurial capabilities of women in small business ventures.

The potential for women operating successfully in entrepreneurial activities is unlimited. In both early-stage activity and established businesses, the entrepreneurial activity of women forms 'an increasingly important part of the economic profile of any country' (Allen et al., 2007, p.9). Therefore, women will continue to venture into new business operations, and their contributions to job and wealth creation around the world will continue to be significant.

REFERENCES

Abhayaratna, J. and Lattimore, R. (2006). 'Workforce participation rates – how does Australia compare?'. Productivity Commission Staff Working Paper, Canberra: Australian Government Productivity Commission.

Allen, I.E., Langowitz, N. and Minniti, M. (2007). *Global Entrepreneurship Monitor: 2006 Report on Women and Entrepreneurship*. London Business School.

Australian Bureau of Statistics (2002). *Characteristics of Small Business*, Catalogue No. 8127.0. Canberra: Australian Government Publishing Service.

Australian Bureau of Statistics (2003). *Women in Trade*. Canberra: Australian Government Publishing Service.

Australian Bureau of Statistics (2004a). *Characteristics of Small Business*, Catalogue No. 8127.0. Canberra: Australian Government Publishing Service.

Australian Bureau of Statistics (2004b). *Australian Census Analytic Program: Indigenous Australians in the Contemporary Labour Market, 2001*, Catalogue No. 2052.0. Canberra: Australian Government Publishing Service.

Australian Bureau of Statistics (2008). *Labour Force, Detailed Quarterly*, Catalogue No. 6291.0.55.003. Canberra: Australian Government Publishing Service.

Bruni, A., Gherardi, S. and Poggio, B. (2004). 'Entrepreneur-mentality, gender and the study of women entrepreneurs'. *Journal of Organizational Change Management* 17(3), 256–68.

Brush, C.G. (1992). 'Research of women business owners: past trends, a new perspective, future directions'. *Entrepreneurship Theory and Practice* 16(4), 5–30.

Brush, C., Carter, N., Gatewood, E., Greene, P. and Hart, M. (2001). *The Diana Project: Women Business Owners and Equity Capital: The Myths Dispelled*. Kansas City: Kauffman Center for Entrepreneurial Leadership, available at: www.esbri.se/diana.asp; accessed 3 February 2010.

Collins, J. (2003). 'Cultural diversity and entrepreneurship: policy responses to immigrant entrepreneurs in Australia'. *Entrepreneurship and Regional Development* 15(2), 137–49.

Deakins, D. (1996). *Entrepreneurship and Small Firms*. London: McGraw-Hill.

Douglas, E.J. and Shepherd, D.A. (2002). 'Self-employment as a career choice: attitudes, entrepreneurial intentions, and utility maximization'. *Entrepreneurship Theory and Practice*, 26(3), 81–90.

Drucker, P.F. (1985). *Innovation and Entrepreneurship*. New York: Harper and Row.

Edelman, L.F., Manolova, T.S. and Brush, C.G. (2008). 'Entrepreneurship education: correspondence between practices of nascent entrepreneurs and textbook prescriptions for success'. *Academy of Management Learning and Education* 7(1), 56–70.

Equal Opportunity for Women in the Workplace Agency (EOWA) (2006). *Census of Women in Leadership: The Status of Women in the Workplace*. Sydney, Australia.

Foley, D. (2003). 'An examination of indigenous Australian entrepreneur'. *Journal of Developmental Entrepreneurship* **8**(2), 133–51.

Frazer, L. and Weaven, S. (2004). *Franchising Australia 2004*. Brisbane: Griffith University.

Frederick, H.H., Kuratko, D.F. and Hodgetts, R.M. (2007). *Entrepreneurship: Theory, Process and Practice*. South Melbourne, Victoria: Nelson Australia.

Goffee, R. and Scase, R. (1985). *Women in Charge: The Experiences of Female Entrepreneurs*. London: George Allen and Unwin.

Hofstede, G. and Hofstede, G.J. (2005). *Cultures and Organizations: Software of the Mind* (2nd edition). New York: McGraw Hill.

Hyytinen, A. and Ilmakunnas, P. (2007). 'What distinguishes a serial entrepreneur?'. *Industrial and Corporate Change* **16**(5), 793–821.

Johnsen, G.J. and McMahon, R.G.P. (2005). 'Owner-manager gender, financial performance and business growth amongst SMEs from Australia's business longitudinal survey'. *International Small Business Journal* **23**(2), 115–42.

Kalleberg, A.L. and Leicht, K.T. (1991). 'Gender and organizational performance: determinants of small business survival and success'. *Academy of Management Journal* **34**(1), 136–61.

Kupferberg, F. (2003). 'The established and the newcomers: what makes immigrant and women entrepreneurs so special?'. *International Review of Sociology* **37**(2), 89.

Legge, J. and Hindle, K. (1997). *Entrepreneurship: How Innovators Create the Future*. South Melbourne: Macmillan Education Australia.

Leibenstein, H. (1968). 'Entrepreneurship and development'. *American Economic Review* **58**(2), 72–83.

Liff, S. and Ward, K. (2001). 'Distorted views through the glass ceiling: the construction of women's understandings of promotion and senior management positions'. *Gender, Work and Organization* **8**(1), 19–36.

McClelland, D.C. (1961). *The Achieving Society*. New York: Van Nostrand.

McKay, R. (2001). 'Women entrepreneurs: moving beyond family and flexibility'. *International Journal of Entrepreneurial Behaviour & Research* **7**(4), 148–65.

Menzies, T.V., Diochon, M. and Gasse, Y. (2004). 'Examining venture-related myths concerning women entrepreneurs'. *Journal of Developmental Entrepreneurship* **9**(2), 89–107.

Minniti, M., Arenius, P. and Langowitz, N. (2005). *Global Entrepreneurship Monitor: 2004 Report on Women and Entrepreneurship*. The Center for Women's Leadership, Wellesley MA: Babson College.

Minniti, M., Bygrave, W.D. and Autio, E. (2006). *Global Entrepreneurship Monitor: 2005 Executive Report*. Babson College and London Business School.

Newton, J., Gottschalk, L. and Wood, G. (2001). *A Model for Success: Women's Entrepreneurial and Small Business Activity in Regional Areas*. Report prepared for the Department of State and Regional Development. Ballarat: School of Business, University of Ballarat.

Rosa, P., Carter, S. and Hamilton, E. (1996). 'Gender as a determinant of small business performance: insights from a British study'. *Small Business Economics* **8**(6), 463–78.

Shane, S. and Venkataraman, S. (2000). 'The promise of entrepreneurship as a field of research'. *Academy of Management Review* **25**(1), 217–26.

Sinclair, A. (1998). *Doing Leadership Differently: Gender, Power and Sexuality in a Changing Business Culture*. Carlton, Victoria: Melbourne University Press.

Still, L.V. (1990). *Enterprising Women*. Sydney: Allen and Unwin.

Still, L.V. (2004). 'Women in management in Australia', in Marilyn J. Davidson and Ronald Burke (eds) *Women in Management Worldwide: Progress and Prospects*, Chapter 16. London: Ashgate, pp. 225–42.

Still, L.V. (2006). 'Where are the women in leadership in Australia?'. *Women in Management Review*, **21**(3), 180–94.

Still, L.V. and Timms, W. (1997). *Women and Small Business: Barriers to Growth*. Report prepared for the Office of the Status of Women, Department of Prime Minister and Cabinet. Canberra: Australian Government.

Still, L.V. and Timms, W. (2000). 'Women's business: the flexible alternative workstyle for women'. *Women in Management Review* **15**(5/6), 272–82.

Still, L.V. and Walker, E.A. (2006). 'The self-employed woman owner and her business: an Australian profile'. *Women in Management Review* **21**(4), 294–310.

Symons, G.L. (1986). 'Women's occupational careers in business: managers and entrepreneurs in France and in Canada'. *International Studies of Management & Organization* **16**(3/4), 61–75.

Wajcman, J. (1999). *Managing Like a Man: Women and Men in Corporate Management*. Cambridge: Polity.

Walker, E. (2003). 'Home-based businesses: setting straight the urban myths'. *Small Enterprise Research Journal* **11**(2), 35–48.

Watson, J. (2003). 'SME performance: does gender matter?'. Annual Conference of Small Enterprise Association of Australia and New Zealand. 28 September–1 October. Ballarat, Victoria, Australia.

Weaven, S., Isaac, J. and Herington, C. (2007). 'Franchising as a path to self-employment for Australian female entrepreneurs'. *Journal of Management & Organization* **13**(4), 345–65.

Wood, G.J. (2006). 'Career advancement in Australian middle managers: a follow-up study'. *Women in Management Review* **21**(4), 277–93.

Wood, G.J. and Newton, J. (2006). '"Facing the wall" – "equal" opportunity for women in management?'. *Equal Opportunities International* **25**(1), 8–24.

Yellow Pages Australia (1996). *Small Business Index: A Special Report on Women in Business*. Melbourne, Australia: Yellow Pages.

3   Brazil
Andrea E. Smith-Hunter

INTRODUCTION

This chapter focuses on the current position of women entrepreneurs in Brazil, covering a number of issues that are pertinent to the literature on women's entrepreneurship in today's environment. Beginning with a look at the overall presence of women and their place in the labour market, it details factors that mobilize women's movement from that sector into the field of entrepreneurship, which includes business ownership and self-employment. Women's progression, as it relates to work, has been attributed to three significant areas: access to resources, factors that propel them from the current position (push factors) and factors that welcome their entry into entrepreneurial fields (pull factors) (Baldez, 2003). Women's labour status in Brazil represents many different identities, interests and issues. With this latter point in mind, this chapter explores what historically has led to women's current labour market position. It traces a journey from the mainstream labour market to the world of self-employment, while simultaneously delving into the economic, sociological and historical explanations that exist for women's positioning in each of these sectors. The chapter continues with an analysis of women's entrepreneurship presence, specifically related to the context in which women entrepreneurs operate in the Brazilian economy. This analysis is intriguing, as it looks at women's labour market position across racial and socioeconomic lines, a perspective that is unique in its contribution to the link of Brazilian women's subsequent steps into the entrepreneurial world.

The burgeoning development of entrepreneurship studies in general, and women entrepreneurship studies in particular, has provided access to an increasing amount of scholarly work exploring issues of entrepreneurship from many perspectives (De Lourdes Villar, 1994; Gilbertson, 1995; Peterson, 1995; Godoy et al., 2000; Robles, 2004; Heriot and Campbell, 2005; Duffy et al., 2006; Smith-Hunter, 2006). The current dynamics for women entrepreneurs from various backgrounds requires that their stories be told from individualistic perspectives, allowing each set of women's unique contributions in their own society to be represented. Telling the story of women entrepreneurs en masse using a broad brush to sweep across women entrepreneurs from various countries, and assuming a common set of characteristics to all, is not indicative of the true picture that exists (Reynolds et al., 2002; Allen et al., 2007). This chapter is thus important at this pivotal period, as it represents a contribution to the literature from the perspective of South American, albeit Brazilian women entrepreneurs – a perspective that is often not presented or, when done, is not always given a context that is pragmatic.

The experience of women's entrepreneurial positioning in Brazil is parallel to the broader framework of women's global entrepreneurship experience that is often explored. This exploration is based on the assumption that relating the two contexts can help in an understanding of women's positioning in various other contexts. Today, Brazil is seen as a fertile and viable option to study entrepreneurship in general and women entrepreneurship in particular, since in addition to being seen as a leader in entrepreneurism (Allen et al., 2007), it is also described as having the world's fourth largest economy with a gross domestic product (GDP) of 812 billion dollars (ibid.). Brief results from a specific study on women entrepreneurs in Brazil are presented in the current chapter as a means to ground the aforementioned discussion in a realm of realism. This chapter pursues these relationships and identifies others that help to explain women's movement from the mainstream labour market of Brazil into the area of entrepreneurship. The chapter ends with a summary of the issues covered, as well as recommendations for women entrepreneurs in the Brazilian context, and others similarly positioned in other parts of the world.

THE POSITION OF WOMEN'S EMPLOYMENT IN BRAZIL

Brazil has made great strides since its independence in 1822 (Alvarez, 1990; Geddes et al., 1992; Dias, 1995), which sought to achieve among other things, advancement for women in various sectors of the society. Historically, married women from the middle and upper socioeconomic class strata of Brazil were reluctant to admit their employment status, for fear that this would reflect poorly on their husbands' duties as adequate financial providers for their households (Andrews, 1988; Patai, 1988; Bak, 2000). The last seven decades in Brazil have shown significant increases in women's participation in the labour market since the latter half of the previous century. While during the 1940s, women represented only 13 per cent of the labour force in Brazil, their participation increased to 21 per cent during the 1970s, rising to 42 per cent during the 1990s (Madalozzo and Martins, 2007). Although women account for the majority of those who are unemployed (Instituto Brasileiro de Geografia e Estatistica, 2008), in 2001, 53 per cent of Brazilian women were economically active (Madalozzo and Martins, 2007). However, whilst the number of men with a formal employment contract reached 48.9 per cent in 2008, for women it was only 37.8 per cent (ibid.).

Occurring simultaneously with the increase with the number of women entering the labour market has been an increase in the educational levels of women employed in the labour market. Recent data shows that from 1992 to 2001, the percentage of women without schooling went down from 18 per cent to 13 per cent, while the percentage of women with more than 11 years of education – secondary degree – went up from 6 per cent to 9 per cent (Madalozzo and Martins, 2007). Women also have a better level of schooling than men. In fact, among working women, 59.9 per cent had 11 or more years of schooling in January 2008, versus 51.9 per cent of men (Instituto Brasileiro de Geografia e Estatistica, 2008).

In the analysis of distribution of employed women among the different economic activities, it is possible to observe that 16.5 per cent were in the group of domestic services; 22.0 per cent in public administration, education, defence, security, health; 13.3 per cent in services rendered to enterprises; 13.2 per cent in industry; 0.6 per cent in construction; 17.4 per cent in trade and 17.0 per cent in other activities (ibid.). Among employed men, there is predominance of participation in industry, 20.0 per cent, and, differently from women, men are more often employed in construction, 12.0 per cent, and have little participation in domestic services, 0.7 per cent (ibid.). The income of working women with a degree is equivalent to 60 per cent of the income earned by men with the same level of schooling (ibid.), a wage gap of 40 per cent. Working women in Brazil are said to occupy approximately 37 per cent of the administrative and managerial positions, but only 3 per cent of the executive positions in the mainstream labour market (Hutn, 2000).

In a recent study, authors Madalozzo and Martins (2007) concluded that the wage gap between genders in Brazil is more pronounced at higher levels of education, confirming the assumption that Brazil is still a patriarchal society, and while women have improved their educational levels, this does not necessarily translate into higher earnings. The issues of sexism are pervasive in the Brazilian society, buoyed by a historical and long-standing belief that women have long occupied and continue to occupy a secondary place in society, where genders are stratified and queued in terms of management levels and wage levels (Metcalf, 1986; Baldez, 2003). This queuing doubly applies to Blacks or Afro-Brazilian women (Andrews, 1988). In addition to gender and race, another issue that impacts women in Brazil is the high level of inequality in income or affluence gap between classes (Rezende, 1998; Alves De Siqueira, 2008). The main victims of the affluence gap in any economy are women who are said to be more likely to exist at a lower income level (Buvinic, 1997), sometimes even living in poverty. This has resulted in the term, the 'feminization of poverty', used to describe the majority of women worldwide, especially in Brazil, who are said to be more likely to live in poverty (Buvinic, 1998; Rezende, 1998). One key element that provides an overarching paradigm of women's main disadvantage is focussed on the differential earnings that exist between them and their male counterparts.

In the same vein, four key reasons have been advanced for the disadvantaged position of women in Brazilian society. First, the lowered human capital position (which refers to the level of education, job skills and experience one has) that women occupy when compared with their male counterparts. Second, the fact that women in the Brazilian labour market are entrenched in industries that pay less than other industries and that are mainly dominated by men. Third, the fact that women experience overall discrimination that results in them not advancing to higher levels in an organization (i.e., the glass ceiling effect, which refers to the invisible barrier that prevents women from being promoted to top corporate positions) and being paid less. Furthermore, even when they are in primarily female-dominated industries in which Brazilian women are concentrated they experience a labour surplus, which further lowers the wages paid in such industries (Skidmore, 2004). Finally, the literature on Brazilian women's labour market position suggests that in addition to the expected reasons that place women at a disadvantage in other countries, such as discrimination, the wage gap, the glass ceiling and gender segregation into 'gendered' (traditionally dominated by a particular gender) occupations, there is the added pressure and effects of sexism, racism and classism having a negative impact on women's position in the country's labour market (Telles, 1994). Thus, any look at the position of women in such an environment has to be examined with this backdrop in mind.

CURRENT POSITION OF WOMEN AND SMALL BUSINESS OWNERSHIP IN BRAZIL

A close examination of women entrepreneurs in Brazil suggests that most are employed in the services industry, followed by manufacturing (which consists primarily of making products with their own hands) and then transportation/communication (National Foundation for Women Business Owners, 1999). A marginal majority are said to be married, with an average number of 2.1 children, operating businesses with an average of 10–50 employees (ibid.). The Brazilian economy boasts a high level of entrepreneurial activity when compared with other countries worldwide (Allen et al., 2007). The same report also indicated that overall, business owners have an activity level of 19.06 per cent for females, as compared with a 28.8 per cent rate for males. A more detailed look at the female statistics indicated that this percentage consisted of 9.61 per cent early-stage entrepreneurial activity (in business less than 42 months) and 9.45 per cent established business owners' level of activity (being in business more than 42 months) (ibid.). The male activity levels showed that the males had a 13.74 per cent early-stage entrepreneurial activity and a 14.77 per cent established business owners' level of activity (ibid.).

In recent years, self-employment and home-based work have expanded opportunities for women's participation in the labour force worldwide, but are characterized by a lack of security, a lack of benefits and low income. In the case of Brazil, 42 per cent of their entrepreneurs are opportunity entrepreneurs (defined as people who take advantage of a recognized opportunity), while 56 per cent of the entrepreneurial population are described as necessity entrepreneurs (defined as people who enter entrepreneurship because other employment options are absent or unsatisfactory) (ibid.). In addition, in Brazil, the female opportunity to necessity ratio is 0.73 compared with the ratio for males of 1.43 (ibid.). One can conclude from this prior statistic that in Brazil, females are more likely to be necessity versus opportunity entrepreneurs when compared with their male counterparts.

Women entrepreneurs in Brazil are on average 40–45 years old, are highly educated with most having a secondary degree or higher, including graduate experience (NFWBO, 1999). In spite of this high human capital potential, women entrepreneurs in Brazil were shown to be less likely than their male entrepreneurs to have the required skills to start a business (Alves De Siqueira, 2008). This sentiment is echoed in another study, which showed that the desire for more business training and education was a major concern for women business owners in that economy (ibid.). Other issues or concerns for Brazilian women owners included economic issues, access to financial capital, cash flow to operate their business, the state of the country's economy and the impact it had on their business, as well as obtaining and keeping good employees (Geddes and Neto, 1992; NFWBO, 1999; Duffy et al., 2006; Djankov et al., 2007). A minority of the women entrepreneurs in Brazil are involved in the international marketplace (NFWBO, 1999), a factor that is said to be needed to grow a business successfully (Jalbert, 2000). Furthermore, the employment pattern of women entrepreneurs in Brazil shows that most are also employed in the mainstream labour market and that some are in fact employed full-time (17.5 per cent) outside of their entrepreneurial ventures. This outside access to financial resources, network structures, customers and ideas in turn aids them in their entrepreneurial ventures.

One distinct perspective that is often presented in women entrepreneurial studies is the problems they experience while operating their enterprises. One main problem women entrepreneurs in Brazil encounter is the many competitors they have, especially in which other women entrepreneurs are the dominant members. Compared with their male counterparts, women entrepreneurs were less likely to work together to establish an adequate network structure. A network structure can be defined as the formal and informal connections of overlapping organizational, family and social memberships that account for their level of success, the resources they have available to them to satisfy their needs, obligations and expectations (Aldrich et al., 1989; Easter, 1996; Hogan, 2001; Coughlin and Thomas, 2002). It has been described as the hidden hand of influence that impacts the development of business markets (Chung and Gibbons, 1997; Hogan, 2001; Choi and Hong, 2002), which includes other business owners. This finding is significant, since an appropriate network structure has been shown to be critical for the establishment and continuation of entrepreneurial ventures.

EXPLORATION OF CONCEPTUAL AND CONTEXTUAL BARRIERS TO FEMALE ENTREPRENEURSHIP

While women entrepreneurs in Brazil continue to experience barriers while pursuing the business of entrepreneurship, various agencies and government organizations in that country have recognized the need to assist the women in transcending some of these barriers. Two dominant research papers that identify the barriers experienced by women entrepreneurs in Brazil highlight similar issues. Economic issues were a top concern, ranging from cash flow problems, to gaining access to bank credit (NFWBO, 1999; Alves De Siqueira, 2008). The earlier study also identified the then economic and political instability as a major concern for women entrepreneurs (NFWBO, 1999). Since then, the economic and political aspects of the Brazilian economy have stabilized, but women in that sector continue to occupy a disadvantaged position, compared with their male counterparts. This disadvantaged position has its roots in a historically patriarchal society (Alvarez, 1990; Bak, 2000; Skidmore, 2004) that continues to see women, more than men, to be affected by poverty, and less likely than their male counterparts to be employed (Corral, 2002). Currently women in the labour force in Brazil are earning returns that are 40 per cent less than their male counterparts, although they have an overall higher educational level (Corral, 2002). This reduced access to financial capital hampers women's ability in that country to accumulate the resources to start and operate their businesses.

Other barriers identified by the women entrepreneurs included: finding good employees, obtaining more training, both on business ownership in general and that related to their industry in particular and the lack of membership organizations that catered specifically to women entrepreneurs (NFWBO, 1999; Smith-Hunter and Leone, 2010). The more recent study looked at Brazilian women entrepreneurs in São Paulo and confirmed previous results, as well as offered new insights. The study cited too much competition, finding good employees and state and federal regulations (the cumbersome and at times bureaucratic process needed to comply with government regulations when operating a business in Brazil) as the top three problems faced by women business owners in that country (Smith-Hunter and Leone, 2010).

It should be noted that the studies mentioned previously kept the variable of gender constant, focussing exclusively on women rather than pursuing male versus female comparisons. Thus, declaring that Brazilian male entrepreneurs do not express the same problematic issues or identify the same barriers would be erroneous. In fact, both

Robben (1984) and Djankov et al. (2007), who looked at multiple gender samples of entrepreneurs in Brazil, identify government regulations, access to financial capital and competition, as barriers applicable to both male and female entrepreneurs in Brazil.

While organizations that provide support to women entrepreneurs in Brazil are limited in their own capacity and not gender-specific, they do exist. Most notably is Sebrae, which has offices across the country and assists all entrepreneurs – both men and women – in initiating and developing their ventures (Sebrae, 2008). Sebrae came into being in 1972 as result of a pioneering initiative from many institutions that encourage entrepreneurship in the country (ibid.). It provides among others things: assistance with preparing a business plan, an assessment of the viability of an entrepreneurial venture and evaluation, which allows interested individuals to assess whether they have the profile to be an entrepreneur, based on their personal characteristics (ibid.). Sebrae has significantly contributed to the development of Brazil, since it lends its support to a segment that accounts for 99.23 per cent of the business of the country and generates 28.7 million jobs in the micro and small enterprises of the country. It assists about 14.9 million ventures, out of which 4.5 million are formal and 10.3 million are informal (ibid.).

As a private entity of public interest that has as its main source of revenue the contribution collected from enterprises, Sebrae has a clear and transparent mission of offering to micro and small enterprises the conditions necessary for their survival, prosperity and active contribution to the country's growth through the generation of jobs and income (ibid.). Sebrae has a philosophy that guides its actions, projects, products and services. Along these lines, efforts concentrate on offering a continuous flow of information of quality by means of courses, consultancy services, training, lectures, seminars, publications, events and several other channels that, integrated into conventional methods and new technologies, create a network of knowledge for micro and small enterprises. The organization believes in the dissemination of knowledge as the main tool for the qualification and the survival of Brazilian entrepreneurs. It also holds the opinion that only through the culture of knowledge and the valuation of the information can entrepreneurs ensure a competitive, efficient and modern management.

The research data indicates that women entrepreneurs' involvement in the entrepreneurial sector of Brazil continues to increase (Allen et al., 2007). This increase does not belie the fact that Brazilian women entrepreneurs continue to experience structural and contextual barriers during the inception and operational stage of their businesses that are gender-specific. These barriers include lack of additional avenues to access financial capital, and organizations that focus exclusively on the needs of the women entrepreneurs in that country and provide outlets where women entrepreneurs can receive additional training to assist them in their businesses.

CASE STUDIES: WHAT DETERMINES SUCCESS?

In spite of the barriers that persist, Brazilian women entrepreneurs have increased in numbers (Allen et al., 2007). This increase includes women who are successful in monetary terms through revenue and women are deemed successful because they have broken through barriers to enter into areas that are considered 'traditionally male dominated' industries. The following section looks at detailed cases of two Brazilian women entrepreneurs, one in a traditional female-dominated industry of the services industry and the other in a non-traditional female industry of industrial manufacturing. By looking at these divergent perspectives, the two stories provide a better understanding of what determines success for Brazilian women entrepreneurs. The women entrepreneurs in these case studies were able to expand their business focus into related diversified areas, pursuing strategies of forward and backward integration. The first story details women entrepreneurs in the 'traditional female area' of hair salons. The second story details a woman entrepreneur who has been successful in a 'traditionally male dominated' industry, by offering a slight but unique change on a previous product that caters to the manufacturing sector.

BOX 3.1   LEILA AND MARILLA

The first case study is that of female entrepreneur, Leila (a married, 38-year-old, mother of two) who first became exposed to the entrepreneurial world at a young age when she would assist her parents in their grocery store family business. By the time she was in her late teens, she was selling cosmetics door to door in her neighbourhood. Simultaneously, she and best friend Marilla (a married, 43-year-old mother of one) started experimenting with various chemicals to develop a product that would make their afro-curly hair more manageable. After 18 months of experimentation, they brought their product to a chemist, who refined it and helped them with the application for a patent for the product. Leila and Marilla then opened a small beauty salon and applied the product to customers' hair. Today, 16 years later, they own three large salons, located in two of the major cities in Brazil. In addition to the salons, they operate a manufacturing facility that produces a whole line of hair and skin products, all developed by them, which they sell independently, as well as use in their hair salons. Leila's favourite story is that the business was started with the sale of a used Volkswagen car for $3000, growing it into a business that currently grosses $20 million annually and employs 350 people. This success has not occurred without obstacles, however. Both women cite government regulations and the patriarchal nature of the society as major obstacles that they still encounter, despite their financial success. Marilla confirmed that bank managers, builders (when they expand to new locations) and suppliers often ask to speak to the 'male owners' of the business. In spite of the sexism they face, Marilla says that one way to circumvent these obstacles that strive to oppress them is to 'educate yourself in general and expand your knowledge base as it relates to your particular industry'. To this end, both women are pursuing their Masters in Business Administration degrees. They also cite 'extensive financial knowledge' as a key criterion to understanding one's business operation. Leila adds that expansive financial success lies in the global arena, by developing a global customer base and a global network structure. To achieve this, they often attend seminars and trade shows in the United States, Europe, Asia and other parts of South America.

BOX 3.2 ISABEL

Isabel's entry into entrepreneurship was less intentional. She had worked for nine years in a manufacturing facility that does the shrink-wrapping of large quantities of goods that are then shipped internationally. Gradually, as she worked in the facility, she derived the idea of offering a product that was a shrink-wrap bag, rather than the basic shrink-wrapped plastic. This new method reduces spoilage and damage to shipped goods and though more expensive, is preferred by a number of companies in Brazil who ship their goods internationally. Currently, Isabel's business has 700 employees and she is one of the very few women in this type of business, which is primarily male-dominated. She boasts that she has the largest female-owned business of its type and is one of the first women to venture into this line of business in Brazil. She adds that success in this business requires you to be aware of the sexism that you will face as a woman entrepreneur and be proactive in thwarting such discrimination that will inevitably come your way. She offers additional advice: 'always educate yourself on what the latest advancement is in your industry; be aware of the international marketplace, take advantage of any new train- ing sessions that are offered that can help to improve your business and take a hands-on approach to the management of your company'. Her final advice is to never dismiss thoughts and ideas proposed by even your lowest-level employees. She reminisces that what propelled her to start the business in the first place was that after she had proposed the then new idea of a shrink-wrap bag, instead of the method being used, to her then supervisor at her old place of employment, he immediately dismissed the idea with a chuckle. Unlike her competitors, she boasts that she has a disproportionately larger number of females in her employ, especially in supervisory and management positions. She points out that female employees are more understanding of her goals and her perspective on developing her business. Isabel (the oldest of nine children) is single, has never been married and has no children, and acts as a mentor to the young girls who are in her employ, often paying school tuition and purchas- ing personal items for their care.

SUMMARY

This chapter draws attention to the need to recognize women entrepreneurs as important contributors to the Brazilian economy. Women entrepreneurs are more likely to operate small businesses and small businesses are seen as important to a nation's economy through the multiplier effect (NFWBO, 1999; Jalbert, 2000; Corral, 2002). The area of entrepreneurship offers an attractive alternative for women in Brazil, since in spite of their higher educational levels, when compared with their male counterparts, they earn less in terms of wages in the mainstream labour market (Corral, 2002; Madalozzo and Martins, 2007). Historically, women have increased their percentages in the labour market and then in the entrepreneurial sector in Brazil. This increased presence has led to responses by government-related agencies, such as Sebrae, to assist entrepreneurs, including women entrepreneurs, to overcome barriers and efficiently and effectively operate their businesses.

Currently, women business owners in Brazil have an activity level of 19.06 per cent and, compared with their male counterparts, they are more likely to be in the services and retail industries. These industries also show a predominance of women participants worldwide. Resolutions that address women entrepreneurial issues in Brazil should do well in focussing on these industries, since they comprise the largest industry in Brazil by gross domestic product (GDP) and labour force participation (World Fact Book, 2009). It is clear from the evidence presented and discussed throughout this chapter that certain characteristics of women entrepreneurs in Brazil are similar to those found for other women entrepreneurs in other geographic regions of the world, reconfirming the perspective that women entrepreneurs worldwide are more alike than they are different.

The preceding results and discussion suggests that future studies could continue to look at a number of perspectives for Brazilian women entrepreneurs: exploration of the factors that lead to economic success in entrepreneurial ventures; the role of government institutions and membership organizations in assisting women to start and operate their businesses; expanding the robustness of the current quantitative results by supplementing them with in-depth qualitative data. Notwithstanding the many challenges faced by women entrepreneurs globally, an understanding of the differences in their characteristics and thus challenges is important in order to paint the multifaceted picture that is the face of the global woman entrepreneur. An understanding of factors that help or hinder women is also an important first step in the design and implementation of policies to aid the advancement of women in the entrepreneurial world. This study offers several contributions to the understanding of the factors underlying the main dimensions that impact women entrepreneurs in today's global marketplace.

REFERENCES

Aldrich, H., P.R. Reese and P. Dubini (1989), 'Women on the Verge of a Breakthrough: Networking Among Entrepreneurs in the United States and Italy', *Entrepreneurship and Regional Development*, 1(4), 339–56.

Allen, I.E., N. Langowitz and M. Minniti (2007), *Global Entrepreneurship Monitor: 2006 Report on Women and Entrepreneurship*, The Center for Women's Leadership at Babson College/London Business School.

Alvarez, S. (1990), *Engendering Democracy in Brazil: Women's Movements in Transition Politics*, Princeton, NJ: Princeton University Press.

Alves De Siqueira, A. (2008), 'Brazilian Women, Invisible Workers: The Experience of Women Street Vendors in Brazil', unpublished dissertation from Kansas State University, Department of Sociology.

Andrews, G. (1988), 'Black and White Workers: Sao Paulo, Brazil, 1888–1928', *Hispanic American Historical Review*, 68(3), 491–524.

Bak, J. (2000), 'Class, Ethnicity and Gender in Brazil: The Negotiation of Workers' Identities in Porto Alegreís 1906 Strike', *Latin American Research Review*, 35(3), 83–123.

Baldez, L. (2003), 'Women's Movement and Democratic Transition in Chile, Brazil, East Germany and Poland', *Comparative Politics*, 35(3), 253–72.

Buvinic, M. (1997), 'Women in Poverty: A New Global Underclass', *Foreign Policy*, 38(September).

Choi, T.Y. and Y. Hong (2002), 'Unveiling the Structure of Supply Networks: Case Studies in Honda, Acura, and DaimlerChrysler', *Journal of Operations Management*, 20(5), 469–93.

Chung, L. and P. Gibbons (1997), 'Corporate Entrepreneurship: The Roles of Ideology and Social Capital', *Group & Organization Management*, **22**(1), 10–31.

Corral, T. (2002), 'Women's Perspectives on Sustainable Development in Brazil', available at: http://www.eolss.net/ebooks/Sample%20Chapters/C16/E1-58-22.pdf; accessed 4 February 2010.

Coughlin, J. and A. Thomas (2002), *The Rise of Women Entrepreneurs: People, Processes and Global Trends*, Westport, CT: Quorum Books.

De Lourdes Villar, M. (1994), 'Hindrances to the Development of an Ethnic Economy among Mexican Migrants', *Human Organization*, **53**(3), 263–8.

Dias, M. (1995), *Power and Everyday Life: The Lives of Working Women in Nineteenth Century Brazil*, New Brunswick, NJ: Rutgers University Press.

Djankov, S., Y. Qian, G. Roland and E. Zhuravskaya (2007), 'What Makes a Successful Entrepreneur? Evidence from Brazil', Center for Economic and Financial Research (CEFIR) Working Paper Series No. w0104.

Duffy, J., S. Fox, B. Punnett, A. Gregory, T. Lituchy, S. Monserrat, M. Olivas-Lujan, N. Santos and J. Miller (2006), 'Successful Women of the Americas: the Same or Different?', *Management Research News*, **29**(9), 552–72.

Easter, G.M. (1996), 'Personal Networks and Postrevolutionary State Building: Soviet Russia Reexamined', *World Politics*, **48**(4), 551–78.

Geddes, B. and A. Neto (1992), 'Institutional Sources of Corruption in Brazil', *Third World Quarterly*, **13**(4), 641–61.

Gilbertson, G. (1995), 'Women Labour and Enclave Employment: The Case of Dominican and Columbian Women in New York City', *The International Migration Review*, **29**(3), 657–67.

Godoy, R., K. O'Neill, K. McSweeney and D. Wilkie (2000), 'Human Capital, Wealth, Property Rights and the Adoption of New Farm Technologies: The Tawahka Indians of Honduras', *Human Organization*, **59**(2), 222–33.

Heriot, K. and N. Campbell (2005), 'Creating a New Program in Entrepreneurship Education: A Case Study in Columbia', *New England Journal of Entrepreneurship*, **8**(1) 65–74.

Hogan, J.M. (2001), 'Social Capital: Potential in Family Social Sciences', *Journal of Socio-Economics*, **30**(2), 151–5.

Hutn, M. (2000), *Women's Leadership in Latin America: Trends and Challenges*, New School University/Inter-American Dialogue, available at: http://www.iadb.org/sds/doc/malaenglish.pdf; accessed 4 February 2010.

Instituto Brasileiro de Geografia e Estatistica (2008), Special PME Study on Women, Social Communication, available at: http://www.ibge.gov.br/english/presidencia/noticias/noticia_impressao.php?id_noticia=1099; accessed 4 February 2010.

Jalbert, S. (2000), 'Women Entrepreneurs in the Global Economy', available at: http://www.cipe.org/programs/women/pdf/jalbert.pdf; accessed 4 February 2010.

Madalozzo, R. and S. Martins (2007), 'Gender Wage Gaps: Comparing the 80s, 90s and 00s in Brazil', *Revista de Economia e Administracao*, **6**(2), 141–56.

Metcalf, A. (1986), 'Fathers and Sons: The Politics of Inheritance in a Colonial Township', *Hispanic American Historical Review*, **66**(3), 455–84.

National Foundation for Women Business Owners (NFWBO) (1999), *Women Business Owners in Sao Paulo, Brazil: A Summary of Key Issues*, prepared by the Center for Women's Business Research and underwritten by IBM.

Patai, D. (1988), *Brazilian Women Speak: Contemporary Life Stories*, New Brunswick, New Jersey: Rutgers University Press.

Peterson, M. (1995), 'Leading Cuban-American Entrepreneurs: The Process of Developing Motives, Abilities and Resources', *Human Relations*, **48**(10), 1193–203.

Reynolds, P., W. Bygrave, E. Autio, L. Cox and M. Hay (2002), *Global Entrepreneurship Monitor, 2002 Executive Report*, The Center for Women's Leadership at Babson College/London Business School.

Rezende, F. (1998), 'The Brazilian Economy: Recent Developments and Future Prospects, *International Affairs*, **74**(3), 563–75.

Robben, A. (1984), 'Entrepreneurs and Scale: Interactional and Institutional Constraints on the Growth of Small-scale Enterprises in Brazil', *Anthropological Quarterly*, **57**(3), 125–38.

Robles, B. (2004), 'Emergent Entrepreneurs: Latino-owned Businesses in the Borderlands', *Texas Business Review*, October, 1–4.

Sebrae (2008), 'Sebrae: An Agent of Development, The Brazilian Service of Support for Micro and Small Enterprises Encourage Brazil's Entrepreneurship and Development', available at: http://www.sebrae.com.br/customizado/sebrae/institucional/sebrae-in-english; accessed 4 February 2010.

Skidmore, T. (2004), 'Brazil's Persistent Income Inequality: Lessons from History', *Latin American Politics and Society*, **46**(2), 133–50.

Smith-Hunter, A. (2006), *Women Entrepreneurs Across Racial Lines: Issues of Human Capital, Financial Capital and Network Structures*, Cheltenham, UK and Northampton, MA, USA: Edward Elgar.

Smith-Hunter, A. and J. Leone (2010), 'Evidence on the Characteristics of Women Entrepreneurs in Brazil: An Empirical Analysis', *International Journal of Management and Marketing Research*, **3**(1), 85–102.

Telles, E. (1994), 'Industrialization Racial Inequality in Employment: The Brazilian Example', *American Sociological Review*, **59**(1), 46–63.

World Fact Book (2009), 'Central Intelligence Agency: The World Fact Book, Brazil: People', available at: https://www.cia.gov/library/publications/the-world-factbook/geos/br.html; accessed 4 February 2010.

4 Canada
Karen D. Hughes

INTRODUCTION

Canada, like many other countries, has seen a significant expansion of activity in entrepreneurship, small business ownership, and self-employment in recent decades (OECD, 2000; Riverin, 2004, 2005). According to the most recent national report from the Global Entrepreneurship Monitor (GEM), Canada is 'one of the most dynamic industrialized countries in terms of entrepreneurial activity', ranking 12th out of 31 industrialized and developing countries (Riverin, 2005, p. 12). Canadian women have been at the forefront of this trend, establishing businesses in growing numbers, and with increasing success, across an expanding range of sectors.

This chapter provides an overview of women's contributions to entrepreneurial growth in Canada, highlighting key trends and successes, while also considering some of the ongoing challenges and barriers they face. Before turning to detail women's growing involvement in the small business sector, we first discuss women's participation in paid employment, as the gains they have made in educational, labour market and legal institutions in recent years have played a critical role in their growing entrepreneurial achievement.

THE POSITION OF WOMEN IN EMPLOYMENT IN CANADA

Canadian women have one of the highest labour force participation rates amongst industrialized nations. In recent decades their education and occupational aspirations have risen dramatically. Today nearly 60 per cent of Canadian women are employed in either a full-time or part-time job, and they have steadily increased their presence in once largely 'male' occupations such as management, law and medicine (Statistics Canada, 2006, p. 113). Social attitudes have also become more supportive of women's employment, and in the legal realm women have better protection from discriminatory practices of the past (Krahn et al., 2007, pp. 166–74, 206–11). This is not to say that gender inequalities have vanished. 'Glass ceilings', work–family conflict and the undervaluing of traditionally female areas of work all remain ongoing concerns. But looking at long-term employment patterns, Canadian women have made notable gains in the workplace, and these gains have been an underlying factor in their entrepreneurial success.

A brief review of labour market indicators illustrates key areas of change and stability. Most striking, perhaps, has been the steady increase of employment rates for all women, especially those who are mothers of pre-school and school-aged children. Whereas in 1976 just 39 per cent of mothers with children under 16 were employed, by 2006, this had risen to 73 per cent. Of note, 70 per cent of such mothers work relatively long hours of 30–40 hours per week (Statistics Canada, 2007, pp. 7–8). Higher education has played a key role in strengthening women's employment attachment and opportunities, with young women (aged 25–44) with university degrees having the highest employment rates (82.3 per cent) (ibid., p. 12). Despite a growing attachment to paid employment over the life course, however, many Canadian women continue to work in traditionally 'female' jobs. According to Statistics Canada's labour force data for 2006, two-thirds (67 per cent) of women worked in one of a number of heavily female-dominated areas, including teaching, nursing/health, clerical, administrative, sales, or service occupations (ibid., p. 9). Women also comprise 70 per cent of part-time workers.

Despite the persistence of traditional patterns, some women have made notable inroads into what historically were considered 'male' domains. In 2006, for example, women made up 52 per cent of business and financial professionals, 55 per cent of doctors and dentists and 36 per cent of all managers (ibid.). Vertical segregation persists, however, with women's presence falling sharply at the CEO management levels and on corporate boards (Hughes, 2000a, 2000b; Catalyst, 2003, 2006). And women have had far less success in boosting their presence in science, engineering and trades-related occupations (Finnie et al., 2001). Nevertheless, women's growing human capital and educational credentials have allowed them to move into more lucrative areas of employment, gaining valuable experience, skills, contacts and financial clout. Illustrating this, the proportion of women who are 'primary breadwinners' in Canadian families, out-earning their husbands, has increased steadily, from just 11 per cent in 1967 to 29 per cent in 2003 (Sussman and Bonnell, 2006).

Many different factors, such as political, legislative, educational and cultural, have contributed to the employment gains made by Canadian women. Certainly the women's movement of the 1960s and 1970s was a key impetus, sparking debate over gender inequalities and leading to a Prime Minister's Royal Commission on the Status of Women (RCSW) (Canada, 1970). Reporting in 1970, the RCSW made numerous recommendations aimed at providing greater education, training and employment opportunities for women. In the years that followed, federal and provincial legislation has addressed a range of discriminatory practices, taking on issues of maternity leave, pay equity, sexual harassment and discrimination on the grounds of sex. Two particularly important milestones were the Canadian Human Rights Act (1978) and Section 15 of the Canadian Charter of Rights and Freedoms (1985), which sought to eliminate gender-based discrimination.

Beyond legislative and political change, education has also played a vital role. From the mid-1970s to the late 1990s, the proportion of employed women with a university degree (Bachelor, Master or Doctorate) quadrupled, jumping from 3.0 per cent to 12.3 per cent. By the early 2000s women were outperforming men at the undergraduate level, earning 56 per cent of all Bachelor degrees (Statistics Canada, 2006, pp. 89, 100). Higher levels of education have also been accompanied by a shift into non-traditional areas of study, especially in law, medicine and business (Krahn et al., 2007, pp. 188–90). All of this has been important for enabling women to enter into more lucrative areas of work. Despite these gains, however, women's access to higher education has been uneven. Older women and First Nations women, for example, are far less likely to hold university degrees, and in recent years, socioeconomic status has reasserted its role in limiting access to post-secondary education. Importantly, given their growing presence in the Canadian population, visible minority women are much more likely to have a university degree, and a much higher presence in non-traditional areas such as business and science (Statistics Canada, 2006, pp. 246–7, 250).

THE CURRENT POSITION OF WOMEN AND SMALL BUSINESS OWNERSHIP

Women have been a central force in fuelling the increasingly important role that self-employment and small business ownership (SE/SBO) has played in the Canadian economy over the past two decades (OECD, 2000; Hughes, 2005). Industry Canada figures show that from the mid-1980s to the mid-2000s, women's entrepreneurship grew by over 200 per cent, with Canadian women entering the small and medium enterprise (SME) sector at twice the rate of their male peers (Industry Canada, 2004, p. 1). Indeed, Canadian women's contribution to the SE/SBO sector has been so significant that a Prime Minister's Task Force on Women Entrepreneurs was struck in November 2002 to explore how best to support and further encourage the growth of women-led businesses (Canada, 2003; Industry Canada, 2005). Based on country-wide consultations with hundreds of business owners, the Task Force (Canada, 2003) report documents the vital contribution and growing diversity of women entrepreneurs. Multi-country reports, such as the GEM, also confirm Canadian women's leadership in the SE/SBO sector (Minniti et al., 2005; Allen et al., 2007). According to the 2006 *GEM Report on Women's Entrepreneurship*, Canadian women ranked 1st amongst G8 countries in prevalence rates for 'established businesses' and 2nd for 'early-stage' entrepreneurial activity, just behind the United States (Allen et al., 2007, p. 11).

Women's influx into the SE/SBO sector can be seen clearly by looking at figures from Statistics Canada, which has tracked these trends since the late 1970s. These figures include both those working as 'employers' in incorporated and unincorporated businesses, as well as those working 'solo' in an incorporated or unincorporated business.[1] Figure 4.1 illustrates the growth of SE/SBO in the Canadian economy, with the number of Canadians engaged in such work effectively doubling from 1979 to 2007, from 1.3 million to 2.6 million. Women's overall share of SE/SBO increased steadily during this time, moving from just one-quarter of all SE/SBOs in 1979 to well over one-third (34.9 per cent) in 2007, a total of 911 900 women.

Who are these women and what types of business are they creating? Industry Canada (2004) provides the most current information available on women's involvement in the SME sector. According to its figures, almost half (47 per cent) of all SMEs in Canada in 2004 had some degree of female ownership, with about 16 per cent of SMEs being female 'majority-owned', 11 per cent female 'minority owned', and 20 per cent 'co-owned' equally by male and female partners (Industry Canada, 2008a, p. 35). In terms of the backgrounds and human capital they bring to their businesses, women, on average, are younger and better educated than their male counterparts. Approximately 32 per cent of women are under the age of 40 (compared with 21 per cent of men) and 54 per cent of women have a graduate or postgraduate education (compared with 47 per cent of men). While women have somewhat lower levels of direct industry experience than men, their backgrounds are still impressive, with 70 per cent of women reporting more than ten years of management experience in their industry (Industry Canada, 2004, 2008a).

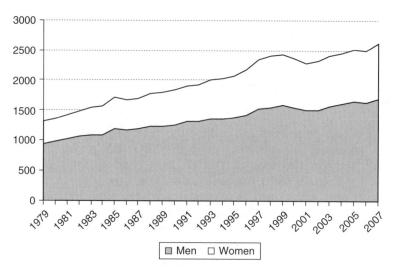

Source: Statistics Canada *Labour Force Survey CANSIM Table 282–0012.*

Figure 4.1   Women and men in self-employment, Canada, 1979–2007 (thousands)

In terms of the businesses they are creating and running, women-led firms make a substantial contribution to the Canadian economy, though there is great diversity in the scale of their operations, as well as key performance differences between female- and male-led firms. Industry Canada (2004) figures for the early 2000s indicate that 'majority women-owned' businesses employed about 570 000 people directly, while engaging another 404 000 people 'on contract'. Together, these majority-owned firms generated combined revenues of $72 billion, representing about 8 per cent of all revenues for the SME sector (ibid., 2004, p. 2). Despite this sizeable contribution, it needs to be kept in mind that most women-owned businesses in Canada, as elsewhere, are small and, on average, tend to be smaller than businesses run by men. According to Industry Canada (2004) figures, 85 per cent of women-owned firms employ fewer than five employees (compared with 79 per cent of men), and about half of women-owned businesses operate as sole proprietorships (compared with 39 per cent of men).

Industrial location is also a key factor in the success of women's enterprises, with many countries showing patterns of high concentration of women-led business in the service sector (Minniti et al., 2005, pp. 16–17). This same pattern holds true in Canada, where women, despite changing educational and employment patterns, are still less likely to operate in knowledge-based, goods-based or resource-based sectors. According to Industry Canada figures for 2001, 80 per cent of women-majority-owned SMEs operated in the service sector (compared with 59 per cent of firms owned by men). Indeed, half of women entrepreneurs operated in just three sectors: wholesale and retail trade (18 per cent), professional services (16 per cent) and information, culture and real estate (16 per cent) (Industry Canada, 2004). In contrast, knowledge-based and manufacturing sectors, which often provider greater economic returns, together account for just 6 per cent of all women-led business.

Finally, in terms of their financial performance, many women in the SE/SBO sector have done well, but there is considerable diversity in terms of economic performance of women entrepreneurs, and a notable gender gap between male- and female-headed firms. Recent Industry Canada (2004) figures show that female-owned businesses had total revenues of approximately $335000 per year in 2000, with net profits of $34000. This compares with male revenues of $706000, and net profits of $65000 per year (ibid., 2004, p. 4). On a percentage basis, this translates to a substantial gender gap, certainly in excess of the wage gap found in paid employment, with female-headed firms generating about 47.5 per cent of total revenues, and 52.2 per cent of net profit, of male-headed firms. Importantly, these figures do not control for key factors such as size, industry and age/stage of the business (e.g., start-up, established). More detailed statistical analysis by academic researchers, however, suggests that a gender gap in performance does persist even when controlling for such factors (see, for example, the summaries of research provided in Industry Canada, 2005; Jennings and Cash, 2006; Orser, 2007).

STRUCTURAL AND CONTEXTUAL BARRIERS TO WOMEN'S SMALL BUSINESS ENTREPRENEURSHIP

Though Canadian women entrepreneurs continue to face many barriers in building their businesses, it must be noted that they have received significant levels of support over the past 15 to 20 years, with federal and provincial governments devoting considerable attention and resources to promoting women's entrepreneurship. In addition to recent initiatives, such as the Prime Minister's Task Force on Women Entrepreneurs (Canada, 2003), there are several long-standing government-funded programmes that operate across the country, providing training, mentoring and financial support to nascent and established women entrepreneurs. Prominent examples include the Women's Enterprise Centres, which operate in the four Western Canadian provinces of British Columbia, Alberta, Saskatchewan and Manitoba. In Eastern Canada, support comes through the Women in Business Initiative run through the Atlantic Canada Opportunities Agency (ACOA). There is also a budding non-government sector of profit and non-for-profit groups catering specifically to women entrepreneurs (see Hughes, 2005, pp. 151–8 for a full review of existing programmes and services). In this sector, one of many excellent examples is Women Entrepreneurs of Canada (WEC), a non-profit organization with over 50000 members. WEC supports women-owned business at the local, national and international level, through networking, events, research, trade missions and an annual conference, Think Big! (WEC, 2008).

Many of these programmes fulfil a dual purpose of both (1) encouraging and promoting business start-up and (2) assisting more established businesses in overcoming barriers to success and growth. Consistent with a well-developed body of academic research, Canadian women appear to face many of the same barriers as female entrepreneurs in other countries, whether it be discriminatory attitudes or preconceptions (e.g., minimizing women's abilities), limited social capital (e.g., underdeveloped personal networks, lack of mentors), or specific challenges in developing their businesses (e.g., work–family conflict, overconcentration in low-return sectors). Indeed, one of the central premises upon which the Prime Minister's Task Force on Women Entrepreneurs was founded was that 'women entrepreneurs face unique challenges and barriers to success' (Canada, 2003, p. 2).

In Canada, several reports have reviewed the question of barriers, though they draw on different sources of information and often come to diverse conclusions as to what these specific barriers are (Belcourt et al., 1991; Canada, 2003; Industry Canada, 2004; for valuable discussions see Hughes, 2005; Jennings and Cash, 2006; Orser, 2007). One of the earliest studies, *The Glass Box: Women Business Owners in Canada*, identified eight 'unique' barriers that women entrepreneurs faced: discrimination by suppliers, creditors and clients; clustering in business sectors with low financial payoffs; limited relevant work experience, management training and experience; a shortage of peer support networks; financial and time constraints in accessing training; conflicting demands of work–family; low support from spousal partners; and insufficient financial returns (Belcourt et al.,1991, pp. 66–9).

More recent reports, such as the Prime Minister's Task Force on Women Entrepreneurs, suggest that many of these same barriers persist, despite the dramatic growth and increased sophistication of women-led businesses. Drawing on existing research and extensive hearings with aspiring and established women business owners across the country, the Task Force noted concerns over a range of issues. Central amongst these were: a lack of access to capital; difficulty developing and maintaining mentoring relationships; exclusion from valuable social networks; a need for business skills training; difficulty accessing business information; inappropriate coordination or targeting of programmes for women entrepreneurs; a lack of knowledge about exporting; and segregation into non-innovative service businesses (Canada, 2003, pp. 7–26).

While acknowledging the importance and persistence of barriers facing women, it must be noted that much existing Canadian evidence is based on women-only, rather than mixed-gender, studies, and thus it cannot be said 'definitively' that these barriers are experienced by women only, or by women across all contexts (Canada, 2003). Indeed, on some issues, such as differential access to business financing, there is debate as to the extent of gender differences. Recent analysis by Orser et al. (2006), for example, based on a large mixed-gender sample, finds that while women-led businesses are smaller, less growth-oriented, and overrepresented in service and retail sectors, there is 'no evidence of discrimination in terms of lending and approval' when controlling for other factors (e.g., industry, business size, etc.). Likewise, representative survey results from Industry Canada (2004), asking both male and female entrepreneurs to self-identify obstacles to business development and growth, suggest that many women and men face similar obstacles depending on business stage. For women entrepreneurs the most commonly mentioned barriers were: finding qualified labour (mentioned by 45 per cent); levels of taxation (40 per cent); instability of demand (33 per cent); low profitability (23 per cent); insufficient financing (22 per cent); government regulation (21 per cent); equipment depreciation (13 per cent); and management skills (7 per cent). Of note, the ranking and relative importance of these barriers was quite similar both for women and men entrepreneurs (Industry Canada, 2004, p. 5).

Thus, while a great deal of evidence suggests that Canadian women do face unique structural and contextual barriers in developing their businesses (especially as they relate to work–family demands, access to social networks, business skills development and industrial location) there is ongoing debate over the extent of gender differences, their origins and the contexts in which they are minimized or sharpened. Further research untangling the nature and extent of barriers faced by Canadian women entrepreneurs is thus a high priority.

STORIES OF SUCCESS

Regardless of the barriers they face, Canadian women have achieved considerable success in starting, developing and growing their businesses. As the Prime Minister's Task Force on Women Entrepreneurs (2003) observed in reviewing recent developments, Canadian women-led business has grown at an impressive rate, becoming more diverse and financially viable, employing significant numbers of Canadians and contributing annually in excess of $18 billion to the Canadian economy (Canada, 2003). Evidence of this success is detailed in a growing body of academic research, policy reviews and popular writing (see, for example, Belcourt et al., 1991; Robertson, 1997; Industry Canada, 1998, 2005; Fenwick, 2002; CIBC, 2005; Hughes, 2005; Jennings and Cash, 2006; Orser, 2007). Together, these accounts document a wide range of success, using both traditional benchmarks (e.g., revenue, net profit, growth) and less conventional measures (e.g., work–family balance, meaningful work).

While there are many different ways of examining women's 'success',[2] one of the most commonly used approaches is to consider 'top performers' or 'leaders' in the SE/SBO sector. In Canada, this can be done by looking at an annual list, 'The 'PROFIT W100: Canada's Top Women Entrepreneurs', which is published by the country's leading business publications, *Canadian Business* and *Profit Magazine*.[3] The most recent list of the PROFIT W100 (Canadian Business, 2008a), which is based on financial results for the fiscal year ending in 30 June 2007, includes a diverse range of women-led business. Many firms, such as Susan Niczowski's 7th-ranked Summer Fresh Salads Inc. or Lise Watier's 8th-ranked Lise Watier Cosmetics, were started and are still run by their original female founders. Other firms began life as a family business, but are now headed by 'next-generation' female family members, such as 3rd-ranked Logistec Corporation, a cargo handling and marine transportation business, run by Madeleine Paquin, or 12th-ranked Italian Centre Shops Ltd., a second-generation family business run by Teresa Spinelli.

Looking at this group of top 100 women-led businesses, a number of features of their businesses stand out. First, we see considerable longevity, with a median year of establishment of 1992 and a median firm age of 16 years. Of note, however, 11 of the top 100 firms have been founded since 2002 and have thus been operating for just five years or less. Not surprisingly, annual average revenues for the W100 are much higher than for women-led SMEs overall, with a median revenue of $8.5 million per year.[4] It bears noting, however, that annual revenues range widely, from $1.5 billion reported for 1st-ranked Rebecca MacDonald, head of the Energy Savings Income Fund (which offers fixed price gas and electricity contracts), to the 100th-ranked Lynn Cook, head of 360 Visibility Inc (an IT consultancy) with $2.7 million of reported revenues. In terms of their contribution to employment, these top 100 businesses together employed over 12 000 Canadians, with 8086 full-time employees and 4408 part-time or contract workers. Again, these averages mask considerable differences, with firm size ranging from 5 to 985 full-time employees, and 0 to 1000 part-time employees and contract workers. Overall firms employed an average (median) of 35 full-time employees and four part-time/contract workers each.

Of special note, given previous discussions concerning the industrial location of women-led business, there is a much different industrial profile to the WP100 (Canadian Business, 2008a). As noted earlier, nearly 80 per cent of majority-owned female-led SMEs in Canada are based in the service sector, while just 6 per cent were in knowledge-based or the manufacturing sectors (Industry Canada, 2004). In contrast, while we still find strong proportions of WP100 businesses located in professional services (23 per cent) and wholesale and retail trade (14 per cent), there are a significant proportion (19 per cent) of businesses in the manufacturing sector. Another 11 per cent are located in health or child care sectors, more traditionally 'female' sectors, but there is also a good presence in more traditionally 'male' dominated sectors, such as transportation (5 per cent) and construction (5 per cent). Moreover, even when women have created businesses in traditionally 'female' sectors, such as food services or personal services, which traditionally have low returns, they have developed these businesses in innovative ways, for example, moving into large-scale manufacturing, developing high 'value-added' products, and pursuing strategies of forward and backward vertical integration.

In order to get a better sense of how some of the top Canadian women have developed their businesses, we conclude by discussing two case studies, one in a more traditionally 'female' sector in food services, and the other in a much less traditionally female manufacturing area.

BOX 4.1   W100 7TH-RANKED SUSAN NICZOWSKI, SUMMER FRESH SALADS INC.

Founded by Susan Niczowski and her mother, Summer Fresh Salads manufactures and sells gourmet salads, dips and appetizers. It is a leading North American supplier to retail and food stores including supermarkets, restaurants and caterers, with revenues of $43 million. Niczowski began the business in 1991 when she spotted a gap in supermarket offerings for nutritious 'fast' foods. Launching production in a 3000 sq ft facility, she started modestly with a narrow product range in high-end salads. With success she expanded to include dips, appetizers, speciality soups and gourmet side dishes. Today Summer Fresh operates in a 63000 sq ft 'state of the art', federally regulated facility, with both organic and kosher certification. Since its inception, Summer Fresh has grown steadily, with revenues of $42 million and 150 full-time employees in the fiscal year ending in 2007.

In terms of assessing Niczowski's success, some key issues stand out. First there is a strong link between her prior work experience and business. University educated, with a BSc in chemistry from the University of Toronto, Niczowski worked for many years as a microbiologist in the food industry for a firm that is now a part of Maple Leaf Foods Inc. This experience no doubt provided essential skills in 'opportunity recognition' and her later business development. Financial and family support also appear to have been critical. Niczowski accessed start-up capital through a $50000 bank loan, but the loan was co-signed by her parents. In start-up phase Niczowski also gained needed resources by selling a 50 per cent stake to another Canadian food supply firm, a stake she bought back in 1999 when the firm was acquired by a publicly traded company. A final key to Niczowski's success appears to be strong product innovation, growth orientation and a value-added focus, which has allowed her to move beyond the often limiting confines of a traditional 'female' sector. Following the motto that 'food is fashion', Summer Fresh constantly updates its offerings with new innovative products and ideas, and provides a library of over 3000 recipes to share with customers.

Sources: Summer Fresh Foods corporate website, http://www.summerfresh.com; Won (2005).

BOX 4.2   W100 20TH-RANKED LEE MCDONALD, SOUTHMEDIC INC.

Started in 1983, Southmedic Inc. operates in a non-traditional industrial sector for women, manufacturing medical devices and distributing surgical speciality products. Currently selling products in more than 62 countries, the company began when Lee McDonald, then working as a hospital nurse in cardiac and trauma units, identified the need for product improvements in existing anaesthesia machines. Designing 'Anaeslock', a patented vaporizer interlock system, McDonald produced early models through a local machine shop. Given the highly regulated nature of the health and medical supply industry, however, she could not sell her product without Health Canada approval and FDA registration, and Southmedic Inc. was born. In just two years, McDonald was successful in distributing her product to 20 countries. She carried on to develop new products (e.g., Vapofil, Aerosol T), moving in 1986 to a 2000 sq ft facility with four employees. By 2005, having undergone numerous expansions, Southmedic doubled its facility to 60 000 sq ft. It now has three divisions, including an R&D division, with 100 full-time and ten part-time/contract employees, and revenues of $18 million for the fiscal year ending 30 June 2007.

In looking at her success, it is notable that McDonald, like Niczowski, established a business with a direct connection to her prior work experience and formal training. This was essential for 'opportunity recognition', though clearly McDonald was also highly innovative, motivated and resourceful in developing her initial products. With respect to industry, McDonald notes that the medical equipment sector offered a great opportunity to run a scalable business, it is 'highly stable', with internationally accepted standards for medical products, thus making it easier to work on volume and sell to foreign markets. It is also more protected from the types of slowdowns and product shifts common in other manufacturing sectors like automotives.

Today Southmedic exports to hospitals in over 60 different countries, including those in the United States, Europe, Scandinavia and Latin America (see Industry Canada, 2008b). Of note, in receiving the 2006 RBC Canadian Women Entrepreneurship Award, McDonald credited her nursing training for her success, noting that it helped hone 'the ability to listen, to analyze situations with speed and caring, to be comfortable with change and unpredictability, and to ask questions' (RBC, 2008).

Sources: Southmedic Inc. corporate website, http://www.southmedic.com; RBC (2008); Ubdul (2008).

SUMMARY

This chapter outlines current trends in women's entrepreneurship in Canada, a country that has seen a dramatic expansion of self-employment and small business activity in recent years. Women's entrepreneurship has taken place amidst a set of broad changes that has significantly reshaped Canadian women's political, economic and family status. Since the 1970s, Canadian women have notably increased their educational achievement and labour force participation. This is particularly true for mothers with young children. In addition to much stronger labour force attachment, Canadian women have also increased their presence within a wide range of occupations, especially in management and the professions (e.g., law, medicine) that were once considered 'non-traditional' for them. At the same time these changes have unfolded, Canadian governments, both federal and provincial, have actively promoted a more 'entrepreneurial economy', providing funding and assistance to those interested in pursuing opportunities in the small business sector. Women have played a key role in fuelling growth in small business ownership, entering the SME sector at twice the rate of their male peers. Governments have been especially encouraging to women entrepreneurs, undertaking initiatives such as the Prime Minister's Task Force on Women Entrepreneurs, and providing funding and advisory support through provincial Women's Enterprise Centres.

Currently, Canadian women make up over one-third of entrepreneurs, a significant change. Though somewhat younger than their male counterparts, they are better educated, and bring impressive management and industry expertise into their ventures. A key feature of women's enterprise today is diversity in the scope and scale of their operations. Despite many high profile 'success' stories, most women-led firms are small, having just a few employees or operating as sole proprietorships. Women's ventures also cluster in traditionally 'female' sectors, such as retail sales and personal services, where financial returns are low and business expansion is difficult. As in other countries, Canadian trends show marked performance differentials between male- and female-led firms (e.g., revenues). Why these exist is the subject of ongoing debate. Some researchers point to gender-specific barriers (e.g., discrimination, lack of access to financing), while others suggest male and female entrepreneurs face similar obstacles. Although the case studies in this chapter illustrate success in both 'traditional' and 'non-traditional' sectors, an analysis of 'top-performing' women entrepreneurs highlights a much stronger propensity to enter into 'non-traditional' areas in knowledge-based and manufacturing sectors, where economic opportunities and returns are high. Hopefully future research can enhance our knowledge about the factors that are most critical for women's entrepreneurial success. Studies that take a more multidimensional view of success, for example, examining not just financial indicators, but also women's satisfaction with their daily work, work–family balance, and the meaning of their ventures, will be especially valuable for understanding Canadian women's strong and growing interest in entrepreneurship, and the growth and vibrancy characterizing this sector in recent years.

NOTES

1. Unpaid family workers are also included in the overall total self-employment rate, though they comprise only a small number of the total category.
2. Research on women entrepreneurs suggests they may have a more multi-dimensional view of success, balancing conventional measures, such as financial growth and performance, with less conventional measures such as personal meaning or work–family balance. For further discussions see Brush (1992); Hughes (2005); Orser (2007).
3. Rankings are determined by gross annual revenue for the most recently completed fiscal year. Gross revenues are defined using generally accepted accounting principles (GAAP). All candidates must submit complete financial statements. To qualify, a company must be headquartered in Canada, with significant Canadian operations; it must be independent (not a division or subsidiary); must have 50 per cent Canadian ownership if privately owned; and operate at arm's length from related companies that have declared their candidacy for the ranking. The nominee must have a senior management role (e.g., CEO, President), contribute significantly to the management or strategic direction of the firm and have a substantial ownership stake relative to the overall structure (see Canadian Business, 2008b).
4. Because of this wide revenue range we report the median rather than the mean as this is less influenced by outlying values.

REFERENCES

Allen, I.E., Langowitz, N. and Minniti, M. (2007), *Global Entrepreneurship Monitor: 2006 Report on Women and Entrepreneurship*, available at: http://www.gemconsortium.org/about.aspx?page=special_topic_women; accessed 4 February 2010.
Belcourt, M., Burke, R. and Lee-Gosselin, H. (1991), *The Glass Box: Women Business Owners in Canada*, Ottawa: Canadian Advisory Council on the Status of Women.
Brush, C. (1992), 'Research on Women Business Owners: Past Trends, a New Perspective and Future Directions', *Entrepreneurship Theory and Practice*, **16**(4), 5–30.
Canada (1970), *Report of the Royal Commission on the Status of Women*, Ottawa: Information Canada.
Canada (2003), *Prime Minister's Task Force on Women Entrepreneurs: Report and Recommendations*, Ottawa.
Canadian Business (2008a), 'The PROFIT W100', available at: http://www.canadianbusiness.com/rankings/w100/list.jsp?pageID=article&year=2007&content=faqen&type=about; accessed 4 February 2010.
Canadian Business (2008b), 'Nomination Information and Methodology'; available at: http://www.canadianbusiness.com/rankings/w100/list.jsp?pageID=article&year=2007&content=faqen&type=about; accessed 4 February 2010.
Catalyst (2003), *The Catalyst Census of Women Board Directors of Canada*, New York: Catalyst.
Catalyst (2006), *2005 Catalyst Census of Women Board Directors of the FP 500*, New York: Catalyst.
CIBC (2005), 'Women Entrepreneurs: Leading the Charge', Toronto: CIBC World Markets, available at: http://www.cibc.com/ca/small-business/article-tools/women-entrepreneurs.html; accessed 4 February 2010.
Fenwick, T. (2002), 'Transgressive Desires: New Enterprising Selves in the New Capitalism', *Work, Employment and Society*, **6**(4), 703–23.
Finnie, R., Lavoie, M. and Rivard, M. (2001), 'Women in Engineering: The Missing Link in the Canadian Knowledge Economy', *Education Quarterly Review*, **7**(3), 8–17.
Hughes, K.D. (2000a), 'Restructuring Work, Restructuring Gender: Women's Movement into Non-traditional Occupations in Canada', in Victor W. Marshall et al. (eds), *Restructuring Work and the Life Course*, Toronto: University of Toronto Press, pp. 84–106.

Hughes, K.D. (2000b), *Women and Corporate Directorships in Canada: Trends and Issues*, Ottawa: Canadian Policy Research Networks.

Hughes, K.D. (2005), *Female Enterprise in the New Economy*, Toronto: University of Toronto Press.

Industry Canada (1998), 'Shattering the Glass Box? Women Entrepreneurs and the Knowledge Based Economy', *Micro-Economic Monitor*, Third Quarter (Special Report), Ottawa: Industry Canada.

Industry Canada (2004), *Small Business Financing Profiles: Women Entrepreneurs* (November), Ottawa: Industry Canada.

Industry Canada (2005), *Sustaining the Momentum: An Economic Forum on Women Entrepreneurs – Summary Report* (March), Ottawa: Industry Canada.

Industry Canada (2008a), *Key Small Business Statistics* (January), Ottawa: Industry Canada.

Industry Canada (2008b), Strategis: Company Profiles, available at: http://strategis.ic.gc.ca/app/ccc/srch/nvgt.do?lang=eng&app=1&prtl=1&sbPrtl=&estblmntNo=123456014084&profile=cmpltPrfl; accessed 5 February 2010.

Jennings, J.E. and Cash, M. (2006), 'Women's Entrepreneurship in Canada: Progress, Puzzles, and Priorities', in Candida G. Brush et al. (eds), *Growth-oriented Women Entrepreneurs and their Businesses: A Global Research Perspective*, Cheltenham, UK and Northampton, MA, USA: Edward Elgar.

Krahn, H.J., Lowe, G.S. and Hughes, K.D. (2007), *Work, Industry and Canadian Society*, Toronto: Thomson Nelson.

Minniti, M., Arenius, P. and Langowitz, N. (2005), *Global Entrepreneurship Monitor: 2004 Report on Women and Entrepreneurship*; available at: http://www.gemconsortium.org/about.aspx?page=special_topic_women; accessed 4 February 2010.

Organisation for Economic Co-operation and Development (OECD) (2000), 'The Partial Renaissance of Self-employment', *OECD Employment Outlook*, Paris: OECD.

Orser, B.J. (2007), *Canadian Women Entrepreneurs, Research and Public Policy: A Review of the Literature*, Ottawa: Telfer School of Management and Foreign Affairs and International Trade Canada.

Orser, B.J., Riding, A.L. and Manley, K. (2006), 'Women Entrepreneurs and Financial Capital', *Entrepreneurship Theory and Practice*, **30**(5), 667–86.

RBC (2008), RBC Canadian Women Entrepreneur Awards: Past Winners, available at: http://www.theawards.ca/cwea/past-winners.cfm; accessed 5 February 2010.

Riverin, N. (2004), *2002 Canadian Report, Global Entrepreneurship Monitor*; available at: http://web.hec.ca/creationdentreprise/CERB_Backup-12-mai-2008/pdf/2004-07GEM2002Canadian-en.PDF; accessed 4 February 2010.

Riverin, N. (2005), *2003 Canadian Report, Global Entrepreneurship Monitor*, available at: http://www.gemconsortium.org/document.aspx?id=387; accessed 4 February 2010.

Robertson, H. (1997), *Taking Care of Business: Stories of Canadian Women Entrepreneurs*, Bolton, Ontario: Fenn Publishing Company Ltd.

Statistics Canada (2006), *Women in Canada: A Gender-based Statistical Report* (5th edition), Ottawa: Statistics Canada.

Statistics Canada (2007), *Women in Canada: Work Chapter Updates 2006*, Catalogue 89F0133XIE, Ottawa: Statistics Canada.

Sussman, D. and Bonnell. S. (2006), 'Wives as Primary Breadwinners', *Perspectives on Labour and Income*, **7**(8), 10–17.

Ubdul, U. (2008), 'Southmedic Turns 25', *Canadian Plastics Magazine* (April).

Women Entrepreneurs of Canada (WEC) (2008), corporate website, available at: http://www.wec.ca/; accessed 4 February 2010.

Won, S. (2005), 'Food Fashion Takes to the Grocers' Aisles', *Globe and Mail Report on Business*, 2 March.

5 China
Jonathan M. Scott, Javed Hussain, Richard T. Harrison and Cindy Millman

INTRODUCTION

Economic restructuring, marketization and privatization have changed the world of work, management and entrepreneurship for women in the People's Republic of China (henceforth referred to as China). The restructuring, privatization and, in some cases, abolition of many state-owned enterprises (SOEs), as a response to international pressures and increasing globalization, have no doubt changed the nature of the culture and social capital in China and in particular will have influenced the nature of gendered relationships in Chinese society. In this chapter we investigate the socio-cultural barriers to women's career paths and economic role in China specifically through a review of women's entrepreneurship, and identify how women have overcome these barriers to start and grow a successful new venture. This builds on our previous primary and secondary data-based research, which has examined the supply of and demand for finance for growth in Chinese women-led firms (Hussain et al., 2010). Conceptually, gender equality can be linked to the communist *danwei*, 'a multi-functional organization which combines productive and reproductive functions', which the reforms envisaged severing, hence potentially leading to increased gender inequality (Stockman, 1994, p. 759). Yet, given widespread low wages, married men and women in China must both work full-time to make ends meet (Cooke, 2004).

Our aim in this chapter is to explore the employment and small business context, then identify constraints facing women in starting up and growing a new venture, and how women have overcome these barriers to succeed in entrepreneurship and entrepreneurial growth. Two previous studies have examined successful women in IT careers in China (Aaltio and Huang, 2007; Xian and Woodhams, 2008), highlighting work–family conflict and the role of *guanxi* relationships or social networks (Aaltio and Huang, 2007). *Guanxi* can be defined as networks or connections, or as Chen and Chen (2004, p. 308) observed, 'personal connections between two or more people'.[1] Work–family conflict has been widely cited in Western literature as a constraint for women entrepreneurs (Jennings and McDougald, 2007) and managers, and would appear to be of salience in the Chinese context despite smaller families due to the one-child policy. Other researchers have explored the critical success factors – such as diversification, internationalization, innovation, quality management, strategy and an entrepreneurial approach – in high-performance Chinese SMEs (Cooke, 2008a), but our chapter is the first that explores successful women's entrepreneurship in China from the perspective of the business owner. We argue that it is critical in this context to understand the role of *guanxi* as it impacts upon women in the labour market (Yueh, 2006) and the nature of gender as a construct and its reality in the society and culture of China (Zheng, 2003). We seek to bring together these disparate but inextricably linked themes by building upon Bourdieu's (1986) forms of capital and how they relate to gender to influence social action and practice in a cross-cultural context (Elam, 2008) and without erroneously treating men's business ownership as a benchmark (Ahl, 2006). In the absence of reliable and consistent primary and secondary data, we draw from a number of key published studies.

THE POSITION OF WOMEN IN EMPLOYMENT IN CHINA

Alongside a raft of equal opportunities legislation, women in China have near parity with men in terms of quantity, if not quality, of participation in the labour market (Cooke, 2004, 2005). Indeed, the quality versus quantity debate is particularly important in the Chinese context. One study found that women's job mobility prospects in China have declined, perhaps due to lower levels of regulation from the state (Cao and Hu, 2007). Indeed, there appears to be discrimination against women, for example, in promotion procedures (Cooke, 2001, 2004), which Cooke (2001, p. 347) ascribes to 'the weakening power of state administrative intervention, the development of the market economy, the looseness of the legislation and the discriminatory nature of some of the regulations themselves'. While commentators such as Cooke (2005) envisage economic reforms and privatization as generating employment opportunities for women, economic restructuring and globalization may actually disadvantage 'older, less educated women workers', which Liu has described as the 'unlucky generation' (Liu, 2007a, p. 151). Recent large-scale factory layoffs are also more likely to affect older women, who are becoming further marginalized. However, while it is clear that there are winners and losers in the globalization process (Stiglitz, 2003), and the losers include older women (Liu, 2007a, 2007b), we would argue that the winners include those women who have fulfilled their entrepreneurial dreams. Nevertheless, there remains concern among analysts about the negative effects of deregulation, privatization and the looser hand of the state. This looser hand of the state, whilst promoting progress and meteoric economic growth has, in the view of Berik et al. (2007), led to a number of disadvantages for women, such as 'disproportionate' numbers of women being made redundant in SOEs and increasing wage inequalities, and hence they argue for 'reprioritizing equity and welfare on the policy agenda'.

This has significant implications for the economic role and social position of women in Chinese society. There is occupational segregation of the workforce by gender (Cai and Wu, 2006), which leads to inequalities in both work and pay. Zhang et al. (2008), however, suggest that in China's cultural context it is women who are married with children (just as in the West – Jennings and McDougald, 1997), who must balance housework and family duties, that experience the greatest levels of such inequalities. Furthermore, there are few 'career breaks' to cover maternity leave and child-rearing obligations, nor is part-time work widely practised (Cooke, 2004, p. 244). Foreign direct investment (FDI) in China has, in the long run, appeared to have provided greater 'wage gains' to men than to women (Braunstein and Brenner, 2007). Shu et al. (2007) found gender differentials in FDI employment, with women concentrated in lower-paid 'export-oriented manufacturing industries' rather than 'high-paying foreign firms and joint ventures'. In the rural context, the process of marketization has shifted men into non-farm jobs while not necessarily excluding women from such jobs, particularly where there are insufficient numbers of male workers (Matthews and Nee, 2000). Elsewhere, job insecurity and harsh 'working conditions' of women migrant workers have been identified (Ngai, 2004), as well as increasing marginalization (Tam, 2008), reinforcing the difficulties faced by migrant workers in China (Feng and Anan, 2003; Liang and Chen, 2003).

Although there is evidence that 91 per cent of businesses have women in senior management roles (Catalyst, 2008), this finding fails to indicate the percentage of women in such businesses and may be, as Cooke (2008b, p. 30) suggests, simply a case of Kanterian 'tokenism' where there is a 'guaranteed seat system' for women but often only one woman senior manager. Indeed, as Catalyst (2008) reported in 2005, 16.8 per cent of legislators, senior officials and managers were women and Cooke (2008b, p. 26) found that, 'only 0.7 per cent of women worked as heads of organizations in 2004, compared with 2.5 per cent of men'. While nine out of ten businesses have women senior managers, only one in six of senior managers and one in four organizational heads were women (Catalyst, 2008; Cooke, 2008b). As we stated earlier, management research in China is bedevilled by a lack of reliable data and so we remain cautious about these figures. Nonetheless, while the quantity of women working appears to be high, the quality of such jobs and the future promotional prospects for many of the women employees are relatively low compared with those of men. Women managers in China must rely upon *guanxi* with those higher up the organization to advance their careers, while there is also emerging a new generation of 'younger and highly educated' women managers with 'a modern outlook' compared with the more 'masculine' middle-aged women managers (Cooke, 2008b, pp. 32–4). An alternative to waged employment, small business ownership is considered in the next section: there is, of course, a possible generational effect in this scenario, in that entrepreneurial careers and business ownership is most likely to appeal to the post-Cultural Revolution generation.

THE CURRENT POSITION OF WOMEN AND SMALL BUSINESS OWNERSHIP

When conceptualizing China as a transition or post-socialist economy, it is important to distinguish between the notion of classic 'entrepreneurship' as an activity engaged in by Kirznerian opportunity-seeking entrepreneurs and business 'proprietorship' (in which there is a lack of reinvestment of retained profits in the business and, therefore, limited growth aspirations – Scase, 2003; Smallbone and Welter, 2009). Some women may have been pushed into small business ownership by labour market disadvantage and may not be classic entrepreneurs. Indeed, Bosma and Harding (2007, p. 15) report that fewer than 40 per cent of Chinese early-stage entrepreneurs were motivated by necessity (push), compared with 60 per cent who were pulled towards opportunity. The ratio of opportunity to necessity entrepreneurship for Chinese men was 1.57 but for women it was only 1.11 (Allen et al., 2008, p. 20). This motivational disparity between men and women business owners in China confirms some of our assumptions about the impact of labour market disadvantage on the level of women's business ownership, both established and new. Moreover, in China, women's careers are often secondary to their husbands', while traditionally it is not normally the case that 'women should be a boss supervising men' (Cooke, 2004, p. 255).

China has high levels of early-stage entrepreneurship, defined as 'owning and managing, alone or with others, a nascent business, or one that has been in operation for 42 months or less' (Allen et al., 2008, p. 6), at 16 per cent of adults, according to the Global Entrepreneurship Monitor (Bosma and Harding, 2007). Indeed, 19 per cent of men and 13.5 per cent of women were early-stage entrepreneurs, and 9.6 per cent of men and 7 per cent of women were established business owners, a total of 28.6 per cent of men and 20.5 per cent of women (Allen et al., 2008, p. 12). In contrast, according to official statistics, 2.5 per cent of women and 3.6 per cent of men in work were owner-managers or self-employed in 2002, and these figures rose to 5.5 per cent and 6.8 per cent in urban areas (Cooke, 2005).[2] Although these figures must be treated with some caution, and we are talking about ownership/self-employment as opposed to recent new venture creation, they do support the GEM findings that the level of women's entrepreneurship is lower than that of men (Baughn et al., 2006; Allen et al., 2008). Such contradictions, official statistical fiction and wide variations in survey results make it incredibly difficult to pinpoint exactly the level of established and nascent small business ownership by women.

STRUCTURAL AND CONTEXTUAL BARRIERS TO WOMEN'S ENTREPRENEURSHIP IN CHINA

Having broadly outlined where women stand in terms of both employment and small business ownership (and this has been necessarily broad given the significant data gaps), we explore below some of the barriers to women starting and growing a new venture in China. To do so, we draw upon Elam's (2008) practice theory-based analytical framework, which builds upon earlier work by Bourdieu (1986) and others. Hence, we have arranged the following meta-analysis in terms of Bourdieu's forms of capital, that is, *economic* capital, *cultural* capital, *social* capital and *symbolic* capital (Bourdieu, 1986), which by implication leads to 'structured social action' (Elam, 200, p. 4). A limitation of this approach is the overly structuralist, rather than agency theory approach of Bourdieu (ibid.), and also the Western European, that is, Francophone, bias of his study and yet it is a sophisticated conceptual framework that enlightens us as to women's barriers. Our contribution to the further development of this conceptual model is that in the Chinese context of the primacy of the family and the indivisibility of society and culture, contrary to the more individualistic and culturally diverse West, we have collapsed Bourdieu's social capital and cultural capital into one overarching concept, of 'socio-cultural capital', which more accurately captures *guanxi* and associated Chinese socio-cultural traditions and norms. Next we explore women's entrepreneurship in China in terms of economic, socio-cultural and symbolic capital.

First, we explore economic capital related barriers including assets and finance. Theoretically, in the Western context, we know that having money and inheritances is a predictor of entrepreneurial start-up and, indeed, liquidity constraints are a major barrier to start-up (Blanchflower and Oswald, 1998). However, given the weaker property rights and lower levels of capital accumulation in China as well as the above emphasized gender inequalities (and the primacy of the husband's career – Cooke, 2004), we can posit that a lack of sufficient economic capital to start a business is likely to be a barrier for many Chinese women *on their own*. In tandem with husbands or family, this we would expect to be less of a barrier. Thus, many Chinese women remain tied to men and depend upon their support for the entrepreneurial venture, for personal capital. That begs the question, what of banks? Bank loans were used by fewer than 4 per cent of Chinese firms in one study (Gregory and Tenev, 2001). Wang (2004, p. 34) revealed that external capital is not accessible to many firms due to 'lagging in the banking system, an inadequate financial structure, lack of a guarantee system'. Smaller, high-growth, private sector firms in China experienced fewer liquidity constraints than larger companies and also preferred the 'informal credit market' (Chow and Fung, 2000, p. 365). However, these authors also found that state-owned banks would not fund small private firms and thus there appeared to be a 'lending bias' (ibid., p. 371), which is likely to extend to women-led firms, unless they access finance informally through *guanxi*. There is little evidence that women experienced 'discouraged borrowing' or undercapitalization or undertook 'bootstrapping' financing strategies. Women, therefore, appear to be no more disadvantaged in obtaining finance than men in China and both women- and men-led firms appear to be significantly stronger in relation to having enough finance to grow than at the start-up phase (Hussain et al., 2010). However, whether or not they can access finance more easily than men (with or without the assistance of men, family or *guanxi*), it appears that financial barriers affect perhaps as many as a third of women entrepreneurs in China (though see Hussain et al., 2006 for a comparative China–UK perspective).

Second, barriers emerging from socio-cultural capital centre largely on *guanxi* relationships, a form of social capital that is highly culturally determined and may be conceptualized as being ethereal or intangible. We found that fewer women use *guanxi* to access finance (Hussain et al., 2010). Why might this be? And might it affect the use of *guanxi* in other business transactions and, therefore, the future performance of the firm? Cooke (2005, p. 21) highlights a major barrier for women managers, which no doubt applies too to women entrepreneurs, in that if they interact too closely with male contacts in their *guanxi* network there may be 'rumours which can be highly damaging to their career because of the relatively low tolerance by Chinese society of close relationships between men and women outside marriage'. Although a rather old study, Hisrich and Fan (1991) found relatively poor levels of education (institutionalized cultural capital, according to Bourdieu, 1986) amongst women business owners, which is being rapidly transformed due to the emergence of a highly educated new generation of entrepreneurs. Education can thus be an enabler rather than a barrier to women's entrepreneurial success.

Third, and finally, symbolic capital-related barriers (which Elam, 2008, p. 47 describes as 'legitimacy, social approval, prestige, status, symbolic power') are highly important in a nation with such a traditional and long-established culture such as China. Women's careers are often secondary to their husbands' (Cooke, 2004, p. 255) and the glass ceiling, or the 'bamboo curtain', may be a significant constraint for women, even in new-technology-based firms (Tan, 2008). On the one hand, where a woman may seek to start a business for reasons of necessity, there are no doubt additional benefits of legitimacy or social approval and status. On the other hand, whether this actually transcends the traditional cultural 'male domination' (Cooke, 2008b, p. 22) is debatable and, despite increasing opportunities, women entrepreneurs face difficulties at the work–family interface in relation to housework (Kitching and Jackson, 2002). Consequently, given that 'reasons for start up are more family oriented, more for assisting their husbands or more for obeying parental requests' (Chu, 2000, p. 82), this finding ties in with the concept of *danwei* (Stockman, 1994). However, on a more positive note, family support for women to start businesses (whether due to social approval or not) would be critical for the subsequent success of the venture, and such support is likely to be present in a highly family-oriented society such as China.

STORIES OF SUCCESS

The above brief review of barriers to women's entrepreneurship has highlighted a unique set of issues related to economic, socio-cultural and symbolic capital that ought to be explored further in future in-depth research and should inform policy-makers in China. Rather than sounding overly negative, this section of this chapter highlights some of the very many stories of success of women's entrepreneurship in China.

BOX 5.1 CHIEF EXECUTIVE, GUANGZHOU

Case A is aged 46 and is Chief Executive of a hair products manufacturer in Guangzhou with over 1000 employees. She graduated from Huanan Science & Engineering University and majored in Chemistry. Her business expanded rapidly about three years ago and increased its yearly revenues to over 2 billion renminbi (RMB) (due to the use of extensive *guanxi*-related networking and contacts), while prior to this the business had remained flat at around 0.2 billion a year during the first ten years or so. She said that, 'Business is a pleasure for me. I need to earn but I do not totally depend on this income. Success is measured in different ways: I think my measure of success has changed as I lived overseas [in the past]. I believe in hard work but not so hard that I do not have a life. Perhaps my comfort level has robbed me of my heritage'.

During the early stage, she relied upon mentors, 'I learnt that mentoring or someone taking an interest in your career is not purely a Chinese phenomenon but equally operates in the West: but in the West mentoring takes place in a university or at an employer and, in the case of China, family and friends may have carried out this role. However, the family and friend mentors may not have the expertise or experience to empower you. So the Chinese system may have more people who are mentored, but this may be not as effective if the standard of mentoring is not so great'.

In terms of relationships, she believed that women have to be 'as tough as men in the business world', and she commented that: 'Men are men wherever they come from, but remember that men are not as innocent as they may appear from their looks; they are equal in mischief to Westerners, if not more. In such an environment, there are a lot of challenges for women and China is not an exception'. She managed to overcome barriers, such as finance, in terms of having the right networks and connections (*guanxi*) and noted that, 'The family's standing and financial position is a key factor in one's success and in my case these two factors just converged'.

When asked what she means by success, as she considers herself a successful woman entrepreneur, she replied that: 'A quick increase in turnover, profit and growth: you cannot wait for things to tick in China. Success in China is linked with one's personal standing, achievements and status: all these three things need to have some level of recognition. And gaining a listing on the stock market is a marker of achievement'. Finally, she said that she believed that 'every business has challenges but in China the business challenge is to make money before everyone else copies your idea, so you need to have money ready to enter and move quickly otherwise you cannot just wait to raise money once you are in the business'. For example, in China every business tries to enter a 'blue sea' (niche market) to be successful before it turns into a 'red sea' (mature market), in which many businesses are fighting for a position in that marketplace.

BOX 5.2   RESTAURATEUR, BEIJING

Case B is a 39-year-old restaurateur in Beijing, with over 87 employees. She has high-school-level education and has been married twice. She was a housewife during her first marriage but after divorce she had to look after herself. She worked for a restaurant for three years prior to starting her own business, using her savings and financial support from her parents, eight years ago. She described her business as 'excellent' and her turnover increased from zero in the first year to almost 1.2 million RMB per year. She achieved strong profit margins of around 65 per cent but her emphasis is on achieving return customers and she noted that, 'Chinese customers and markets are unforgiving: there is no loyalty without standard, quality and value for money, they just move on if they do not get satisfaction. I have to perform and perform every evening to keep my reputation, customers and business'.

She emphasized that, 'I learnt that I need to keep myself happy. I married again four years ago. My husband has his own export business and that suits me well. We have one child. I do spend more time with my child now. I think it is important but my parents are so much help. I have to work late sometimes too and that is a problem. Business does takes time and energy out of one's life. Nothing comes free in life: that is what I have learnt'. She trained her employees as she was the only one who had the cooking skills at start-up. She said that, 'Chinese employees have not learned how to work independently and they need to be monitored and that means that so many businesses are small and cannot grow'. Traditionally, she explained, 'A woman is always behind a man's success. Men are gamblers and women are a more stable force. Historically, women are seen just as a good time by men, and sometimes they cannot cope when a woman is a boss'. And yet the culture has changed today: 'Family only takes you seriously if you are successful: failures are not welcomed'.

She highlighted the importance of *guanxi* to overcoming barriers to her success: 'There were so many social contacts but a few were like gold dust: they knew how suppliers tick and how government officials work, they were able to provide me with real useful contacts and that was the greatest help. Breaking into certain networks in China is difficult, but once you do, all you need are the right contacts. These contacts interact and feed one another; that is where there is a challenge for a woman in China. Success depends on finding the right niche and knowhow: if these two can be brought together then it is magic. I have been lucky in that I managed to network, find a niche market where there was no competition when I started, but things are becoming difficult as more Chinese return from abroad with competence and skills'.

SUMMARY

The significant economic restructuring of the Chinese economy has transformed the playing field for women in the context of a generational shift of economic opportunities from the old to the young (in a sense, an 'opportunity redistribution'), a quality versus quantity debate and very mixed experiences for women of different social, spatial, demographic and other backgrounds. For some, mainly older, women in the 'unlucky generation', opportunities for working altogether have been significantly restricted due to the closure of factories and large-scale redundancies that accompanied the privatization process (Berik et al., 2007; Liu, 2007a, 2007b). For younger women, there have been new job opportunities. However, although almost as many women as men work in China, for some this is by necessity due to low wages. Furthermore, there is low representation in more senior roles often due to opaque promotional procedures (Cooke, 2001, 2004, 2005, 2008b; Catalyst, 2008), compounded by poor job mobility prospects (Cao and Hu, 2007), occupational segregation (Cai and Wu, 2006), work and pay inequalities particularly for married women with children (Zhang et al., 2008) and for those working in externally owned, FDI-funded plants (Braunstein and Brenner, 2007; Shu et al., 2007), and in particular for women migrant workers (Feng and Anan, 2003; Liang and Chen, 2003; Ngai, 2004; Tam, 2008). The 'bamboo curtain' (Tan, 2008) and the economic opportunities now open to many women (Cooke, 2005) have influenced the creation of many new ventures that are women-led. However, many of these are clearly necessity entrepreneurs (Bosma and Harding, 2007; Allen et al., 2008) because of the extreme labour market disadvantages and inequalities highlighted above. Levels of business ownership among men remain higher than among women as in many other countries, although not to the same extent as elsewhere (Cooke, 2005; Baughn et al., 2006; Bosma and Harding, 2007; Allen et al., 2008). Our stories of success highlight that, although men dominate *guanxi* networks, family background (and support from parents and spouses), experience, training, education and finance are key success factors influencing the performance of women-led firms.

While we have attempted to undertake our investigation using a gender-neutral lens of analysis and have avoided adopting the 'masculine' as a benchmark or norm (Ahl,

2006), it is certainly clear that within the domain of employment and (non-owner) management, gender equality is largely absent. However, we suggest that entrepreneurship and business ownership as a domain, whilst having a number of significant barriers relating to economic, socio-cultural and symbolic capital, offer greater opportunities to women than many forms of paid employment. Forms and types of entrepreneurship in China, like elsewhere, are heterogeneous (from 'weaving' and selling garden produce – Kitching and Jackson, 2002 – to high-growth technology firms) and, therefore, there are entrepreneurial activities that can at best be described as 'exploitive', 'lifestyle', or 'unrewarding'. A substantial programme of further research is necessary in order to build upon a small number of studies that have already cleared the ground in terms of women's entrepreneurship in China. More reliable and country-wide, but disaggregated, statistics on small businesses would be a welcome start, including information on the gender of the owner manager(s). Research questions for smaller-scale, qualitative work would surely include how to facilitate women entrepreneurs to take the first step to start their new venture but also, more importantly, how to ensure that they are successful.

NOTES

1. Furthermore, Chen and Chen (2004, p.308) highlighted a typology (as with social capital – bridging, bonding, etc.): 'family ties (kinship), familiar persons (e.g., former classmates and colleagues), and strangers (with or without common demographic attributes)'.
2. Here the discrepancy between the figures presented may be because the official figures do not count a plethora of micro-businesses, for example, or due to the methodology of GEM (i.e., counting aspirations to start a business and engagement in activities that will lead to starting a business, which may be a part-time and/or home-based business). There are significant definitional problems involved when attempting to unpick or interpret figures relating to business ownership or entrepreneurship.

REFERENCES

Aaltio, I. and Huang, J. (2007) 'Women Managers' Careers in Information Technology in China: High Flyers with Emotional Costs?', *Journal of Organizational Change Management*, **20**(2): 227–44.
Ahl, H. (2006) 'Why Research on Women Entrepreneurs Needs New Directions', *Entrepreneurship Theory and Practice*, **30**(5): 595–621.
Allen, I.E., Elam, A., Langowitz, N. and Dean, M. (2008) *GEM 2007 Report on Women and Entrepreneurship*, Babson Park, MA: Babson College.
Baughn, C.C., Chua, B.-L. and Neupert, K.E. (2006) 'The Normative Context for Women's Participation in Entrepreneurship: A Multicountry Study', *Entrepreneurship Theory and Practice*, **30**(5): 687–708.
Berik, G., Dong, X.-Y. and Summerfield, G. (2007) 'China's Transition and Feminist Economics', *Feminist Economics*, **13**(3/4): 1–33.
Blanchflower, D. and Oswald, A.J. (1998) 'What Makes an Entrepreneur?', *Journal of Labor Economics*, **16**(1): 26–60.
Bosma, N. and Harding, R. (2007) *Global Entrepreneurship Monitor: GEM 2006 Summary Results*, Babson Park, MA: Babson College.
Bourdieu, P. (1986) 'The Forms of Capital', in J. Richardson and C.T. Westport (eds), *Handbook of Theory and Practice in the Sociology of Education*, Westport, CT: Greenwood Press.
Braunstein, E. and Brenner, M. (2007) 'Foreign Direct Investment and Gendered Wages in Urban China', *Feminist Economics*, **13**(3/4): 213–37.
Cai, H. and Wu, X. (2006) 'Social Changes and Occupational Gender Inequality', *Chinese Sociology & Anthropology*, **38**(4): 37–53.
Cao, Y. and Hu, C.-Y. (2007) 'Gender and Job Mobility in Postsocialist China: A Longitudinal Study of Job Changes in Six Coastal Cities', *Social Forces*, **85**(4): 1535–60.

Catalyst (2008) *Women in Emerging Markets*, New York: Catalyst.

Chen, X.-P. and Chen, C.C. (2004) 'On the Intricacies of the Chinese *Guanxi*: A Process Model of *Guanxi* Development', *Asia Pacific Journal of Management*, **21**(3): 305–24.

Chow, C.K.-W. and Fung, M.K.Y. (2000) 'Small Businesses and Liquidity Constraints in Financing Business Investment – Evidence from Shanghai's Manufacturing Sector', *Journal of Business Venturing*, **15**(4): 363–83.

Chu, P. (2000) 'The Characteristics of Chinese Female Entrepreneurs: Motivation and Personality', *Journal of Enterprising Culture*, **8**(1): 67–84.

Cooke, F.L. (2001) 'Equal Opportunity? The Role of Legislation and Public Policies in Women's Employment in China', *Women in Management Review*, **16**(7): 334–48.

Cooke, F.L. (2004) 'Women in Management in China', in M. Davidson and R.J. Burke (eds), *Women in Management Worldwide*, Aldershot: Ashgate.

Cooke, F.L. (2005) 'Women's Managerial Careers in China in a Period of Reform', in V. Yukongdi and J. Benson (eds), *Women in Asian Management*, Abingdon: Routledge, pp. 11–24.

Cooke, F.L. (2008a) 'Competition and Strategy of Chinese Firms: An Analysis of Top Performing Chinese Private Enterprises', *Competitiveness Review: An International Business Journal incorporating Journal of Global Competitiveness*, **18**(1/2): 29–56.

Cooke, F.L. (2008b) 'The Changing Face of Women Managers in China', in C. Rowley and V. Yukongdi (eds), *The Changing Face of Women Managers in Asia*, Abingdon: Routledge.

Elam, A.B. (2008) *Gender and Entrepreneurship: A Multilevel Theory and Analysis*, Cheltenham, UK and Northampton, MA, USA: Edward Elgar.

Feng, W. and Anan, S. (2003) 'Double Jeopardy? Female Rural Migrant Labourers in Urban China: The Case of Shanghai', in B. García, R. Anker and A. Pinnelli (eds), *Women in the Labour Market in Changing Economies: Demographic Issues*, Oxford: Oxford University Press.

Gregory, N. and Tenev, S. (2001) 'The Financing of Private Enterprise in China', *Finance & Development: The Quarterly Magazine of the IMF*, **38**(1).

Hisrich, R.D. and Fan, Z. (1991) 'Women Entrepreneurs in the People's Republic of China: An Exploratory Study', *Journal of Managerial Psychology*, **6**(3): 3–12.

Hussain, J., Millman, C. and Matlay, H. (2006) 'SME Financing in the UK and in China: A Comparative Perspective', *Journal of Small Business and Enterprise Development*, **13**(4): 584–99.

Hussain, J., Scott, J.M., Harrison, R.T. and Millman, C. (2009) 'Enter the Dragoness: Firm Growth, Finance, *Guanxi*, and Gender in China', *Gender in Management: An International Journal*, **25**(2): 137–56.

Jennings, J.E. and McDougald, M.S. (2007) 'Work–Family Interface Experiences and Coping Strategies: Implications for Entrepreneurship Research and Practice', *Academy of Management Review*, **32**(3): 747–60.

Kitching, B.M. and Jackson, P.A. (2002) 'Female Entrepreneurs in a Transitional Economy: Businesswomen in China', *International Journal of Entrepreneurship and Innovation*, **3**(2): 145–55.

Liang, Z. and Chen, Y.P. (2003) 'Migration, Gender, and Returns to Education in Shenzhen, China', in B. García, R. Anker and A. Pinnelli (eds), *Women in the Labour Market in Changing Economies: Demographic Issues*, Oxford: Oxford University Press.

Liu, J. (2007a) 'Gender Dynamics and Redundancy in Urban China', *Feminist Economics*, **13**(3/4): 125–58.

Liu, J. (2007b) *Gender and Work in Urban China: Women Workers of the Unlucky Generation*, Abingdon: Routledge.

Matthews, R. and Nee, V. (2000) 'Gender Inequality and Economic Growth in Rural China', *Social Science Research*, **29**(4): 606–32.

Ngai, P. (2004) 'Women Workers and Precarious Employment in Shenzhen Special Economic Zone, China', *Gender and Development*, **12**(2): 29–36.

Scase R. (2003) 'Entrepreneurship and Proprietorship in Transition: Policy Implications for the SME Sector', in R. McIntyre and R. Dallago (eds), *Small and Medium Enterprises in Transitional Economies*, Basingstoke: Palgrave Macmillan, pp. 64–77.

Shu, X., Zhu, Y. and Zhang, Z. (2007) 'Global Economy and Gender Inequalities: The Case of the Urban Chinese Labor Market', *Social Science Quarterly*, **88**(5): 1307–32.

Smallbone, D. and Welter, F. (2009) *Entrepreneurship and Small Business Development in Post-Socialist Economies*, Cheltenham, UK and Northampton, MA, USA: Edward Elgar.

Stiglitz, J. (2003) *Globalization and its Discontents*, London: Penguin.

Stockman, N. (1994) 'Gender Inequality and Social Structure in Urban China', *Sociology*, **28**(3): 759–77.

Tam, M. (2008) 'Marginalization or Empowerment? Rural Migrant Women in China's Changing Political Economy', paper presented at the annual meeting of the ISA's 49th Annual Convention, Hilton San Francisco, CA.

Tan, J. (2008) 'Breaking the "Bamboo Curtain" and the "Glass Ceiling": The Experience of Women Entrepreneurs in High-tech Industries in an Emerging Market', *Journal of Business Ethics*, **80**(3): 547–64.

Wang, Y. (2004) 'Financing Difficulties and Structural Characteristics of SMEs in China', *China & World Economy*, **12**(2): 34–49.

Xian, H. and Woodhams, C. (2008) 'Managing Careers: Experiences of Successful Women in the Chinese IT Industry', *Gender in Management: An International Journal*, **23**(6): 409–25.

Yueh, L. (2006) 'Social Capital, Unemployment and Women's Labour Market Outcomes in Urban China', in H. Sato and S. Li (eds), *Unemployment, Inequality and Poverty in Urban China*, **1**(3): 285–316.

Zhang, Y., Hannum, E. and Wang, M. (2008) 'Gender-based Employment and Income Differences in Urban China: Considering the Contributions of Marriage and Parenthood', *Social Forces*, **86**(4): 1529–60.

Zheng, W. (2003) 'Gender, Employment and Women's Resistance', in E.J. Perry and M. Seldon (eds), *Chinese Society, 2nd edition: Change, Conflict and Resistance*, Abingdon: Routledge, pp. 158–82.

6 Denmark

Suna Løwe Nielsen, Kim Klyver and
*Majbritt Rostgaard Evald**

INTRODUCTION

'A "passion for equality" is often pointed out as a special marker of the Nordic societies' (Holli et al., 2005, p. 148), including gender equality. Also, Hofstede (1980) has positioned Denmark as a nation dominated by a feminine discourse in preference to a masculine one. It implies values of relationship building on quality of life as well as less emphasis on competiveness and wealth generation. Finally, Denmark is characterized by the Scandinavian welfare model. It is a model of comprehensiveness, which covers everyone in terms of social security and benefits. It provides women with flexibility and rights autonomously from their husbands.

These contextual dimensions of the Danish society can be expected to have an impact on women entrepreneurship. The aim of the chapter is to give insight into how women entrepreneurs of the Danish welfare state manage to succeed as entrepreneurs/small business owners in spite of barriers that exist. Particularly, it addresses the gap between gender equality perceptions and practices, which tends to dominate the gender situation in Denmark, and how this gap influences the dynamics of women's entrepreneurship.

THE POSITION OF WOMEN IN EMPLOYMENT

Within the Scandinavian countries, equality was especially emphasized during the post-Second World War period by social democratic governments. Policies were primarily focused on toning down class differences, but gender equality was also considered. Within this process, the obligations of the welfare state were extended into areas that earlier had been considered to belong to the private sphere. For instance, child and elderly care, healthcare and hospitals, a social security net and education became universally provided by a public system (Borchorst, 1999).

The Scandinavian welfare model, with its special social benefits that cover women's conventional obligations, has provided an opportunity for greater numbers of women to enter the labour force. As a result, Denmark and Sweden experienced a large-scale entry of women into the labour market in the 1960s, with Norway following a decade later. For most women of the Scandinavian countries this move has been a positive one. Today, Danish women are no longer merely a reserve army of labour; they hold a significant and all-important position in the labour market. In 2007, the employment rate for women was 71.5 per cent compared with an employment rate of 78.8 per cent for men (Statistics Denmark, 2008a). Moreover, the employment rate for women has increased from 68.6 per cent in 1997, while the employment rate for men actually decreased in the same period. Overall, the unemployment rate has decreased from 7.3 per cent to 3.5 per cent for women and from 4.1 per cent to 3.1 per cent for men. Thus, Danish women have gained an increasingly larger share of the labour market.

However, the working patterns of Danish men and women differ, with 25 per cent of men self-employed or working as top managers, compared with only 10 per cent of women (Statistics Denmark, 2008b). Furthermore, women in general are working fewer hours than their male counterparts. In 2007, 56 per cent of women senior managers worked more than 37 hours per week compared with 75 per cent of the men senior managers (ibid.). Although the proportion of senior managers working more than 37 hours per week has increased for both men and women during the last ten years, it has risen significantly more for women senior managers.

Also, among blue-collar workers, men work more hours than women. In 2007, 27 per cent of male blue-collar workers worked more than 37 hours per week. This was the case for only 13 per cent of the women blue-collar workers (ibid.). Furthermore, women blue-collar workers do more part-time work. Interestingly, this gap between men's and women's working routines has increased during the last ten years. Seemingly, Danish women still have some obligations at home that prevent them from competing on equal terms with men in the labour market, or they may prioritize differently between work and family.

Women are becoming economically independent and they have, to a higher extent than previously, the opportunity of self-realization through work. However, the changes have resulted in a shift from the private to public dependence of women. Also, dual family structures have emerged in which women and men participate more on equal terms in family care and breadwinning; structures, which have positive as well as negative consequences (Orloff, 1996). The maternity and parental leave policies are considered to be the cornerstones of 'woman-friendly' policies in the Scandinavian social democracies (Leira, 1998). Through a comprehensive system of public economic assistance and different kinds of leave schemes, Danish society has attempted to reduce the drawbacks associated with combining pregnancy, children and work (Kautto et al., 2001). However, child care is still one of the areas in which there is room for improvements in regard to gender equality. The supply and the nature of child care services influence the two sexes very differently (The Nordic Council of Ministers, 1999). For instance, inflexible opening hours of nursery schools demarcate women in participating as fully as men in employment, as women still have the primary responsibility for the family (Haas, 2003); 'women continue to bear the overall responsibility for organizing and facilitating the reconciliation of work and family' (Borchorst, 2001, p. 204). Thus, women are very dependent on the child care system and its opening hours.

The critics of the Scandinavian welfare model identify a gap between gender equality perceptions and practices. Typically, Danes believe that gender equality has been achieved (Borchorst, 2001) and there is a consensus that this debate and regulations concerning gender equality are not necessary anymore (Borchorst and Dahlerup, 2003). The general opinion is that the feminist movement of the 1970s took care of these problems and solved them by making gender equality an official policy of the Danish government. This resulted in a law on equal pay for equal work for female and male employees, and a law on gender equal treatment in the labour market in 1976.

Yet, although the debate on gender equality has taken place for decades, a significant salary gap still exists between female and male managers. In 2007, male managers earned 28 per cent more than female managers (Statistics Denmark, 2008c); ten years ago, the gap was 30 per cent. At the same time, women have a tendency to fulfil the roles they have always played. Previously, they were taking care of their families in the private sphere. Today, many Danish women are employed in the public sector taking care of the elders, children and ill individuals of society. In the fourth quarter of 2007, approximately 68 per cent of the employees within the area of public and personal services were women (Statistics Denmark, 2008d), many of whom held competences within the social service areas. For example, in 2005, 333 women became Bachelors of Health Care in Denmark compared with 161 men (Statistics Denmark, 2008e).

Further, the overall level of education between women and men has been balanced during recent years. More and more Danish women are being educated in areas that before were dominated by male students, such as psychology, medicine, dentistry, law and architecture (Madsen, 2006). The Head of Studies at Copenhagen University commented on the situation: 'A number of very prestigious advanced educations have been overtaken by girls. It concerns all the very popular courses – those where you have to have very good grades' (ibid., p. 3).

Thus, in conclusion, even though Denmark seems to have won the battle of gender equality, this equality is in some ways an illusion. Inequality remains a product of women and men working in separate areas, which is further reinforced by women and men working at different levels in the hierarchies.

THE POSITION OF WOMEN IN ENTREPRENEURSHIP/SMALL BUSINESS OWNERSHIP

Worldwide, fewer women than men are involved in early-stage entrepreneurial activities (Allen et al., 2008) and this section addresses entrepreneurial activity among women in a Danish context. The distinct pattern of gender equality outlined above also affects the levels and ways of women's participation in entrepreneurship/small business ownership.

Early-stage entrepreneurial activity involves individuals who are either in the process of starting a business or running a business younger than 3.5 years. In 2007, 8.17 per cent of men on average within high-income countries[1] were involved in early-stage entrepreneurial activities compared with just 4.34 per cent of women. For Denmark, these figures are slightly higher for women and lower for men. In 2007, 4.6 per cent of Danish women were engaged in early-stage entrepreneurial activities compared with 6.2 per cent of Danish men (see Figure 6.1). This may indicate that the relatively high participation rate of Danish women in the labour force is reflected in the level of entrepreneurial activity among women.

Although, over the last seven years, male involvement has decreased from 10.03 per cent in 2001 to 6.21 per cent in 2007, within the same period women's involvement has been around 3–4 per cent. The male–female ratio has through the years been close to 2 with the highest ratio of 2.8 in 2003 and the lowest of 1.4 in 2007. From a longitudinal perspective, Danish men are therefore becoming less entrepreneurially active, whereas the level of entrepreneurial activity among women is more stable. In an investigation of women entrepreneurs, the Danish Enterprise and Construction Authority (2003) found

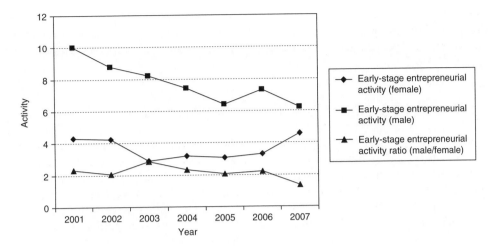

Source: Global Entrepreneurship Monitor (Denmark).

Figure 6.1 Early-stage entrepreneurial activity

that women's and men's association with the labour market did not differ significantly before entering into entrepreneurship. However, surprisingly, relatively more women entrepreneurs had a job in the private sector before they moved into entrepreneurship. Furthermore, women entrepreneurs earned more in their previous job compared with men. Finally, the investigation showed that on average women entrepreneurs were older than men when initiating their first business.

In general, Danish women prior to becoming entrepreneurs have a higher income, are better educated and are older than their male counterparts. It therefore may be expected that women are better qualified to start their own business. However, investigations show that this is not the case. Danish women entrepreneurs had a lower survival rate than male entrepreneurs: within the period 1994–2000, only 29 per cent of businesses started by women survived. The survival rate for men entrepreneurs in the same period was 33 per cent (ibid.). Survival rates also vary across industries. Women have, for instance, the highest survival rate in service industries and they also more often initiate businesses within the areas of retailing and service compared with men. When controlling for other factors, such as industry, age and education, the difference in survival rate between women and men entrepreneurs becomes insignificant. Therefore, it can be concluded that women's lower survival rate is not merely a product of their gender; other factors such as the industry in which they choose to operate also matter.

Another interesting result is that women entrepreneurs with children below seven years old are less likely to survive in business compared with men in a similar situation (ibid.). Seemingly, the higher the child care responsibilities of women entrepreneurs, the lower their success rate. The fact that the degree of child care responsibilities means less to men once more supports the assertion that Danish women retain the primary responsibility of the family. Women entrepreneurs are also less likely to work more than 37 hours per week compared with their male counterparts (Statistics Denmark, 2008b), which also supports the above interpretation. Interestingly, internationally, women entrepreneurs are, however, significantly more likely to establish solo companies compared with men. Analysis of international GEM data from 2004 (available at www.gemconsortium.org) shows that 52.6 per cent of women entrepreneurs establish solo companies; the figure for men is 45.5 per cent.

STRUCTURAL AND CONTEXTUAL BARRIERS

Dual family structures, a comprehensive welfare system and economic independence provide the central ingredients to ease Danish women's participation in economic wealth generation from employment, intrapreneurship or entrepreneurship. Paradoxically, mapping out the landscape of the barriers confronting Danish women entrepreneurs, many of the same ingredients also appear to be variables hindering women in becoming successful entrepreneurs. The central barriers fall in to three categories: (1) structural barriers of society; (2) cultural and social barriers and (3) psychological barriers. Several barriers of entrepreneurship are not gender-specific and emphasis is placed on barriers being prominent among women entrepreneurs.

Structural Barriers of Society

A central barrier in Danish society is the welfare system itself, which aims to achieve gender equality by promoting social support activities that cover the traditional responsibilities of women. Still, women tend to hold competences and work within the areas reflecting the traditional responsibilities, often within the public sector. Considering the link between prior knowledge and opportunity recognition (Shane, 2000), the Danish welfare system can be assumed to limit and exercise control over many entrepreneurial opportunities interesting to women. Or at least, the welfare state becomes a key competitor to Danish women in initiating ventures within industries of social support. This might hinder Danish women's entry into an entrepreneurial career.

A second fundamental barrier to women entrepreneurs, pregnancy, is biologically exclusive to women, but enhanced by a societal support system that tends to position women entrepreneurs worse off in terms of maternity and parental leave compared with women employees. The public system and the associated strong labour unions tend to be built on the preferences of a 'job-taker' culture, not the culture of 'job-making'. Problems related to pregnancy are intensified by the fact that women entrepreneurs are likely to establish solo companies. Hence, women are in need of a replacement when being on maternity leave. This is for many reasons a highly complicated exercise, since entrepreneurial networks are often associated with the personality of the entrepreneur. Thus, when the entrepreneur takes a break from the venturing activities, the network may crumble away. Finally, Danish women entrepreneurs often employ other women, who may also become pregnant (The Ministry of Economics and Business Affairs, 2000).

Cultural and Social Barriers

Socially constructed norms, beliefs and values of society determine the extent to which entrepreneurship is perceived feasible and desirable among its members (Shane, 2003).

Denmark relatively early on enacted a welfare state and emphasized gender equality, and today many Danes believe gender equality has been established. However, this issue is still open for discussion because gender equality has not been established in all aspects in Denmark. A belief in gender equality in the absence of gender equality practices creates barriers for women entrepreneurship. One result is that sparse attention is given by local communities, banks, educational institutions, mass media, the counselling system and so on to the special needs, motives and circumstances of women entrepreneurs. In spite of the fact that Denmark is known as a culture marked by feminine values, these agencies tend to attach the same values and expectations to women entrepreneurship as to male entrepreneurship, being based on masculine values and success criteria, such as profit, innovation and growth (The Ministry of Economics and Business Affairs, 2000).

However, there are many indicators that Danish women are often motivated by a holistic approach emphasizing the facilitation of a synthesis between family and entrepreneur-making (Korsgaard and Neergaard, 2007). The 'holistic way' means that key motives of women in entrepreneurship are a desire for independence in terms of flexibility in time and obligations, harmonic living and other soft success criteria (The Ministry of Economics and Business Affairs, 2000). These motives have to be viewed in the light of the fact that Danish women entrepreneurs are driven by opportunity in preference to necessity; they do not run towards entrepreneurship due to the absence of others career options. In fact, Denmark is one of the highest ranking countries in terms of opportunity-driven women's entrepreneurship (Allen et al., 2007). Consequently, women entrepreneurs call for support that emphasizes the unique circumstances and competences of women, as well as role models that are reflections of themselves. This is substantiated by statistical analysis of data collected by MEGAFON for The Confederation of Danish Industry (DI) among approximately 1600 women and men entrepreneurs/small business owners (Petersen and Sørensen, 2008). The authors were given access to the raw statistical data and analysis showed that it is a general perception that women entrepreneurs in Denmark have difficulties finding mentors and role models.

The cultural discourse emphasizing masculine success values reflects that Danish women in general are still locked in by traditional gender roles. This is problematic. The world of the mother and the world of the entrepreneur are both often regarded as being demanding in time, effort and commitment, as well as reflecting different meaning, cues, constraints and opportunities. However, in women's entrepreneurship the two worlds often have to exist side by side. Potential barriers related to holding multiple roles reinforce inconsistent action, psychological and physical work overload, stress, lack of control, high coordination cost, and so on (Pratt and Foreman, 2000). For instance, barriers of holding the multiple roles of 'woman' and 'entrepreneur' reflect that women work less hours as entrepreneurs than men, and thus (as previously mentioned) their success rate is lower than their male counterparts, especially when they have young children.

Finally, an important cultural dimension of the Danish society is the Jante Law. The law reflects the Scandinavian countries' socialistic and communitarian orientation. It covers ten rules of conduct, which structure behaviour away from individual conduct and towards group conformity. Examples of the rules are: 'You shall not believe you are something' and 'You shall not believe you are greater than we'. The socializing effect of these rules are known to punish people who do not conform, for instance, by staging their own entrepreneurial show. Women are expected to organize family and work and entrepreneurship is assumed not to work well together with family. Danish women entrepreneurs can be expected to experience the Jante Law even more strongly than male entrepreneurs. Consequently, as indicated by analysis of the data collected by MEGAFON, significantly more women than men entrepreneurs/small business owners agree that the number of women entrepreneurs is relatively low in Denmark, because the Danish population in general frowns on women who give equal priority to work and family.

Psychological Barriers

Psychological variables that influence an individual's propensity to exploit opportunities and risk are often pointed to as a major psychological barrier (Simon et al., 1999). Analysis of the MEGAFON data reveals that it is a general assumption among Danish entrepreneurs/small business owners that too few Danish women dare to run the risk involved in entrepreneurship. Maybe the unwillingness to engage in risky activities has to be seen in the light of women's family obligations, that is, they not only place themselves in the situation of the unknown but also their families. However, the DI research most of all indicates that according to the women entrepreneurs/small business owners it is primarily weak self-efficacy that keeps women away from entrepreneurship. Women underestimate their own competences and business ideas; they do not believe they have what it takes to successfully perform entrepreneurial tasks.

STORIES OF SUCCESS

The dark side of the story of women's entrepreneurship in the Danish welfare state has been detailed above and many potential barriers to women entrepreneurship exist in Denmark. However, this is by no means the whole story. Despite the barriers, successful women entrepreneurs have flourished in Danish society, and more are on their way. Recognizing their successes and telling the stories about these women is crucial in a society in which the Jante Law is dominant. In the following, two stories of success are presented and the factors underlying that success are discussed.

BOX 6.1   'THE SKY IS THE LIMIT'

In 1994, two young recently educated designers, Naja Munthe and Karen Vedel-Simonsen, started the well-known design company Munthe plus Simonsen. They launched their first collection in 1995 and have since won several awards for their designs and business talent. In 2004, they were awarded Veuve Clicquot's award: 'Business Women of the Year'. The media were, however, not that interested in their designs and talents, rather the story about two young women who came from nothing to conquer the Danish fashion scene. 'It was extremely difficult to come through with our message. Especially being women designers, because you are just considered to be sewing girls making dresses'. Many expected them to fail.

Previously, in 1991, a set assignment at the School of Design in Kolding con-
vinced the two women that they were something unique. Driven by a desire to
express themselves in a creative manner, a few years later they initiated their
own business and developed their own collection. The collection became a
huge success. The business expanded with a tremendous speed although the
two young women basically were against commercialization, which they saw as
the enemy of creativity. 'We took pride in not being commercial. Nobody should
tell us how to design or sell our products'. To them, the explanation behind their
success was that they believed in themselves: 'Never take no for an answer.
You have to keep on going. Only one thing is for sure. A lot of doors are closed.
But they can be opened'. The two women had two mottoes that inspired them
in their daily operations: 'The sky is the limit' and 'Anything is possible'.

The growing firm was, however, a challenge to the two women. To them,
business development and cash flow management were secondary tasks.
They emphasized their design and having an interesting lifestyle. Spending was
used to hire Cindy Crawford, and create fancy shows, dinners, showrooms, and
so forth. It was a busy time of their lives. Karen gave birth to a child, but she
only stayed at home for two weeks as she was too eager to continue being an
entrepreneur.

When earnings dropped, spending continued to grow. In 2006, they were in a
deep business crisis, ending up with a suspension of payments, and they were
confronted with the Jante Law. People said: 'Don't fly higher than your wings
can carry you. What did we say? You could not go on like this'. The two women
realized that they and the growth of the business had to be tempered. A business strategy balancing design values and commercializing issues rescued the
company from bankruptcy and the business got back on track.

Today, the two entrepreneurs are emphasizing the 'holistic' approach to
entrepreneurship. As Karen says in a recent interview: 'What is next? Is life
quality to have 200 employees and be just as big as Christian Dior? No, it is not.
I have two small kids, and I am in a phase of life in which many find themselves
when they are getting close to 30. It means there are things in regard to the firm
from which I have to withdraw. Instead, I am concentrating on our designs and
being a mom'.

Source: The case is developed based on an interview with Karen Vedel-Simonsen.

BOX 6.2   ADVERTISING WOMEN OF WORLD-CLASS (WELTKLASSE)

In 2005, two women, Jeanett Kaare and Charlotte Stougaard Espensen,
opened their own advertising and public relations firm Weltklasse. Before starting their own business, they both had been employed in the same advertising
firm; nevertheless, they were looking for new challenges that allowed them to

fully express their creativity. After some months of consideration and precise calculations, they chose to take the leap into self-employment and independent entrepreneurship, and their families supported them.

After a few days, the telephone began to ring and their calendar was quickly filled up with meetings. The two women's dream of their own advertising and public relations firm was becoming a reality as assignments kept coming in. Everything happened so quickly and after six months the two women employed their first staff member: 'Wow! What a milestone to reach. Therefore, we clapped our hands in delight'. Moreover, after one-and-a-half years they employed six staff and their locations were further extended. 'The problem for many entrepreneurs is that goals and ambitions are set too low. Of course one should not believe that trees grow into the sky, but it is much more fun to run after the almost unreachable'.

From the very beginning they decided that a shorter maternity leave made sense. 'We always knew that one of us would eventually be pregnant, and early on we agreed that our maternity leave should be four months. We insist on the ability to combine our professional life with the natural consequences of being a woman'. In fact, the two women perceive their gender to be an advantage in regard to their entrepreneurial activities. 'We never really considered our gender as a problem when we decided to start our own company. On the contrary, we actually saw it as an advantage, making our advertising agency something completely different from the competitors'.

The two women were located in a science park with 50 other firms. Immediately after beginning their business, they introduced themselves to the other firms and offered their services: 'The science park was a place populated with men in dull suits. People did not advertise their activities and products. We thought this was a shame, for many things happen that deserve to be known outside the researchers' own circles. Therefore we contacted the firms, and the result was terrific'. During the first year, 50 per cent of the turnover came from firms located in the science park. Since, the turnover has grown and now the share from the science park is only one-third.

From the start the two women were very conscious about self-promotion, which also explains the name of the company: 'Weltklasse': 'You have to believe it yourself if you want your customers to believe it. Especially in our business, self-belief and high self-esteem are decisive factors because we feed from giving our customers a boost in self-confidence'. The two women's strategy was to make use of micromarketing in which you use few resources to get into the media with a few good stories. Their strategy was a success and everyone wanted to know who the two colourful and loud girls were, as their firm was nothing like the other ordinary advertising and public relation firms.

Source: The case was developed based on an interview with Jeanett Kaare and Charlotte Stougaard Espensen.

Looking at the two stories of success and how the four women overcome the identified barriers, it is foremost evident that they have extensive self-confidence and self-efficacy. They strongly believe that they have the required competences to execute the entrepreneurial process. In fact, the sky is the only limit of their entrepreneurial competences, or at least they act on this assumption. Seemingly, the identified psychological barriers of weak self-efficacy and unwillingness to take risks among Danish women entrepreneurs are challenged by these two stories. This may explain why they are stories of success. After all, research shows that confidence in an ability to perform is central to success (Ajzen, 1991).

Both stories deal with women who dare to break with what is expected of them. They were confronted with a pressure not to become entrepreneurs; a pressure that expressed itself through the Jante Law and people's prejudices of women's roles. For example, the perception is that women do not run successful growth businesses, they wait for others to recommend them – they do not approach new customers. Nevertheless, these women became entrepreneurs as they are driven by a passionate interest in and deep enjoyment of what they do as entrepreneurs. They engage in entrepreneurship for its own sake, not as a response to some outer expectations of success, growth and profit. The inner drive makes them willing to engage in risky activities even though they have family obligations and other opportunities of employment. Also, they break with the socially constructed norms, beliefs and values that seem to direct the society they have been born and raised in. Contrary to many other women, they perceive independent entrepreneurship as feasible and desirable, and even more vitally they make use of a successful strategy for breaking down other people's socially constructed norms, beliefs and values.

It is also interesting that the women in the case studies differ from most female start-ups by the fact that they are not solo entrepreneurs. Instead, an entrepreneurial team is the departure point of the processes. Considering the barriers related to pregnancy, maternity and parental leave, and women's conventional role of being responsible for the family, the team way of organizing can be argued to make them stronger. On the other hand, in both cases the entrepreneurial team consisted of women; women who may all be confronted with the aforementioned barriers. It is interesting how the two Weltklasse women from the very beginning made a rule that limited the problems related to pregnancy, that is, 'maternity leave is four months and no longer'.

Finally, considering the discussed gap between gender equality perceptions and practices, the two success stories underpin the general perceptions among the population in Denmark, that is, the Scandinavian welfare state leaves room for women to be independently successful within the arena of work and wealth creation. Yet, the stories also indicate that in order to be successful, the women also have to tone down the obligations of pregnancy and family caring and emphasize the more male-oriented values of success, growth and 'being a lone cowboy'. For example, Karen Vedel-Simonsen only took two weeks of maternity leave after giving birth to her first child. Economic crises, however, made her stop, reflect and search for a balance between being an 'entrepreneur' and 'mom'. Her new entrepreneurial life took into consideration the unique circumstances of being a woman. As we can see, the fact that the two success stories deal with women entrepreneurs who in some ways live under the premises of the values of male entrepreneurship highlights the gap between gender equality perceptions and practices that exists in entrepreneurship within a Danish context.

SUMMARY AND RECOMMENDATIONS

This chapter has mapped out the landscape of the topic of women entrepreneurs in the Danish welfare state. Specifically, it has been sensitive to the circumstances in which Danish women entrepreneurs are embedded and in particular the structural, cultural and psychological barriers they experience as entrepreneurs. In spite of these barriers, we have identified that plenty of successful women entrepreneurs exist, and we have given examples of how four of these women have overcome the aforementioned barriers.

The analysis demonstrates a gap between gender equality perceptions and practice. The typical Dane perceives gender equality to be an integrated fact of the Danish society. Also, for a long period of time regulations and laws have existed that support this perception. However, these are not extensively implemented and practiced in the labour market. There is much evidence to indicate that Danish women and men do not have equal opportunities in regard to engaging in entrepreneurship and surviving as an entrepreneur. As a result, successful women entrepreneurs tend to act based on the premises of male entrepreneurial values, such as success, profit and 'being a lone cowboy'. They are generally unable to combine the two roles of 'entrepreneur' and 'women' in a balanced and holistic way.

Thus, we argue that a profound challenge is needed to address the unequal opportunities, motives and barriers of women and men in entrepreneurship. Understanding the differences and similarities between men and women entrepreneurs is fundamental in closing the gap between gender equality perceptions and practices. Further, to close this gap effectively, we need to build a culture, infrastructure, policy programmes and welfare system that take into account the unique circumstance of Danish women entrepreneurs, which can improve the quality and survival rate of these entrepreneurs. Following are some recommendations of the key changes that need to be made to support the development of women's small business ownership in Denmark.

Suggestions to Fill the Gap

A free advisory system tailored to women's entrepreneurship
In Denmark, entrepreneurs are offered free advice on certain topics throughout the start-up process. This support, however, is dominated by a masculine approach to entrepreneurship, such as growth generation and profit. We suggest that these advisors are offered training in understanding women entrepreneurship and that a higher proportion of these advisors are women themselves, in such a manner that the ratio of men and women advisors mirrors the ratio of men and women entrepreneurs. A more targeted free advisory system can support women entrepreneurs in overcoming the unique barriers they are confronted with and motivate more women to pursue an entrepreneurial career.

Equal maternity and parental conditions for employees and entrepreneurs
In order to make the entrepreneurial career choice feasible and desirable for women, it is necessary to eliminate as many factors as possible that differentiate women employees from women entrepreneurs, specifically differences in maternity and parental conditions. After all, the analyses show that Danish women are still considered mainly responsible

for organizing and facilitating the reconciliation of work and family. Also, biological conditions make pregnancy a major issue to consider in regard to women entrepreneurship. It is important, to both women and men, that services such as social support are provided equally regardless of women's choice of career. Young women should not reject an entrepreneurial career because it would be in conflict with having a family. We therefore suggest that Denmark creates equal maternity and parental conditions for employees and entrepreneurs. For now, private business owners pay into a joint maternity settlement agreement to insure that all employees in the private sector are secured on equal terms in regard to maternity leave. A likely settlement agreement may also be constructed for the business owners themselves.

Evaluate the Scandinavian welfare state's influence on women entrepreneurship
The analysis shows that the Scandinavian welfare state enhances as well as constrains women entrepreneurship. Through its comprehensive social support system it gives women space and flexibility to participate in economic wealth-generating activities via employment, intrapreneurship or entrepreneurship. At the same time, much indicates that the state controls many of the entrepreneurial opportunities relevant to women. Also, some of the welfare benefits are not tailored to support women entrepreneurs. For instance, the opening hours of nurseries limit the flexibility of women entrepreneurs. We suggest that a further understanding of the positive as well as negative tensions between the Scandinavian welfare state and women entrepreneurship is reached. In other words, the influence of the welfare state on women entrepreneurship has to be evaluated.

Encourage women to start their business in teams
The last suggestion is not directly related to the gap between perceptions and practice, but is more biologically grounded. We suggest that younger women entrepreneurs consider and prepare for how their business should survive if they become pregnant. A pregnancy results in an absence from work and someone has to manage the business meanwhile, such as taking care of the existing networks. The most obvious way of dealing with that issue is to start businesses in teams, where the team members can cover for each other.

NOTES

*   We want to thank MEGAFON and The Confederation of Danish Industry (DI) for their support of this research by letting us access the valuable survey data.
1.   These high-income countries include Austria, Belgium, Denmark, Finland, France, Greece, Hong Kong, Iceland, Ireland, Israel, Italy, Japan, Netherlands, Norway, Portugal, Puerto Rico, Slovenia, Spain, Sweden, Switzerland, United Kingdom and United States.

REFERENCES

Ajzen, I. (1991), 'The theory of planned behavior', *Organizational Behavior and Human Decision Processes*, **50**(2), 179–211.
Allen, I.E., Langowitz, N. and Minniti, M. (2007), *GEM 2006 Report on Women and Entrepreneurship*, Global Entrepreneurship Monitor.

Allen, I.E., Elam, A., Langowitz, N. and Dean, M. (2008), *GEM 2007 Report on Women and Entrepreneurship*, Babson Park, MA: Babson College.

Borchorst, A. (1999), 'Feminist thinking about the Welfare State', in M.M. Ferree, J. Lorber and B.B. Hess (eds), *Revisioning Gender*, Walnut Creek, CA: Rowman Altamira, pp. 99–127.

Borchorst, A. (2001), 'Still friendly: Danish women and welfare state restructuring', *Social Politics*, **8**(2), 203–5.

Borchorst, A. and Dahlerup, D. (2003), 'Ligestilling – hvad er problemet?', in A. Borchorst and D. Dahlerup (eds), *Ligestillingspolitik: Som diskurs og praksis*, Frederiksberg: Samfundslitteratur, pp. 9–28.

Danish Enterprise and Construction Authority (2003), *De nye virksomheder – 4. statistiske portræt af iværksæt-tere*, Copenhagen: Danish Enterprise and Construction Authority.

Haas, L. (2003), 'Parental leave and gender equality: lessons from the European Union', *Review of Policy Research*, **20**(1), 89–114.

Hofstede, G. (1980), *Culture's Consequences*, Beverley Hills: Sage.

Holli, A.M., Magnusson, E. and Rönnblom, M. (2005), 'Critical studies of Nordic discourses on gender and gender equality', *Nordic Journal of Women's Studies*, **13**(3), 148–52.

Kautto, M., Fritzell, J., Hvinden, B., Kvist, J. and Uusitalo, H. (2001), 'Introduction: how distinct are the Nordic Welfare States?', in M. Kautto, J. Fritzell, B. Hvinden, J. Kvist and H. Uusitalo (eds), *Nordic Welfare States in the European Context*, London: Routledge, pp. 1–13.

Korsgaard, S. and Neergaard, H. (2007), 'Mompreneurs mod strømmen – om balance mellem familieliv og arbejdsliv i iværksætteri', *Tidskrift for arbejdsliv*, **9**(1), 28–43.

Leira, A. (1998), 'Caring as social right: cash for child care and daddy leave', *Social Politics*, **5**(3), 362–78.

Madsen, T.N. (2006), 'Kvinder styrer mod toppen af samfundet', *Newsletter of A4*, **30**(10), 3–6.

Orloff, A. (1996), 'Gender in the welfare state', *Annual Review of Sociology*, **22**(1), 51–78.

Petersen, S.K. and Sørensen, T.M. (2008), 'For få kvinder I Danmarks vækstlag, *Indsigt*, **3**, 5–7.

Pratt, M.G. and Foreman, P.O. (2000), 'Classifying managerial responses to multiple organizational identi-ties', *Academy of Management Review*, **25**(1), 18–42.

Shane, S. (2000), 'Prior knowledge and the discovery of entrepreneurial opportunities', *Organization Science*, **11**(4), 448–69.

Shane, S. (2003), *A General Theory of Entrepreneurship: The Individual–Opportunity Nexus*, Cheltenham, UK and Northampton, MA, USA: Edward Elgar.

Simon, M., Houghton, S.M. and Aquino, K. (1999), 'Cognitive bias, risk perception, and venture formation: how individuals decide to start companies', *Journal of Business Venturing*, **15**(2), 115–34.

Statistics Denmark (2008a), www.statistikbanken.dk/AKU2, 1 April.

Statistics Denmark (2008b), www.statistikbanken.dk/AKU5, 1 April.

Statistics Denmark (2008c), www.statistikbanken.dk/LON01, 1 April.

Statistics Denmark (2008d), www.statistikbanken.dk/AKU33, 1 April.

Statistics Denmark (2008e), www.statistikbanken.dk/U31, 1 April.

The Ministry of Economic and Business Affairs (2000), *Iværksætterkvinders vilkår: Erhvervsfremme Styrelsens analyse: Iværksætterkvinder nu og i fremtiden*, Copenhagen, The Danish Ministry of Economic and Business Affairs.

The Nordic Council of Ministers (1999), *De nordiske velfærdssamfund*, The Nordic Council of Ministers, pp. 43–4.

7 Fiji
Gurmeet Singh, Raghuvar Dutt Pathak and Rafia Naz

INTRODUCTION

This chapter explores women's entrepreneurship in the Fiji context. It commences with an overview of entrepreneurship in the economic development of a country. Entrepreneurship is a new area and is considered an important ingredient in the modern global economic development recipe (Kirschoff and Phillips, 1989; Keeble et al., 1990; Audretsch and Fritsch, 1991). According to the 2007 World Bank Group Entrepreneurship Survey, there exists a significant relationship between entrepreneurial activity and the key indicators of economic and financial development and growth, the quality of the legal and regulatory environment and governance of an economy. This survey by the World Bank has measured entrepreneurial activity in 84 developing and industrial countries around the world in the period 2003–05 (Klapper et al., 2007). US studies alone exhibit 90 per cent of employment growth originating from the entrepreneurial sector of the economy (Morris et al., 1996) and this applies to other countries as well where entrepreneurship has gained importance in pursuit of growth (Hoy et al., 1992). Growth in this context refers to a significant increase in sales, profits, assets, employees and locations. Unfortunately, this sort of growth is not very visible in Pacific Island countries and some studies conducted by Singh (2000), ADB (2001), Timothy (2002), Singh (2006), Van Gelder et al. (2007) and Singh et al. (2007) are testimony to this fact.

Many countries of the world are actively seeking ways and means to promote entrepreneurship (Singh and Belwal, 2008). In developing countries women entrepreneurs are taking a leading role in helping their respective governments to establish and develop strong SMEs that contribute significantly towards poverty reduction. More and more small firms are now expanding globally (Delaney, 2004). Globally, more women are entering the business field. No doubt ever-increasing global competition presents challenges to companies big and small and their choice to take work abroad can be risky, especially for smaller companies that lack resources to fall back on, if a particular venture falls through (Haapaniemi, 1998; Weeks, 2008). Still, we cannot deny the fact that with more small businesses taking advantage of the outsourcing trend (Engardio, 2006) natives working overseas also create new markets and opportunities for home companies to sell their products overseas, creating what some would call a 'win–win' scenario (Strauss, 2004). Here women, who make up the majority of the small-scale entrepreneurs especially in developing countries could be the major beneficiaries (Blackman, 2000). This is because women are often marginalized in many developing countries and improving the life of women implies a significant impact on the lives of their families.

Also in the case of SMEs, factors such as age, gender, education and training, family background, ethnicity, religion, network membership and motivation (in addition to other structural and competitive factors) play an important role in influencing entrepreneurs' behaviour and decision-making (Porter, 1980; Gartner, 1988; Brush, 1997; Orhan and Scott, 2001). Women entrepreneurs appear to be motivated to start their own business in order to be their own boss, to get job satisfaction, for economic independence or for an opportunity to be more creative (Kandasaami and Tibbits, 1993). But, despite the increase in global ownership by women entrepreneurs, they still face numerous barriers, which this study will highlight. Therefore, to illustrate this, the results are presented and four case studies of women whose firms have achieved success within their fields are described. Finally, the chapter concludes with a summary of the arguments raised and further recommendations for policy action and support.

POSITION OF WOMEN IN FIJI

The Bureau of Statistics (2007) report presents the 2004–05 Household Survey of Employment and Unemployment for Fiji. It shows that women comprise 31 per cent of the labour force. In analysing the contribution of females in each industrial sector, it is seen that in agriculture, forestry and fishing, they make up 22 per cent, mining and quarrying 5 per cent, manufacturing 3 per cent, electricity and water 7 per cent, construction 5 per cent, hotel, retail and restaurants 41 per cent, transport, storage and communication 13 per cent, finance, real estate and business 34 per cent and community, personal and social services 41 per cent (ibid.). In terms of specific activities, women account for 19 per cent of employers, 27 per cent of wage earners, 25 per cent of the self-employed, and 37 per cent of salary earners. Further, and perhaps not surprisingly, women are involved in 99 per cent of household activities.

POSITION OF WOMEN IN SMES

A recent SME survey shows that of the 14 560 registered businesses in Fiji, 19.2 per cent of them are operated by women, 44 per cent by Indo-Fijian women, 34 per cent by Fijian women and 22 per cent by women of other ethnic origins (Chandra and Lewai, 2005). Females in self-employment make up 24 per cent, family workers comprise 42 per cent and 37 per cent are salary earners. In the formal sector 5 per cent of registered businesses (in both rural and urban areas) are run by females (Bureau of Statistics, 2006). The study shows that most of the female registered businesses were crop and horticultural farming and services while men were involved in dairy, crop and poultry production (ibid.). Chandra and Lewai's (2005) study of 150 informal businesses show that 28 per cent were run by women. Garcia (2004) also highlights the contribution of women in the economy and states that women's role is integral to the functioning of small-holding farms and carrying out the work of sustenance.

The Fiji government has established the National Centre for Small and Micro Enterprise Development (NCSMED) (a statutory organization) in 2002, to coordinate assistance to SMEs and to provide services to entrepreneurs. The Centre merged with the government's National Micro-Finance Unit (NMFU) in early 2004. According to Luse Kinivuwai, Director of the Centre's Microfinance Unit, the Centre released loans totalling FJD$2.66 million by the end of July 2005 (NCSMED Newsletter, 2005), in the NMFU scheme. Eighty-five per cent of the clientele are women (Kinivuwai, 2005).

The government of Fiji is fully committed to ensuring that women participate fully in the socioeconomic development of the country, which is reflected in the 'Strategic Development Plan 2007–11'. In 1999 it endorsed the national Women's Plan of Action (WPA) 1999–2008, which had five overall goals for advancing the economic, legal and political status of women (Government of Fiji, 2006). Despite the initiatives in place, however, there are still a number of challenges facing women entrepreneurs: these challenges restrict women's ability to survive in the entrepreneurial market. Despite the initiatives, more funding is still channelled to male counterparts. Savenaca Narube, the Governor for the Reserve Bank of Fiji, comments that Fiji lacks statistics on SMEs. Therefore, from 2006, banks and other financial institutions have been asked to provide them with data to allow for better decision and policy-making to promote growth in this sector (*The Fiji Times*, 2 November 2007).

Studies conducted in different South Pacific countries by Croulet and Sio (1986), Ritterbush (1986), Finney (1987, 1988), Fairbairn (1988), Hailey (1988), Mamman (1993), Yusuf (1998), Baldacchino (1999) and Schaper (2002) have found that entrepreneurs in the region portray different characteristics from their counterparts in the West. Fiji is one such island country of the South Pacific region where a growing number of families are settled in crowded urbanized settlements around towns and although the number of professional workers is said to be increasing, the rate of economic development and social change has not been sufficient to create an environment wherein every citizen has the opportunity to earn a decent living (Hailey, 1987). The small size of this country, predominantly strong family orientation and overall education level of women, reflect social structures that differ from many developed countries. The business environment for women entrepreneurs also reflects the complex interplay of different factors that ultimately result in the disadvantaged status of women in society. Moreover, little is known about performance of women-owned businesses in Fiji except the recent studies by Singh (2006) and Singh et al. (2007).

There are a number of difficulties faced by women entrepreneurs in Fiji. These include:

- poor access and/or control over land and resources necessary for entrepreneurial activities;
- costs of basic infrastructure, capital and regulatory services (which, in turn, alienate many women who have little access to finance to meet expenses);
- lack of help with planning;
- lack of skilled trainers who can relate family obligations and commitments to development;
- lack of support systems for women (such as extension services and specific credit facilities);
- little understanding of market forces and variables that determine production;
- jobs that women enter, that is, enterprising activities, tend to be labour-intensive with marginal profits;
- little access to training due to time, geographical and financial commitments related to reproductive, social and economic roles;

- systematic biases that make it difficult for women to obtain certain levels of education and employment;
- cultural variables that exclude women from particular employment fields;
- government commitments that aim at assisting women through equity and anti-discrimination clauses have not been translated into programmes;
- and finally lack of basic formal education opportunities in some countries to offer both confidence and awareness. (Pacific Women's Resource Bureau [PWRB] 1999)

Many problems of SMEs in the Pacific have been reported to relate to environmental factors. Fairbairn (1988) cites the following obstacles: capital shortage, transportation, weak domestic markets and traditional obligations. Singh (1992) and Briscoe et al. (1990) included the problem of lack of government support. Carroll (1986) adds other external factors affecting small businesses as relating to socio-cultural conditions. Kinivuwai (2005) mentions that microfinance services in Fiji have attracted more women recipients, and suggests that coordination of programmes with other microfinance programmes in the country is prudent to avoid repetition and competition.

EXPLORATION OF CONCEPTUAL AND CONTEXTUAL BARRIERS TO FEMALE ENTREPRENEURS

Following the analysis of the issues affecting women entrepreneurs it was seen that women entrepreneurs work under the same macro-level framework as their male counterparts. However, there is greater need to understand the gender biases embedded in society that limit women's mobility, interactions, active economic participation and access to business development services. Women contemplating becoming entrepreneurs are facing daunting challenges everywhere (Phillips and Kirchhoff, 1989). Also, women entrepreneurs in many developing countries face greater obstacles in achieving success because their businesses tend to be small and grow less quickly compared with male entrepreneurs (Cooper et al., 1994; Cliff, 1998). Credibility of women heading their businesses is also one important factor that is being mentioned over and again (Baron et al., 2001).

A survey conducted with women entrepreneurs in Fiji (Singh, 2006) revealed that almost 85 per cent of women reported that they had acceptance among family, friends and relatives as an entrepreneur. It was further found that almost 64 per cent of the women did not believe that they faced any gender bias in society by being an entrepreneur, and 76 per cent felt they had ample time for managing business over family responsibilities. Though there are no gender biases among the family and acquaintances, almost 55 per cent of women did report a lack of cooperation on the part of business partners; for example, banks, suppliers and marketing intermediaries and so on. Interestingly, almost 74 per cent of the respondents reported a lack of coordination among women entrepreneurs. It can be concluded that the women have enough acceptance in Fiji as entrepreneurs. For these women, networking among women entrepreneurs would have been a real benefit.

The survey attempted to investigate the business environment in terms of five factors viz. availability of funds, business infrastructure, gap between demand and supply of credit, role of bank and financial institutions and competition with male entrepreneurs. It was found that almost 83 per cent of women entrepreneurs have had disagreement with regard to easy availability of funds for starting up their business ventures. As regards availability of business infrastructure in Fiji, 33 per cent of them were satisfied, 22 per cent remained neutral and 44 per cent were not satisfied. Regarding the gap between the demands made for bank credit by SMEs and supply of funds by the banks, 59 per cent of women reported a gap, while 38 per cent rated these banks poor in terms of their support for SMEs' day to day operations. Furthermore, only 25 per cent of women reported that they did not find male entrepreneurs difficult to compete with.

The government of Fiji claims to have launched many schemes for the development of women's entrepreneurship in the country. The statistics for the inadequacy of training and updates pertaining to the promotion of women entrepreneurship show that 72 per cent of women entrepreneurs do not get any form of training. However, the survey by Singh and Belwal (2008) revealed that in general they have limited awareness of such schemes. Eleven per cent of the women entrepreneurs were unable to comment on these schemes and 74 per cent expressed disagreement about the availability of such schemes. Further, 75 per cent were not happy with the role of government machinery in support of women entrepreneurship and almost 48 per cent reported a gap between the government policy and its implementation.

A large majority (92 per cent) of women stated that the government did not ask their advice in framing policies, which means that schemes are being created without the input of those people for whom the schemes are designed. This may explain why women entrepreneurs do not know about or benefit from such initiatives.

To the utmost advantage of entrepreneurship, 78 per cent of the entrepreneurs attributed the SME registration process in Fiji as simple, while at the same time almost 32 per cent of them complained of extremely high tax rates impeding entrepreneurial growth. The legal system was found supportive for entrepreneurship with 57 per cent of the respondents reporting it as safeguarding the interests of women, although 73 per cent of the respondents denied the presence of the demarcated special SME zones for women entrepreneurs that the government claim to provide. There were mixed responses with regard to entrepreneurs having easy access to market intelligence, where 46 per cent found difficulty, 11 per cent remained neutral and 43 per cent found easy access. Respondents evaluated each of the 14 infrastructural facilities on a scale of 1 to 7, the lower numbers representing 'Critical Problem' and the higher numbers representing, 'Not a Problem'. The researchers have calculated an average for each problem, with a low average score implying a relatively difficult problem and a high average score implying a relatively easy one (Table 7.1).

Further analysis looked at the degree of agreement between women entrepreneurs with regard to these issues; they simply reveal the degree of agreement on their evaluation (Table 7.2).

It is evident that the availability of markets, raw materials, warehousing, know-how and opportunities for exports are the most important problems faced by women entrepreneurs in Fiji.

Table 7.1   Infrastructural facilities-related problems

Factors (Problems)	Average	Rank
Promotional assistance from government	3.25	1
Supportive vocational training programmes	3.34	2
Availability of finance	3.35	3
Transport	3.59	4
Telecom	3.98	5
Availability of skilled employees	4.09	6
Subsidies	4.14	7
Availability of raw material	4.52	8
Availability of know-how	4.65	9
Electricity	4.73	10
Opportunities for exports	4.73	10
Warehousing	4.75	12
Availability of markets	4.91	13
Import facilities	5.02	14

Source: Authors' own data analysis.

Table 7.2   Agreement on the infrastructural facilities-related problems

Factors (Problems)	Rank
Availability of markets	1
Availability of raw material	2
Warehousing	3
Availability of know-how	4
Opportunities for exports	5
Availability of skilled employees	6
Availability of finance	7
Import facilities	8
Electricity	9
Subsidies	10
Promotional assistance from government	11
Supportive vocational training programmes	12
Transport	13
Telecom	14

Source: Authors' own data analysis.

CASE STUDIES: WOMEN ENTREPRENEURS IN FIJI

The following case studies are about the successful entrepreneurs in Fiji and some of the government initiatives taken to provide assistance and uplift the status of women in entrepreneurship.

BOX 7.1   CHANDRA LEKHA

The first case study is of Chandra Lekha, who applied for a loan with Fiji Development Bank. Chandra Lekha is an entrepreneur based in Vunidawa, Naitasiri. In 1993, she faced the most difficult time of her life when her beloved husband passed away. She was left with the sole responsibility of taking care of her two children. That same year she faced the huge consequences of Cyclone Kina that drastically affected her 87-acre farm, house and other buildings. She was very distressed and left to return after a year with firm determination to start work on her farm again. Mrs Chandra Lekha applied for a loan at the Fiji Development Bank, who approved her loan, and following approval she started repair work on the farm, buildings and other infrastructure. With the loan that she received from the FDB, she was able to purchase ten head of cattle to commence work at the farm.

Today, she owns 31 cows that produce milk and employs two labourers and casual workers. The earnings from the dairy products help her sustain a living. She believes that to remain in business you have to be committed.

BOX 7.2   ANASAINI ADIQISA

Our second case study focuses on Anasaini Adiqisa, who is an entrepreneur based in Makoi, Nasinu. In 1998, she decided to open a small second-hand clothing outlet from her home in Makoi. Since she could not operate well from home, afterwards she moved to the flea-market in Suva, but here she battled with stiff competition from Value City. As her business could not survive in that location, in January 2002, Anasaini purchased a second-hand clothing outlet (EziBuy Second Hand Clothing), in another location. As a result of heavy customer demand, she approached the Fiji Development Bank for a loan. With the loan that she received she ordered clothes from her supplier in Australia and one local supplier in Fiji. She received a certification from 'Start Your Own Business Training' and since then has managed her business well, due to the knowledge and skills that she acquired in the training. Anasaini says to those thinking of starting a new business: work hard and achieve your goals.

BOX 7.3   MOHINI PRAKASH

Our third case study example is of Mohini Prakash, an entrepreneur based in Tuvu, Lautoka. She hails from a poor background and was previously working in a garment factory. When the garment factory closed down, she started her own small-scale tailoring business from home and afterwards moved to the city area to rent a shop. Mohini learnt about the microfinance loan scheme from a nearby shoe shop entrepreneur and applied for her first loan in 2004, after which she has received three loans and has successfully been able to purchase stock for her business and at the same time fund her husband for the purchase of a van to start his van business. She is currently doing well and hopes to expand her business further by owning her own shop and serving more than 200 clients. She attributes her success to hard work, creativity and customer-focused attitude.

BOX 7.4   TULIA VEIKOSO

Our fourth case example is of Tulia Veikoso, an entrepreneur based in Nauluvata Settlement. She is the mother of three children. In 2001 she approached the NMFU with the possibility of starting a canteen business. Tulia was told to complete a training course, after which she was awarded her first loan. From this loan she bought groceries and stocked her home to target 30 households. She has taken her third loan and used that to further expand the business. Currently she operates a shop in Reservoir Road, Suva, and has out-sold her competitors forcing one rival to close shop. Tulia does not lend easily, is very careful with her money and manages her canteen well. Her intention is to own a supermarket.

SUMMARY AND RECOMMENDATIONS

Based on the survey results (presented in Tables 7.1 and 7.2) and from the examples of success stories (Boxes 7.1 to 7.4), the following policy initiatives need to be taken immediately for promoting women's entrepreneurship in Fiji. In order to develop the skills/qualifications of women entrepreneurs, training and development programmes should be available. These training and development programmes should equip them with theoretical knowledge as well as practical skills. Second, an awareness campaign is needed for women to gain an insight into the different types of programmes and funding sources that are available. Third, high interest rates, which are a major hindrance, need to be looked into. There should be incentives set in place to develop and motivate women, for instance special/low interest rates. Fourth, there should be a clear demarcation of SME zones, and warehousing facilities should be provided. Fifth, many women do not have access to markets and raw materials, they lack awareness and information, funds to purchase materials, support from the government, networking, and experience prejudice and stereotyping from society with regards to products sold by women either locally or for exports. Affirmative action policies should be strengthened to empower women, and the community at large should be educated on the role of women in society and their contribution to the economy. There is also a need for promotional campaigns and social marketing on the problems and challenges faced by women entrepreneurs and the issue of stereotyping/prejudice against women entrepreneurs in society.

In conclusion, entrepreneurship is an important issue for the long-term sustainability and development of the economy and the people in Fiji. The contribution of women should not be underestimated and this issue demands serious attention. As a result, although family and friends appear supportive of women entrepreneurs, business partners are far less supportive and are blocking women's progress. Women have been marginalized due to stereotyping and negative biases/attitudes, cultural issues, poor networking and support. There is a need to incorporate affirmative action policies and gender mainstreaming to develop women and promote equal employment in all spheres, from policy formulation to implementation. It is crucial that support in the form of skills workshops, training and development programmes, education and awareness, coupled with strong policies backing women in their work, low interest rates, and more sources of funding availability is created. This should be the stepping stone towards ensuring that women are empowered and they are not marginalized, that is, society at large accepts and values their potential to contribute towards their own development and towards the development of the economy in general.

BIBLIOGRAPHY

ADB Key Indicators (2001), 'Growth and change in Asia and the Pacific employment indicators', ADB, available at: http://www.adb.org/documents/books/key_indicators/2001/default.asp; accessed 9 February 2010.

Ahl, H. (2006). 'Why research on women entrepreneurs needs new directions', *Entrepreneurship Theory and Practice*, **30**(5), 595–621.

Allen, E., Langowitz, N. and Minniti, M. (2007), *Global Entrepreneurship Monitor: 2006 Report on Women and Entrepreneurship*, available at: http://www3.babson.edu/CWL/upload/GEM_2006_Report.pdf; accessed 9 February 2010.

Audretsch, D.B. and Fritsch, M. (1991), 'Market dynamics and regional development in the Federal Republic of Germany', Discussion Paper No. IV, 92–6, Berlin: Wissenschaftszentrum.

Baldacchino, G. (1999), 'Small business in small islands: a case study from Fiji', *Journal of Small Business Management*, **37**(4), 80–84.

Baron, R.A., Markman, G.D. and Hirsa, A. (2001), 'Perceptions of women and men as entrepreneurs: evidence for differential effects of attributional augmenting', *Journal of Applied Psychology*, **86**(5), 923–9.

Blackman, J.A. (2000), 'Entrepreneurs: interrelationships between their characteristics, values, expectations, management practices and SME performance', Gold Coast: Griffith University.

Briscoe, R., Nair, G.S. and Sibbald, A. (1990), *Enterprise Support Organizations for the South Pacific: Problems and Proposals*, Honolulu: PIDP East West Center.

Brush, C.G. (1997), 'Women-owned businesses: obstacles and opportunities', *Journal of Development Entrepreneurship*, **2**(1), 1–24.

Brush, C., Carter, N., Gatewood, E., Greene, P. and Hart, Myra (2006), 'The use of bootstrapping by women entrepreneurs in positioning for growth', *Venture Capital, An International Journal of Entrepreneurial Finance*, **8**(1), 15–31.

Bureau of Statistics, Fiji (2006), unpublished statistics, Fiji, in E. Singh (2006), *Women Agribusiness Entrepreneurs in Fiji – Challenges and Prospects*.

Bureau of Statistics (2007), *Fiji Island Bureau of Statistics Report on the 2004–05 Employment and Unemployment Survey*, Fiji: Vanuavou Publications. Report data analysed and prepared by Wadan Narsey, available at: http://www.statsfiji.gov.fj/censandsurveys/EUS%20report.pdf; accessed 9 February 2010.

Carroll, J. (1986), *Entrepreneurship and Indigenous Business in the Republic of Marshall Islands*, Honolulu: PIDP East West Center.

Carter, S. and Bennett, D. (2006), 'Gender and entrepreneurship', in S. Carter and D. Jones-Evans (eds), *Enterprise and Small Business*, London, Prentice Hall.

Carter, S., Shaw, E., Lam, W. and Wilson, F. (2007). 'Gender entrepreneurship and bank lending: the criteria and processes used by bank loan officers in assessing applications', *Entrepreneurship, Theory and Practice*, **31**(3), 427–45.

Center for Women's Business Research (CWBR) (2008a), 'Key facts about women-owned businesses', available at: http://www.womensbusinessresearch.org/facts/index.php; accessed 9 February 2010.

Center for Women's Business Research (CWBR) (2008b), 'Businesses owned by women of color growing faster than the overall economy: employment, sales also on the rise', available at: http://www.imdiversity.com/vil lages/woman/business_finance/women_of_color_business_1104.asp; accessed 9 February 2010.

Chandra, D. and Lewai, V. (2005), *Women and Men of Fiji Islands: Gender Statistics and Trends*, Demographic Report No. 10, University of the South Pacific and Fiji Bureau of Statistics, Fiji.

Cliff, J.E. (1998), 'Does one size fit all? Exploring the relationship between attitudes toward growth, gender, and business size', *Journal of Business Venturing*, **13**(6), 523–42.

Cooper, A., Gimeno-Gascon, F.J. and Woo, C. (1994), 'Initial human and financial capital as predictors of new venture performance', *Journal of Business Venturing*, **9**(5), 371–95.

Croulet, C. and Sio, L. (1986), *Indigenous Entrepreneurship in Western Samoa*, Honolulu: PIDP East West Center.

Delaney, L. (2004), 'Small businesses are going global', 30 September, available at: http://www.smallbiztrends. com/2004/09/small-businesses-are-going-global.html; accessed 9 February 2010.

Engardio, P. (2006), 'The future of outsourcing: how it's transforming whole industries and changing the way we work', 30 January, available at: http://www.businessweek.com/magazine/content/06_05/b3969401.html; accessed 9 February 2010.

Fairbairn, I.J. (1988), *Island Entrepreneurs: Problems and Performance in the Pacific*, Honolulu: PIDP East West Center.

Fielden, S. and Davidson, M. (2005), *International Handbook of Women and Entrepreneurship*, Cheltenham, UK and Northampton, MA, USA: Edward Elgar.

Fiji Development Bank (FDB) (2003–06), 'Annual Report 2003–06', Suva: FDB.

Finney, B. (1987), *Business Development in the Highlands of Papua New Guinea*, Research Report Series No. 6, Honolulu: PIDP East West Center.

Finney, B. (1988), 'Culture and entrepreneurship in the highlands of Papua New Guinea', in T. Fairbairn (eds), *Island Entrepreneurs: Problems and Performance in the Pacific*, Honolulu: PIDP East West Center.

Garcia, Z. (2004), 'Impact of agricultural trade on gender equity and rural women's position in developing countries', available at: http://www.glow-boell.de/media/de/txt_rubrik_5/SuS_Garcia.pdf; accessed 9 February 2010.

Gartner, William B. (1988), 'Who is an entrepreneur? is the wrong question', *American Journal of Small Business*, **12**(4), 11–32.

Global Gender Gap Report, 2007, available at: http://www.weforum.org/pdf/gendergap/report2007.pdf; accessed 9 February 2010.

Government of Fiji (2006), 'Strategic Development Plan 2007–2011', Parliamentary Paper No. 92 of 2006, Fiji: Ministry of Finance and National Planning, available at: http://www.mfnp.gov.fj/Documents/Draft_Strategic_%20Development_%20Plan_2007-2011.pdf; accessed 12 February 2010.

Haapaniemi, P. (1998), 'The mice that roared – globalization of small companies – Little Big Corp: The Smaller Company Goes Global', *The Chief Executive*, September, available at: http://findarticles.com/p/articles/mi_m4070/is_n137/ai_21200397; accessed 9 February 2010.

Hailey, J.M. (1987), 'Entrepreneurs and indigenous business in the Pacific', Honolulu: PIDP East West Center.

Hailey, J. (1988), 'Fijian entrepreneurs: indigenous business in Fiji', in T. Fairbairn (eds), *Island Entrepreneurs: Problems and Performance in the Pacific*, Honolulu: PIDP East West Center.

Hoy, F., McDougall, P.P. and Dsouza, D.E. (1992), 'Strategies and environments of high-growth firms', in D. Sexton and J.D. Kasayda (eds), *The State of the Art of Entrepreneurship*, Boston, MA: PWS-Kent, pp. 341–57.

Kandasaami, T. and Tibbits, G.E. (1993), 'An empirical investigation of women small business owners. Fostering small enterprise growth', Joint SEAANZ and IIE National Small Enterprise Conference, University of Newcastle: Institute of Industrial Economics.

Keeble, D., Potter, J. and Storey, D.J. (1990), 'Cross-national comparisons of the role of SMEs in regional economic growth in the European community', working paper, SME Centre, University of Warwick.

Kinivuwai, L. (2005), 'Developing micro finance in Fiji: challenges and successes', available at: http://www.engagingcommunities2005.org/abstracts/Kinivuwai-Lucy-final.pdf; accessed 9 February 2010.

Kirschoff, B.A. and Phillips, B.D. (1989), 'Examining entrepreneurship's role in economic growth', *Frontiers of Entrepreneurship Research*, Wellesley, MA: Babson College.

Klapper, L. et al. (2007), 'Entrepreneurship and firm formation across countries', available at: http://knowl edge.wharton.upenn.edu/papers/1345.pdf; accessed 9 February 2010.

Mamman, A. (1993), 'Big man, wantoks and liklik business man', *Administration for Development*, **1**(1), 20–33.

Morris, H.M., Pitt, Leyland F. and Berthon, Pierre (1996), 'Entrepreneurial activity in the Third World informal sector, the view from Khayelitsha', *International Journal of Entrepreneurial Behavior and Research*, **2**(1), 59–76.

NCSMED (2005), *SME News, The Newsletter of NCSMED*, 3, 1–12.

NFWBO (1997) in CWBR (2008b), 'Businesses owned by women of color growing faster than the overall economy: employment, sales also on the rise', available at: http://www.imdiversity.com/villages/woman/business_finance/women_of_color_business_1104.asp; accessed 9 February 2010.

OECD (1998), *Women Entrepreneurs in Small and Medium Enterprises*, OECD, Paris.

Orhan, M. and Scott, D. (2001), 'Why women enter into entrepreneurship: an explanatory model', *Women in Management Review*, **16**(5), 232–43.

Pacific Women's Resource Bureau (PWRB) (1999), 'Gender and entrepreneurial development for women: a situation analysis' (Fiji, Papua New Guinea, Samoa, Tonga, Vanuatu), produced By Pacific Women's Resource Bureau Secretariat of the Pacific Community, Noumea, New Caledonia in association with Forum Secretariat, Suva, Fiji.

Phillips, B. and Kirschoff, B.A. (1989), 'Formation, growth and survival: small firm dynamics in the US economy', *Small Business Economics*, **1**(1), 65–74.

Porter, M.E. (1980), *Competitive Strategy: Techniques for Analyzing Industries and Competitors*, New York: Free Press.

Ritterbush, S. (1986), 'Entrepreneurship and business venture development in the Kingdom of Tonga', Honolulu: East-West Center.

Schaper, M. (2002), 'The future prospects of entrepreneurship in Papua New Guinea', *Journal of Small Business Management*, **40**(1), 78–83.

Singh, A. (1992), 'Small business management in Fiji: the reasons for success and failures of small business', unpublished assignment, Massey University, Palmerston North.

Singh, G. and Belwal, R. (2008), 'Entrepreneurship and SMEs in Ethiopia: evaluating the role, prospects and problems faced by women in this emergent sector', *Gender in Management: An International Journal*, **23**(2), 120–36.

Singh, S.B. (2006), 'The performance of small and medium-sized enterprises (SMEs) in Fiji: the interplay between entrepreneurial characteristics, organizational structure and corporate culture', unpublished Masters thesis, The University of the South Pacific, Fiji.

Singh, T. (2000), 'Problems of small business management', unpublished Masters thesis, The University of the South Pacific, Fiji.

Singh, T., Pathak, R.D., Kazmi, A., Sharma, B. and Terziovski, M. (2007), 'An empirical study of small business organizations in Fiji using a competency-based framework', *South Asian Journal of Management*, **14**(2), April–June.

Strauss, S. (2004), 'Globalization is good for (small) business', *USA Today*, 17 May, available at: http://www.usatoday.com/money/smallbusiness/columnist/strauss/2004-05-17-globalization_x.htm; accessed 9 February 2010.

The Fiji Times (2007), 'SMEs can help growth', available at: http://www.fijitimes.com/story.aspx?id=73486; accessed 9 February 2010.

Timothy, D. (2002), *Small Business Management*, New York: Prentice Hall.

Van Gelder, J.L., De Vries, R.E., Frese, M. and Goutbeek, J.P. (2007), 'Differences in psychological strategies between failed and operational business owners in Fiji', *Journal of Small Business Management*, **45**(3), 388–400.

Weeks, J.R. (2008), 'A connotation for control: women business owners seeking balance and growth', Institute of Small Business and Entrepreneurship Conference (ISBE), held on 5–7 November, available at: http://www.womenable.com/userfiles/downloads/Weeks_isbe_balance_and_growth.pdf; accessed 9 February 2010.

Women and Equality Unit (2008), 'Working and Living', in M. McAdam and S. Marlow, *The Business Incubator and the Female High Technology Entrepreneur: A Perfect Match?*, available at: http://www.nwbc.gov/ResearchPublications/documents/2008ICSBPaper.pdf; accessed 20 February 2010.

Yusuf, A. (1998), 'Small business development and survival in the South Pacific: barriers and strategic responses', *The Journal of Entrepreneurship*, **7**(1), 49–65.

8 India
Tanuja Agarwala

INTRODUCTION

The female population in India is approximately 48 per cent of the total population of over a billion (RGCSI, 2001). Women, therefore, constitute almost half the human resource potential available in India. Since India attained independence in the year 1947, several positive developments have significantly improved the status of women. Yet, women's potential has not been fully integrated into the socioeconomic mainstream of the country. Gender disparities in education, literacy rate, cultural barriers to knowledge acquisition by women, and social barriers to participation of women in workforce, have contributed to this state of affairs (Naidu and Chandralekha, 1998; Basargekar, 2007). This chapter explores the barriers that women in India confront in setting up their entrepreneurial ventures and the role that the state machinery and other associations have played in encouraging women's entrepreneurship in the country. The chapter also presents success stories of two Indian women entrepreneurs.

THE POSITION OF WOMEN IN EMPLOYMENT IN INDIA

The importance of socio-political and economic empowerment of women has been emphasized in India since Independence, and it has also been achieved to some extent. Several factors such as industrialization, globalization, urbanization and legislation, have played an important part in women's empowerment (Singh, 1993; Kollan and Parikh, 2005). There have been substantial improvements in the educational status of Indian women and female literacy rates showed an upward increase, from 39 per cent in the year 1991 to 54 per cent in 2001 (RGCSI, 2001). Educational progress among women has resulted in higher involvement of women in activities such as teaching, research, engineering and medicine, as well as an increase in their enrolment in higher technical and professional education (Table 8.1). The percentage of Indian women employed in managerial and administrative occupations (1.6 per cent of total female employment in 2004–05), and in professional and technical occupations (3.6 per cent of total female employment in 2004–05) has increased over the years (NSSO, 2004–05).

Indian women have made a mark in almost all traditionally male bastions, be it judiciary, administrative services, politics, or business. Though overall female participation in the labour force (i.e., those willing to be economically active) in India registered a marginal increase between 1993–94 and 2004–05, the percentage of female workforce engaged in economic activity in India (i.e., those engaged in employment), as indicated by Workforce Participation Rate (WFPR) for women, remained constant at around 28 per cent between 1993–94 and 2004–05 (Table 8.2). Table 8.3 illustrates the Labour Force Participation Rate (LFPR) for urban as well as rural educated women (gradu-

Table 8.1   Enrolment of women in higher technical and professional education

Technical and Professional Courses*	Year			
	2001	2002	2003	2004
Engineering/technology/architecture	154041	NA	NA	165316
Medicine	115557	NA	NA	145302
Business management, journalism, law, music, social work, etc.	41279	81206	NA	94160
Total enrolment in professional/technical courses (degree and above level)	413000[a]	460000[a]	494000[a]	NA

Note: * Includes enrolment at graduate, postgraduate, and Doctoral level; a. as on 30 September; NA = not available.

Sources: University Grants Commission (UGC), *Annual Report* for various years; University Grants Commission (UGC), *Basic Facts and Figures*, 1995–96 to 2000–01.

Table 8.2   Female participation in labour force and workforce in India

Female Labour Force Participation Rate (LFPR)* and Estimates of (millions) Labour Force			Female Work Force Participation Rate (WFPR)* and Estimates of (millions) Employment		
Year	Female (rural and urban)		Year	Female (rural and urban)	
	LFPR[a] (per cent)	Labour Force[a]		WFPR[b] (per cent)	Employment[b]
1990–91	25.7	104.6	1987–88	28.5	106.5
1993–94	28.7	123.1	1993–94	28.6	121.0
1999–00	25.8	125.1	1999–00	25.9	122.9
2000–01	25.2	123.8	2000–01	25.0	123.0
2001–02	NA	NA	2001–02	27.4	133.5
2004–05	29.4	139.4	2004–05	28.7	135.8

Note: * Labour Force Participation Rate/Workforce Participation Rate is the size of labour force/ workforce as percentage of total population.

Sources:
a.   National Sample Survey Organization (NSSO): Sarvekshana, Vol. XX, 1993–94; Report No. 458, *Employment and Unemployment Situation in India, 1999–2000*; Report No. 476, *Employment and Unemployment Situation in India, 2000–01*; and Report No. 515, *Employment and Unemployment Situation in India, 2005*.
b.   National Sample Survey Organization (NSSO): Report No. 481, *Employment and Unemployment Situation in India, 2001–02*; and Report No. 515, *Employment and Unemployment Situation in India, 2004–05*.

ate and above) increased between 1999–2000 and 2004–05. The WFPR for the urban educated (graduate and above) women, was 28 per cent in 1993–94, and marginally improved to 29 per cent in 2004–05 (Table 8.3).

According to the employment figures available, overall employment in the organized sector in India has gone down, but the number of women working in the organized sector has increased (Table 8.4).[1] The statistical figures are encouraging with respect to the

Table 8.3   Labour force and workforce participation rates for educated females*

Labour Force Participation Rate (LFPR) for Educated (Graduate and Above) Females[a]			Work Force Participation Rate (WFPR) for Educated (Graduate and Above) Females[b]		
Year	Rural	Urban	Year	Rural	Urban
1993–94	44.80	35.50	1993–94	29.30	28.20
1999–00	40.28	30.24	1999–00	27.80	25.20
2004–05	46.81	35.02	2004–05	34.50	29.00

Note: * Figures represent size of the labour force/workforce of given educational level as percentage of population of that educational level.

Sources:
a.   National Sample Survey Organization (NSSO): Report No. 409, *Employment and Unemployment Situation in India, 1993–94*; Report No. 455, *Employment and Unemployment in India, 1999–2000, Key Results*; and Report No. 515, *Employment and Unemployment in India, 2004–05*.
b.   National Sample Survey Organization (NSSO): Sarvekshana, Vol. XX, July 93–June 94, 50th Round; Report No. 458, *Employment and Unemployment in India, 1999–2000*, 55th Round; Report No. 575, *Employment and Unemployment in India, 2004–05*, 61st Round.

Table 8.4   Employment in the organized sector

Year	Employment (in lakhs*)			Percentage of Women Employment to Total
	Public	Private	Total	
1991	190.57	76.76	267.33	14.10 (28 lakhs)
2001	191.38	86.52	277.89	17.81
2002	187.73	84.32	272.06	18.43
2003	185.80	84.21	270.00	18.40
2004	181.97	82.46	264.43	18.66 (50 lakhs)

Note: * Unit in the Indian numbering system equal to 100000.

Source: Directorate General of Employment and Training, Employment Review for various years.

status of women in India. However, a significant number of women are still illiterate and the majority continues to work in the unorganized sector, such as farms, construction and small-scale manufacturing industries or in village, household and cottage industries. According to the 2001 National Census, almost 60 per cent of the female population in India was in the working age group (that is, between 15 and 64 years), yet only 27 per cent women were engaged in gainful economic activity (Table 8.2), indicating a huge untapped potential.

THE CURRENT POSITION OF WOMEN AND SMALL BUSINESS OWNERSHIP

The proportion of women business owners has increased over the years across the world. Entrepreneurship is a powerful tool to facilitate the direct participation of women in

Table 8.5   Percentage distribution of employment of women by status

Year	Employment Status of Women				
	Self-employed			Regular employees	Casual labour
	Total	Rural	Urban	Total (rural and urban)	Total (rural and urban)
1993–94	56.7	58.5	45.4	6.3	37.0
2000–01	57.2	59.3	44.4	7.1	35.7
2001–02	57.2	58.9	44.1	8.0	36.8

Sources: National Sample Survey Organization: Report No. 481, *Household Consumer Expenditures and Employment–Unemployment Situation in India, 2001–2002*; Report No. 515, *Employment–Unemployment Situation In India, 2004–2005.*

income-generating activities. Literature suggests that women entrepreneurs impact the political, socio-cultural and economic affairs of a country (Jalbert, 1999). Internationally one in ten women are self-employed (McClelland et al., 2005).

The entrepreneurial world in India has been largely male-dominated (Singh, 1993), with women's participation in entrepreneurial activity starting in the early 1970s (Ganesan et al., 2002). After more than 30 years, the number of women in entrepreneurial activity is still not encouraging, although it is difficult to accurately estimate the number of women entrepreneurs in India. The national-level household survey by National Sample Survey Organization (NSSO) provides some information on women entrepreneurs under the broad category of self-employment (Table 8.5). These self-employment figures include both own account and establishment figures and hence may not be accurate estimates. Though more than 50 per cent of the total women workforce engaged in economic activity were self-employed, they are largely engaged in small household work such as stitching, making pickles and so on. As more women become educated and acquire technical expertise the type of product lines/service activities selected by women entrepreneurs has diversified, and includes specialized entrepreneurial ventures with advanced technologies.

According to a survey of 1994–95 of registered small-scale industries for the year 1992–93, there were only 7.69 per cent women entrepreneurs compared with 5.15 per cent in the Second All India Census for the base year 1987–88.[2] At the time of the Third All India Census of Small Scale Industrial (SSI) Units (base year 2001–02), the total number of enterprises owned by women increased to 1 063 721, which accounted for around 10.11 per cent of total small-scale enterprises. Out of these 137 534 (10 per cent) were registered and 926 187 were unregistered.[3] Approximately 60 per cent of them represented small-scale units, 15 per cent represented large-scale units and the rest comprised cottage and micro-enterprises (Basargekar, 2007).

Certainly, self-employment among women is important for the economy of a country and the initiatives taken by the government of a particular country can increase the participation of women in entrepreneurial activities.

Role of Government in Promoting Women's Entrepreneurship

The government of India (GOI) recognized the importance of small and medium enterprises in the economic development of the country fairly early. The office of the Development Commissioner (DC), Ministry of Small Scale Industries (SSIs) was established as early as 1954 and within this office the Ministry of Micro, Small and Medium Enterprises (MSMEs) was set up in 2007 by merging the Ministry of Agro and Rural Industries and Ministry of SSIs.[4] The major thrust areas of the office of the DC (MSMEs) is to provide technological support, marketing and credit support, collateral-free loans, taxation benefits, entrepreneurial development and training programmes through various institutes, reservation of products for exclusive manufacture, purchase and price preferences, instituting awards, capacity building, assistance for exports, amongst others. The central and state governments of India have taken several measures to provide incentives and facilities to new as well as existing women entrepreneurs in order to promote women entrepreneurship. In addition, the MSMEs has instituted several special schemes for empowerment and promotion of women entrepreneurs (see Table 8.6).

To achieve its objective of the empowerment of women, the GOI has developed partnerships with financial institutions, nationalized banks, NGOs, training institutions and industry associations. Financial institutions and nationalized banks have set up special cells to extend loans to assist women entrepreneurs in starting their ventures. Various state- and national-level institutions, such as National Bank for Agriculture and Rural Development (NABARD) and Small Industries Development Bank of India (SIDBI), have made special provisions to provide opportunities and incentives to women entrepreneurs entering SMEs. Several institutions are involved in promoting Entrepreneurship Development Programmes (EDPs) for women, including the Small Industries Service Institutes (SISIs) and National Institute of Entrepreneurship and Small Business Development (NIESBUD). In addition, technical institutions like polytechnics and engineering colleges are imparting entrepreneurship education and also providing the necessary technical training, with some NGOs also involved in similar efforts (Ganesan et al., 2002).

Associations of existing women entrepreneurs who are reasonably well established in the SME sector have also played an important role in the dissemination of benefits of government schemes to women entrepreneurs (Rani and Rao, 2007). Some prominent associations are the Federation of Indian Women Entrepreneurs (FIWE), Consortium of Women Entrepreneurs of India (CWEI), Indian Council of Women Entrepreneurs (ICWE), FICCI Ladies Organization, Association of Lady Entrepreneurs of Andhra Pradesh (ALEAP) and Association of Women Entrepreneurs of Karnataka (AWAKE). These associations provide several services to women entrepreneurs, such as counselling and incubation services for prospective entrepreneurs, special incentives and training for women entrepreneurs, getting access to credit, giving guarantees for loans obtained by member entrepreneurs, providing platforms for marketing of products at national and international levels, undertaking market research, professional guidance on legal compliance and best entrepreneurship awards.

The result of government-promoted schemes for women entrepreneurs has been the emergence of women entrepreneurs on the economic scene in recent years. But the progress made in encouraging women into entrepreneurial vocations has not been very

Table 8.6   Special schemes of Ministry of Small and Medium Enterprises (MSMEs) for women entrepreneurs

MSMEs Schemes	Specific Initiatives
Special women cell by Small Industries Development Organization (SIDO)	Assistance to women entrepreneurs facing specific problems Support for marketing of goods through exhibitions Free display scheme for SSIs Units to help SSI exporters access overseas markets
Small Industries Development Bank of India (SIDBI)	Credit on soft terms Training for credit utilization and credit delivery skills for executives of voluntary organizations working for women
Trade Related Entrepreneurship Assistance and Development (TREAD) Scheme for women implemented by the Ministry in cooperation with nationalized banks, training institutions and NGOs	GOI grant of up to 30 per cent of the total project cost to non-governmental organizations (NGOs) for promoting entrepreneurship (through counselling, training, tie-ups for marketing, etc.) among target groups of women Entrepreneurship training programmes through selected training institutes and NGOs Grant of up to Rs5 lakhs per project to national entrepreneurial development institutions (EDIs) such as National Institute of Entrepreneurship and Small Business Development (NIESBUD), Small Industries Services Institutes (SISIs), and so on for designing training modules for women entrepreneurs, conducting project evaluation studies, etc.
Credit Guarantee Fund Scheme for Micro and Small Enterprises (2000)	Flow of credit to SMEs by lending institutions without collateral security Guarantee cover of up to 80 per cent of the loan for MSEs operated and/or owned by women
Entrepreneurship Development Programmes (EDPs)	Earmarking 20 per cent of the training courses conducted by MSMEs development institutions exclusively for women entrepreneurs at nominal fees
Promotional package by central and state government organizations (2007) for MSEs run by women	Help in selling in overseas markets Facilitating participation in international trade fairs/exhibitions Promoting products manufactured by women entrepreneurs by organizing exhibitions, trade shows and *gram melas* (village fairs)
Government incentives to small-scale units of women entrepreneurs	Incentives for marketing of goods Small-scale units registered with National Small Industries Corporation (NSIC) extended government's Price and Purchase Preference Policy through reservation of certain products by the government for exclusive purchase from the SSI sector and price preference up to 15 per cent in case of selected items

Sources: http://www.laghu-udyog.com/schemes/sidoscheme.htm; http://www.laghu-udyog.com/schemes/wenterpre.htm; accessed 9 February 2010.

significant. Several socioeconomic barriers and unfavourable conditions continue to place limits on participation of women in economic activities and often hinder the emergence of entrepreneurial talents (Naidu and Chandralekha, 1998; Sinha, 2003, 2005; Kollan and Parikh, 2005).

EXPLORATION OF STRUCTURAL AND CONTEXTUAL BARRIERS ENCOUNTERED BY WOMEN

Entrepreneurial individuals, such as renowned industrialist the late Sir J.R.D. Tata, have played an important role in the economic development of India. Women entrepreneurs contribute to the economic growth and competitiveness of a developing country. Shahnaz Hussain, Vandana Luthra, Kiran Mazumdar Shaw are some examples of successful women entrepreneurs, but the number of women in the list of notable entrepreneurs and examples of great enterprises promoted and nurtured exclusively by women in India is conspicuously low.

There are several reasons why not many women enter into business. The entrepreneurial literature suggests that women confront a variety of challenges in developing and running a business (McKay, 2001) and some of these hurdles have been identified as being greater for women than men. These challenges include obtaining capital (Buttner and Moore, 1997), acquiring appropriate training (Walker and Joyner, 1999), lack of knowledge of skills required to develop business, resistance from relatives, friends and family (Babaeva and Chirikova, 1997), problems in overcoming cultural conditioning (McKay, 2001), obtaining credit and start-up financing, cash flow management in early operations, and financial planning (Scott, 1996), having fewer informal support systems and networks (Stevenson, 1986), being accepted, lack of role models, difficulty in gaining confidence of clients and suppliers (Hisrich and Brush, 1984) and gender discrimination (Kleiman, 1998).

Entrepreneurship, therefore, is anchored in a socio-cultural context and the major barriers confronted by women entrepreneurs in India may be broadly classified under three categories:

1. *Socio-cultural barriers.* Traditionally women in India are expected to shoulder most of the household and care-giving responsibilities, even when they take up full-time employment. To establish and manage a business involves high financial and emotional cost for women, as they have to fight family opposition and social constraints, while at the same time developing adequate business skills. Women entrepreneurs in India also face public prejudice and gender bias. These factors create overwhelming obstacles for women even when credit, capital and skills are made available to them.
2. *Economic barriers.* Women seeking to establish their own venture find it difficult to secure finance since they are unable to furnish collateral security. Though women in India have the right to own, acquire and dispose of any financial asset, only a small minority actually have access to these assets since the society is predominantly patriarchal. Financial institutions are generally reluctant to sanction loans to women independent of a male head or a guardian, although various government schemes, the role of NGOs and women's associations have changed this scenario (as discussed in the 'Role of government in promoting women's entrepreneurship' above). Inability to obtain finance acts as a barrier for women leading to slow start-up rates. Several studies have found that although government programmes exist to help women entrepreneurs financially, women often complain of a lack of access to financial capital from institutional lenders and have to rely on family and friends (e.g., Dhillon, 1993; Verheul and Thurik, 2001).

3. *Educational barriers.* Historically, the educational level of women in India has been lower than men as indicated by the literacy rate. More recently the gender gap has narrowed, though participation of women in professional training courses continues to be relatively low. Limited access to educational opportunities and lack of adequate training places limits on employment opportunities and the employability of women, their access to information about market trends, latest technology, various schemes of assistance, and so forth (Basargekar, 2007). This, combined with problems arising from the lack of prior employment and managerial experience faced by many women, also leads to problems in terms of market-entry choices and start-up problems (Naidu and Chandralekha, 1998).

Thus, several barriers have been responsible for preventing women from taking up gainful employment. Das (1999) found that cash flow problems were the most frequently cited bottleneck for women entrepreneurs, followed by 'inadequate working capital', 'lack of managerial experience', 'lack of time', 'marketing' and the like. The following section presents stories of two women entrepreneurs from India, the barriers they confronted and how they overcame these barriers and established a successful enterprise.

STORIES OF SUCCESS

To understand the experiences of women entrepreneurs in India when establishing their ventures, in-depth interviews were conducted with two women entrepreneurs. Women who owned businesses by virtue of inheritance or family responsibility were not included since they were unlikely to encounter the usual barriers faced by those who start their venture independently. The two women interviewed by the author had different social, educational, and economic backgrounds (Table 8.7). These success stories stand out as examples of how difficulties and barriers can be overcome by sheer determination and hard work.

Table 8.7   Background variables of successful women entrepreneurs interviewed

Serial No.	Demographic Variables (Socioeconomic Variables)	Mrs Kamala*	Ms Sunayana*
1	Age	40 years	40 years
2	Marital status	Widowed	Single (never married)
3	Education	Class 12th from a village in Uttar Pradesh	BA (Hons) Economics (University of Delhi) and MBA (Marketing)
4	Prior work experience/ professional status	Nil	Three-and-half years in a multinational firm
5	Social background	Rural	Urban
6	Parents' background	Farmer, not educated	Engineer in government of India service. Both parents educated
7	Type of enterprise	Sole proprietorship	Partnership
8	Family responsibilities	Main earning member of the family	None
9	Reason for starting business	Economic necessity	Challenge and self-actualization

Note: *Names have been changed to protect identity.

BOX 8.1   MRS KAMALA

Mrs Kamala runs a home-based boutique of ready-made ladies Punjabi suits in Delhi, India. The boutique, which started in 1991, today has an annual turnover of Rs1300000 (2007–08). There are ten employees – six full-time and four part-time. In addition, embroidery jobs are also contracted to independent crafts-people on a payment basis.

Mrs Kamala had just finished school when she got married to a small-time timber-merchant in 1985 at the age of 18 years. In 1986, she became a mother. Her husband was an alcoholic and hardly had any earnings. After a couple of years of marriage, his work ended. Mrs Kamala started stitching clothes for her neighbours initially, to bring up her child, pay for her husband's treatment, and also keep the household fires burning. Mrs Kamala was widowed in 2001. Thus, necessity drove her to start her tailoring set-up.

Mrs Kamala received the maximum guidance and support from Bharatiya Yuva Shakti Trust (BYST), an NGO promoted by top industrialists and the Confederation of Indian Industry (CII). BYST gave her a soft loan in 1995, and also assigned a mentor for her in the year 1996. Mrs Kamala credits her success to BYST and to her mentor. Mrs Kamala received the Citicorp Micro Entrepreneur Award for the year 2007. Her success story has featured in news-papers and national television. She has been appointed on the mentor panel of BYST and shares her experience with others, which has motivated many women. Mrs Kamala is a member of the Consortium of Women Entrepreneurs of India (CWEI) and is associated with several NGOs like Prayas, Sanjivani and SSIs.

Barriers faced:

- resistance and opposition from an orthodox family, restrictions on mobil-ity, lack of family/spousal support, balancing work with household duties, lack of self-confidence (socio-cultural barriers);
- lack of formal education, no prior work experience or training in trade, no business skills, lack of knowledge about financial aspects (educational and training barriers);
- lack of financial support, difficulty in obtaining loan (financial barriers);
- lack of information about how to start, where to apply for a loan or obtain training, whom to ask for help (lack of information/access to networks);
- delayed payments by shopkeepers, difficulties in interacting with shop-keepers and suppliers (gender-related barriers).

BOX 8.2　MS SUNAYANA

Ms Sunayana started a telemarketing firm in partnership with her childhood friend in the year 1994. With a management degree under her belt, she was a successful executive with a multinational firm. However, her desire to be independent and to experiment led her to take the risk. Her enterprise was the result of the need for self-actualization and the challenge of creating a venture.

The company, which was started with 'zero finance' and 'no employees or infrastructure except a telephone in a rented space in a friends' business centre', had a turnover of Rs20 lakhs[a] in its second year of operation. The firm became a private-limited firm in 1999. From 2000 onwards, the growth was very fast with the company turnover reaching Rs2 crores[b]. By 2005, the company had a turnover of Rs20 crores. The firm started by hiring housewives as telecallers in 1994 and the employee count had reached 1700 in 2005.

Telemarketing as a concept was just emerging in 1994 and firms were keen to experiment with the idea. Getting clients was not too difficult for Ms Sunayana's firm. She also tapped her professional contacts for the purpose. By 2000, the firm had evolved into a domestic Business Process Outsourcing (BPO) operation. The domestic BPO market was beginning to grow and seizing the opportunity the partners chose to cash out. The firm sold out in 2005.

Barriers faced:

- lack of support, resistance and opposition from family (especially father), who did not approve of leaving a 'good' career with a multinational firm for the risk and insecurity of business (socio-cultural barrier);
- lack of domain knowledge and prior experience in the sector, lack of knowledge about financial matters in setting up a venture (educational barriers);
- difficulty in securing loans, no collateral to offer (economic barriers);
- could not socialize to build networks (lack of access to networks);
- not taken seriously by banks and clients, faced with sexual overtones when dealing with clients, difficulty in obtaining finance (gender bias).

Note:　a. Unit in the Indian numbering system equal to 100 000; b. a unit in the Indian numbering system equal to 10 000 000.

Mrs Kamala – Coping with Barriers

The barriers were overcome mainly with the support that Mrs Kamala received from BYST and various government schemes for women entrepreneurs. The BYST mentor gave her guidance on both professional and personal issues, helped her market her products, get contracts and provided her with information about the Entrepreneurship

Development Programmes organized by SSIs, trade fairs and entrepreneurship awards in which she could participate. Kamala relied on friends for moral support and also became a member of CWEI, which helped her gain access to information and networking opportunities. According to Kamala she overcame socio-cultural and educational barriers by 'seizing every opportunity to learn, drawing on life experiences, making mistakes and learning from them, determination, hard work and never taking "no" as final from anyone'.

Ms Sunayana – Coping with Barriers

Ms Sunayana managed to overcome most barriers through 'learning from mistakes, personal strength, hard work, professional attitude, and determination'. Government schemes were not relevant to her since her firm had grown very big when she considered taking finance. To overcome lack of knowledge of finance, she attended some courses. She also travelled to the United States to understand operations of BPO firms. Support from friends in industry who were advisors to her firm also helped.

SUMMARY AND RECOMMENDATIONS

The success stories discussed above suggest that irrespective of socioeconomic background or nature of enterprise, women found it difficult to obtain finance and, therefore, used their own savings to start their venture. They also lacked knowledge of business and related experience and sought guidance in their business venture. Both entrepreneurs also reported gender discrimination and prejudice. However, as their businesses progressed, both the women perceived the challenges as less intense. Ms Sunayana remarked that 'beyond a point people look at you for business reasons – not as a woman' and that 'the road became smoother once they had achieved some degree of success'. Both Ms Sunayana and Mrs Kamala attributed their success to 'hard work', thus, reinforcing research findings (Handy et al., 2007).

Research studies report that the major obstacles encountered by women entrepreneurs during the business establishment phase were working capital, equity finance, marketing and gender bias (Ganesan et al., 2002). While the evidence for overt discrimination against female entrepreneurs is mixed (Carter and Brush, 2004), women in a number of countries have listed lack of respect or not being taken seriously as among the barriers that they have faced in their ventures (Bliss et al., 2003). According to Ganesan et al. (2002) women continue to encounter problems as their businesses progressed, but the problems are mentioned less frequently than at start-up. When the business has been launched women are able to manage many difficulties such as working capital, finance and the like, as they enhance credibility by demonstrating results. However, some problems continue in the running of the enterprise; these include, for example, marketing products in a predominantly male-dominated market.

It is evident from the above case studies that women within the same country experience similar types of barriers irrespective of socioeconomic or educational background, though the actual manifestation of these barriers may differ. The nature of socio-cultural barriers was different for Mrs Kamala and Ms Sunayana. This may be explained by the fact that Mrs Kamala was a 'forced entrepreneur' or a 'conventional' (Goffee and Scase, 1985), since she was compelled by circumstances such as financial difficulties (push factors) to start the business. On the other hand, Ms Sunayana was a 'created entrepreneur' (pull factors) or an 'innovator', whose goal was to be independent, and who was motivated by challenge, personal achievement and the urge to try something new.

The case studies and available research literature suggest that women's entry into entrepreneurship seems to be a complex mix of constraints and opportunities, of external coercions and subjective aspirations (Bruni et al., 2004). It would be interesting to discover whether socioeconomic factors may facilitate the understanding of how entrepreneurial barriers and challenges are experienced and managed by women entrepreneurs starting their ventures. Identifying the constraints and limitations, which prevent women from starting their own businesses, is an important aspect of development research (Das, 1999).

Despite situational constraints, more women are entering the field of entrepreneurship in India and their contribution to economic activity is well established. However, a great deal remains to be achieved with respect to economic empowerment of women. Since women confront a set of challenges, it calls for a range of initiatives to facilitate women's entrepreneurship. These include training on business skills and financial matters, EDPs, confidence-building measures, credit and loan facilities and assistance in marketing of products (Kantor, 2001; Sinha, 2003, 2005). Most of these initiatives have already been adopted by the GOI and almost all documents of state policy make a recommendation for women's role in economic development (Ganesan et al., 2002).

Various GOI schemes directed towards women entrepreneurs have made an important contribution to the growth of women's entrepreneurship. NGOs like BYST play an important role in the development of women entrepreneurs by assigning mentors, providing access to information networks, extending EDPs and business skills training. Some measures that can contribute greatly towards women's empowerment are presented below (Kantor, 2001; Sinha, 2005):

1. Government must develop policies for supporting women-owned SMEs through legal and fiscal measures, providing skills training, and community outreach programmes to disburse information about government schemes.
2. NGOs and women's associations must work to influence government policies for improvement of opportunities available to women entrepreneurs.
3. Service providers should provide counselling and mentoring programmes for women entrepreneurs at the establishment stage as well as post-start-up, and help them gain access to networks of women business owners such as FLO (FICCI [Federation of Indian Chamber of Commerce and Industry] Ladies Organization), SEWA (Self Employed Women's Association), CWEI (Consortium of Women Entrepreneurs of India), and so on.
4. Staff in various organizations (such as banks) involved with women entrepreneurship development should undergo gender sensitization.
5. Universities can play an important role by providing trainers for EDPs, conducting research and seminars on women entrepreneurs, and disseminating information about the importance of women in the economic development of the country.

The government, NGOs, women's associations and private sector industry leaders have played an exemplary role in the development of women's entrepreneurship in India. Several schemes for women and several initiatives by NGOs, women's associations and the corporate sector are already in place. Yet, the outcome has not matched expectations. Moreover, women entrepreneurs from different socioeconomic backgrounds have different characteristics, and one policy cannot address the needs of all groups (Gillani, 2004). This distinction has not been made at policy level. Moreover, it is important to monitor the implementation of all schemes and evaluate the effectiveness of various measures in achieving their objectives. For this, the partnership between the government, NGOs, women's associations and the corporate world in service delivery needs to be strengthened. The role of community-level interventions is also highly desirable for changing the socially defined man–woman roles.

NOTES

1. The organized sector includes all the establishments in the public sector and non-agricultural establishments employing ten or more persons in the private sector.
2. http://www.laghu-udyog.com/ssiindia/statistics/statusSSI.htm); accessed 9 February 2010.
3. http://www.laghu-udyog.com/ssiindia/census/sumryres.htm; accessed 9 February 2010.
4. http://dcmsme.gov.in/sido/sido.htm; accessed 9 February 2010.

REFERENCES

Babaeva, L. and A. Chirikova (1997), 'Women in business', *Russian Social Science Review*, **38**(3), 81–92.
Basargekar, P. (2007), 'Women entrepreneurs: challenges faced', *The ICFAI Journal of Entrepreneurship Development*, **IV**(4), 6–15.
Bliss, R.T., L. Polutnik and E. Lisowska (2003), 'Women business owners and managers in Poland', in J. Butler (ed.), *New Perspectives on Women Entrepreneurs*, Greenwich, CT: Information Age Publishing, pp. 225–41.
Bruni, A., S. Gherardi and B. Poggio (2004), 'Entrepreneur-mentality, gender and the study of women entrepreneurs', *Journal of Organizational Change Management*, **17**(3), 256–68.
Buttner, E.H. and D. Moore (1997), 'Women's organizational exodus to entrepreneurship: self-reported motivations and correlates with success', *Journal of Small Business Management*, **35**(1), 34–47.
Carter, N. and C. Brush (2004), 'Gender', in W. Gartner, K. Shaver, N. Carter and P. Reynolds (eds), *Handbook of Entrepreneurial Dynamics: The Process of Business Creation*, Thousand Oaks, CA: Sage Publications, pp. 12–25.
Das, M. (1999), 'Women entrepreneurs from southern India: an exploratory study', *Journal of Entrepreneurship*, **8**(2), 147–63.
Dhillon, P.K. (1993), *Women Entrepreneurs: Problems and Prospects*, New Delhi: Blaze.
Ganesan, R., D. Kaur and R.C. Maheshwari (2002), 'Women entrepreneurs: problems and prospects', *Journal of Entrepreneurship*, **11**(1), 75–93.
Gillani, W. (2004), 'No policy framework to address women entrepreneurs', *Daily Times*, 16 July, available at: http://www.dailytimes.com.pk/default.asp?page=story_17-4-2003_pg7_23; accessed 10 February 2010.
Goffee, R. and R. Scase (1985), *Women in Charge: The Experiences of Female Entrepreneurs*, London: Macmillan.
Handy, F., B. Ranade and M. Kassam (2007), 'To profit or not to profit: women entrepreneurs in India', *Nonprofit Management and Leadership*, **17**(4), 383–401.
Hisrich, R.D. and C. Brush (1984), 'The woman entrepreneur: management skill and business problems', *Journal of Small Business Management*, **22**(1), 31–36.
Jalbert, S.E. (1999), 'The global growth of women in business', *Economic Reform Today*, **3**, 8–11.
Kantor, P. (2001), 'Promoting women's entrepreneurship development based on good practice programmes: some experiences from the North to the South', SEED Working Paper No. 9, Geneva: ILO.
Kleiman, C. (1998), 'Women entrepreneurs are a big loss to corporations', *St Louis Post*, Dispatch, C5.

Kollan, B. and I.J. Parikh (2005), 'A reflection of the Indian women in entrepreneurial world', Working Paper No. 2005-08-07, Working Paper Series of the Indian Institute of Management, Ahmedabad (IIMA), India.

McClelland, E., J. Swail, J. Bell and P. Ibbotson (2005), 'Following the pathway of female entrepreneurs: A six-country investigation', *International Journal of Entrepreneurial Behaviour & Research*, **11**(2), 84–107.

McKay, R. (2001), 'Women entrepreneurs: moving beyond family and flexibility', *International Journal of Entrepreneurial Behaviour & Research*, **7**(4), 148–65.

Naidu, V.J. and K. Chandralekha (1998), 'Barriers to women's development', in P.R. Reddy and P. Sumangala (eds), *Women in Development: Perspective from Selected States of India*, Vol. 2, Delhi: B.R. Publishing Corporation, pp. 841–87.

National Sample Survey Organization (NSSO) (2004–05), Report No. 458, 'Employment and Unemployment in India, 1999–2000'; and Report No. 515, 'Employment and Unemployment in India'.

Rani, B.S. and D.K. Rao (2007), 'Perspectives on women entrepreneurship', *The ICFAI Journal of Entrepreneurship Development*, **IV**(4), 16–27.

Registrar General and Census Commissioner of India (2001), *Census of India*.

Scott, C.E. (1996), 'Why more women are becoming entrepreneurs', *Journal of Small Business Management*, **24**(4), 37–44.

Singh, K.P. (1993), 'Women entrepreneurs: their profile and motivation', *Journal of Entrepreneurship*, **2**(1), 47–58.

Sinha, P. (2003), 'Women entrepreneurship in North East India: motivation, social support and constraints', *Indian Journal of Industrial Relations*, **38**(4), 425–43.

Sinha, S. (2005), *Developing Women Entrepreneurs in South Asia: Issues, Initiatives, and Experiences*, United Nations Economic and Social Commission for Asia and the Pacific (UNESCAP), Trade and Investment Division, Bangkok: UNESCAP.

Stevenson, L.A. (1986), 'Against all odds: the entrepreneurship of women', *Journal of Small Business Management*, **24**(4), 30–36.

Verheul, I. and R. Thurik (2001), 'Start-up capital: does gender matter?', *Small Business Economics*, **16**(4), 329–45.

Walker, D. and B.E. Joyner (1999), 'Female entrepreneurship and the market process: gender-based public policy considerations', *Journal of Developmental Entrepreneurship*, **4**(2), 95.

9 Lebanon
Dima Jamali and Yusuf Sidani

INTRODUCTION

This chapter explores the socioeconomic context for female entrepreneurship in the Lebanon. Starting with a brief background overview on the rates of female economic activity and the status of female entrepreneurship in Lebanon, we move through an interpretive qualitative methodology to assess the perceptions of a sample of female entrepreneurs regarding micro- and macro-level factors affecting female entrepreneurship in the Lebanese context. The literature on female entrepreneurship has traditionally focussed on the micro level, including an exploration of the distinctive characteristics of female and male entrepreneurs in terms of motivation, personality traits, or experience. However, more systematic attention has been accorded in recent years to the influence of macro-level factors on entrepreneurship generally, and female entrepreneurship specifically (e.g., Baughn et al., 2006; Verheul et al., 2006). We believe that both sets of factors are important to provide a comprehensive understanding of female entrepreneurship in a particular context, consistent with the integrative multi-level research design advocated by Davidsson and Wiklund (2001) and more recently by Bruin et al. (2007).

There is indeed little doubt that determinants of female entrepreneurship lie in a complex interplay of micro- and macro-level factors. Gender differences have indeed been documented in relation to self-perception (Anna et al., 2000), opportunity recognition (e.g., Eckhardt and Shane, 2003), decision-making styles (Baker and Nelson, 2005), and network structures/networking behaviour (McManus, 2001). This micro-level emphasis has been counterbalanced in recent years by some attention to the economic, legal, normative and societal environments influencing entrepreneurship, supporting the thesis of entrepreneurship embeddedness in specific socio-cultural contexts (Baughn et al., 2006; Bruin et al., 2007). Our purpose in this chapter is to highlight the dynamic interplay of those two sets of factors in influencing the female entrepreneurship experience in the Lebanon, recognizing from the outset the embeddedness of entrepreneurship in indigenous socio-cultural systems, which invariably mould and shape the experience and expression of entrepreneurship in that context.

THE POSITION OF WOMEN IN EMPLOYMENT IN LEBANON

Lebanon is an Arab country and a founding member of the Arab League. Females in the traditional Arab culture have been viewed mostly in terms of their roles as mothers and caretakers of the home. The socio-political and economic changes impinging on the Arab world over the past few decades, however, have affected this perception to varying degrees in different Arab contexts. Lebanon is among the few Arab countries that have allowed women to increasingly assume functions outside the traditional mother–home

Table 9.1   Female economic activity rate in Lebanon and selected world regions

2008	Female Economic Activity Rate (%)	As % of Male Rate
Lebanon	32.4	41
Arab States	26.7	34
Developing countries	52.4	64
OECD	50.3	72
World	52.5	67

Source: HDR (2008).

roles. This is due to several reasons, many of which are peculiar to Lebanon (Sidani, 2002). In the first instance, Lebanon has traditionally been more open to the West compared with other Arab countries. In addition, the heavy migration of men, in search of better pay and work opportunities, to the Arab Gulf oil-producing countries in the 1980s and 1990s has been reflected in shortages in the male workforce and catalyzed an influx of women into non-traditional jobs. In the wake of the civil war in 1990, further economic changes necessitated that women participate more aggressively in the country's development. Worsening economic conditions implied that many homes could only survive if supported by dual-career couples (Jamali et al., 2005). Hence, over the past decades, significant consideration has been accorded to the role of women in Lebanon, resulting in relative progress and an influx of women into new sectors.

Perceptions of Lebanon as a country where women have long enjoyed freedoms and rights that their counterparts in neighbouring Arab countries have been striving for do not, however, reflect the complete picture. Statistics about women's participation in the economic, educational and political spheres are somewhat depressing. On the one hand, educational enrolment of women has steadily improved with women's post-secondary educational enrolment nearing 50 per cent in both public and private educational sectors. For example, more than half of all university students are women, 53 per cent in 2001 (World Bank, 2005). On the other hand, the economic involvement of women does not fare as well. While the economic activity rate of women has increased from 17.5 per cent level in the early 1970s, it has nonetheless been estimated at a modest 32.4 per cent in 2007 (41 per cent of the male rate – HDR, 2008). Furthermore, the estimated earned income for women was USD2701 in 2005 compared with USD8585 for men (ibid.). The participation of women in public life also remains marginal. A meagre 4 per cent of the Lebanese parliament members are women and women lead only two out of more than 700 municipal councils (Sha'rani, 2004). Table 9.1 summarizes relevant indicators pertaining to the economic activity of women in Lebanon in comparison to selected world indicators.

THE POSITION OF WOMEN AND SMALL BUSINESS OWNERSHIP IN LEBANON

Very few reliable statistics are available documenting the rates of female entrepreneurship in Lebanon. A recent study by Pistrui et al. (2008) suggests that although entrepreneurship is not an exclusively male activity in Lebanon, the rate of female entrepreneurial activity in the country was estimated at a modest 15 per cent. This estimation is consistent with earlier studies, which documented that in 2002 self-employed women constituted 11.6 per cent of the female labour force, which is significantly less than the rates of self-employment for men (estimated at 29.6 per cent of the male labour force) (ESCWA, 2004). Based on trend analysis and in the absence of official and reliable statistics about rates of female entrepreneurship in the country, it is safe to assume that there have not been significant changes in these rates over the past few years.

Earlier studies also document the concentration of Lebanese women entrepreneurs in the small trade and service industries and their reliance on personal and family savings to support their new ventures (IFC, 2007; Samaha, 2007). Husseini (1997) reports that Lebanese women entrepreneurs have smaller-sized businesses compared with men and are disadvantaged in terms of securing external bank financing. Very few indeed resort to external sources of financing as suggested by the IFC (2007), which reported in a recent study that Lebanese women comprised about 35 per cent of micro credit borrowers in contrast to a rate of 60 per cent for most of the Arab world. This is further reinforced by the results of another study (IFC and CAWTAR, 2007) where Lebanese women entrepreneurs reported concerns relating primarily to access to capital and the high cost of public services.

Lebanese women entrepreneurs are similarly disadvantaged in terms of access to business networks, given that they comprise a very small percentage of the memberships and boards of almost all syndicates and chambers of commerce and/or industry (Sha'rani, 2004). This may translate into fewer opportunities for networking, partnering, identifying new opportunities, and expanding new ventures. Lebanese women entrepreneurs are also likely to be constrained by a patriarchal culture (Haddad, 2003) that continues to ascribe caring and family responsibilities to women and that is permeated by various traditional masculine stereotypes (Sidani, 2002; Jamali et al., 2005; Jamali, 2009; Jamali and Abdallah, 2010). Lebanese society indeed accords primary importance to the role of the family, with strong family ties cemented and sustained in what is still considered as a collectivist culture (Sidani, 2002).

It is also worth mentioning that all Lebanese entrepreneurs, irrespective of gender, have faced significant hurdles and constraints in recent years, in light of a daunting economic recession (for example, gross public debt stood at 177 per cent of GDP in June 2004 – IIF, 2005) and a serious political stalemate. Recent World Bank statistics suggest that Lebanon ranks relatively low in relation to the ease of starting a business (99 out of 181 regional and high-income OECD economies) and that the costs and minimum capital required to start a business are very high in comparison to regional and high-income economies (World Bank, 2009). These contextual conditions have no doubt exacerbated the difficulties experienced by women entrepreneurs specifically, rendering it even more difficult to navigate and manoeuvre in the complex labyrinth of Lebanese society.

EXPLORING MICRO AND MACRO FACTORS AFFECTING FEMALE ENTREPRENEURSHIP

The most popular themes in entrepreneurship research have traditionally revolved around micro-level factors including opportunity recognition and motivation. Gender differences in opportunity identification have been linked to differences in human capital variables including education and work experience, with men documented to leverage significantly higher levels of prior industry or entrepreneurial experience as well as experience in managing employees than women (Boden and Nucci, 2002; Carter and Williams, 2003; Carter and Brush, 2005). The evidence presented above suggests that there has been some progress in Lebanon by way of bridging gender gaps in relation to educational attainment, although women continue to leverage less work experience in view of their modest labour force participation rates and punctuated and interrupted work histories and careers. Aside from seeking independence and challenge, women's motivations for pursuing entrepreneurship have also been related in the Lebanese context to the restricted structure of opportunities in the labour market, labour market discrimination or glass ceiling career problems, with self-employment often perceived as a survival strategy, or as a means of providing flexibility in work scheduling and reconciling multiple roles (Jamali et al., 2005; Jamali, 2009). Many women entrepreneurs indeed admit choosing an entrepreneurial career path as a survival strategy, given experienced setbacks and discrimination in previous employment, or otherwise to gain control over their work routines and schedules in pursuit of work–life balance and increased family satisfaction (Jamali, 2009).

At the macro level, Lebanese women entrepreneurs continue to operate within a peculiar set of patriarchal norms and with limited institutional support. A number of recent studies relating to the Middle East and Lebanon have aptly highlighted the coexistence of contrasting paradigms of modernity and traditionalism, female entrepreneurship amidst male dominance and continued pervasive female submissiveness within gendered values and patriarchal norms (Al Lamky, 2007; Jamali, 2009). Women continue to be ascribed primarily to caretaker functions and roles within the household (Jamali et al., 2005; Jamali, 2009; Jamali and Abdallah, 2009) and they continue to perceive themselves as accountable to male scrutiny, stereotypes and traditional leadership prototypes (Al Lamky, 2007; Neal et al., 2007). Lebanese women entrepreneurs are moreover severely disadvantaged in terms of accessing and securing funding for their new ventures (Husseini, 1997). Although financing for new entrepreneurial ventures has been a key area of concern across the Middle East for both men and women (World Bank, 2009), women have had even more constrained access to venture capital, financial angels or investment banks. Financial institutions are also generally reluctant to provide funding at start-up levels, and bankruptcy legislation in Lebanon does not encourage risk taking (ibid.). The Lebanese government has been pursuing various initiatives to encourage foreign direct investment in the country with pieces of legislation relating to intellectual property, anti-dumping and increased competition, but initiatives to tackle support for entrepreneurial activity have been modest at best.

The above discussion makes clear the complex interweaving and entanglement of micro- and macro-level variables even as we tried to set a distinction between the two. For example, push-factor-type motivations are inextricably linked to labour market constraints. Lebanese women are inclined to pursue entrepreneurship not simply out of desire and personal aspirations but also in view of labour market discrimination, glass ceiling career barriers, or as a means of providing flexibility in work scheduling and reconciling multiple roles, or securing an extra income for the family. Similarly, performance and growth of entrepreneurial ventures are likely to be affected by societal role expectations and availability of family support, particularly in relation to caretaking functions as well as the status, desirability and credibility society attaches to women's employment, self-employment and business success. Performance and growth of female entrepreneurial ventures in Lebanon are also no doubt affected by the country's economic, socio-cultural and legal environments, limited government intervention and support and unique legal, banking and regulatory institutional constellations. Hence, micro- and macro-level variables certainly interweave to shape the general experience of female entrepreneurship in the Lebanese context.

STORIES OF SUCCESS

The interplay of micro- and macro-level factors is highlighted in the two case studies below, which stem from the narratives of two successful women entrepreneurs in Lebanon.

BOX 9.1   AISHA

I started this business together with my husband in the early 1980s. The main driver was the need to secure additional income for our family. Our children were all at the university. I had more time given the fact that my children were older and did not need my continuous attention. I used to work before I got married and in the early years of my marriage, but I had to exit from the workplace after I gave birth to my eldest child. After leaving the workforce for 20 years or so, the time was ripe for me to go back. My husband and I thought it was a good idea to start another business. He was already employed in the government and had a consulting business that he ran so he could not devote time to the new venture. I was willing and able to take the initiative. That was in the 80s. The initial funding came from our family savings. But that was not enough. We had to purchase the premises of the training centre [vocational training centre, offering educational services, relating to computing, accounting and languages] and we did this through an instalment plan given by the previous owner. It took us almost two years to settle. Bank financing was not an option at the time. Things haven't been going as well for the past few years because of the political and economic instability. We're still making money but it is not close to what it was in the late 1990s. Many of the problems that I faced are related to the environment: (1) at a personal level, lack of support from the extended family who thought it was not appropriate for me to leave and neglect my kids in pursuit of this business opportunity; (2) lack of a governmental vision for our sector together with corruption. Corruption has really hurt us; the governmental agencies have given permits for similar institutions with no proper control, standards, or supervision; (3) lack of financial support was and still is a problem. I want to move into different premises, larger and in a different area, but I cannot because of the capital requirements. Things have changed in

---

the past 20 years. I would say that now the notion of women business owners is more accepted but the work of women in general is not appreciated in our society. I have a strong belief in my abilities. During the first few years, I faced many problems but with dedication and persistence we were able to do very well. Personal factors, including ambition, perseverance and determination are the key ingredients for success.

BOX 9.2   SONIA

I was the first in the university, so ambitious and distinguished. [Sonia was consistently an honours student while at university.] I decided to work for several years just to get the required experience and then to open my own office. The main reasons are challenge and seeking independence. While working as an accountant in a company, I was exposed to important experiences as well as the chance to meet a lot of potential future clients. Moreover, a new law was implemented that permitted an accountant who had more than seven years of experience in this domain to participate in the syndicate and to open his/her own audit office. So I decided to exploit this opportunity and to have my own business. Push factors: wage; I was not well paid compared with my colleagues and flexibility. Pull factors: I was always looking to be independent, to run my own business and to take control of my life and my career. The initial funding came from my family; my brother supported me financially and emotionally. Moreover, he introduced me to a lot of clients. Financially, at the beginning my net income was not higher than my previous salary but recently my income is more than sufficient. The three main obstacles that I think a woman entrepreneur will face in running this kind of business are time, time needed will invariably affect family and social life, and tends to be interpreted as time taken away from childcare responsibilities; family perception and approval; plus male stereotyping of entrepreneurship. Most people perceive the woman entrepreneur as a female having male characteristics, for example, dominance, strength. How did I overcome these constraints? I am so dedicated to my work, I spent most of my time working in the office. It was badly perceived by my family especially when returning late or working Saturday and Sunday. I think that women entrepreneurs can be so successful in life, can run the business better than men because they are more devoted to their work, more determined to succeed and ascertain their capabilities than men. Personal factors are more important than external factors.

SUMMARY

This chapter has explored the socioeconomic context for female entrepreneurship in Lebanon. The insights reveal the interplay of micro- and macro-level factors and the need to account for both in providing a comprehensive account of the female entrepreneurship experience in the Middle Eastern context. While opportunities facing women entrepreneurs tend to be identified at the micro level (e.g., opportunity identification and strong motivation), and related to personal characteristics (e.g., self-efficacy, resilience and autonomy), these are invariably nested within the contours of a woman's life and overall experiences. For example, the entrepreneurial identities of the two Lebanese women (Aisha and Sonia) were certainly affected by prevailing societal norms and expectations in the sense that they seem to have internalized the caretaker role expectations dominant in Lebanese society, resulting in feelings of guilt when pursuing entrepreneurship despite high levels of aspiration and determination. Moreover, it was difficult to isolate women's motivations from macro-level push factors such as economic stagnation, labour market constraints and the need for double-income families.

Furthermore, the insights drawn and compiled in this chapter support the embeddedness of entrepreneurship and its context specificity, highlighting the strong salience of normative constraints facing women entrepreneurs in this peculiar Middle Eastern context, to the extent of undermining their full and fair engagement in entrepreneurship in the current market economy. They also suggest the usefulness of institutional theory as a relevant theoretical lens in the context of entrepreneurship research and that role conflicts are inevitable when norms and practices are so embedded and engrained. Yet our findings do not lend support to blind institutional conformity, suggesting room for active agency in response to institutional constraints as reflected in the resilience and determination of the interviewees to persist with their new ventures despite the pressures encountered. The findings therefore echo recent writings in entrepreneurship, which have alluded to the embeddedness of entrepreneurship in specific institutional contexts, the greater sensitization of women to normative support, while also integrating the relevance of agency in entrepreneurial accounts (Baughn et al., 2006; Aidis et al., 2007).

Going forward, the main challenge for the Lebanese government in the intermediate term is to establish 'a level playing field' for working women in general, as in enacting anti-discrimination legislation and equal pay regulation to alleviate the constraints that prevent women from engaging in the full range of socioeconomic activity. With respect to women entrepreneurship specifically, the government can provide various services including information, advice and training for women aiming to be self-employed. Access to capital is also important, as in provision of small loans, or seed corn funding to encourage the growth of female-owned micro-enterprises. Legislation is clearly important as in alleviating complex bureaucratic procedures that may put women off at the start of their ventures. Societal values and standards, of course, are most important, but this is part of a longer-term challenge that we face at the level of ordinary increasingly educated and sophisticated citizens.

REFERENCES

Aidis, R., Welter, F., Smallbone, D. and Isakova, N. (2007), 'Female entrepreneurship in transition economies: the case of Lithuania and Ukraine', *Feminist Economics*, **13**(2), 157–83.
Al Lamky, A. (2007), 'Feminizing leadership in Arab societies: the perspectives of Omani female leaders', *Women in Management Review*, **22**(1), 49–67.

Anna, A., Chandler, G., Jansen, E. and Mero, N. (2000), 'Women business owners in traditional and non-traditional industries', *Journal of Business Venturing*, **15**(3), 279–303.

Baker, T. and Nelson, R. (2005), 'Creating something from nothing: resource construction through entrepreneurship bricolage', *Administrative Science Quarterly*, **50**(3), 329–66.

Baughn, C., Chua, B. and Neupert, K. (2006), 'The normative context for women's participation in entrepreneurship: a multi-country study', *Entrepreneurship Theory and Practice*, **30**(5), 687–708.

Boden, R.J. and Nucci, A. (2002), 'On the survival prospects of men's and women's new business ventures', *Journal of Business Venturing*, **15**(4), 347–62.

Bruin, A., Brush, C. and Welter, F. (2007), 'Advancing a framework for coherent research on women's entrepreneurship', *Entrepreneurship Theory and Practice*, **31**(3), 323–39.

Carter, N. and Brush, C. (2005), 'Gender', in W. Gartner, K. Shaver, N. Carter and P. Reynolds (eds), *Handbook of Entrepreneurial Dynamics: The Process of Business Creation*, Thousand Oaks, CA, Sage Publications, pp. 12–25.

Carter, N.M. and Williams, M.L. (2003), 'Comparing social feminism and liberal feminism: the case of new firm growth', in J.E. Butler (ed.), *New Perspectives on Women Entrepreneurs*, Greenwich, CT: Information Age Publishing, pp. 25–50.

Davidsson, P. and Wiklund, J. (2001), 'Levels of analysis in entrepreneurship research: current research practice and suggestions for the future', *Entrepreneurship Theory and Practice*, **25**(4), 81–99.

Eckhardt, J. and Shane, S. (2003), 'Opportunities and entrepreneurship', *Journal of Management*, **29**(3), 333–49.

ESCWA – Economic and Social Commission for Western Asia (2004), 'Where do Arab women stand in the development process? A gender-based statistical analysis', New York: United Nations.

Haddad, N. (2003), 'Entrepreneurship in small industries in the Arab countries', Proceedings of the Expert Group Meeting on Creation of Indigenous Entrepreneurship, ESCWA, Damascus.

Human Development Report (HDR) (2008), *Gender-related Development Index*, New York: United Nations Development Programme.

Husseini, R. (1997), 'Promoting women entrepreneurs in Lebanon: the experience of UNIFEM', *Gender and Development*, **5**(1), 49–53.

IFC – International Finance Corporation (2007), *Gender Entrepreneurship Markets (GEM). GEM Country Brief-Lebanon 2007*, Washington: International Finance Corporation, World Bank Group.

IFC and CAWTAR – International Finance Corporation and Center for Arab Women for Training and Research (2007), *Women Entrepreneurs in the Middle East and North Africa: Characteristics, Contributions and Challenges*, Washington: International Finance Corporation, World Bank Group.

IIF – Institute for International Finance (2005), *Corporate Governance in Lebanon – An Investor Perspective*, Task Force Report, Washington: IIF Equity Advisory Group.

Jamali, D. (2009), 'Constraints and opportunities facing women entrepreneurs in developing countries: a relational perspective', *Gender in Management: An International Journal*, **24**(4), 232–51.

Jamali, D. and Abdallah, H. (2010), 'Diversity management rhetoric versus reality: insights from the Lebanese context', in M.F. Özbilgin and J. Syed (eds), *Managing Gender Diversity in Asia: A Research Companion*, Cheltenham, UK and Northampton, MA, USA: Edward Elgar.

Jamali, D., Sidani, Y. and Safieddine, A. (2005), 'Constraints facing working women in Lebanon: an insider view', *Women in Management Review*, **20**(8), 581–94.

McManus, P.A. (2001), 'Women's participation in self-employment in Western industrialized nations', *International Journal of Sociology*, **31**(2), 70–97.

Neal, M., Finlay, J., Catana, G. and Catana, D. (2007), 'A comparison of leadership prototypes of Arab and European females', *International Journal of Cross-cultural Management*, **7**(3), 291–316.

Pistrui, D., Fahed-Sreih, J., Huang, W. and Welsch, H. (2008), 'Entrepreneurial-led family business development in post-war Lebanon', USASBE 2008 Proceedings, 0847-0862.

Samaha, N. (2007), 'Arab women entrepreneurs outpace Westerners by some measures', *Daily Star*, 10 June, Beirut, Lebanon.

Sha'rani, A. (2004), 'The Lebanese women: reality and aspirations', available at: www.lcw-cfl.org/Roots.shtml; accessed 20 February 2010.

Sidani, Y. (2002), 'Management in Lebanon', in Malcolm Warner (ed.), *International Encyclopedia of Business and Management*, 2nd edition, London: Thomson Learning, pp. 3797–802.

Verheul, I., Van Stel, A. and Thurik, R. (2006), 'Explaining female and male entrepreneurship at the country level', *Entrepreneurship and Regional Development*, **18**(2), 151–83.

World Bank (2005), *The Status and Progress of Women in the Middle East and North Africa*, Washington: World Bank Middle East and North Africa Socioeconomic Development Group.

World Bank (2009), *Doing Business in Lebanon* available at http://www.doingbusiness.org/ExploreEconomies/?economyid+109; accessed 11 February 2010.

10 New Zealand
Marianne Tremaine and Kate Lewis

INTRODUCTION

Women in New Zealand have always worked, and work, both paid and unpaid, has been important for their autonomy and sense of identity. Maori (the name of New Zealand's indigenous people) women, before and after colonization, were the weavers and the cooks and cared for children, but could also be healers and warriors and gardeners – depending on the need or the season or their individual skills.

Europeans began to come to New Zealand for whaling and sealing and to trade for food and other goods. But colonization, with large numbers of immigrants, did not begin to happen until the 1830s and 1840s. Settlers came in family groups and also as single men looking for work in bush clearing and farming or trades, with some (though far fewer) single women, who worked mainly in domestic labour. Although there were upper-middle-class settlers who sought to preserve the niceties of Britain's privilege, they were a minority. Most settlers came from working-class backgrounds seeking to improve their lives and opportunities in New Zealand.

For many decades, the New Zealand economy was based on agriculture, through to the 1950s when growing urbanization shifted the balance and people began to move to the towns and cities for work, as society became more industrialized. On farms, married women had worked as farmers shifting stock and helping with the physical work, as well as cooking for the shearers and providing morning and afternoon tea for any visitors. In the cities, women had more opportunity to find paid part-time work in factories and service industries. The typical career options for women were as office workers, nurses or teachers, but society's expectations of the time were that women would give up paid employment when they married.

Despite the fact that New Zealand had been the first country to grant women the vote in 1893, even as late as the 1970s there were barriers to women's entrepreneurship caused by bank managers refusing loans to females, unless they had the support of male guarantors. This chapter explores the ways that the situation has changed in New Zealand from 1970 until the present. Women have begun to feel pressure to return to work after having children and to feel that their identity rests on their work achievements. Typically, women's unpaid work has been treated as invisible and undervalued, seen simply as what women ought to do to comply with social norms and expectations.

Complex changes have taken place in the last three decades. While the numbers of women in paid employment have continued to increase, many women are unwilling to compromise their other roles and have turned to entrepreneurship to gain more control over their lives and have the flexibility that can help them achieve rewarding work, yet also meet unpaid obligations such as caring for children, doing the accounts for the family business, or carrying out voluntary work. With the growing diversity that Pacific Island, Asian and other immigrants have brought to New Zealand, the variety of obstacles facing women seeking employment has also increased and entrepreneurship has been one way that some women have created suitable employment for themselves.

The next section of this chapter will scope out the current situation of women in employment in New Zealand and explain some of the factors that have led to these outcomes. We will then discuss the structural and contextual barriers that women in New Zealand have had to face in establishing their own businesses and give specific examples of ways these barriers have been overcome by particular entrepreneurial women in this country. Finally, we will highlight specific recommendations that, if implemented, could make a difference by helping to eliminate barriers and obstacles confronting potential female entrepreneurs. So, first, let's turn to the position of women in employment as it is now.

THE POSITION OF WOMEN IN EMPLOYMENT IN NEW ZEALAND

The major changes that have taken place in terms of women's employment since 1970 are:

- legislative changes;
- an ideological shift in public policy that has moved to strongly encourage women into paid work;
- a large and continuing increase in the proportion of women in the workforce; along with
- an increasing diversity of working women, both in terms of ethnicity and the range of age groups represented.

To begin with, here is a survey of the most influential legislative changes that have taken place. The major changes affecting women in employment are the Government Services Equal Pay Act 1960 and the Equal Pay Act 1972, the Race Relations Act 1971, the Human Rights Commission Act 1977 and the 'good employer' provisions of the State Sector Act 1988.

Much of this legislation was instigated and supported by the activities of feminist groups. The need for equal pay for equal work and equal opportunities for women in employment and education were the first two issues initiated by the women's movement in New Zealand (Women's Rights Committee, 1975). However, the equal pay legislation proved ineffective in closing the gap between men and women in terms of their relative earnings. Partly as a result of submissions detailing dissatisfaction with the outcome of the equal pay legislation and the treatment of women at work the report of the Select Committee on Women's Rights, published in 1975, recommended the establishment of the Human Rights Commission (ibid.). The Select Committee's report explained that the work of the Human Rights Commission should include the responsibility to focus on eradicating gender-based discrimination. The Human Rights Commission has an Equal Employment Opportunities Commissioner on its staff whose role includes seeking to improve and support opportunities for women. The Human Rights Commission also has the machinery of a tribunal for hearing complaints. However, preventing complaints from arising in the first place is far preferable, if it can be achieved.

The 'good employer' provisions of the State Sector Act 1988 comprise one particularly important prevention strategy in terms of combating discrimination against women at work in the public service and government agencies. In Part V, Section 56 (2), the Act stipulates that personnel policies should include an equal opportunities programme and recognition of the employment requirements of women along with a need to recognize the needs of Maori people, ethnic minorities and people with disabilities. The critical factor introduced in this legislation has been that Chief Executives of government departments are reviewed on the basis of their achievements in meeting these requirements along with all the other requirements of the Act (Part III, Section 43, Clauses 1 & 2). This accountability has made the good employer provisions far more effective in improving public sector workplaces than would have been the case otherwise as it has encouraged Chief Executive Officers to prioritize efforts to address discrimination alongside other institutional goals.

At the same time as legislation has been making workplaces more receptive to the needs of women, attitudes towards women working have been changing, particularly government attitudes. Kahu and Morgan (2007) cite a Ministry of Women's Affairs (2002) report on work–life balance as evidence for their view that 'In New Zealand the government is increasingly vocal in its desire to increase women's participation in the workforce as a means to increase productivity and stimulate economic growth' (p. 55). Kahu and Morgan consider that government rhetoric sees paid work as a kind of basis for citizenship, demonstrating an increasingly dominant economic rationalist discourse that values only what is done for money. As Kahu and Morgan's (2007) article shows, women have internalized the pressure from social and government attitudes into a sense of returning to work after the birth of children as something they ought to do or even feel compelled to do.

Given changing social and government attitudes and the sense women have that they should work, it is not surprising that the proportion of women in the workforce has been increasing rapidly, from 39 per cent to 60 per cent between 1971 and 2001, although it is still much lower than the 74 per cent of men in work. There were almost 200 000 more women in work in 2001 than in 1991. In the early 1990s, growth in part-time work for women exceeded growth in full-time work but since then the situation has been reversed and numbers of women in full-time work have grown more rapidly than in part-time work, even though women are three times as likely as men to work part-time (Statistics New Zealand, 2005).

Another of the dramatic changes is in the diversity of women represented in the workforce. Changes in immigration policies have broadened possibilities for intending immigrants beyond point systems for those meeting specific criteria and members of preferred occupations, to also include provisions for prospective entrepreneurs with significant sums of money to invest in the New Zealand economy. Asian and European women are the most likely to be employers or self-employed, rather than Maori or Pacific Island women (ibid.).

However, women's participation in the labour force remains lower than men at all ages and is more subject to life-cycle factors. As well as a drop in the proportion of women working between the ages of 25 and 40 when they are likely to be having and raising children, women also tend to leave the workforce at an earlier age than men from the age of 50 upwards. Nevertheless, the generation of women who have come into the workforce in the 1960s and 1970s, who have seen work as an important part of their lives rather than secondary to having children, are staying in the workforce in their 50s and 60s. The proportion of 60- to 64-year-old women in the labour force increased from 17 to 42 per cent between 1991 and 2001 (ibid.).

In the year ended March 2007, the proportion of employed women in professional and managerial occupations was recorded in the Labour Market Statistics, 2007, as 29 per cent (11.2 per cent categorized as legislators, administrators and managers, 18 per cent classified as professionals, according to the New Zealand Standard Classification of Occupations) (Department of Labour, 2007).

THE CURRENT POSITION OF WOMEN AND SMALL BUSINESS OWNERSHIP

In the context of small and medium-sized enterprises (SMEs) women as a specific group have only attracted significant research interest in the last two to three decades. In the 1970s, second-wave feminism aroused a desire for institutional and political change and led to the establishment of women's pressure groups such as the Women's Electoral Lobby and The Society for Research on Women. This kind of social change influenced researchers to see women as a separate group who could not simply be assumed to have the same characteristics or needs as men. Unsurprisingly then, a major focus in research-ing women and SMEs has been the type of research necessary to establish the importance of a previously unrecognized group. That is, research that counts the numbers – in this case of women involved (to establish their presence), of trends in female participation in self-employment (to demonstrate increases), and of 'difference' in either experiences or performance (between the group under study, women, and others, i.e., males). As such, the focus on women has manifested itself in projects that have dealt with two specific sub-sets of women: those that can be called entrepreneurs or owner-managers in their own right, that is, female entrepreneurs, or women who are in business in partnership with a spouse, that is, copreneurs (Marshack, 1993).

The proportion of women who are self-employed in New Zealand is growing. According to 2006 New Zealand Census data from the government agency Statistics New Zealand, 36 per cent of all those in self-employment are women (an increase of 7 per cent since 1991). This figure represents 17 per cent of the total number of women in the workforce (Statistics New Zealand, 2007). Census data also indicates that women repre-sented 31 per cent of all employers, 35 per cent of all self-employed without employees, and 58 per cent of unpaid family workers (MWA/MED, 2008).

In New Zealand 97 per cent of enterprises employ 19 or fewer people and 89 per cent employ five or fewer. Out of the total number of enterprises 68 per cent have no employ-ees (ibid.). Consistent with that, 'not employing others' is the most common status for both self-employed males and females in New Zealand. Women are also more likely to be unpaid family workers, less likely to be employers and on average own and/or manage firms with slightly fewer employees than men (ibid.). The range of industries that women start enterprises in is also narrower than it is for men (ibid.). Asian and European women are more likely to be self-employed in New Zealand than those who are Maori or Pacific (ibid.). In terms of educational attainment, self-employed women are qualified similarly to their employee counterparts (male and female). However, those women working as unpaid workers in family businesses are likely to be less qualified than those self-employed in other ways (ibid.).

A large number of self-employed women (31 per cent) in New Zealand work part-time, compared with only 14 per cent of self-employed men. A similar disparity occurs when data relating to earnings of male and female self-employed individuals is examined. Women, on average, earn significantly less than men (ibid.). This is no doubt linked to the presence of greater numbers of women working part-time, and potentially to the choice by some women to work fewer hours in order to balance family commitments (Cheyne and Harris, 2005).

EXPLORATION OF CONCEPTUAL AND CONTEXTUAL BARRIERS TO FEMALE ENTREPRENEURSHIP

There are a broad range of business assistance initiatives funded by government to encourage and support business start-up and operations in New Zealand. These are delivered by New Zealand Trade & Enterprise[1] (often in partnership with other agencies) and many of these programmes include women as a target group. However, New Zealand cannot be described as having any niche entrepreneurship or business assistance policies designed specifically for women. A number of non-governmental agencies (e.g., the Chambers of Commerce) and private providers (e.g., The Small Business Company[2]) also deliver a variety of business assistance initiatives. In terms of provision or programmes specifically designed for women, the Her Business Group[3] is a leader in this area. Its portfolio of offerings includes a magazine, facilitated networks, business club, conference and businesswomen of the year awards.

A significant amount of research suggests that women on the whole face barriers accessing capital and mobilizing start-up resources, start businesses using less capital than men and are less likely to use bank loans compared with men at start-up. Those who argue for these points include a number of well-known international researchers, such as Hisrich and Brush (1984), Riding and Swift (1990), Brush (1992), Orser and Foster (1994), Carter et al. (1997), Carter and Rosa (1998), Verheul and Thurik (2001). This list of sources suggests that similar conclusions regarding the financial disadvantages women face at start-up have been made across a considerable time period and in a variety of countries (including Australia, United States, United Kingdom and Canada). In the Australian context (as the situation most closely comparable to New Zealand), Still and Timms (2000) found that women in small business in Australia 'suffered deficient access to debt and equity finance through networks, banks and the finance sector' (p. 277).

Substantial research has investigated the perceived barriers to women in dealing with banks, and has focused on determining whether gender stereotypes and discrimination are the main causal factors. As a by-product of that relatively narrow focus, there has been some information collected about the nature of the interaction between women and banks and perceptions of reasons why the relationship is often negative. Riding and Swift (1990) and Haines et al. (1999) argued that the pervasive belief that women face greater difficulties obtaining bank credit than men is supported by the popular media, professional literature, lobby organizations and academic literature. However, there is significant empirical evidence that does not support the allegation of gender bias (e.g., Riding and Swift, 1990; Buttner and Rosen, 1992; Haines et al., 1999). Two reasons put forward to explain this conflicting evidence are that research results in the area are highly sensitive to the methodology employed and that the heterogeneity of women-owned businesses is not taken into account (Carter and Rosa, 1998; Haines et al., 1999). Indeed, studies are often single gender in nature and would appear to rely disproportionately on anecdotal evidence, rather than on gender-comparative empirical studies.

An example of findings from a comprehensive investigation of a gender-comparative nature regarding the finance experiences of male and female entrepreneurs are those of Verheul and Thurik (2001). They concluded that: female entrepreneurs are more likely to have less experience with financial management; female entrepreneurs spend less time networking, which may deprive them of important information concerning the acquisition of finance; female entrepreneurs are more likely to work in the service sector, which is characterized by relatively small initial investments requiring a small amount of financial capital; and women are assumed to be more risk averse and risk aversion implies a reliance on equity instead of bank loans.

Indeed, it would appear that as time has gone on and more research has been carried out, there has been a shift from a perception of discrimination on the part of banks. Instead there now seems to be some research that suggests women often understand why they have been rejected for a loan better than researchers think, and that the reasons are often to do with competencies or experience rather than being related to gender. For example, Carter and Rosa (1998) found in their research that banks were not guilty of discrimination, instead socialization and the work-related experiences of women put them at a disadvantage compared with their male counterparts. Of the 600 UK firms involved in the research, the authors found that women who had been rejected by banks for loans did not directly attribute this to gender discrimination, and few applicants of either gender blamed the lender for the refusal. Part of this subtle shift in understanding is the realization that whilst outreach is essential on the part of banks, women also need to learn how to develop financial relationships and a support network (i.e., there is a dual educative process). Part of this continued 'misunderstanding' on the part of both women and banks has been described by Orser and Foster (1994) as 'discontinuity that is detrimentally affected by gender', that is, 'the lack of coherence between the evaluative criteria used in traditional lending models to determine the eligibility of business loan applicants and the characteristics of those seeking business loans' (p. 11).

In terms of research on women SME owner/managers and finance in New Zealand, there is little empirically based literature on women per se (most appears gender neutral), and even less that is comparative in nature (Dupuis and de Bruin, 2004). Often information about women in SMEs is gathered as a by-product of a broader research focus or they are treated as a group of interest within the SME sector as a whole. Cameron and Massey (1999) argued that the small business 'finance gap' has changed over the years (due to the emergence of new financial institutions and changing attitudes towards the sector). Nevertheless, whilst loan finance is described as being more readily available, there is still a lack of equity finance (especially of start-up capital and venture capital).

Therefore, that situation exists for women as SME owners, or potential owners, as well as for men. A similar conclusion had been reached by Williams (1987) who found that women faced no more difficulties obtaining finance than all other small business owners.

Fay and Williams (1993a and 1993b) used a random sample of 200 branches of four major trading banks in New Zealand and found some evidence that women encountered credit discrimination in seeking start-up funding, but that the situation is not necessarily the fault of banks. Often women experienced greater difficulties than men in acquiring the skills and knowledge necessary to conform to the loan criteria of banks. Duff (1998) replicated the methodology of this work and failed to find evidence that supported the hypothesis that gender influenced the decisions of bank officers regarding loans. These findings are consistent with some of the international literature: research in New Zealand has signalled that whilst women do lack access to capital, this disadvantage is either caused or exacerbated by their corresponding lack of knowledge and training (MWA/MED, 2008). As a consequence, women often enter industries or enterprises where entry barriers are low and prior experience or knowledge is not a prerequisite.

STORIES OF SUCCESS IN OVERCOMING BARRIERS

Choosing examples from the diversity of female entrepreneurs is demanding, because there are so many interesting possibilities to choose from. There are musicians, designers, artists, writers and others working in the creative industries. There are many consultants who have professional training and have decided to leave an unrewarding environment and gain more control over their working lives by 'hanging their shingle' [going into business for themselves] and selling their skills; there are women working in tourism and hospitality and there are women in farming or those who add value to primary produce.

Three examples cannot do justice to the exciting range of business activity, but they will help show some ways that barriers can be overcome. Women themselves have often talked of a lack of confidence as a barrier (MWA/MED, 2008). However, in conversation about their businesses they often show a steely determination and an impressive commitment that drives them forward. They do seem to be able to gain access to funding, either from family or from the bank and presumably those who finance them are impressed by their passion for their business idea as well as their financial projections. Both push and pull factors are in evidence with one young woman saying that she started on the path to self-employment when she entered the working world at 16 and saw how many people were unhappy and bored in their jobs, and another saying that she wanted to link her job with her lifestyle and her lifestyle with her job and did so by developing her own range of products and setting up a gallery and store where she could display and sell them.

The three case studies demonstrate a similar range of push and pull factors in the businesses developed by Wendy, a consultant, Ruth, a caterer and food writer and Cathy, who produces organic milk and yogurt with her husband in the family business.

BOX 10.1   WENDY

Wendy's story began almost ten years ago when the university department she worked in as a lecturer was in the process of being restructured. She, along with two other staff members, was told that of their three jobs only two would remain at the end of the repositioning process. After taking in the news, Wendy decided that she had no desire to wait for her fate. She would prefer to choose her own future. So, although she had two children and a musician husband who made an important contribution to the household with cooking and childcare, but tended to cost money rather than make money, and all of whom depended on her as the breadwinner, she became a consultant specializing in research and analysis, writing reports for government departments. Her training as a qualified lawyer was a helpful background and she readily gained work and gained a reputation for reliability, excellent writing skills and being able to work well with other staff.

Her major barrier has been finding and maintaining a suitable office, as an office away from home where she can concentrate is one of her personal necessities for work. Finance was not a huge barrier as her work did not require a great deal in terms of set-up costs, but she has found it difficult to gain continuity of work while guarding against becoming overwhelmed with work. Finding an office that was not too costly has been her major barrier and she has shifted office once, but both offices have been compromises. However, she enjoys the freedom her work gives. She can decide on the jobs that she wishes to accept, she can decide for herself when to take a holiday. She has flexibility and autonomy and has taught herself to enjoy the brief times when she is without work as opportunities, rather than becoming anxious about when her next contract will happen. Now her network of contacts is so strong that she has only to make a few calls to let prospective employers know that she is available and they let her know what is coming up that they need her to help work on. Although she could not have anticipated that she would become a self-employed consultant when she was working at the university, the new life suits her desire for independence and control. For her, consultancy has been the ideal solution. She has created her own tailor-made job, rather than having to fit into another less than satisfactory job.

BOX 10.2   RUTH

By contrast, Ruth's work in catering was a passion that had been part of her family background, as her mother was a good cook and her father was a grocer and a baker's son, so they talked about food in the family. She wanted her own business, so in her 20s she went through the process of racking her brains about what it was that interested her most and once she decided it was food, became a restaurateur for ten years before moving into catering. In her catering business, she has 35 permanent staff and 150 casual staff. She is seldom in the kitchen, but has a kitchen manager who reports to her. She has a cooking school where a test chef is in charge of the recipes, which they brainstorm together. Her operation is in the countryside on a property called Springfield, which is often a venue for weddings and has some accommodation for guests or cooking school attendees.

Ruth feels that as an entrepreneur you have to be prepared to take a risk. She sees it as helpful to analyse the risk factors in advance. Only small parts of her undertakings have ever failed so they have been easy to put to one side. She writes books and magazine articles and newspaper columns on food and cooking and works long hours as catering is a seven-day-a-week business. She would not expect anyone on the staff to do anything she wouldn't be prepared to do herself. Her aim is that everything they do should be of high quality. She says that knowing the staff really well as she does can be a problem. When she has to let someone know that what they've done is not acceptable, she has to think her way carefully round the situation to protect the relationship. With such a busy life, she says that being organized at home is really important. Ruth counsels other entrepreneurial women that trying to do everything is impossible and it is wise to organize others to do as much of the work as is practicable.

BOX 10.3   CATHY

Cathy's business is also based on food, but has an underlying philosophical basis as well. In the 1980s, Cathy and her husband developed an interest in the Green Party movement in Europe and in sustainability. Rudolf Steiner's teaching encouraged her to find a safe, healthy sustainable lifestyle that she could control. She is from Ngati Raukawa (a Maori tribe) so she was also influenced by Maori beliefs in relation to the earth and the sky and nurturing the land and she, along with her husband and their business partner, decided to run their farm organically, without chemicals and pesticides. In the 1980s New Zealand was going through a recession so unemployment figures were rising, especially for Maori, and running one's own business did not seem any more of a risk than working for an organization. The major risk was the assumption that New Zealand would follow trends in Europe and people would want to buy organic food. Fortunately, after some time, the organic movement did gain momentum in New Zealand and demand for their products increased (Gillies, 2006).

The first 12 years were hard trying to meet bank repayments but their belief in their principles sustained them. Cathy enjoys living on the land, being true to her values and having self-determination and autonomy in the way they run the business. She says to start a business you have to be committed to what you are doing. Discipline, a focused approach and dogged persistence are required for problem-solving. You need to make sacrifices and to be prepared to be totally immersed in work. Family finance, as well as their own, was used to buy the farm and that family support was another motivation to succeed. Cathy has spent time getting out into the community to talk about the business and let people know about the health benefits from the products and the benefit to the environment of sustainable farming. Her joy in the business comes from doing something that she believes in, that she knows is worthwhile, that is making a contribution to the well-being of people and the environment (ibid.).

SUMMARY AND RECOMMENDATIONS

The feminist movement of the 1970s and 1980s created better employment situations for women and gave employers and women themselves the notion that there should be gender equality in employment. However, despite the passing of equal pay legislation, women's earnings in New Zealand as a proportion of those of their male counterparts are still only 87 per cent (Sutherland, 2008). Women have moved from being encouraged to be homemakers and stay-at-home mothers in the 1950s and 1960s to feeling a social push to return to work after having children and make a contribution to the economy. Nevertheless, women do wish to have flexible working conditions that will enable them to attend to family responsibilities and this desire for flexibility and autonomy has been one of the drivers that has encouraged women into setting up their own businesses.

Barriers for women entrepreneurs have been shown to be lack of confidence, lack of finance and fear of risking failure, along with a lack of networks and business knowledge (MWA/MED, 2008). The barriers can be overcome by gaining information, by persistence and determination, by being prepared to make sacrifices and being disciplined. The rewards are an enormous sense of achievement as well as having autonomy and control over one's own work:

- Many organizations push women into entrepreneurship, because of a reluctance to provide flexible work and part-time job opportunities. Organizations should consider possibilities for part-time work, even at senior levels of management, rather than assuming that anything different from the norm is not possible.
- Women tend to lack confidence in their entrepreneurial ability because of the risk. Interested entrepreneurs should discuss the risks with others and plan for the risks rather than trying to ignore them.
- Government should support a network that helps women prepare a business plan and make contact. The Ministry of Women's Affairs should explore the feasibility of setting up a website with advice on business planning and contacts for women who wish to explore becoming entrepreneurs.

NOTES

1. www.nzte.govt.nz; accessed 12 February 2010.
2. www.tsbc.co.nz; accessed 12 February 2010.
3. www.herbusinessmagazine.com; accessed 12 February 2010.

REFERENCES

Brush, C.G. (1992), 'Research on women business owners: Past trends, a new perspective and future directions', *Entrepreneurship Theory and Practice*, **16**(4), 5–30.

Buttner, E.H. and Rosen, B. (1992), 'Rejection in the loan application process: Male and female entrepreneurs' perceptions and subsequent intentions', *Journal of Small Business Management*, **30**(1), 58–65.

Cameron, A. and Massey, C. (1999), *Small and Medium-sized Enterprises: A New Zealand Perspective*, Auckland: Longman.

Carter, S. and Rosa, P. (1998), 'The financing of male- and female-owned businesses', *Entrepreneurship and Regional Development*, **10**(3), 225–42.

Carter, N.M., Williams, M. and Reynolds, P.D. (1997), 'Discontinuance among new firms in retail: The influence of initial resources, strategy, and gender', *Journal of Business Venturing*, **12**(2), 125–45.

Cheyne, J. and Harris, C. (2005), 'Women and self-employment', in C. Massey (ed.), *Entrepreneurship and Small Business Management*, Auckland, New Zealand: Pearson Education, pp. 228–39.

Department of Labour (2007), *Labour Market Statistics, 2007*, available at: http://www.stats.govt.nz/publications/workknowledgeandskills/labour-market-statistics-2007.aspx; accessed 11 February 2010.

Duff, S. (1998) 'The influence of bank loan officers' attitudes on funding decisions', Palmerston North, New Zealand: Massey University, unpublished research report.

Dupuis, A. and de Bruin, A. (2004), 'Women's business ownership and entrepreneurship', in P. Spoonley, A. Dupuis and A. de Bruin (eds), *Work and Working in 21st-century New Zealand*, Palmerston North: Dunmore Press, pp. 154–79.

Fay, M. and Williams, L. (1993a), 'Gender bias and the availability of business loans', *Journal of Business Venturing*, **8**(4), 363–76.

Fay, M. and Williams, L. (1993b), 'Sex of applicant and the availability of business start-up finance', *Australian Journal of Management*, **16**(1), 65–72.

Gillies, A. (2006), 'Bio-farm Products Ltd: entrepreneurship, innovation, leadership and strategy', in M. Mulholland (ed.), *He Wairere Pakihi, Maori Business Case Studies*, Palmerston North: Te Au Rangahau, Maori Business Research Centre, Massey University.

Haines Jr., G.H., Orser, B.J. and Riding, A.L. (1999), 'Myths and realities: An empirical study of banks and the gender of small business clients', *Canadian Journal of Administrative Sciences*, **16**(4), 291–307.

Hisrich, R.D. and Brush, C.G. (1984), 'The woman entrepreneur: Management skills and business problems', *Journal of Small Business Management*, **22**(1), 30–37.

Kahu, E. and Morgan, M. (2007), 'Weaving cohesive identities: New Zealand women talk as mothers and workers', *Kotuitui: New Zealand Journal of Social Services Online*, **2**, 55–73.

Marshack, K.J. (1993), 'Coentrepreneurial couples: A literature review on boundaries and transitions among copreneurs', *Family Business Review*, **VI**(4), 355–69.

MWA/MED – Ministry of Women's Affairs and Ministry of Economic Development (2008), *Women in Enterprise: A Report on Women in Small and Medium Enterprises in New Zealand*, Wellington, New Zealand: MWA/MED.

Orser, B.J. and Foster, M.K. (1994), 'Lending practices and Canadian women in micro-based businesses', *Women in Management Review*, **9**(5), 11–19.

Riding, A. and Swift, C. (1990), 'Women business owners and terms of credit: Some empirical findings of the Canadian experience', *Journal of Business Venturing*, **5**(5), 327–40.

State Sector Act (1988), Part III, Chief Executives, Section 43, Review of Performance of Chief Executives, available at: http://gpacts.knowledge-basket.co.nz/gpacts/public/text/1988/se/020se43.html; accessed 11 February 2010.

Statistics New Zealand (2005), *Focusing on Women*, Wellington, New Zealand: Statistics New Zealand.

Statistics New Zealand (2007), *2006 Census Employment Status Data*, Wellington, New Zealand: Statistics New Zealand.

Still, L.V. and Timms, W. (2000), 'Women's business: The flexible alternative workstyle for women', *Women in Management Review*, **15**(5), 272–82.

Sutherland, J. (2008), 'Suffrage New Zealand style – white or red anyone?', *NZCOSS Network News*, September, p. 4.

Verheul, I. and Thurik, R. (2001), 'Start-up capital: "Does gender matter?"', *Small Business Economics*, **16**(4), 329–45.

Williams, L.E. (1987), 'Women in business: Bank finance and discrimination', Dunedin: University of Otago, unpublished dissertation.

Women's Rights Committee (1975), *The Role of Women in New Zealand Society*, Wellington: Government Printer.

11 Pakistan
Jawad Syed

INTRODUCTION

The number of women entering small business ownership has increased significantly across the world (see e.g., Ericksen, 1999; Hughes, 2003; Fielden and Davidson, 2005). However, research into the experiences of small business owners remains focused on a relatively small number of established markets. This chapter seeks to examine the contexts and experiences of women entrepreneurs engaged in small businesses in Pakistan.

With a population of more than 167 million (July 2008 est.) and an increasingly empowered middle class, Pakistan is the 6th most populous country in the world. Pakistan is a developing economy (per capita GDP of less than $2600 – 2007 est.), which has suffered from decades of internal and international political disputes and economic instability since its independence in 1947. However, since 2001, economic reforms including privatization of the banking sector, foreign economic assistance and renewed access to global markets have generated macroeconomic recovery. Spurred by gains in the industrial and service sectors, the country has experienced GDP growth in the 6–8 per cent range in 2004–07 (CIA, 2008).

From a gender equality perspective, Pakistan is a country where patriarchal customs and practices seem to be firmly embedded in the society and in the workplace (Syed et al., 2009). However, despite such challenges, the recognition of women as employees and business owners is just gaining ground. While recognizing the socio-cultural and structural barriers to women's small business ownership, this chapter's focus is on Pakistani women's success in overcoming such barriers. By identifying contextual challenges as well as women entrepreneurs' stories of success, the chapter seeks to demonstrate the degree of success achieved by Pakistani women.

THE CURRENT POSITION OF WOMEN IN EMPLOYMENT

Pakistan has one of the lowest rates in the world of female participation in economic activity. Compared with neighbouring Iran and India, where female labour force participation rate (for females aged 15 and older) is as low as 38.6 per cent and 34 per cent respectively, Pakistan's female economic activity rate lags behind at 32.7 per cent (UNDP, 2007). According to United Nations' *Human Development Report*, an overwhelming majority of economically active women in Pakistan are working in agriculture (65 per cent) followed by services (20 per cent) and industry (16 per cent). Female professional and technical workers represent only 26 per cent of total workers. Furthermore, the proportion of estimated female to male earned income is only 29 per cent (PPP US$ female 1.059, male 3.607). The gender gap is also visible in education (ibid.). Since 1951, the number of illiterate Pakistanis has doubled, but the number of illiterate women has tripled (Bari, 2000). In 2005, the female literacy rate was reported to be less than 33 per cent, compared with about 45 per cent male literacy rate (UNDP, 2007).

However, despite these challenges, there is some evidence of improvement in women's participation in economic activities. For example, Arif and Sheikh (n.d.) note that the number of females in Pakistan's labour force increased from 1.8 million in 1973 to 5.9 million in 1997–98. In 1981 the female labour force participation rate (crude, for all age groups) was 2.1 per cent. It moved up to 13.3 per cent by 2005–06 (FBS, 2006).

Furthermore, the female unemployment rate in Pakistan dropped from 16.5 per cent in 2001–02 to 8.4 per cent in 2006–07. Yet, the rate is still substantially higher than the male unemployment rate of 4.5 per cent, indicating that women are less successful in securing job opportunities than men (FBS, 2007; IFC, 2007). It may be noted that female economic activity in Pakistan is mainly concentrated in agriculture (65 per cent) followed by services (20 per cent) and industry (16 per cent) (UNDP, 2007).

Pakistan is a signatory of the Millennium Development Goals, thus affirming its commitment to empower women and eliminate gender inequality by 2015 (Subohi, 2006). Pakistan's Small and Medium Enterprise (SME) Policy 2007 also states that special attention will be given to women entrepreneurs and other disadvantaged groups. The policy aims to increase the share of women-owned SMEs to 6 per cent.

WOMEN AND SMALL BUSINESS OWNERSHIP

According to the Economic Census of Pakistan, women-owned businesses represent about 2.4 per cent of a total 3.2 million enterprises in Pakistan (FBS, 2006). Most of the women-owned businesses are really small, that is, with a turnover less than Rs1 million and/or investment less than Rs0.5 million (FBS data, cited in Amjad, 2007). Table 11.1 offers an account of enterprises in Pakistan by gender and type. According to these statistics, female (as well as male) entrepreneurship is clearly concentrated in the household sector. The ratio of male to female enterprise is about 2.5 in the household sector; however this ratio jumps to about 34 in the corporate sector.

SMEs are estimated to represent more than 80 per cent of the non-agricultural labour force in Pakistan (SMEDA, 2005). There is, however, a dearth of data on women-owned businesses in Pakistan. According to a 2005 report by the United Nation's Convention on the Elimination of all Forms of Discrimination against Women, the category of 'self-employed' women in Pakistan has increased from 11.7 per cent in 1997–98 to 15.7 per cent in 2001–02 (CEDAW, 2005).

Table 11.1   Status of enterprise by type and gender

Type	Male	Female
Household	127338	52295
Corporate	1773	51
Proprietors/Partners	2776893	18312
Total	2906004	70658

Source: Based on FBS (2006).

A study undertaken by the International Labour Organization (ILO) of 150 women entrepreneurs in Pakistan found 39 per cent of women engaged in small enterprises (employing less than 100 workers) and 9 per cent in medium-size enterprises (employing between 100 and 250 workers) (Goheer, 2003). The study reveals that women entrepreneurs in the SME sector provide greater employment to women, with female-owned businesses having an average of eight female employees and seven male employees. Also, it suggests that women's entrepreneurship in Pakistan is often an issue related to social class. For example, upper class, highly educated women are generally more capable of starting up their own small and medium businesses as they possess both the capital and the knowledge to do so. Women in urban areas are in a better position to foster businesses due to easier access to opportunity and information. The study revealed that 73 per cent of the women entrepreneurs started their businesses from personal savings and over 50 per cent belonged to upper tiers of education. However, the majority of women entrepreneurs tend to work in traditional sectors, such as boutiques, parlours and bakeries, along with apparel, handicrafts, jewellery and other similar businesses (ibid.).

STRUCTURAL AND CONTEXTUAL BARRIERS

Previous research has identified manifold challenges to women's entrepreneurship in Pakistan. These challenges range from lack of access to education, information and finance to patriarchal and gender discriminatory traditions and routines embedded in the society (e.g., Shabbir, 1995; Roomi, 2005a, 2005b). Together, these factors tend to severely inhibit women's ability to develop leadership skills and to own and manage their own businesses. The female literacy rate, for example, is alarmingly low, that is, 36 per cent. Furthermore, only 6.6 per cent of girls enrol at the high school level, reducing further to 1.2 per cent at the university level. This diminishes the chances of women emerging as entrepreneurs and senior executives in organizations.

Gender Stereotypes

Research suggests that in Pakistan, women's full economic potential is not being tapped due to deeply rooted discriminatory socio-cultural values and traditions, embedded particularly in the institutional support mechanisms (Roomi, 2005a). The United Nations Development Programme (UNDP, 1996) points to a strong inside–outside dichotomy in Pakistan, where women are restricted to the 'inside' space of their homes and households. This 'inside' reference restricts females from access to education, employment, training opportunities and social services, and the dichotomy continues to prevail in Pakistan. In the labour market (the 'outside'), lower educational attainment coupled with social norms of restricted mobility confine women to a limited range of employment and training opportunities and lower wages. Mobility constraints also undermine the ability of women to take a role in the market place as an entrepreneur or as a paid worker. According to the ILO study (Goheer, 2003), women entrepreneurs in Pakistan consider gender-related issues as most challenging in the business start-up process: 28 per cent of the challenges identified were marketing related, 26 per cent were family related and 16 per cent were government related.

The stereotyped reproductive image of women limits their role to the home and the family, playing only an auxiliary part in economic activity (Roomi, 2005a; Syed, 2008). An extremely patriarchal perspective on Islamic female modesty restricts women's mobility, limits social networks and imposes a check on their economic activity. Although, in the past two decades, the number of women joining the formal economic sectors has been increasing, equal opportunity in the workplace still remains elusive (Sajjad and Raza, 2007, p. 3). For example, several women entrepreneurs in Sajjad and Raza's study identified the conflict between their roles as a family person and as an entrepreneur. One woman entrepreneur in their study thus remarked: 'My family thinks that it is not safe for a woman to operate from outside the house. I need to market my product more aggressively but I can only go out if accompanied by my husband who has his own business to look after too' (ibid., p. 6).

Goheer (2003) argues that the business environment for women in Pakistan reflects the complex interplay of two groups of factors. The first is made up of socio-cultural, tribal and religious elements. This aspect of the environment is anchored in the patriarchal system and clearly manifested in the lower status of women. The second group of factors derives from the first group, taking the form of constitutional and legal structures, regulatory arrangements and institutional mechanisms. This category is contemporary rather than traditional, so it is cosmetically impartial.

Similarly, in his study on women entrepreneurs in Pakistan, Roomi (2005a) asked the interviewees to describe the gender-related challenges they faced in start-up and growth phases as well. The study identifies spatial mobility as the most challenging task for starting up a business. According to Shabbir (1995), the restricted spatial mobility has two dimensions: the first relates to the actual physical limitation to move around because of the inadequacy of transportation facilities, and the second relates to the actual ability of women to move around freely because of socio-cultural, tribal and religious reasons.

There is, however, some change in attitudes with the passage of time. In urban areas of Lahore, Islamabad and Karachi, for example, it is not uncommon to see women who work in offices from 9 to 5. However, in view of the problem of mobility (caused by, for example, social restrictions, lack of adequate transport facilities), women entrepreneurs generally restrict their businesses to 'feminine' professions, such as education, health and beautification where they provide services mostly to women customers, or in the garments/textile sector where they have women employees to manufacture products for women customers (Roomi, 2005a). It may be noted that the 'uneducated males' represent the majority of the labour force in Pakistan, who are less than willing to accept the authority of women. Another gender-related challenge for women is to prove their credibility to the suppliers and customers. Especially, if they work in the non-traditional sectors, neither suppliers nor customers take them seriously and doubt these women's ability to achieve their business targets (Shabbir, 1995).

Indeed, economic necessity is forcing more and more women to engage in some sort of employment, without relieving them of their traditional roles. However, it must be acknowledged that the situation is also improving because of women's tremendous determination and courage. They are entering in fields as diverse as education, health, IT, engineering and textiles (Khatoon, 2002).

The Neglect of Small Businesses

Economic policy in Pakistan has been traditionally biased towards the elite and the large-scale sector (Haque, 2006). Small businesses have grown up as an informal sector, which is neglected by the state in its quest to protect the large formal sector (Zaidi, 2005; Haque, 2007). Consequently there is a tension between the big push for industry and the neglect of small businesses. For most of the time in Pakistan's economic history, 'enterprise' for the government was synonymous with large industry only. Various policy measures, such as tariff protection and import licensing schemes, rather than enhancing productivity or encouraging industrialization for growth, adversely affected the prospects of entrepreneurship in the country (Hussain, 1999; Zaidi, 2005).

Since the late 1970s, Pakistan has experienced various phases of denationalization/privatization and encouragement of private sector. However, the large-scale manufacturing sector has always been a governmental priority; a number of heavy industries were opened up that were given numerous incentives including tax holidays. Thus, the small-scale manufacturing sector in Pakistan has developed in the context of a difficult industrialization process; where import substitution strategies led to an unbalanced sectoral composition and caused further bias in favour of large-scale capital-intensive production methods (Haque, 2007). Although the informal sector and the small-scale sector have been continuously ignored in Pakistan's economic policies, it is a fact that today almost 40 per cent of business takes place in the informal sector. Still, the small-scale enterprise and industry continue to remain a second priority. The neglect of the small-scale sector on part of the government is also evident from the fact that even today the actual growth rate of the sector is not computed the way it is done for the large-scale sector. Instead it is merely imputed (Zaidi, 2005; Haque, 2007).

Access to Finance

The per capita income of women in Pakistan is the lowest in the region (PPP US$1059) making it difficult for women to finance their businesses (UNDP, 2007). While women are entitled to property under the Islamic Shariah, research reveals that women own less than 3 per cent of plots in (sampled) villages (UNICEF, 2007), hence restricting their access to collateral assets and subsequently finance. Cooperatives, personal savings and family support are the main sources of finance for women entrepreneurs (IFC, 2007). This is also confirmed by Roomi's (2005a) study of 256 women entrepreneurs in Pakistan, which suggests that the biggest challenge these women faced in the start-up phase is the access to capital followed by lack of business management skills and bureaucratic government regulations. Also, in the development (growth) phase, the access to finance was considered to be the most difficult challenge followed by the access to the market and lack of technical skills.

According to a report by The Association of Chartered Certified Accountants (Sajjad and Raza, 2007), the usual sources of seed capital for women entrepreneurs are personal savings, income from the sale of personal jewellery, or loans from family members and relatives. The report notes that while the growth potential of female-owned enterprises is constrained by the lack of availability of formal finance, there is also a factor of reluctance of women entrepreneurs to access bank finance. The major reasons for this reluctance were found to be fear of default, high interest rates, past (unpleasant) experiences with the banks, difficulties in raising collateral and guarantors, lack of awareness of financing schemes, high risk averseness, social barriers and lack of an effective lobby. Among other challenges, the report also identifies social and cultural problems as well as the taboos of society as deterrents in provision of finance to women entrepreneurs.

Because of these problems, lower-income women in particular find it difficult to establish new businesses. In Karachi, for example, women's complaints primarily relate to male-dominated banks and companies that often turn away aspiring women entrepreneurs, as well as the difficulty of dealing with important officials in the government and the private sector. According to Hummaa Ahmad, editor of a leading English newspaper in Pakistan: 'For many start-up businesses run by women, it's really the chicken and the egg situation. How does a woman with a very good business plan also begin something where a substantial collateral is required?' Ahmad remarks that relatively successful businesswomen include those backed by family wealth and support (cited in *Asia Money*, 2005).

Access to Markets and Networks

Women-owned businesses in Pakistan are mainly in the informal sector with low turnover rates, which makes it difficult to reach new markets. Furthermore, the ability to expand into new markets requires experience, professional skills and market-oriented contacts. Issues related to gender are also a deterrent in establishing new contacts. According to Gillani (2003), women tend to stay in a 'comfort zone movement', mostly doing business with clients they know. This is also supported by Goheer (2003) whose study suggests that the majority of women entrepreneurs tend to operate within the same markets, with only a few (7 per cent and 11 per cent respectively in Goheer's sample) extending their business to national and international level.

Research has also highlighted the issue of gender-specific deficits in the social networking and outreach of women entrepreneurs even in industrialized countries (Aldrich, 1989; Cooper et al., 1995). The problem is also evident in Pakistan where there are stringent socio-cultural and physical barriers to women's mobility and meetings at a place away from their homes. According to Roomi (2005a), the majority of women entrepreneurs in Pakistan feel there is a lack of networks to exchange information and seek advice on common business-related issues. As the bulk of women-owned businesses in Pakistan operate on a micro and small scale, they rarely take part in existing business networks. Most SME networks are male-dominated; there are only a few networks (discussed in the next section) that have attempted to reach out to women entrepreneurs.

RESOURCES AND ENABLERS

Government Policy

The modern institutional environment in Pakistan has a cosmetic emphasis on gender equality; however, there is a huge gap between the rhetoric and reality of equal opportunity in the workplace. For example, Article 25 of the Constitution of Pakistan (1973) guarantees equality of rights to all citizens irrespective of sex, race and class and also empowers the government to take action to protect and promote women's rights. But actual practices discriminate against women's economic activity as producers and providers of services (Goheer, 2003).

The regulatory process that governs SMEs in Pakistan is complex, which is rather discouraging for women entrepreneurs who also face mobility and other socioeconomic constraints. Acknowledging the loss of human potential due to gender inequality, the Ministry for Women's Development (Government of Pakistan) seeks to provide training and support to empower women. For example, in collaboration with the UNDP, the Ministry has embarked on a National Plan for Action with a focus on women and the economy. Similarly, the 2006 SME Development Policy drafted by the Ministry of Industry, Production and Special Initiatives has a special focus on women-owned SMEs (SMEDA, 2006). Women-targeted finance programmes have been established by institutions such as the Agricultural Development Bank, the First Women Bank Limited (FWBL), the Pakistani Poverty Alleviation Fund (PPAF), the SME Bank, First MicroFinanceBank, the Khushhali Bank and other public and private sector organizations. Several programmes have been initiated to provide loans to SMEs by the government, civil society organizations and international development agencies. For example, the PPAF (which is also supported by the World Bank), with women consisting of 40 per cent of its 7 million beneficiaries, is an endowment of $100 million and is a wholesale lender to NGOs engaged in providing micro-financing that has presence in 94 districts across Pakistan (IFC, 2007).

Support from Businesses and NGOs

Entrepreneur women's associations in Pakistan are mainly limited to medium-size businesses, while micro- and small enterprises rarely belong to any type of association. A prominent businesswomen's association in Pakistan is the Pakistan Association of Women Entrepreneurs, which was registered as an NGO in 1985. The Women Chambers of Commerce and Industry, represented in various cities including Karachi, Lahore and Rawalpindi-Islamabad, also serve as important institutions safeguarding and representing businesswomen's interests.

The national Rural Support Programmes Network (RSPN) offers support mechanisms for women entrepreneurs mostly in rural and semi-urban underprivileged areas of Pakistan. Also, The Aga Khan Rural Support Programme (AKRSP) has initiated women micro-enterprise support programmes (e.g., Shubinak and Hunza Threadnet in the Northern Areas and Chitral). Hunza Threadnet, with more than 3000 female beneficiaries, has initiated capacity-building programmes for micro- and small enterprises. Similarly, the Sarhad Rural Support Programme (SRSP) and the Thardeep Rural Development Programme (TRDP) have been supporting women entrepreneurs through micro-credit services and capacity-building initiatives. Several NGOs such as Asasah, Sungi, Hawwa and Behbood have been supporting women entrepreneurs mostly in rural and semi-urban areas.

The United States Agency for International Development (USAID) has allocated $66 million for its strategic plan of 2003–07 to support economic empowerment targeting SME development (IFC, 2007). Similarly, The Canadian International Development

Agency (CIDA) offers micro-credit loans and training to women. Additionally, the Aga Khan Development Network created the First MicroFinanceBank Limited (FMFB) with a specific focus on SMEs operated by women. The ILO has also been working with FWBL to directly finance women micro-borrowers in rural areas (FWBL, 2005). Similarly, the World Bank is implementing an initiative in coordination with the government of Pakistan to facilitate women's mobility, which would also help increase their access to information and markets. The International Finance Corporation has recently undertaken research on women's access to finance in Pakistan, identifying financial and non-financial policy initiatives and recommendations (IFC, 2007).

Individual Motivation

Notwithstanding the contextual barriers and enablers, there is ample evidence that women entrepreneurs use their own agency to operate and manage their own businesses. Individual motivations, however, vary from person to person. For example, based on their qualitative interviews with 33 female participants of an entrepreneurship development programme run in the metropolitan city of Karachi, Shabbir and Di Gregorio (1996) revealed that women decided to start a business in order to achieve three types of personal goals: *personal freedom, security* and *satisfaction*. Freedom seekers were those women who had experienced some kind of frustration or dissatisfaction in their paid work, and who now wanted to start their own business in order to have the freedom to choose the type of work, hours of work, work environment and the people they worked with. Security seekers were those women who, triggered by some personal mishap (such as death or retirement of their husband), wanted to start a business in order to maintain or improve their and their family's social and economic status. An important reason why most of these women opted for their own business rather than paid work was the flexibility that self-employment offered in terms of location (close to home, working from home) and hours of work, to which paid jobs could not cater. Satisfaction seekers were mostly housewives, with no previous work experience, who wanted to start a business in order to prove to themselves and to others that they were useful and productive members of society. Shabbir and Di Gregorio (ibid.) argued that structural factors influencing start-up may be divided into three categories: internal resources, that is, women's qualification and work experience; external resources, that is, finance and location; and relational resources, that is, family, employees, suppliers and customers. However, the impact of structural factors on women's ability to start a business varies according to the dominant personal goal. The relationship between women's personal goals and structural factors influencing start-up helps in understanding why some women, despite apparently unfavourable circumstances, succeed in starting a business, whereas others even under apparently favourable circumstances may not do so.

STORIES OF SUCCESS

Barriers to women's entrepreneurship cover the whole spectrum of business development, from pre-start-up to maturity. However, despite the barriers faced by women entering and operating small businesses, their stories are frequently ones of success (see e.g., Ericksen, 1999; Cantando, 2006). This section offers a snapshot of Pakistani women's stories of success and the organizations that helped them in establishing their business.

SMEDA's Women Entrepreneurs Development Cell

The Small and Medium Enterprise Development Authority (SMEDA) was established in 1988 by the Government of Pakistan to develop SMEs in the country. In order to meet the needs of women entrepreneurs, SMEDA established the Women Entrepreneurs Development Cell (WEDC) in 2002. The following is an account of the key projects undertaken by the WEDC:

Women Business Incubation Center (WBIC)
This project aims to provide practical support to women entrepreneurs including help in developing the infrastructure and various service packages to improve female participation in economic development. The infrastructure support includes, for example, the provision of fully furnished, air conditioned offices/display areas along with administrative support. The establishment of a female-managed facility in Lahore has served to establish women entrepreneurs' presence in the market, for example, by expanding from home-based business to commercial office, or starting their business, and an opportunity to market their products through a display centre along with access to instant business management solutions. SMEDA is currently planning to expand the network of WBICs to other regions.

Women Entrepreneurs Information Network (WIN)
Given that a vast majority of females have little access to information of incentives and initiatives introduced by private sector or government bodies for women entrepreneurs' business development (Goheer, 2003), SMEDA launched Pakistan's first exclusive women entrepreneurs' web portal, Women Entrepreneurs Information Network. The Network has been designed to bridge the resource gaps for women in business through ready access to information, export markets and increased networking opportunities.

Furthermore, the WEDC regularly organizes training programmes covering management, technical and skill development sessions for women entrepreneurs, whereby hundreds of women have benefited from these training sessions (e.g., SMEDA, 2008).

The First MicroFinanceBank Limited

With an aim to promote the development of an active privately based micro-finance industry in Pakistan, The First MicroFinanceBank Limited (FMFB) was established in 2001. The Bank is owned by the Aga Khan Development Network. The Bank operates with the underlying long-term principles of outreach and sustainability, aiming to reach out to those who are currently not able to receive adequate financial services, throughout the country, in rural as well as urban areas. The target audience is vulnerable groups, especially women.

The FMFB is the embodiment of the concept of micro-loans as a means to spur development in developing countries. The loans are quite small relative to normal financial

BOX 11.1   LOK VIRSA BOUTIQUE, LAHORE

Adeeba Talat got married at the age of 15. She had hardly finished her matricu-
lation at that time. She is 40 now, the mother of five children, and running her
own business for the last ten years. Adeeba was very fond of dress designing
from the beginning, and her mother-in-law encouraged her to start designing
and selling clothes. She was short of money and wanted to be independent
as well. Hence she decided to start her own business, and she chose crochet
lace clothes to start with. The idea caught on quickly as it was relatively new
in the market and public response was very good. This gave her some business confidence and she decided to expand by making outfits to be sold in
the market. She made a verbal contract with a local shopkeeper to sell her
clothes by displaying at his shop. This turned out to be a very bad experience.
The treacherous shopkeeper sold her clothes but never paid her. She was
not the only one who became the victim of a male retailer. Many of her friends
told her that their small initiatives had met with the same fate. Disgruntled and
disappointed, Adeeba decided not to use this marketing channel any more but
resolved to carry on with her business. She changed her strategy and started
direct marketing by participating in the local exhibitions and fairs. A moderate
response in the beginning soon turned into a good stream of orders.

   These days she serves a number of clients, but produces only to order. Her
husband manages the marketing and sales, while she manages designing and
production. Adeeba intends to expand her business and enter into the export
market. The main purpose behind earning more money is to send her son
abroad for higher education. She has recently sent some designs to her sister
who lives in the United States and is expecting to get some orders from there.

Source: Kamyab Women, Gallup Cyber Letter on SME, July–October, 2004, available at: www.
gallup.com.pk/sme/SMEjul04.pdf; accessed 20 February 2010.

BOX 11.2   SEWING MACHINE TO SEWING TRAINING
INSTITUTE, CHITRAL

Islamabad, Pakistan, 27 November 2007 – The First MicroFinanceBank's
client, Ms Sifat Gul from Gharam Chashma, Chitral, won the 'Best National
Micro-Entrepreneur Award – Female' at the recently organized Citi-PPAF
Micro-entrepreneurship Awards 2007 ceremony in Islamabad. The award
recognizes the extraordinary contributions that individual micro-entrepreneurs
have made to the economic sustainability of their families as well as their communities.

   The award winner Sifat Gul, faced with economic problems, began her
journey a couple of years ago by approaching the FMFB for a loan to purchase
a sewing machine and become a tailor. However, she was soon able to diversify

her small home-run business into a full training institute to harness the sewing and embroidery skills of the young women in her community. Today, she plans to construct a separate building for her training institute and has partnered with other organizations that purchase her products and exhibit them in city centres.

Through a prudent use of the micro-finance facility, Sifat has been able to increase her own household income. It has also empowered her to play a positive role in mobilizing her community to bring about a social change in their surroundings. Today, not only does she have the basic amenities of life including good-quality access to education, housing and health facilities for her entire household but also trains and empowers many young women to earn their livelihoods. Coming from the remote, mountainous area of Chitral, hers is a story of true woman empowerment as she stepped up to earn a livelihood and was later elected as a female councillor, revolutionizing the surroundings by playing a pivotal role in mobilizing common interest projects such as Community Based Schools, village pipeline repair and road repair projects. Initially faced by strong resistance and opposition from her family to start a business, Sifat Gul with the support of the FMFB and her sheer commitment, confidence and hard work succeeded in bringing a positive change in her household and continues to be a social change agent.

Source: http://www.bwtp.org/news/november2007/firstmicrofinance-bank.pdf; accessed 15 February 2010.

arrangements, but provide access to capital that was not possible due to economic, cultural or historical reasons. The Bank offers a full range of financial products, such as deposits and loans but also transfer of funds. It provides different loan products, adapted to its diverse clientele, in urban and rural regions. The most attractive of its loan schemes is its group loan, using village banking methodology, which is available in rural areas. Other loans include urban group loans, business committee loans and house improvement loans (available to five or more borrowers in village or women organizations). The Bank has expanded to over 100 branches in just five years and is currently found in four major provinces as well as Northern areas of the country.

SUMMARY AND RECOMMENDATIONS

Based on the literature, the chapter has discussed a number of challenges faced by women entrepreneurs in Pakistan, which include:

- gender discriminatory stereotypes, attitudes and routines;
- inadequate structural and institutional support (e.g., micro-financing schemes; legal enforcement and monitoring; training and development); and
- lack of information (e.g., access to finance, markets and networks, literacy, technical and management skills).

The chapter has discussed that because of patriarchal traditions and social stereotypes, women entrepreneurs in Pakistan face greater challenges in starting and managing their own businesses. The deeply rooted discriminatory socio-cultural traditions are also embedded in the institutional support mechanisms. Consequently, there are inadequate legal and financial structures provided by the government and the civil society to encourage women's entrepreneurship in Pakistan.

However, despite such barriers, the stories of Pakistani women's success suggest that once such women are given access to adequate resources (e.g., training and finance), they are very capable of starting the motor of economic development. Indeed, this dream cannot be realized without raising consciousness among policy-makers, investors and bankers, and women and men generally that women's entrepreneurship represents an untapped reservoir for job creation, economic growth and social cohesion. To achieve that aim, the following steps may be considered:

1. *An enlightened religio-cultural approach to gender equality.* There is a need to promote an enlightened, gender-egalitarian approach to the status and roles of women in Pakistani society (see Syed, 2008). Such an approach may be realized through an integrated promotion of gender equality in socio-political and religious discourses, academic texts, media and public policy. It can help change the stereotypical images of women in the society, encourage family support and help women both in venturing into and managing business. Also, tribal and religious taboos on women's mobility outside their home need to be publicly contested and demolished. Media can play an important role by portraying an egalitarian image of the 'Muslim woman', who has a right equal to her male counterpart to acquire knowledge through education, to own property and to manage her own business.

2. *Structural and institutional support.* Since women have generally less access to external funding than men, their businesses tend to be concentrated in the services sector, requiring small initial capital outlay and less technical knowledge. In line with its initiatives of the FWBL and PPAF, the government may reinforce and expand flexible banking policies especially for women. This will be particularly useful given the unavailability of collateral to women entrepreneurs. Public–private partnership can be one possible way forward to achieve that aim. Furthermore, policy-makers may consider designing and implementing positive discrimination policies to put women entrepreneurs on a level playing field with their male counterparts. For example, the State Bank of Pakistan may encourage banks to design and advertise products customized to women's needs and constraints and to allocate amounts in the total lending portfolio for women entrepreneurs (Sajjad and Raza, 2007). Similarly, the government may play a vital role in providing/enforcing women-friendly work structures and services as more women would be able to embark upon business initiatives.

3. *Facilitation of women's mobility outside their homes.* Women's mobility outsides their home can be facilitated through a number of measures, for example, by providing adequate public transport for commutation. This is particularly important in Lahore, Karachi and other urban areas where more and more women are coming out to work, and the need for transportation facilities by women has increased dramatically (Shabbir, 1995). Indeed, families would not like their women to commute if there are inadequate commutation options available. Similarly, childcare facilities

and flexible work arrangements can be provided in organizations to facilitate female employment.

4. *Support networks.* In order to promote women's entrepreneurship, established women entrepreneurs may develop and expand their networks to help budding women entrepreneurs, particularly those operating at the micro-level. Such networks may also help in identifying and filling in any marketing and management gaps. The existing networks may review their strategies and activities to play an important role in women entrepreneurs' business development. For local markets, such support may be in the form of help with forecasting market and financial trends. Business support institutions may develop a mechanism to support women entrepreneurs in tapping international markets. Last but not least, women entrepreneurs themselves will need to adopt a more proactive approach to learning their own profession, its financing and marketing, and designing and implementing efficient and effective management plans.

5. *Attention to context.* Research suggests that women-only training can play an important role in developing women's leadership skills, and in the enhancement of their careers (Vinnicombe and Singh, 2003). In view of the Islamic institution of female modesty, women-only training opportunities can be deployed to enhance business management skills in Muslim entrepreneurs. Women-only entrepreneurship training programmes in addition to other support mechanisms such as mentoring and coaching can provide women with an opportunity to learn business management in a socially acceptable environment (Roomi, 2005b). This context-specific approach may also be considered in other aspects of entrepreneurship, for example, interest-free Islamic micro-financing.

6. *Recognition of individual differences.* Finally, taking into account individual differences, understanding the different goals that women may have for business ownership and the relationship between these goals and the structural factors that influence start-up can be of great help to researchers as well as policy-makers working to promote women's entrepreneurship (Shabbir and Di Gregorio, 1996). This understanding can lead to the development of policies and programmes of support that not only recognize that there are different goals that women have for wanting to start a business but also that their needs and experiences may vary according to their particular goals for business ownership.

REFERENCES

Aldrich, H. (1989), 'Networking among women entrepreneurs', in O. Hagan, C. Rivchun and D. Sexton (eds), *Women-owned Businesses*, New York: Praeger, pp. 103–32.

Amjad, A. (2007), 'Role of WBIC in women entrepreneurship development', presentation by the Project Director, Women Business Incubation Center, SMEDA.

Arif, G.M. and K.H. Sheikh, (n.d.), 'Women's employment concerns and working conditions in Pakistan', PIDE Workshop Paper, available at: http://www.ilo.org/wcmsp5/groups/public/---ed_mas/---eval/documents/publication/wcms_110147.pdf; accessed 16 February 2010.

Asia Money (2005), 'Women at work in Pakistan', **16**(2), March 2005.

Bari, F. (2000), *Women in Pakistan: Country Briefing Paper*, Manila: Asian Development Bank.

Cantando, M. (2006), *The Woman's Advantage: 20 Women Entrepreneurs Show You What it Takes to Grow Your Business*, Chicago, IL: Kaplan.

CEDAW (2005), *The Convention on the Elimination of all Forms of Discrimination against Women*, Pakistan Report, August.

CIA (2008), *The World Factbook: Pakistan*, available at: https://www.cia.gov/library/publications/the-world-factbook/geos/pk.html; accessed 11 February 2010.

Cooper, A.C., T.B. Folta and C. Woo (1995), 'Entrepreneurial information search', *Journal of Business Venturing*, **10**(2), 107–20.

Ericksen, G.K. (1999), *Women Entrepreneurs Only: 12 Women Entrepreneurs Tell the Stories of their Success*, New York, NY: John Wiley.

FBS (Federal Bureau of Statistics) (2006), *Pakistan Labour Force Survey 2006*, Islamabad: Government of Pakistan.

FBS (Federal Bureau of Statistics) (2007), *Pakistan Labour Force Survey 2007*, Islamabad: Government of Pakistan.

Fielden, S.L. and M.J. Davidson (2005), *International Handbook of Women and Small Business Entrepreneurship*, Cheltenham, UK and Northampton, MA: USA: Edward Elgar.

FWBL (2005), *Annual Report 2005, First Women Bank Limited*, available at: http://www.fwbl.com.pk/cr1.html; accessed 15 February 2010.

Gillani, W. (2003), 'No policy framework to address women entrepreneurs', *Daily Times*, Lahore, 17 April.

Goheer, N.A. (2003), *Women Entrepreneurs in Pakistan: How to Improve their Bargaining Power*, Geneva: International Labour Organization.

Haque, N. (2006), 'Awake the sleeper within: releasing the energy of stifled domestic commerce!', PIDE Working Papers No.11, Islamabad: Pakistan Institute of Development Economics.

Haque, N. (2007), 'Entrepreneurship in Pakistan', PIDE Working Paper No. 29, Islamabad: Pakistan Institute of Development Economics.

Hughes, K.D. (2003), 'Pushed or pulled? Women's entry into self-employment and small business ownership', *Gender, Work and Organization*, **10**(4), 433–54.

Hussain, I. (1999), *Pakistan: the Economy of an Elitist State*, New York: Oxford University Press.

IFC (International Finance Corporation) (2007), 'Gender entrepreneurship markets, GEM Country Brief: Pakistan', Paper No. 44197, February.

Khatoon, A. (2002), 'Women entrepreneurs in Pakistan', *Economic Review*, 7, 22–3.

Roomi, M.A. (2005a), 'Women entrepreneurs in Pakistan: profile, challenges and practical recommendations', paper presented at the 51st ICSB Conference, Washington, DC, June, available at: http://www.sbaer.uca.edu/Research/icsb/2005/164.pdf; accessed 15 February 2010.

Roomi, M.A. (2005b), 'The impact of women-only entrepreneurship training in Islamic society', paper presented at the 28th National Conference of the Institute for Small Business and Entrepreneurship, Blackpool, UK, 1–3 November.

Sajjad, A. and A. Raza (2007), *Access to Finance for Female Entrepreneurs in Pakistan*, a report by The Association of Chartered Certified Accountants Pakistan.

Shabbir, A. (1995), 'How gender affects business start-up: evidence from Pakistan', *Small Enterprise Development Journal*, **6**(1), 25–33.

Shabbir, A. and S. Di Gregorio (1996), 'An examination of the relationship between women's personal goals and structural factors', *Journal of Business Venturing*, **11**(6), 507–30.

SMEDA (2005), 'Small and medium enterprises in Pakistan', presentation by SMEDA delegate on 20 May 2005 available at: www.sbp.org.pk/bpd/Conference/Day_One/SME_in_Pakistan.ppt; accessed 15 February 2010.

SMEDA (2006), *SME-led Economic Growth – Creating Jobs and Reducing Poverty*, Small and Medium Enterprise Development Authority, Government of Pakistan.

SMEDA (2008), 'Pakistan: business training for women by SMEDA', 31 January, available at: http://www.fibre2fashion.com/news/textile-news/newsdetails.aspx?news_id=49222; accessed 15 February 2010.

SME Policy (2007), *SME-led Economic Growth – Creating Jobs and Reducing Poverty*, SMEDA, Ministry of Industries, Production and Special Initiatives, Government of Pakistan.

Subohi, A. (2006), 'Competition driven sustained growth', *Daily Dawn*, Karachi, 16 October.

Syed, J. (2008), 'A context-specific perspective of equal employment opportunity in Islamic societies', *Asia Pacific Journal of Management*, **25**(1), 135–51.

Syed, J., M. Ozbilgin, D. Torunoglu and F. Ali (2009), 'Rescuing gender equality from the false dichotomies of secularism versus Shariah in Muslim majority countries', *Women's Studies International Forum*, **32**(2), March–April, 67–79.

UNDP (United Nations Development Programme) (1996), Preparatory Assistance (PA) Document Number: PAK/96/016 – *Facilitating Women's Mobility*, Islamabad: UNDP.

UNDP (United Nations Development Programme) (2007), *Human Development Report 2007–08: Fighting Climate Change*, New York: UNDP.

UNICEF (United Nations Children's Fund) (2007), *The State of the World's Children: Women and Children*

– *the Double Dividend of Gender Equality*, available at: http://www.unicef.org/sowc07/docs/sowc07.pdf; accessed 15 February 2010.
Vinnicombe, S. and V. Singh (2003), 'Women-only management training: an essential part of women's leadership development', *Journal of Change Management*, **3**(4), 294–306.
Zaidi, A. (2005), *Issues in Pakistan's Economy*, Karachi: Oxford University Press.

12 Portugal

Christina Reis

INTRODUCTION

This chapter investigates the socioeconomic context for self-employed women within Portugal and it begins with an overview of the Portuguese labour market. The position of women in the Portuguese labour market is remarkable for their full-time employment and their contextual development of attaining domestic support. Regarding occupational segregation, women tend to be concentrated in a few sectors and vertical segregation becomes more masculine at higher hierarchical levels (Guerreiro, 1996; MTSS, 2002). Having described women's positioning within the Portuguese labour market, the focus shifts to business enterprises. Regarding acquisitions of capital and restrictions in Portugal, there are interventional policies supported by the Portuguese government (QREN, 2007), which show potential for augmenting Portuguese women's entrepreneurship. These interventions propose training, consultancy services, technical assistance and access to other enterprises' networks for information that may contribute to the successful start of a new business. However, it is still too early to know the relevance of these governmental interventions on the increase in successful self-employment, a trend that should be analysed not only at the start-up level but also at the level of business sustainability. Since the construction of the entrepreneur in Portugal is male (Ahl, 2007), it is necessary to reflect on the situations of women who have been recognized as successful entrepreneurs in their local cultural and socioeconomic contexts. Not all women have the same experiences, and there are many standpoints and voices (Billing and Sundin, 2006). To illustrate these struggles, therefore, two case studies are presented. Finally, the chapter concludes with a brief summary and suggestions for the development of business for self-employed women particularly related to policies and their sustainability are discussed.

THE POSITION OF WOMEN IN EMPLOYMENT IN PORTUGAL

In Portugal, approximately 55.8 per cent of the female population of working age (i.e., over 15 years old) are in formal employment or self-employed (INE, 2006). Employment rates for women and men over 15 years old are 62 per cent and 73.9 per cent respectively (ibid.). In the context of developed economies, Portugal has a labour market with a higher rate of full employment when compared with the average of the European Union. This difference is particularly evident in the case of female employment when compared with the European Union average of female employment, which is 57.3 per cent, whereas Portugal is 4.3 per cent higher (Eurostat, 2006).

In Portugal women prevail in intellectual and scientific professions by 57.2 per cent, in administrative positions by 61.2 per cent, services and sales by 68.3 per cent, and among non-qualified occupations by 62.5 per cent (INE, 2006). However, despite the process of modernization experienced by Portugal during the last 30 years, science has been institutionalized as a male-dominated profession (Amâncio, 2003). The proportion of women in the labour force has increased in most sectors but occupational segregation remains largely unchallenged. Women tend to be concentrated in a few sectors, particular in health and social services and the clothing industry and it is unusual to find women in male-dominated sectors such as the motor or the building industries (MTSS, 2002). Indeed, Guerreiro (1996) suggests that vertical segregation is accentuated and becomes more masculine at higher hierarchical levels.

The position of women in the Portuguese labour market is characterized by their full-time employment and their contextual development of attaining domestic support. The high percentage of full-time employment in Portugal, which strongly contrasts with the other Southern European countries (Spain, Italy and Greece), cannot be easily explained (Hakim, 2000). However, in Hakim's large longitudinal study, which compares preferences among women cross-nationally in respect to employment, she cannot explain the differences for Portugal in relation to the other countries '[it is not clear] why it differs from the pattern in the other three southern European countries, and why full-time work rates are so high in the absence of any institutional supports and child care services that are considered essential elsewhere in Europe' (p. 172).

Ruivo (1998) regards the low level of earnings in Portugal as the main reason why it is necessary for many families to have two incomes. Even so, this is not the case with high-income Portuguese women (whether self-employed or otherwise) and these women are more likely to employ low-waged domestic servants. In addition to domestic servants, domestic support from female relatives is another characteristic of the Portuguese situation. According to Reis (2004) the class structure seems to be polarized into two extremes. One extreme includes the women who are professionally qualified, self-employed or materially protected by their own family members. At the other extreme, women offer themselves to other families for work in lower-skilled and poorly paid jobs in the domestic sphere, in the manufacturing sector and in the agricultural sector. Although the proportion of workers in the agricultural sector in Portugal has decreased heavily since the beginning of the 1990s, it is still much larger than in most other European countries (Fink, 1999). Many female servants hail from other nations such as the Ukraine and Brazil, or from rural backgrounds, and represent the first generation in urban areas. Either these women did not have easy access to education or their families did not push them towards professional training because they were supposed to work for the family and on the farms. This situation is also connected to Portugal's relatively late industrialization (ibid.).

Since payment in Portugal is low in general (Baukloh, 2001), and especially in the manufacturing industry (Eurostat News Release, 2001), female domestic servants see themselves as having a similar status to female workers in manufacturing. If they provide domestic services on a normal, regular basis, they get an employment contract that offers at least some social protection. Female domestic servants who have a labour contract organized by the local labour authority, have the possibility of flexible work (i.e., doing several hours in different families' houses), which unskilled manufacturing work does not always offer. The legal and cultural status of domestic work continues to be low, but not in the same sense as before because it is better regulated and offers similar social protection (see Hampson, 1997) to jobs in manufacturing or the service industries. However, the work of domestic servants continues to be systematically performed by women and beyond the public eye, because it is work usually done in the home and subject to all the disadvantages of a relationship of personal dependency and of demeaning tasks. Some women combine the help of domestic servants with that of other females from their kinship. Leonardo (1987) explains about female kinship work: 'even the wealthiest women must negotiate the timing and venue of holidays and other family rituals with their kinswomen' (p. 449). Kinship work is an alternative to paid domestic support and additional to the wide use of female servants in Portugal; kinship work (normally performed by the mother of the wife) seems to be very important and taken for granted. Women do not rely exclusively on institutional child care but replace this with female servants whom they trust, or sometimes with female relatives.

The Portuguese market is regulated by legislation and covers direct and indirect acts of sex discrimination. Therefore overt discrimination is illegal. However, the 'gender pay gap' is still significant in various contexts and women continue to earn considerably less than men on average (Blau and Khan, 2007). In Portugal, the higher the level of qualifications, the higher the income differences between men and women. This situation is particularly noticeable at higher management levels, where women earn 24 per cent less than men in their basic salaries and 30 per cent less in general remuneration gains (MTSS/DGEEP, 2005).

Within Portugal, only 26.7 per cent of all managerial positions are occupied by women. From 1995 to 1999, however, there was a 27 per cent increase in women in management (MTSS, 2002), although women's participation in management decreases with age. Women in management (under 30 years old) account for 32.6 per cent; aged 31–40 years old 28.9 per cent; 41–50 years old 16.2 per cent; and 50 and over 22.5 per cent (MTSS, 2002). From this brief outline on gender and the Portuguese professional labour market, it emerges that although women occupy more than 50 per cent of intellectual and scientific professions and administrative positions, they still experience vertical segregation at higher hierarchical levels. Certainly it is evident that in Portugal, as well as in other countries, in order to obtain recognition, autonomy and flexibility, women frequently choose to enter entrepreneurial careers (e.g., Mallon and Cohen, 2001).

THE CURRENT POSITION OF WOMEN AND SMALL BUSINESS OWNERSHIP

There are limited data for women's entrepreneurial activity in Portugal and the existing data has not been updated since 2004/06. Nevertheless the following section elaborates the current position of self-employed and small-business-owning (SE/SBO) Portuguese women. The latest available data for Portugal from the Global Entrepreneurship Monitor (GEM) report are from 2004 as Portugal is not included in the GEM 2006 report.

Regarding new start-up companies, the Total Entrepreneurial Activity (TEA) for the average rate in the 34 countries covered in the GEM (2004) report dropped to 7.0 per cent. The TEA rate in Portugal followed this general downwards trend, with a significant reduction from 7.1 per cent in 2001 to 4.0 per cent in 2004, signifying that only four people in every 100 aged 18–64 years in the country were actively involved in starting or managing a new firm. According to the GEM 2004 report, Portugal ranked 28th of the 34 countries in TEA. The average TEA rate was lower in Europe than in the other regions, with the EU country average lower than for the non-EU European countries. Portugal ranked only 13th of the 16 EU members, with a TEA rate significantly lower than countries such as Poland, the United Kingdom and Ireland. Furthermore, the GEM 2004 report provided details about the most important entrepreneurial segment in Portugal, the consumer-oriented sector, with 71 per cent of all female entrepreneurs in Portugal engaged in this sector. By contrast, only 18 per cent of female entrepreneurs in Portugal had entrepreneurial activities in the transformation sector (construction, manufacturing, transportation and wholesale distribution), 11 per cent in the business service sector and none within the extractive sector.

Regarding female entrepreneurship, the GEM report says that:

> [a]s with all other GEM 2004 countries, Portugal has more male than female entrepreneurs. However, the proportion of female entrepreneurs in Portugal is substantially higher than in most other countries, with 48 per cent of all entrepreneurs in Portugal being female. This compares to a national average of 38 per cent for the other GEM 2004 countries. (Ibid., p. 7)

It is striking how Portugal is rated differently from all other countries in terms of gender equality and the GEM 2004 report says '[t]here is near gender equality in entrepreneurship in Portugal' (ibid., p. 41). This concluding remark for Portugal is perplexing because there is no explanation for this unique overall difference for Portugal. The gender 'near equality' is explained by the lack of structural development of entrepreneurial activity in the country as a whole. It is possible that there are other cultural constraints influencing these conclusions, such as the Portuguese tendency towards risk aversion (Hofstede, 1991) and that men in general are less entrepreneurially proactive than in other countries in comparison to women of the same nationality. However, these observations are merely speculative. Even so, differences in the type of business and income generation between male and female entrepreneurial activity can be dramatically large. Although the differences in income levels do not sustain the gender differences argument, income levels may offer a better explanation for the differences in gender representation for Portugal, that is, 'Women entrepreneurs tend to come uniformly from all levels of income in Portugal, while male entrepreneurs are predominantly from the upper income levels' (ibid.).

Statistics Portugal provides the most current information available on women's involvement in small business ownership in Portugal. Regrettably, this study has not been updated since 2006. The survey compares the entrepreneurial activity by gender for the last trimester of 2005 and the first trimester of 2006. According to Statistics Portugal (SE/SBO), women in the Portuguese economy are represented in all age groups but are far behind men in terms of entrepreneurial activity (Guerreiro, 1996). According to Statistics Portugal, women decrease in entrepreneurial activity with age in opposition to men who increase their entrepreneurial activity with age. It is in the younger group of women entrepreneurs that the representation is higher. Women less than 30 years old represent 22 per cent of all entrepreneurs in this age group, whereas their representation decreases by half of this percentage beyond age 40 (Figure 12.1).

It is also important to look at the educational level women reached before they started their businesses. The secondary education of Portuguese women entrepreneurs is only 26 per cent compared with the 41 per cent average of other women in the European Union.

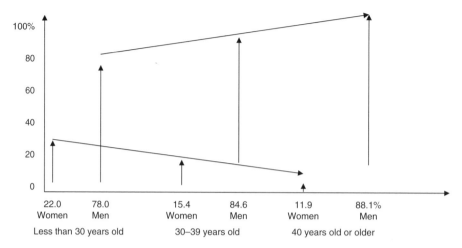

Source: Figures adapted from Statistics Portugal.

Figure 12.1   Start-up entrepreneurs in 2002

Portuguese women entrepreneurs who hold technical or university degrees account for only 16 per cent while the average in the European Union is 20 per cent (Statistics Portugal, 2006). Although the GEM (2004) report suggests that there is evidence for all GEM countries that a person is more likely to be an entrepreneur if he or she possesses more formal education, this information is not broken down by gender. 'This finding is reproduced in Portugal, where the proportion of entrepreneurs with at least secondary or vocational education is higher than in the Portuguese population as a whole' (GEM, 2004, p. 7).

A 61.5 per cent majority of women were employees before starting their own busi-ness, versus 49 per cent of the men in the same circumstances (Statistics Portugal, 2006). However, regarding management experience prior to starting their enterprises, men have 21.9 per cent more experience than women. Again, the higher representation of women is in the lowest age group, that is, women younger than 30 (ibid.).

It is worth noting that 10 per cent of women entrepreneurs developed start-up enter-prises because they were unemployed, while this situation accounts for only 3.9 per cent of men (ibid.). Scase and Goffee (1989) suggest that women searched for self-employment because they regarded it as a means for obtaining a certain degree of autonomy and 'it enables them, if only for limited spheres of their lives, to discard their roles as mothers and wives and to take on independent identities associated with their business' (p. 118).

The rate of women managers of small businesses with fewer than ten employees is 28 per cent, in businesses with between ten and 500 employees 21.7 per cent and in large companies with more than 500 employees 23.2 per cent (MTSS, 2002). However, there are no national data for women owners of business specifying how many people they employed on contracts or directly.

Finally, the source of advice on starting a small business is also important. For women who started their business 20 years ago, friends were crucial to their decision-making during the start-up period. Family and friends accounted for 46.8 per cent, professional contacts 43.1 per cent, while other advisees such as financial institutions accounted for only 4.7 per cent (Statistics Portugal, 2006). Most small business owners, 87.2 per cent in 2002, started their companies with their own savings and only 3.3 per cent had financial support from public organizations (ibid.). It must be noted that these figures do not specify key factors such as gender, age and stage of the business. There is also no reference to the representation of women's SE/SBO revenues and their portion of total revenues for the small business enterprises sector. The same situation can be observed for the industrial location of women entrepreneurs' business and for the degree of female ownership, meaning whether the small business enterprises are 'majority-owned' or 'co-owned' equally by male and female partners.

EXPLORATION OF CONCEPTUAL AND CONTEXTUAL BARRIERS TO FEMALE ENTREPRENEURSHIP

Portuguese women entrepreneurs continue to face various barriers to starting up and maintaining their venture enterprises. During the past decade, Portugal has had several changes in government and political controversies have helped retard business development. It was not until 2005 that a stable government (socialist), elected by a popular majority, occupied the Portuguese parliament. Furthermore, while for 20 years in other developed countries (e.g., Canada) women have received noteworthy levels of government support, it was not until 2007 that Portugal devoted resources to promoting women's entrepreneurship

The National Strategic Reference Framework (QREN), interventional policies developed under this latest governmental agenda, seems to show potential for incrementing Portuguese women's entrepreneurship in Portugal. Although QREN is designed for both men and women, it includes a programme devoted solely to women. This programme, directed to start-ups that show potential in developing innovative business, promotes funding for women entrepreneurs through conquests. However, there is no specific programme assisting more established women entrepreneurs in overcoming barriers to success and growth.

There are other women's enterprise associations[1] that organize business events and meetings as well as providing access to other international associations. In addition, these associations inform women how to access entrepreneurial networks, training, consultancy services and technical assistance. The Industrial Portuguese Association (AIP) is the main entrepreneurial Portuguese association; while it presents similar information to the above associations, it is gender neutral. Some daily news writers (e.g., Afonso, 2007; Ferreira, 2007) describe a belief, widespread in Portugal, that there is no longer any need for women's entrepreneurial associations. Ferreira (2007) interviewed the president of the APME, Ana Silva, by asking her provocatively whether there was *still* the necessity in Portugal for an Association of Women's Entrepreneurs. She replied:

> There is an absolute necessity. If we have a look at the directive board of entrepreneurial associations we can see there are no women represented there. Moreover, women as entrepreneurs have a different vision of entrepreneurial issues and we think we need to transmit this message independently from gender neutral associations. (Adapted and translated from Portuguese)

In this specific situation Ana Silva emphasized the feminine identity:

> We have a different leadership style from men, because women are differently connected with Earth through maternity. Women think long term and work in different ways by looking at space and time differently; this is the reason for women to work well in groups. Their ancestral functions in the family and in the community gave them great strategic vision, which is fundamental in enterprise, and a great capacity to deal with business conflicts. (Adapted and translated from Portuguese)

Silva's perspective on gender identity has its merits; in everyday business interaction, however, women entrepreneurs may risk being manoeuvred into a defensive position rather than enjoying the business advantage she describes. Defensive tactics may emerge when identities are not recognized. However, gender identities shift with context (Burke et al., 2003) and the issue for Portuguese women entrepreneurs is that many individuals are not aware of the barriers faced by self-employed women.

In many contexts employment is constructed around the idea that the worker is a man, who has his day-to-day needs met by a female partner who takes primary responsibility for caring for children or other dependants, allowing him to follow an unbroken career (Wilson, 1999). Partners' attitudes have been discussed in the literature as a barrier for entering and staying in entrepreneurship (Fielden and Dawe, 2004). Such processes blind people to societal inequalities in power and status (Wilson et al., 2007). In this sense, individuals may not see alternatives to the way they deal with their gender subordination. For them, it seems to be natural: other ways of organizing their lives are unthinkable and may not even seem moral. They see women's work in terms of the needs of the job, being a woman, being a man, morality, the proper way to behave, working as a family team, that is, each doing what they are best at (Reis, 2004). Individuals of the oppressed gender often fail to see alternatives to the way their lives are organized, or even to admit they are themselves subordinated (Mill, 1876): 'Frequently such women feel guilt and a sense of failure' (Mulholland, 1996, p. 146). Moreover, their expectations of being a woman make them feel 'normal'; these ideas are already formed by their societies' dominant ways of thinking. Men and women act in 'good faith', and do not see the harm they do to their lives, and, therefore, they do not aim at reflection and changes. Some argue that 'ideology' is a concrete system of representation that positions the subject, and this is the reason why: 'ideology is so hard to pin down or unravel: because it constantly re-interprets while only claiming to re-present reality' (Williamson, 1978, p. 74). Regarding issues of class hierarchies, Derrida (1981) claims that one element in any binary opposition is always privileged over the other and this is what it produces, social and cultural hierarchies (e.g., man–woman). Some other authors (e.g., Prasad, 2005) following Foucault's (1972) notion of discourse perceived as categorizing meaning, explore ideals or subjectivity in discourse (e.g., the legitimacy of the arguments of a speech) and challenge the interpretation of dominant discourses about what is said and not said in respect to management practices.

The assumption that the field of entrepreneurship is masculine has been challenged at both the conceptual level and at the level of everyday life experience (e.g., Allen and Truman, 1993; Guerreiro, 1996; Fielden and Davidson, 2005). Self-employed women face a range of conceptual and structural barriers. In general, the biggest obstacle to career advancement for women is the attitudes, perceptions and behaviours of their male colleagues (Morrison, 1992; Ragins et al., 1998; Shein, 2007). Men's beliefs in their manhood are reinforced by the construction of the entrepreneur as male, rendering women's identity invisible (Ahl, 2007).

Statistics Portugal (2006) offers a list of barriers although they are not broken down by gender. However, for women business owners the most relevant barriers are: management training, getting funding, establishing contacts with clients, finding suppliers and getting adequate personnel. In general, 69 per cent of the entrepreneurs had no management training before starting their business ventures. Getting funding was not important for a 43 per cent plurality of entrepreneurs and somewhat important for some by 29 per cent. Establishing contact with clients was not important for most entrepreneurs by 42.2 per cent and somewhat important for some by 34.55 per cent. Finding suppliers was for most entrepreneurs not important by 64 per cent. Getting adequate personnel is also distributed between being very important for some entrepreneurs by 33.6 per cent and for others not important by 38.9 per cent.

Other reports (e.g., GEM, 2004) are also gender neutral and have similar results to the ones described above. However, there are observational and qualitative data suggesting that women do face unique structural and contextual barriers in developing their business. Therefore, there is an imperative need for further research of gender differences, informing the nature and the extent of barriers faced by Portuguese women entrepreneurs.

Since gender differences in Portugal have been strongly decremented in history, origins and contexts (Amâncio, 1994), before the existence of the few governmental interventions as well as non-profit associations self-employed women relied on the establishment and sustainability of their own business with little support and relied heavily on a range of personal resources. Indeed, in this context, professional women who progressed in their entrepreneurial careers often found creative avenues for achievement (Apter, 1993). Women entrepreneurs' stories have features somehow supported by the literature, whose statistics gender-neutral reports do not disclose. Therefore, the next paragraphs introduce a general literature review of women's individual experiences with the purpose of understanding the two case studies in this chapter.

The history of the concept of entrepreneurial ideology supports the view that an entrepreneur is a person capable of creating a successful economic opportunity or an innovator of a business venture (Say, 1803; Schumpeter, 1934; Schultz, 1961; Hisrich and Peters, 1998). Self-employment can be cultural and contextualized within labour market positioning and experiences (Bannock, 1981; Marlow et al., 2005) and the competences gained through experience seem to be important for the entrepreneur's business success (Henry et al., 2005; Reijonen and Komppula, 2007). Therefore, entrepreneurial success may be influenced by education and training interventions (Gibb, 1987).

Some authors (e.g., Storey, 1994; Hundley, 2001) argue that entrepreneurial capital is acquired before starting a new business venture and is largely due to the proximity of supportive mentorship. Mentorship is an important aspect in supporting the development of women in their professional lives. However, research indicates that self-employed women lack entrepreneurial female role models (Ahl, 2007) and therefore often have to rely on male figures as mentors. Acker (2008) discusses the analogy of helpful men and the lack of feminist support in the academic world. A woman 'must have the characteristics of a stranger, that is, the characteristics of a man or at least a genderless, neutered creature . . . authoritative, domineering, a bit condescending, unconcerned and even unaware of the trivia of keeping daily life going' (p. 289).

It is interesting to note Acker's speculative thoughts about how women attracted the attention of devoted male supporters. Among several suggestions relating to self-employed women are the following points: self-employed women are 'fortunate to have either marriages or very close relationships with men with similar . . . interests' (p. 292); wealthy sponsors; helpful friends; lovers; colleagues; access to their professional circles; and other social support (e.g., professional organizations).

CASE STUDIES: ENGAGING WITH ENTERPRISE

As shown above, individuals have different ways of negotiating resources and adopting entrepreneurial identities in the context of local geographical and environmental opportunities and constraints. In this section, two case studies of self-employed Portuguese women are described. Both women had useful male mentors and in some instances had to emphasize their femininity to gain recognition. Each explains how she achieved a flourishing sustainable business in a time of worldwide economic crisis. Their names have been changed for purposes of anonymity. Although the women presented here come from different backgrounds, they have a lot in common, particularly their overcoming difficulties in developing their enterprises.

BOX 12.1   MARIA

The first case study example is that of female entrepreneur Maria, founder of a successful clothing and costume jewellery company in its early stages of internationalization. Maria is 49 years old and started her business when she was 19. She employs on average 140 employees. Maria's childhood and adolescence were troubled by dissatisfaction with the fact that her family made her work at a local factory, but she did not know what direction to take to improve her situation. When she reached the age of 19 she met her boyfriend, who lived in another town. Since she was working, she had enough money to rent a room in another town but she had to find a new job in order to survive. This was when her boyfriend provided the support she needed to make a radical life change. She left her mother's home and moved to her boyfriend's town. He had a sister who was a high-school teacher of the subject she was unable to pass in her home town where she was studying, and his family rented her a room for an insignificant rent. She only had to pay for herself, her food and other basic expenses. After Maria completed high school, her boyfriend and his sister decided to open a business and included Maria in this venture. They needed a business requiring a low investment that would earn them money, so they decided to open a wool business that sold hand-made pullovers, which were fashionable at the time. Although these pullovers could be found in shops selling yarn for hand-made pullovers, there were no shops in the region specializing in

---

hand-made pullovers. In the meantime her boyfriend's sister was relocated to teach in another town and her boyfriend got another job. As a result, Maria took over full responsibility for the shop, as she was the only one without a job, and the shop was left for her to manage alone. Maria said: 'Everything started here. At the time I felt good working alone. I never got along working with someone else. After these events, I felt that I had gained some stability in my life and I felt good about myself. I was doing what I enjoyed and I felt that the business was improving day by day. I was happy and I had the will to continue to make progress with this business'. During this time, Maria still thought about continuing her studies but her exams did not go well and she decided to apply all her energy to the business she was enjoying. She bought costume jewellery, which she matched with the pullovers in this first shop. She said: 'I am very feminine. I have a passion for female accessories. The proceeds from the sweaters were enough to pay the shop's expenses. This combination of costume jewellery and woollens opened my eyes to my future business'. Maria was not satisfied with her business partnership. Her business partners did not care about or help with the development of the shop. She continued to manage the shop alone. She decided to work towards starting her own business and found a small 8 m^2 space to open a new shop. Her ex-boyfriend helped her find the new shop and provided some backing. 'I didn't have money to buy the shop and I couldn't get a loan. The owner offered to let me pay for the shop in monthly instalments. I negotiated with the owner and agreed to buy everything in the shop, I mean all baby clothes. I could pay a certain amount of rent every month to pay for the shop. I sold all the baby clothes at a reduced price and did some redecoration. Everything was very simple. I started by selling some costume jewellery and in the same day I opened the shop I sold everything. The shop was empty'. She considered it important to recount another detail of overcoming the first barriers at this phase in her life. The money to buy the first jewellery and the money for the shop that her boyfriend sponsored came from her family, more specifically her materially disadvantaged mother. 'My mother never believed I would have any luck with the business because I was very unstable but I said, you lend me the money or I am not your daughter any more'. Maria bought and sold new stock every week. She had more money so she bought more goods. However she spoke about many of the barriers she had to overcome in order to achieve the position she has today. 'I made many trips at night to get in to Lisbon by early morning and come back the same day. In those days, it took four hours to get to Lisbon (while it today takes around two-and-a-half). I made this effort to get the goods to sell the next day. It was this way for a long time. Only later after some years did I have an employee to keep the shop open while I was on these trips'. Maria saw her business expanding step by step as she made these efforts to overcome the barriers. The shop prospered and she had to think about a larger distribution network. 'I could never make plans for the future. I know that the product exists but I have to check whether it is for sale in certain places. If it does not exist I will open a shop there to sell it. I never plan anything'. She describes how she expanded her business: 'I overcame barriers by saving money. I had to save as much as possible. By saving, I mean that I made soup with part of a cabbage and did not go to the supermarket to buy the whole cabbage. I had to save as much as possible and I had a red line. I had to feel this red line. I have to see whether I can advance the business or not and if the expenses are higher, I am obviously not going to take the risk. At that time I was more isolated than insecure because I was expanding my business. I thought, I am alone but I am progressing. I work for what I get. At that time there were no imports like there are today and my business was "peanuts". I used to sell many Indian clothes and I used to travel by train to Paris for a week. I crossed the water by ferry boat, filled the bags and after a week I was back with those clothes to sell. This was how I got things through and the business expanded'. She also described her night trips to get the goods for the next day in her shops. She recommended: 'Things that do not require a large investment but perseverance in our dreams are the most important ones. You have to make sacrifices. Persistence may be connected to sacrifice. I am not sure, but I think sacrifices are always necessary at different levels'. However, Maria warned that even with the new Portuguese government policies, things may not be easier today. 'Things are more difficult today for new starters even if women have access to credit. On the one hand, women entrepreneurs have access to people and studies to help them; on the other hand they are confronted with higher competition and global products. It is more difficult to bring something new into the market or to find a niche in a market; this is where one makes money'. Finally, in relation to domestic support Maria concluded: 'I always had a full-time, live-in maid and this is why I can be here at the company. She is 60 years old and is a second grandmother to my children. She does the housework, does the shopping and takes care of everything necessary'.

BOX 12.2   FRANCISCA

The second case study example focuses on Francisca, a founder of a car leasing company also in its early stages of internationalization. Francisca is 48 years old and started her business in the very male-dominated car repair and petrol sector when she was 27 years old. She employs on average 30 employees. Francisca started work as a company telephone operator and later she moved to an office. She did simple office work at a car repair company for nine years. In the meantime she moved to another company in the rent-a-car sector. 'My parents were divorced and I lived with my mother. I had financial difficulties and I decided to move to another job. I was in charge of buying cars for the company I used to work for and when I was negotiating with a man (a friend I met during car sports events, now deceased), he offered me work at his own company. He invited me to open two rent-a-car franchises in two towns'. She knew how the automobile sector operated but she did not know the car rental business. 'After three years, two friends of mine (one was a director of a financial company and the other had a car dealership), asked me to join them to open a corporate car leasing company. This was new in the market. I like challenges and I immediately agreed to start this venture. The director of the financial company did not go ahead with the business and I opened the company I own today with the other friend. My business partner believed in me and through him I got the necessary money to start this venture. If I had gone to the bank alone to ask for a loan, I would not have got anything at the time even if I had told them that I was a very good professional. This friend gave me courage and told me that I should work for myself and not for others. He had a strategy for our corporate leasing company since he knew that the company would benefit from government advantages. He also knew the car rental sector. This is the way life goes. After this, our company became successful'. Francisca then decided to set up a joint venture with a multinational car rental company to enlarge her market share. She recounted how she overcame the barriers and expanded her business. 'I had this joint venture for ten years. For five years, the business was alright, but in the next five years things didn't go well. Today we have an economic crisis and the strategies of this large company did not match ours. Therefore, I decided to continue my business alone'. 'Everybody in the company was satisfied but these were difficult moments for me since I was finishing ten years of a marriage with another company. We are now doing our own franchising and we are opening corporate leasing dealers in the north and south of Portugal. We are also expanding in the area of tourism. I can see new possibilities in that area'. While Francisca started her corporate leasing company with a business partner (friend), she had to overcome many barriers to start this new business: 'I left all my personal life behind me. I knocked on every door to start this business. It was exhausting and most of the time the people treated me badly and closed the door in my face. I cried a lot, but at the same time I said to myself that I could do it. Many companies told me, we do not do business with women. In this area, other people were already in operation and I had to deal with men and only men. They made my life hell and they gave me the wrong advice. I had to pay back the money every month my friend got for me and I had to think where I was going to get the money to pay what I owed. When I had a car not leased in the business, I was anxious as I had to rent it to make a profit. We never know the people we are renting cars to and this means taking high risks. Today everyone has a credit card, but at that time we might rent a very expensive car to someone who had no money to pay for it. It was difficult to change the mentality of our clients so that they could lease a car instead of owning it. The car sector is constantly changing but we are expanding and internationalizing'. In relation to domestic support Francisca said: 'I have a full-time maid who takes care of everything at home. She cooks the meals and we just sit down and eat. In addition the school takes care of everything and picks the children up at home.'

SUMMARY

This chapter investigates the socioeconomic context for self-employed women within Portugal. Although since 2007 there have been new interventional policies to encourage more women to start up new firms, the impact of these initiatives on women's engagement and the sustainability of their enterprises is yet to be seen. The quite unique and brave Portuguese women who broke the 'glass ceiling' (Moore and Buttner, 1997) in traditional male sectors apparently removed some barriers for other women to enter the same business sector. However, the younger generation of women do not seem to follow their self-employed predecessors in these traditional male-dominated sectors (MTSS, 2002). Interventional policies and programmes may encourage women to enter typical male sectors where growth opportunities are widespread, but this may not necessarily remove the barriers women face. This is well illustrated within male-dominated industries such as car rental and the oil industry.

Certainly, important lessons can be extracted from the case studies presented in this chapter. Male role models and mentors seem to have been important for these women and these supportive men provided personal loans and offered flexible terms of repayment and offered them knowledge and ideas during business start-up. Further, these same men opened doors for these women, granting them access to higher-level business networks. However, when these women were on their own, they experienced hardships with other relationships and friends, where sharing and collaborative problem-solving was problematic. To conclude, what emerges from these case studies is that for women to fit into the Portuguese contextual ideological sense of entrepreneurial success, they need to have the 'street sense' necessary to deal with its 'unwritten' features. There were two main concerns that had to be managed strategically: the start-up of their companies and maintaining sustainability. Both women initially lacked access to bank loans and needed to find someone who would believe in their capabilities and trust them with their private money. They found male sponsors and mentors who helped them to meet their ends. Additionally, while family helped them, this support was not the main financial impulse in their business. For the sustainability of their business, they found respectful local husbands from traditional Portuguese families. They got married and managed their private lives with the support of home helpers (other socially disadvantaged women), who otherwise were only available to socially privileged women.

It is possible that today, with the interventional policies within the governmental framework of QREN, more women will start new businesses. They have gained easier access to loans sponsored by government intervention, entrepreneurial training, consultancy services, technical assistance and access to the networks of other enterprises. Even so, this is no guarantee that they will have successful enterprises. The start-up and sustainability of their enterprises will demand careful supportive interventions, since there are invisible long-term established gender tensions in the Portuguese socioeconomic context. Taking into account the present economic crisis, the recommendations from the women entrepreneurs in the two case studies are that the future of women entrepreneurs in Portugal may be even more unstable than when they started their enterprises. For although government policies may foster success stories of women entrepreneurs, global competition is fiercer than ever.

NOTE

1. Institutions of public interest, non-governmental and non-profit: Association of Entrepreneurial Women in Portugal (AMEP), connected with other women's international networks such as Business and Professional Women (BPW); see http://www.amep.pt/. AMEP is also connected with the Network of Entrepreneurial Women WorldWide (NEWWW): http://www.newww.org/default.aspx and the World Association of Women Entrepreneurs: http://www.fcem.org/www/en/qadoc.asp?arid=3. See also the National Association of Women Entrepreneurs (ANA): http://www.ane.pt/.

REFERENCES

Acker, J. (2008), 'Helpful Men and Feminist Support: More than Double Strangeness', *Gender, Work and Organization*, **15**(3), 288–93.

Afonso, G. (2007), 'O empreendedorismo feminino cresce, mas e invisivel'/'Female Entrepreneurship Grows but is Invisible', Associacao Portuguesa para a Qualidade, ECSI.

Ahl, H. (2007), 'Sex Business in the Toy Store: A Narrative Analysis of a Teaching Case', *Journal of Business Venturing*, **22**(5), 673–93.

Allen, S. and C. Truman (1993), *Women in Business: Perspectives on Women Entrepreneurs*, London, New York: Routledge.

Amâncio, L. (1994), *Masculino e Feminino A Construção Social da Diferença*, Portugal: Edições Afrontamento.

Amâncio, L. (2003), 'Gender and Science in Portugal', *Portuguese Journal of Social Science*, **1**(3), 185–94.

Apter, T. (1993), *Professional Progress: Why Women Still Don't Have Wives*, London: Macmillan Press.

Bannock, G. (1981), *The Economics of Small Firms: Return to the Wilderness*, Oxford: Basil Blackwell.

Baukloh, A.C. (2001), 'Portugal: Vom autoritären Korporatismus zum demokratischen Pluralismus', in W. Reuter and P. Rütters (eds), *Verbände und Verbandssysteme in Westeuropa*, Opladen: Leske und Budrich.

Billing,Y.D. and E. Sundin (2006), 'From Managing Equality to Managing Diversity. A Critical Scandinavian Perspective on Gender and Workplace Diversity', in A.M. Konrad, P. Prasad and J.K. Pringle (eds), *Handbook of Workplace Diversity*, London, Thousand Oaks, New Delhi: Sage Publications.

Blau, F. and L. Khan (2007), 'The Gender Pay Gap: Have Women Gone as Far as They Can?', *Academy of Management Perspectives*, February, 1–23.

Burke, P.J., T.J. Owens, R. Serpe and P.A. Thoits (2003), *Advances in Identity Theory and Research*, New York: Springer.

Derrida, J. (1981), *Positions*, London: Athlone Press.

Eurostat (2006), *EU Labour Force Survey*, Luxemburg, Office des Publications Officielles des Communautés Européennes.

Eurostat News Release (2001), 'Hourly labour costs in industry and services in 1999. Member States labour costs differ by a factor of up to four. Euro-zone and Japan higher than USA', No. 28/01, 12 March.

Ferreira, A.R. (2007), 'A Banca em Portugal e uma Mentira'/'The Portuguese Banks are Unfaithful', Correio Manha.

Fielden, S.L. and M. Davidson (2005), *International Handbook of Women and Small Business Entrepreneurship*, Cheltenham, UK and Northampton, MA, USA: Edward Elgar.

Fielden, S.L. and A. Dawe (2004), 'Entrepreneurship and Social Inclusion', *Women in Management Review*, **19**(3), 139–42.

Fink, M. (1999), 'Atypische Beschäftigung in Großbritannien', in E. Talos (ed.), *Aptypische Beschäftigung. Internationale Trends und sozialstaatliche Regelungen*, Wien: Manz.

Foucault, P. (1972), *The Archaeology of Knowledge and the Discourse on Language*, New York: Pantheon Books.

GEM (2004), *The Global Entrepreneurship Monitor, Portugal Executive Report*, Nova Forum.

Gibb, A.A. (1987), 'Enterprise Culture – Its Meaning and Implications for Education and Training', *Journal of European Industrial Training*, **11**(2), 3–38.

Guerreiro, M.D. (1996), *Famílias na Actividade Empresarial*, Lisbon: Celta Editora.

Hakim, C. (2000), *Work–Lifestyle Choices in the 21st Century: Preference Theory*, Oxford: Oxford University Press.

Hampson, J. (1997), 'Social Protection and Social Insurance in Portugal', in J. Clasen (eds), *Social Insurance in Europe*, Bristol: Policy Press.

Henry, C., F. Hill and C. Leitch (2005), 'Entrepreneurship Education and Training: Can Entrepreneurship Be Taught? Part I', *Education+Training*, **47**(2), 98–111.

Hisrich, R.D. and M.P. Peters (1998), *Entrepreneurship*, 4th edition, Boston, MA: Irwin, McGraw Hill.

Hofstede, G.H. (1991), *Cultures and Organizations: Software of the Mind*, London, New York: McGraw-Hill.

Hundley, G. (2001), 'Why Women Earn Less than Men in Self-employment', *Journal of Labor Research*, **12**(4), 817–29.

INE (2006), *Inquerito ao Emprego/Employment Survey*, Portugal.

Leonardo, M. di (1987), 'The Female World of Cards and Holidays: Women Families and the Work of Kinship', *Signs*, **12**(3), 440–53.

Mallon, M. and L. Cohen (2001), 'Time for a Change? Women's Accounts of the Move from Organizational Careers to Self-employment', *British Journal of Management*, **12**(3), 217–30.

Marlow, S., D. Patton and M. Ram (2005), *Managing Labour in Small Firms*, London, New York, Routledge.

Mill, J.S. (1876), *L'assujettissement des femmes*, Paris: Guillaumin.

Moore, D.P. and E.H. Buttner (1997), *Women Entrepreneurs: Moving Beyond the Glass Ceiling*, Thousand Oaks: Sage Publications.

Morrison, A.M. (1992), *The New Leaders*, San Francisco, CA: Jossey-Bass

MTSS (2002), Ministerio do Trabalho e Solidariedade Social/Ministry of Employment and Social Security, Estatisticas/Statistics, Portugal.

MTSS/DGEEP (2005), *Quadro de Pessoal/Framework of Personnel* – translated, Portugal.

Mulholland, K. (1996), 'Entrepreneurialism, Masculinities and the Self-made Man', in D. Collinson, and J. Hearn (eds), *Men as Managers, Managers as Men: Critical Perspectives on Men, Masculinities and Management*, London, Thousand Oaks, New Delhi: Sage Publications.

Prasad, P. (2005), *Crafting Qualitative Research*, New York: M.E. Sharpe.

QREN (2007), Quadro de Referencia Nacional Estrategico/National Strategic Reference Framework, Portugal.

Ragins, B.R., B. Townsend and M.C. Mattis (1998), 'Gender Gap in the Executive Suite: CEOs and Female Executives Report on Breaking the Glass Ceiling', *Academy of Management Executive*, **12**(1), 28–42.

Reijonen, H. and R. Komppula (2007), 'Perceptions of Success and its Effect on Small Firm Performance', *Journal of Small and Enterprise Development*, **14**(4), 689–701.

Reis, C. (2004), *Men Working as Managers in a European Multinational Company*, Munich and Mering: Rainer Hampp Verlag.

Ruivo, M.P. (1998), 'Why is Part-time Work so Low in Portugal and Spain?', in J. O'Reilly and C. Fagan (eds), *Part-time Prospects. An International Comparison of Part-time Work in Europe, North America and the Pacific Rim*, London, New York: Routledge.

Say, J.B. (1803), *A Treatise on Political Economy, Distribution and Consumption of Wealth*, New York, NY: A.M. Kelley Publishers.

Scase, R. and R. Goffee (1989), *Reluctant Managers: Their Work and Lifestyles*, London: Unwin Hyman.

Schultz, T. (1961), 'Investment in Human Capital', *The American Economic Review*, **51**(1), 1–17.

Schumpeter, J. (1934), *The Theory of Economic Development*, Cambridge, MA: Harvard University Press.

Shein, W.E. (2007), 'Women in Management: Reflections and Projections', *Women in Management Review*, **22**(1), 6–18.

Statistics Portugal (2002, 2005, 2006), *Factores de Sucesso das Iniciativas Empresariais*, DEE/Servico de Estatisticas das Empresas.

Storey, D. (1994), *Understanding the Small Firm Sector*, London: Routledge.

Williamson, J. (1978), *Decoding Advertisements: Ideology and Meaning in Advertising*, London: Marion Boyars.

Wilson, F. (1999), 'Genderquake? Did You Feel the Earth Move?', *Organization*, **6**(3), 529–41.

Wilson, F., S. Carter and E. Shaw (2007), 'Bank Loan Officers' Perceptions of Business Owners: The Role of Gender', *British Journal of Management*, **18**(2), 154–72.

13 Russia
Anna Shuvalova

INTRODUCTION

The emergence of a small and medium enterprise sector and conditions that support new businesses are key elements in any new market economy, and entrepreneurs or business owners are essential actors (Aidis et al., 2005, p. 1). Russia's entrepreneurial potential stems from vast supplies of natural resources and a well-educated population (Wells et al., 2003). Ageev et al. (1995, p. 375) view Russian entrepreneurship 'on the leading edge of radical economic and political transformation of the society that should lead to new business developments, and improved quality of life'. Russian women, well educated and represented in the labour force in large numbers, are positioned to be key contributors to this transformation.

Culture and political-economic history affect the potential for entrepreneurship (Mueller and Goic, 2002, p. 399) as they define the way people regard the place of women in society, and therefore influence women entrepreneurs' self-perception and shape their behaviour by imposing certain visible and invisible rules of social etiquette. Aidis et al. (2005, p. 1) believe that women entrepreneurs are of special significance in a transition context, because they tend to more frequently employ other women, which helps to reduce the effect of discrimination against women in the labour market, and because female business owners can serve as role models for younger generations by demonstrating new opportunities for employment.

This chapter begins by looking at the historical, legal and cultural context of Russia and its effect on the position of Russian women in employment and social life. It distinguishes four historical periods: the tsarist period – from the nineteenth century till the revolution of 1917; the Soviet period, post-Revolution; the transition period, starting with Gorbachev's perestroika from 1987 to 2000; and the modern period from 2000 to 2007. The following section gives an overview of female entrepreneurship in Russia, providing some statistical data; the numbers of women in small businesses and their activity according to industry sector; and the women's personal characteristics and motives. The subsequent section discusses structural and contextual barriers to female entrepreneurship, which arose mainly from underdeveloped institutions and business infrastructure. The next section describes three stories of successful women entrepreneurs and the final section summarizes the information discussed in the chapter and gives some recommendations for Russian women who aspire to become entrepreneurs.

THE POSITION OF WOMEN IN EMPLOYMENT IN RUSSIA

Tsarist Period

Patriarchal traditions in Russian society were very strong during the tsarist period. The prevailing attitude held that a woman's single most important function was to give birth to offspring, that motherhood was her supreme role, biologically determined for her by God – the ultimate authority in tsarist Russia. The legislation of the time precluded women from holding government offices, seeking political appointments, and engaging in economic management or professional occupations such as the law, architecture and engineering (Tonchu, 1998).

In 1861, when Alexander II enacted the Emancipation Reform that abolished serfdom, many more Russians, including Russian women from the peasant classes, found that they could earn a decent living in the city plying a trade or marketing their skills. Initially, the law allowed women to work in public and government organizations only in secretarial positions: as typists, stenographers, typesetters or bookbinders. They were also permitted to work as midwives, pharmacists, telephonists, doctors, or shop clerks. However, women in trade were often judged harshly by many members of society, who saw economic activity by women as undermining moral principles (Riasanovsky, 2000).

Academia was one notable exception: the first President of the Russian Academy of Sciences, and the first woman to head an Academy of Sciences anywhere, was Catherine Vorontsova-Dashkova in 1784 (Troyat, 1980). Perhaps because of such examples, even in tsarist times, there were some extraordinary women whom nothing could stop from displaying entrepreneurial talent. There were women, mainly from the aristocratic class, who proved themselves especially bright in the fields of education and culture: they organized brilliant literary and musical salons, published journals and participated in literary and public activities. Sometimes they even headed industrial enterprises following their husband's, father's or brother's death. Women worked in different trading institutions, opened kindergartens, made prints using lithographs, organized charity societies for poor women and orphans and sometimes ran their own shops (Tonchu, 1998).

Soviet Period

The revolution of 1917, which wanted to destroy everything old, attempted to change the patriarchal tradition. During the first years of Soviet power there was a boom in policies and practices with respect to equal rights for men and women (Ziryanov, 1994, p. 124). The Soviet government passed laws that protected women's work and motherhood and encouraged women's equal participation in the labour force by creating the infrastructure that provided the possibility to combine work with family and domestic responsibilities. Many day nurseries, kindergartens and summer camps for scholars were created (Sukovataya, 2002a, p. 42) and the policy of 'illiteracy liquidation', which covered women as well as men, allowed women to become a notable part of a workforce and enlarged their place in the labour market (Ziryanov, 1994, p. 147). Through the 1970s and 1980s the share of women in employment was around 51 per cent (Aivazova,

Table 13.1   Share of women in certain professions

Profession	Share of Women (%)
Economists and accountants	87
Teachers	74
Doctors	66
Engineers	60
Agriculturists	45
Researchers	40
Manual workers and labourers	50
Stockmen	70
Conveyer operators	90
Weavers	97
Cleaners, nannies and sick-nurses	98

Source: Gruzdeva and Chertihina (1986).

1998), as authorities guaranteed the right to equal pay for equal work, maintained a relatively high minimum wage, generous maternity leave and day care benefits (Brainerd, 2000, p. 149). In addition, there were official trade unions that defended the rights of workers.

Although the number of qualified women was increasing they were still overrepresented in semi-skilled and low-skilled professional occupations, where wages were low. These included labourers in industrial, construction and agricultural enterprises, stockmen, machine-tool and conveyer operators, weavers, cleaners, nannies and sick-nurses (Gruzdeva and Chertihina, 1986; see Table 13.1).

However, although the Soviet Union boasted full employment and a high percentage of women in the labour force, the level of emancipation achieved by Soviet women was exaggerated. During the Soviet period men occupied the leading positions in politics, economy and society, and women were the last to be hired and first to be fired. Even in industries with a high percentage of female employment such as light industry, food processing, teaching and medicine, men were usually responsible for supervision and decision-making while the women had 'auxiliary roles'. In 1986 approximately 700 of 5000 job designations were still closed to women (Wells et al., 2003, p. 63). The shares of women in different managerial positions are shown in Table 13.2. Women earned less than men: in 1989 the proportion of average female to male monthly wages in the Russian republic was 69 per cent (Brainerd, 2000, pp. 151–5).

Women participated in the Soviet political and bureaucratic system. They accounted for 33.1 per cent of deputies in local administration in 1939 and constituted 26 per cent of deputies in the Supreme Soviet in 1952. By 1971 their share reached 45.8 per cent in local administration and 31 per cent in the Supreme Soviet. However, often they were merely in token positions (Wells et al., 2003, p. 62), as they were prevented from entering those levels of political system where decisions were made (Aivazova, 1998). There were only 20.9 per cent of women in the Party, 2.8 per cent in the Central Committee of the Party and the Political Bureau (Politburo – the highest government body in Soviet Union) constituted 100 per cent men (Aivazova, 1998).

Table 13.2   Share of women in different managerial positions

Position	Percentage of Women
Junior researchers	51
Senior researchers	23
Professors and members of the Academy	8.8
Primary school directors	74
Secondary school directors	21
Industrial enterprises' directors	6
Shop superintendants	24
Collective farms' (*kolkhoz*) directors	2

Sources: People's Economy in the Women and Children in the USSR (statistical reference work) (1963); *The Party's Life* newspaper (1965) and *USSR* newspaper (1966) both cited in Aivazova (1998).

Transition Period

The transition to a market economy brought rising prices, increasing unemployment, growing poverty and declining living standards (Wells et al., 2003, p. 64). Privatization of the economy and the demise of the Soviet state were responsible for the wide downgrading of the economic status of women in Post-Communist Russia (Izyumov and Razumnova, 2000, p. 4). Further, the removal of the regulations maintained by the Soviet authorities caused the return of patriarchal attitudes towards women that prevailed prior to the communist era.

Typical reforms during the transition included wage and price liberalization, trade liberalization, privatization of state-owned enterprises, tax and legal reforms. The central wage-setting system was abandoned and replaced by the decentralized informal plant-level negotiations (Brainerd, 2000, p. 158). The trade unions had lost their influence on employers and could not provide protection for employees; after the collapse of the Soviet Union the distribution of jobs passed from the state to private employers (Izyumov and Razumnova, 2000, p. 5). The safety nets of the old system were dismantled and many benefits, such as crèche facilities, medical benefits and maternity leave, previously offered by the state began to disappear. The breakdown of state control over enterprises enabled employers to discriminate against women more openly. Women were increasingly viewed as expensive and unreliable employees and were frequently the first to be laid off (Wells et al., 2003, p. 65).

All these factors resulted in a higher rate of unemployment among women (ibid.) and in 1992, their total number among the officially registered unemployed increased from 43 000 to 417 000. Throughout the 1990s, women's share of official unemployment was approximately two-thirds, fluctuating between 63 and 73 per cent (Federal State Statistics Service, 1992, 1999), although the true extent of unemployment in Russia is much higher than indicated by the official numbers due to widespread compulsory part-time employment, forced early retirements and other factors. Further, the main feature of female unemployment was the high level of educated women (Tonchu, 1998, p. 112).

The system of social security that could provide support for the unemployed was

Table 13.3   Share of women employed in the sectors of economy dominated by women

Sector	Share of Women in 2007 (%)	Share of Women in 2000 (%)
Education	80.8	79.0
Public health and social services	80.3	82.4
Hotels and restaurants	79.6	83.9
Consumer services	70.2	52.0
Finance	68.7	65.1
Trade	60.8	59.6

Source: FSSS (2007c).

destroyed. Unemployment along with rampant inflation led to a slump in the total income of the family, so the needs of women as well as of men to earn additional income have grown. In such conditions starting and running a business, or becoming self-employed, becomes one of the few possibilities left for women to overcome the increasing discrimination in the labour market during the transition period and to contribute to the alleviation of poverty (Wells et al., 2003, p. 67).

Modern Period

In 2007 women made up 49 per cent of the working population in Russia (FSSS, 2007a), although women constituted 63.3 per cent of registered unemployed people (FSSS, 2007b). The average wage of Russian women in 2005 was 39 per cent lower than the average wage of Russian men (Trofimova, 2007) and the number of women in high-paid jobs (more than 25 000 roubles per month) was only 25.2 per cent (ibid.). Women are still concentrated in low-paid jobs, typically in such sectors as public health, education and social services, except for those who work in finance (ibid.). The share of women employed in different sectors of the economy is shown in Table 13.3.

CURRENT POSITION OF WOMEN AND SMALL BUSINESS OWNERS

In the beginning of transition (second half of 1980s) the purpose of female self-employment was the maintenance of the family and was considered as an additional income. Women were employed on individual garden-plots, growing products for small-scale street vending and for domestic consumption. Also, women's activities comprised crafts such as sewing, knitting and embroidery, which did not require capital investment, did not give a big turnover and did not have a large market. But some women progressed from the sphere of small-scale production and entered into the sphere of entrepreneurship (Babaeva and Chirikova, 1996, p. 57).

Women started to enter entrepreneurship in 1991 and the overwhelming majority of them joined the ranks of 'informal' one-person businesses in activities such as the resale of consumer goods, shuttle trade and home-based businesses (nursing, sewing,

Table 13.4   Industrial segregation of Russian women entrepreneurs

Sphere	Share of Female Businesses (%)
Consumer services	60
Light industry	45
Catering	40
Retail trade	40

Source: Babaeva and Chirikova (1996, p. 72).

repair, cleaning, day-care, tutoring) (Izyumov and Razumnova, 2000, p. 8). Alternative registered businesses were derived from the privatization of state enterprises where women held top management positions, that is, the service sector, catering, food and textile industries. By 1996, of the 12 million people in Russia engaged in small business of various kinds, both informal and registered, an estimated 35 per cent were women (Babaeva, 1998, p. 137). However, the official Russian statistics do not give information about the participation of women in entrepreneurship.

Women's businesses still lag behind their male rivals' by sales, revenue and employee number indices, most likely because women usually own businesses in relatively low-revenue, low-labour-intensity industries. The small size of female enterprises is due also to their restricted access to capital – a worldwide phenomenon. Moreover, women prefer to allow more time for themselves and their family, rather than pursue high profits and growth (Babaeva and Chirikova, 1996). These and other factors predetermine the small size of women-owned businesses, causing concentrations of women entrepreneurs in particular sectors, as shown in Table 13.4.

More recently women-led businesses have started to branch out into traditionally male-orientated business sectors, such as manufacturing and construction (Chirikova, 2002, p. 148), although women are not yet visible in the rapidly growing field of small computer-based businesses: sales of computers, software development, data processing and Internet commerce (Izyumov and Razumnova, 2000, p. 16).

The latest data (Gorbulina, 2006) indicates that the share of women entrepreneurs in Russia amounts to almost 40 per cent of the total. Other sources (Vorobyeva, 2008) assert that women make up 80 per cent of small business leaders. In 2007, 6.6 per cent of women were self-employed, with 1.1 per cent being employers, compared with 8 per cent and 1.7 per cent of men, respectively (FSSS, 2007d). According to the Vice-President of the Trade and Industry Committee, Russian women today employ a quarter of Russia's labour force. The rate of growth of women-owned business is 1.7 per cent higher than the same rate in male-owned firms (Pletneva, 2008).

A demographic profile of Russian women entrepreneurs showed that the average age was 41 years, 65 per cent were married, 24 per cent divorced or separated, 3 per cent widowed and 8 per cent never married (Chirikova, 1998, p. 32). One of the particular features of Russian women entrepreneurs is that they are highly educated, with 80 per cent having attained a university degree, although areas of higher education vary widely, as is shown in Table 13.5.

Most of Russian women entrepreneurs can be classified as opportunistic or needs-based entrepreneurs: for 80 per cent of women the choice of the entrepreneurial route

Table 13.5   Education of Russian women entrepreneurs

Area of Education	Percentage Among Women Entrepreneurs
Humanities and fine arts	30
Engineering	27
Finance and economics	15
Science	13
Business	5
Medicine	4
Law	3
Other	3

Source: Chirikova (1998, p. 45).

Table 13.6   Motives of Russian women entrepreneurs

Motive	Percentage of Respondents Who Cited this Motive
Self-realization	40
Personal interest	35
Material stability and money	30
Concern for the people around	25
Professional improvement and promotion	20
Self-assertion	15

Source: Babaeva and Chirikova (1996, p. 78).

was driven more by the external circumstances rather than their own desire. Business itself, in the form of striving for profit, was the main driving force for only for 20 per cent of women (Babaeva and Chirikova, 1996, p. 76) and the motivation of women entrepreneurs is dominated by psychological rather than economical factors (GEM, 2007, p. 7). The most cited motives for Russian female entrepreneurs are shown in Table 13.6.

EXPLORATION OF STRUCTURAL AND CONTEXTUAL BARRIERS TO FEMALE ENTREPRENEURSHIP

In transition economies the influence of the institutional and legal contexts on entrepreneurship is greater than in market economies (Aidis et al., 2005, p. 3). Aidis et al. (ibid., p. 4) suggest that while formal institutions can create the opportunity fields for entrepreneurship, informal institutions can strongly influence the collective and individual perception of entrepreneurial opportunities. Informal institutions such as cultural norms and values shape the way into entrepreneurship and more specifically women's intention to set up a business. Several contextual factors that affect entrepreneurial potential of women can be identified:

- cultural influences;
- level of economic development;
- legislation;
- banking system;
- corruption of authorities;
- criminality of business environment.

The cultural values of a society are deeply rooted and therefore less influenced by experiences of recent economic and political systems and events. Culture has a strong influence over a wide variety of human behaviours including entrepreneurial behaviour (Mueller and Goic, 2002, p. 442) and with regard to female entrepreneurship public attitudes may also restrict participation in economic activities (Aidis et al., 2005, pp. 5–6). Cultural norms, traditions and religion all together mould the presuppositions concerning the roles of men and women. Cultural contextual barriers encountered by women in the establishment and development of business consist of the persistence of social stereotypes, which imply that entrepreneurship is not an appropriate occupation for a woman, as it is not compatible with the role of mother and wife. These stereotypes are rooted in historically strong patriarchal traditions in Russian society. Sukovataya (2002b, pp. 70–75) argues that the existence of myths about women entrepreneurs is the price for entrepreneurial success, that is, that a woman either cannot succeed in business because she cannot take quick decisions and is reluctant to take risk, or has to sacrifice her femininity, sexual attractiveness and family harmony.

Market insufficiency and economic instability caused general uncertainty in every sphere of business (Kuznetsov and Kuznetsova, 2003). Weak institutions and the need to reframe laws, which takes time and expertise, led to a shortage of capital, high transaction and start-up costs. Direct assistance programmes and venture capitalists were scarce; a combination of state regulations and banking policies placed credit out of reach for small and medium-sized enterprises (Kuznetsov and Kuznetsova, 2003). Having dismantled banks in 1917, it would take post-Soviet Russia time and effort to regrow normal, healthy financial institutions and in the interim, small businesses struggled with restricted access to bank capital because of the instability and high risks of the financial markets (Aidis et al., 2005). For 92 per cent of Russian respondents, capital availability was problematic (NFWBO, 1995) and the limited access to financial resources was aggravated by the discriminative attitude of bankers towards women entrepreneurs (Chirikova, 1998). However, sometimes women preferred not to take credits because they were reluctant to increase their risks (Shuvalova, 2009, p. 154).

A special difficulty for women entrepreneurs in Russia was the juridical registration of business, which was a long process, badly organized and often involved bribing (Radaev, 1994). In the latter years this process was improved thanks to the appearance of numerous law firms that helped start-up firms to go through the tedious process of registration more quickly (Chirikova, 2002). However, the registration process remains time-consuming because companies have to register with several authorities: the average time necessary for the registration of a branch or a representative office is approximately five weeks from the date of filing the necessary documents with the accreditation body (Federal Tax Service, 2009). Tax legislation has also been seen as a serious difficulty by the majority of the women entrepreneurs because of its ambiguity, instability and a high tax burden (Aidis et al., 2005). Frequent changes in tax legislation have rendered it difficult for entrepreneurs to keep up to date and to understand what they needed to do. The introduction of new legislation has involved the cost of compliance, as it distracted women entrepreneurs from business activities, diverting resources from more productive activities.

Women entrepreneurs are often excluded from male business networks, as most of them are informal and involve male activities: 'There is a certain loneliness to being a woman in charge of a big enterprise here. Being the boss means men finally take you seriously, but there are other obstacles, not least the tradition among some male business leaders of holding meetings in steamy saunas, with prostitutes and vodka laid on' (Belova, interviewee cited in Stephen, 2006). In addition, the growing competition in Russian markets, which implied that 'one has to fight for every client' (see Galina in Shuvalova, 2009, p. 239), can be related to the structural barriers. Interestingly, business owners thought that it was easier to start up a business in 1990s as the market was yet unsaturated and 'every announcement found a response from the consumer' (ibid.).

Rampant corruption represents another substantial obstacle for women entrepreneurs. They can be denied licences, permits, office space and access to materials unless substantial bribes are paid (Kuznetsov and Kuznetsova, 2003). As Estrin et al. (2005, p. 22) wrote, 'the chaotic business environment that existed while a legal and institutional framework was being developed also gave many opportunities for *nomenklatura*-based networking, and led to an increase in corruption, a failure to enforce property rights and the rise of mafias'. The participants of one author's research (Shuvalova, 2009, p. 41) complained that 'it's impossible to decide any issue without a bribe'. The World Bank report (Kupreshenko, 2008) concluded that Russia is regarded as one of the most corrupt states. To organize a business a Russian entrepreneur, on average, has to go through 12 procedures, get permissions from 50 officials, spend 29 days for registration and pay 200 dollars. The agencies that give the most problems to Russian entrepreneurs are legal bodies; consumer organizations take the second place and fire control, the third place. According to Kupreshenko (ibid.) corruption in Russia has grown and changed in the last few years: entrepreneurs spend less on ordinary bribes, but more on kickbacks (*otkati*) – payments to officials for their assistance in arranging state orders for enterprises.

A common belief in Russia is that organized criminals control much of the Russian economy, and also that these problems exist in no other country (Kuznetsov and Kuznetsova, 2003). The denunciation of capitalists as common gangsters was a key point of communist propaganda that many citizens may simply be clinging to as a way of rationalizing their own economic inertia. Whatever the cause, many entrepreneurs feel obliged to pay for private security, and many others conceal income, export capital, use offshore accounts and evade excise duty (ibid.).

The social context inherited from the Soviet era poisoned many minds against business. As Estrin et al. (2005, p. 23) wrote, 'The culture has been strongly opposed to entrepreneurial activity – little distinction was made in the media or public perception between entrepreneurs and criminals'. Aversion to business and commerce because it is believed to amount to illegal activity still persists, although it is diminishing as more citizens join in, or benefit. Most women doing legitimate business in Russia choose underserved sectors avoiding categories perceived to be more hostile, intensely competitive or fraught with risks (Barsukova, 2001). An example of a risky, intensely competitive business might be selling imported luxury cars; imported luxury gloves or cosmetics, or organic produce, or speciality foods, would be viewed as 'safer for a woman'.

CASE STUDIES: STORIES OF SUCCESS

The following section describes the stories of three women entrepreneurs who succeeded in different spheres of business: trade and restaurants, printing, and audit. They attributed their success to different factors, such as luck, interpersonal and leadership skills, intuition, professionalism and strategic thinking.

BOX 13.1   GALINA

Galina's involvement in entrepreneurship started with an 'acquaintance with Hari Krishna on the underground' (Shuvalova, 2009) at the age of 19 – she was given a book about Hindu religion and an invitation to come to the temple. At that time she was studying mechanization of calculation and statistics and worked as a technical constructor, not enjoying it at all. After four months she left her job (she lied that she had to go to another city to marry to get the permission for dismissal from the Ministry of Labour), joined the 'brotherhood' as she called it and started to trade with esoteric literature. As she had a shortage of money she started to speculate with children's walkie-talkies, selling them at twice the price she had bought them for. Then she decided to speculate with something else and organized a small family business with her husband, which was buying old computers, repairing and selling them. After acquiring the starting capital through their computer business and selling off their flat, they diversified their business into a range of activities, which included selling land and country houses; selling cars; and importing cars from Ukraine. Then when economic stagnation and competition undermined most of their businesses, they invested all their money into the shares of a company, which later became notorious for the biggest financial fraud in Russian history.[1] Galina was trying to prevent her husband from participating in the risky stock exchange game, but he did not listen and they lost everything. One day Galina left her husband, leaving him all the property they had, taking only her child and 700 US dollars. She rented a flat for 350 US dollars and used the remaining 350 US dollars as starting capital for a new business of her own. Following the advice of the spiritual leader of the 'brotherhood', who was very entrepreneurial and promoted the idea of earning money for spiritual goals, Galina started to trade with Indian silver jewelleries and essences in an esoteric shop. This was at a time (1994–95) when oriental culture, including philosophy, design and food, had just started attracting the attention of Russian consumers, and Galina was one of the first to spot this trend. She was travelling to China to buy teapots and souvenirs and was earning a margin of 300–500 per cent by selling them to tearooms and directly to consumers. Then the owner of a vegetarian restaurant offered Galina a tea-shop as a department of his restaurant. In two years Galina became a partner and co-owner of the restaurant. Galina believes that intuition, social skills and quick wit, which helped her in her travelling, are the key elements of her success.

BOX 13.2   LUDMILA

Ludmila started her audit business as a result of her career development and regards it a 'directed fortuity' (Shuvalova, 2009). She studied economic cybernetics in the Moscow Institute of Economics and Statistics and then worked in the Ministry of Defence as a junior researcher. She had her first managerial experience in the Research Institute of Instrument-making, working as a chief of computing studies centre. After 1991 she left the Institute and was offered a job of accountant in a small private firm. In a year she was promoted to the post of chief accountant. Then she studied for an auditing qualification and was employed as an economist in a big bank. Then through personal networks she was offered a job in the department of internal audit in a petrol company and soon became the chief of the department. After the crisis of 1998 she changed her job again, being recommended for the post of deputy director of an audit firm. Then when that firm started to fall to pieces, because she felt responsible to the clients and employees, she created her own audit company inside a big holding company that produced spirits and belonged to her client. Initially this holding was her only client and then she expanded her business using the recommendation of the holding's director and gave him a part of the profit. She built a very clever juridical structure of business, which consisted of an independent audit company that provided audit conclusions and a consulting firm that had a contract for the management of the department of internal audit of her client holding, and offered audit maintenance. Such a structure allowed her to economize on taxes and to provide two kinds of services to the client holding without breaking the law. Ludmila believes that the key secrets of success in business are to be attractive, to 'present yourself successfully from the very beginning', to maintain good relationships with everyone, to care about the prosperity of the clients and 'a little bit of luck'.

BOX 13.3   MARINA

Marina created her printing company because she had had an interest in printing and advertising from a young age. She had a degree in journalism and worked as an editor prior to starting business. She calls herself a 'qualified manager' rather than entrepreneur, though she does not deny having an entrepreneurial talent. She distinguishes between a manager, for whom 'it is not important whether he is working for his own money or for somebody else's' (Shuvalova, 2009), and an owner of capital, for whom it is not important in what sphere he works and who transfers his capital to the spheres with higher yield. She had to become an entrepreneur because at that time there was no employment in the sphere she was interested in, and because she needed more money to maintain her child after her divorce. She was a pioneer in quality printing in Russia. She took a bank loan, as she presented a convincing business plan and proved to be a reliable client by paying off her mortgage credit in time. She bought very expensive equipment in Germany, which did not have equivalents in Russia and gave her a strong competitive advantage. It was the time when glossy magazines had just appeared in the Russian market, and Russian publishers of *Elle, Cosmopolitan, Vogue* and other famous magazines became Marina's clients. Her company has grown to employ 5000 people and inevitably attracted the attention of the authorities who wanted to 'have a hand in a tasty morsel'. She had to sell her company in 2003 because she was 'in the epicentre of a political conflict', when the Ministry of Press wanted to take her company. She even had to live with bodyguards 24 hours a day and had to send her son to study in the UK. But finally she managed to sell the company for a good price. Now she works in the top management of a company in the same sphere of business. Marina believes that the quality of the product, planning ahead, professionalism, clever motivation of employees and an innate disposition to entrepreneurship are key elements of business success.

These three examples show women engaged in different types of businesses: trade, service and production. They based their success on different principles: for Galina it was intuition and social skills; for Ludmila it was self-representation, networking and professionalism and for Marina it was quality, analytical entrepreneurial thinking and charismatic leadership.

SUMMARY AND RECOMMENDATIONS

Russian women have always wanted to play an active role in society. In the tsarist period they did it through organizing music and literature salons, supporting artists and taking an active part in cultural life. During the first years of Soviet government they worked on equal terms with men breaking down the gender segregation of labour. After the war they entered into the scientific sphere and highly qualified jobs, gaining knowledge and professional skills and increasing their human capital. Now they bring their talents into the sphere of management and entrepreneurship and, although they are not yet very large in numbers and face many problems, they are proving capable of managing successful businesses. In addition, despite the persistence of certain sceptical attitudes to female entrepreneurs they are gaining more and more attention, popularity and respect.

The qualitative research conducted by the author, who interviewed 30 women entrepreneurs from Moscow (Shuvalova, 2009, p. 172), showed that the psychological profile of women entrepreneurs include such characteristics as: the need for achievement (22 women), interpersonal skills (26), intuition (23), diligence (19), resilience (18), self-assurance (18), honesty (17), restlessness (16), leadership skills (13), ambition (12), fatalism (11). The qualities traditionally attributed to entrepreneurs, such as risk propensity and locus of control, were not reported by the respondents. In contrast, 17 of them expressed risk aversion, and only seven of them used bank credit. The women from the sample were motivated by factors similar to those that were attributed to Russian female entrepreneurs in general (see Table 13.6). In addition to the motives discovered by Babaeva and Chirikova (1996) the research conducted by the author (Shuvalova, 2009) discovered other motives: creation, independence, achievement, recognition, ownership, fulfilling a dream, psychological rehabilitation, leadership, 'thirst for change' and promotion of an idea or philosophy. Concern for others proved to be one of the most important motives (Shuvalova, 2009, p. 207).

However, Russian women entrepreneurs have had to overcome many difficulties and the majority turn to entrepreneurship not out of choice but out of need. In the newly created private sector of the Russian economy, women entrepreneurs operate under conditions of adversity. Most of this adversity is not female-specific, but rather related to the small business sector situation in Russia. The factors of this adversity are the prolonged macroeconomic crisis, domination of the economy by large monopolistic structures, high level of government corruption (Izyumov and Razumnova, 2000), a criminal business environment (Kuznetsov and Kuznetsova, 2003), social prejudices (Sukovataya, 2002b), shortage of capital (Chirikova, 1998) and ambiguity of legislation (Aidis et al., 2005). The uniqueness of the situation is that Russian women are on average markedly better educated than men (Tonchu, 1998), but unlike male entrepreneurs, many of which 'graduated' from the school of the black-market economy, few women had any business experience before Russia's free-market transition (Estrin et al., 2005, p. 15). This lack of basic business skills among aspiring women entrepreneurs, rather than direct gender discrimination, makes them the underprivileged players in the new Russian economy (Babaeva, 1998, p. 141).

In the conditions of the transition economy, when there is no system that regulates business, success depends highly on people themselves. Informal institutions become especially important in transition economies because formal institutions are weak and unstable. For example, in unstable and unclear legal environments, networks and contacts play a key role in helping entrepreneurs to mobilize resources and to cope with the constraints imposed by highly bureaucratic structures and often unfriendly officials (Chirikova, 1998, pp. 231–45). The examples of Galina and Ludmila (Shuvalova, 2009) illustrated that two women found business opportunities through personal informal networks. Networking depends greatly on social and interpersonal skills (Baron and Markman, 2000, p. 108), as they help effective interaction with others. Specific social skills, such as the ability to read others accurately, make favourable first impressions, adapt to a wide range of social situations and be persuasive, can influence the quality of these interactions. Women entrepreneurs showed an amazing mastery of those skills (Chirikova, 1998; Shuvalova, 2009) and stressed the importance of being pleasant and attractive, caring about other people, being engaged in business and having empathy and emotional intelligence. The change in the value system of society and the shift towards democratic principles contributes to the appearance of a new type of entrepreneur, who uses inspiring charismatic leadership strategies instead of traditional aggressive methods (Chirikova, 2002, p. 168).

Women entrepreneurs see business as a system of human relationships rather than an organizational structure or an instrument of earning money (Shuvalova, 2009, p. 161). Intuition helps women to develop and maintain good and trustful relationships with people, to find like-minded partners and investors and to select reliable employees (pp. 269–305). Intuition also helps women to spot a trend and to be alert to business opportunities, especially in the conditions of an unstable economy, when standard methods of forecasting are unreliable. It does not mean that women entrepreneurs rely exclusively on intuition: they use logic and analytical thinking when dealing with bankers and officials and when solving juridical issues.

The overall conclusion reached is that love and faith were perceived by the respondents to be the most important conditions for success. According to the women interviewed it was their love and/or faith that gave them the energy to do their work, the strength to overcome difficulties, a stimulus for achievement and the empathy to build good personal relationships with employees, clients, partners, investors and even competitors. Love and faith are equally at the core of other factors of success. Love for humankind, that is, a humanitarian outlook, is the key to interpersonal skills; effective human resource management; the pledge of integrity; the serene confidence that maintains inner harmony, providing sources of motivation and strong desire. Faith empowers women to be charismatic inspiring leaders, to ignite others with their vision, to enhance commitment to business; together with advanced knowledge and outcomes, faith or adherence to cherished principles leads to the creation of a good reputation for the company and its leader. Faith that they will succeed, together with intuition and deep-seated motivation, were believed by the respondents to have 'made them lucky' (in Russian, *udacha* means both luck and success). In this way the women in the three case studies believed they could influence outside circumstances by adopting the right mental and behavioural attitude toward external conditions. Furthermore, having love and faith made the women feel successful, as they stated that their inner satisfaction constituted for them the essential, overriding criterion of success (Shuvalova, 2009, pp. 242–95).

NOTE

1. Company 'MMM' was the biggest financial pyramid of 1990s; the shares of the company were bought by 10 million Russian people. In 1997, the company was declared bankrupt, most of the depositors lost their money and the leader Mavrodiy disappeared until 2003 when he was arrested and given five years in prison.

REFERENCES

Ageev, A.I., Gratchev, M.V. and Hisrich, R.D. (1995), 'Entrepreneurship in the Soviet Union and post-socialist Russia', *Small Business Economics*, **7**(5), 365–76.
Aidis, R., Welter, F., Smallbone, D. and Isakova, N. (2005), 'Female entrepreneurship in transition economies: the case of Lithuania and Ukraine', *Feminist Economics*, **13**(2), 1–41.

Aivazova, S.G. (1998), 'Freedom and equality of Soviet women', in S.G. Aivazova (ed.), *Studies of Political Theory and History*, Moscow: RIK, pp. 66–99.

Babaeva, L.V. (1998), 'Russian and American women entrepreneurs', *Socis*, **8**, 134–45.

Babaeva, L.V. and Chirikova, A.E. (1996), 'Women in business', *Socis*, **3**, 55–89.

Baron, R.A. and Markman, G.D. (2000), 'Beyond social capital: how social skills can enhance entrepreneurs' success', *The Academy of Management Executive*, **14**(1), 106–17.

Barsukova, S. Yu. (2001), 'The models of success of women in Soviet and post-Soviet periods: ideological myth creation', *Socis*, **2**, 75–82.

Brainerd, E. (2000), 'Women in transition: changes in gender wage differentials in Eastern Europe and the former Soviet Union', *Industrial and Labor Relations Review*, **54**(1), 138–62.

Chirikova, A.E. (1998), *Woman at the Head of the Firm*, Moscow: Institute of Sociology of Russian Academy of Science.

Chirikova, A.E. (2002), *Female Entrepreneurs in Russia: Conceptual Approaches and Directions of Research*, Moscow: Russian Panorama.

Estrin, S., Klaus, E.M. and Bytchkova, M. (2005), 'Entrepreneurship in transition economies', in M.C. Casson (ed.), *The Oxford Handbook of Entrepreneurship*, Oxford, UK: Oxford University Press, pp. 3–34.

Federal Tax Service (2009), 'Registration of businesses in Russia', available at: http://base.consultant.ru/cons/cgi/online.cgi?req=doc;base=LAW;n=95575;fld=134;dst=4294967295.

FSSS – Federal State Statistics Service (1992, 1999), *Men and Women of Russia*, Statistical Reference Book, Moscow: Goskomstat.

FSSS – Federal State Statistics Service (2007a), 'Employment by sex and occupation', available from: http://www.gks.ru/bgd/regl/B08_13/IssWWW.exe/Stg/d1/05-09.htm; accessed 16 February 2010.

FSSS – Federal State Statistics Service (2007b), 'Number of unemployed', available at: http://www.gks.ru/bgd/regl/b08_11/IssWWW.exe/Stg/d01/06-08.htm; accessed 16 February 2010.

FSSS – Federal State Statistics Service (2007c), 'Share of women in overall employed population by type of economic activity', available at: http://www.gks.ru/bgd/regl/B08_13/IssWWW.exe/Stg/d1/05-07.htm; accessed 16 February 2010.

FSSS – Federal State Statistics Service (2007d), 'The composition of employment in the population according to employee standing in the principal workplace', available at: http://www.gks.ru/bgd/regl/b08_30/IssWWW.exe/Stg/d010/labor224.htm; accessed 16 February 2010.

GEM – Global Entrepreneurship Monitor (2007), *Report on Women and Entrepreneurship* released by The Center for Women's Leadership at Babson College, available at: http://www.gemconsortium.org/document.aspx?id=681; accessed 15 February 2010.

Gorbulina, I. (2006), 'Women's small and medium enterprises – path to overcome poverty', paper presented at the APEC Women Leaders Network Meeting, Vietnam, 2006, available at: http://www.scribd.com/doc/4294394/Irina-Gorbulina-Womens-Small-and-Medium-Enterprises-Path-to-Overcome-Poverty; accessed 16 February 2010.

Gruzdeva, E.B. and Chertihina, E.S. (1986), 'Professional employment of women in the USSR and their wages', *Working Class and Modern World*, **3**, 57–60.

Izyumov, A. and Razumnova, I. (2000), 'Women entrepreneurs in Russia: learning to survive the market', *Journal of Development Entrepreneurship*, **5**(1), 1–19.

Kupreshenko, N.P. (2008), 'Influence of corruption on economic relations in Russian Federation', *Taxes* (special edition), pp. 19–34.

Kuznetsov, A. and Kuznetsova, O. (2003), 'Institutions, business and the State in Russia', *Europe-Asia Studies*, **55**(6), 907–22.

Mueller, S.L. and Goic, S. (2002), 'Entrepreneurial potential in transition economies: a view from tomorrow's leaders', *Journal of Developmental Entrepreneurship*, **7**(4), 399–415.

NFWBO – National Foundation for Women Business Owners (1995), *Women Owned Businesses: Breaking the Boundaries – Progress and Achievement of Women Owned Enterprises*, Silver Spring, MD: NFWBO.

People's Economy in the USSR newspaper (1966), Moscow, pp. 683–710; cited in Aivazova (1998).

Pletneva, S. (2008), 'Business women start up and win', *Personnel Management*, **10**, 6–24.

Radaev, V.V. (1994), *Russian Entrepreneurship in the View of Experts*, Moscow: Russian World.

Riasanovsky, N.V. (2000), *A History of Russia*, Berkeley: UC Berkeley.

Shuvalova, A.S. (2009), 'Russian female entrepreneurs', a thesis submitted for the degree of Doctor of Philosophy, Brunel University, March 2009.

Stephen, Ch. (2006), 'Making a clean sweep', *Irish Times*, **13**, 6 September.

Sukovataya, V.A. (2002a), *Female Entrepreneurship in Soviet and Post-Soviet History*, Minsk: EGU.

Sukovataya, V.A. (2002b), 'Businesswomen: myths and reality', *Socis*, **11**, 69–77.

The Party's Life newspaper (1965), 3, p. 10; cited in Aivazova (1998).

Tonchu, E. (1998), *The History of Female Entrepreneurship in Russia*, Saint Petersburg: Posidelki.

Trofimova, Zh. (2007), 'Businesswomen on secondary roles', *Russian Business-Newspaper*, **598**, 3 April 2007, available at: http://www.rg.ru/2007/04/03/zhenshiny.html; accessed 16 February 2010.
Troyat, H. (1980) *Catherine the Great*, New York: E.P. Dutton.
Vorobyeva, D (2008) 'Businessmen or businesswomen?', *Modern Entrepreneur*, **4**, pp. 12–19.
Wells, B.L., Pfantz, T.J. and Bryne, J.L. (2003), 'Russian women business owners: evidence of entrepreneurship in a transition economy', *Journal of Developmental Entrepreneurship*, **8**(1), 59–73.
Women and Children in the USSR (1963), Moscow, p. 123; statistical reference work.
Ziryanov, P.N. (1994), *The History of Russia*, Moscow: Prosveshenie.

14 South Africa
Babita Mathur-Helm

INTRODUCTION

The present chapter addresses the context of gender empowerment through entrepreneurship for women in South Africa (SA). It begins by introducing the initiatives led by the government to implement opportunities, policies and strategies to promote and develop small businesses, with the special focus on women entrepreneurs. The chapter provides clarity by examining the labour market trends and women's economic status and their contributions within the country's economy. Subsequently, it discusses the current position of women and small business ownership within SA, by pointing out how discrepancies based on different racial, cultural and ethnic backgrounds impact women's advancement in business. Next, some primary constraints to the expansion of women entrepreneurs in SA are discussed, which leads to an exploration of facts about how these barriers and constraints were overcome by them, and how they were converted into success stories. Hence, the chapter takes a look at some of South Africa's women who have gained respect for their entrepreneurial spirit and achievements, by illustrating their success stories in the form of case studies. The chapter summarizes the analysis and discussions raised and concludes by providing recommendations for future research and action.

The availability of entrepreneurs may be considered the most important prerequisite for the economic development of a country (O'Neill and Viljoen, 2001). In 1995, the government of South Africa realized the importance of developing entrepreneurship and supporting small businesses, by drawing up a White Paper clearly stating the national strategy for the development and promotion of small businesses (DTI, 1995). The strategy aimed to take the economy to a higher road, through creation of small, medium and micro-enterprises (SMMEs) as an important means to addressing the challenges of job creation, economic growth and equity. The White Paper distinctly elucidates the development of entrepreneurs and, more specifically, the development of female entrepreneurs, through supportive structures, while the South African culture still needs to illustrate that.

Worldwide, women-owned businesses are the fastest-growing segment of new business start-ups (Mattis, 2004) and numerous opportunities exist for businesswomen in South Africa, especially as entrepreneurs and business owners. The government has started recognizing the need for aligning women and their contributions to the national effort for a faster development and shared economic growth. Moreover, the process is stimulated by the female representation of 43 per cent in the country's national cabinet and 37 per cent in the parliament. Yet, despite the focus on a range of initiatives promoting and supporting women's economic empowerment and entrepreneurship, such as more job creation, economic growth and the implementation of Broad-based Black Economic Empowerment (BBBEE) (Balshaw and Goldberg, 2005), women entrepreneurs remain at the periphery of South Africa's national economy. Hence, this rapid increase in the number of women-owned business start-ups has yet to prove that the South African government has been successful in creating more gender-balanced businesses and marketplaces.

The Department of Trade and Industry (DTI, 2006) report indicates that gender inequality inhibits businesswomen from fully participating in private sector development. O'Neill and Viljoen's study (2001) revealed that male-owned businesses outnumber female-owned businesses by more than two to one, suggesting that women own approximately only 33 per cent of the existing businesses in South Africa (Scarborough and Zimmerer, 2000).

Black women predominantly run the largest single self-employed segment and small business segment, according to the labour force survey of 2005, suggesting relatively low participation of black women entrepreneurs in value-adding business opportunities. Furthermore, white women entrepreneurs in South Africa are significantly better placed than their black counterparts, as they are more qualified and skilled. This is not surprising as the pre-democratic South Africa denied education to black people and the majority of black women were domestic workers. It was always difficult for them to acquire further skills, and to get small loans to sustain their small businesses. Nonetheless, considering the intention of the present government to utilize and accelerate SMMEs as a good option for increasing employment as well as providing opportunities, especially to black women, the banks and financial institutions have started to play a role in supporting the small, unlisted, non-VAT registered businesses.

THE POSITION OF WOMEN IN EMPLOYMENT IN SOUTH AFRICA

In order to comprehend the differential effects of distribution of economic resources of women and men, it is essential to examine the economic position of women and their contributions and status within the country's economy. However, due to limited data on women-owned businesses and women's economic contributions to the economy, it is difficult to support and help women to grow in small businesses.

Decades of patriarchy and subordination of women within the political, economic and social domain, has led their income, economic position and employment status to the edge of the country's economy. Socially, women in South Africa were always identified as inferior to men and were assigned the position of minors in both public and private spheres of life (Mathur-Helm, 2004). Moreover, South African culture never recognized its professional women as 'focused business women', rather it encouraged and glorified the image of its professional women in traditional roles (ibid.) and the trends still remain unchanged.

According to Casale and Posel (2002), presently in South Africa women are progressively entering the labour market despite the rising probability of not being able to find regular employment. Furthermore, this rise in unemployment among women has been associated rather with women being increasingly pushed into the labour market, rather than being pulled into it, due to eroding male income in the households. The fact that a growing number of women live with unemployed men or are single leads them to become the breadwinners in households. Subsequently more women are choosing to remain unmarried, out of a relationship and child-free (Mathur-Helm, 2006).

The historical figures suggest that in 1960 women in South Africa accounted for only 23 per cent of the labour force. By 1985 the number of women in the labour force rose to 36 per cent and by 1991 their number had reached 41 per cent (Casale and Posel, 2002; DTI, 2005). From the study of 1991 and 1996 Census and the Household Surveys in 1996 and 1997, Klasen and Woolard (2000) found a rise in the proportions of the female labour force and that an increasing number of jobs in 1999 were occupied by women.

Currently, women constitute 52.1 per cent of South Africa's population that accounts for 41.3 per cent of the employed labour force (Grobler, 2007). About 70 per cent of the economically active female labour force is employed in agriculture, that is, about 47 per cent of the total agricultural labour force of South Africa.

Informal sector work has contributed to more than half of the female self-employment growth rate between 1995 and 1999. The increase in recorded female employment is due to the growth of self-employment in the informal sector despite problems, such as low earnings, little protection and insecure working conditions. Registered self-employment increased dramatically and particularly for women from a much smaller base. Yet female labour force participation and women's share of employment in informal sector employment are underestimated (Casale and Posel, 2002), hence not much has been documented despite their economic contributions.

Increasingly, black women and black men in South Africa have been entering the labour market since 1999, due to the significant number of working age black people catching up on previously missed education. Hence, the labour supply of both women and men has grown in the post-apartheid South Africa (Klasen and Woolard, 2000), with an increase in women's employment, which has been proportionally greater. While the phenomenon has escalated women's status as an economically active population, a sharp decline has been found in the number of white men in the labour force and their income, owing to a rise in white male unemployment in the country.

In 2005, a survey of employers and the self-employed businesses in South Africa (Statistics South Africa, 2006) found an estimated 1.7 million non-VAT registered businesses in the country, of which approximately 91 per cent were owned by Black Africans. Sixty-eight per cent of the population in the survey indicated unemployment as the main reason for starting a business. A little more than 94.8 per cent of people who ran a non-VAT registered business were the single owners of their self-owned businesses.

THE CURRENT PERSPECTIVES ON WOMEN AND SMALL BUSINESS OWNERSHIP IN SOUTH AFRICA

While literature on women entrepreneurs in the developing countries is limited (DTI, 2006), evidence suggests that women entrepreneurs in developed countries have a number of advantages over their counterparts from the developing countries. These advantages are access to support from women mentors and role models, easier access to formal training in the areas of business planning and organization and information on financial lending and borrowing. In South Africa, women are held responsible for the most part for the family and household work (Mathur-Helm, 2006), hence they are often found juggling roles between personal and professional lives. Moreover, most professional women in South Africa contemplate starting their own small businesses to escape from corporate politics, however, for various reasons they do not always take that route.

A previous study by Erwee (1994) illustrated that in post-apartheid South Africa women increasingly took initiatives to start and manage their self-owned businesses with the help of the Small Business Development Corporation. However, Mathur-Helm (2006) found women to be more comfortable in secure permanent jobs, hence avoiding venturing into small business enterprises. While in demanding jobs they may complain about the unpleasant and demanding day to-day work pressures, but to leave that security for a self-owned business has always been a difficult challenge. It is women who are unemployed and are struggling to find work within a respective career who are the ones most likely to enter into a self-owned business. Nonetheless, according to Erwee (1994) more women are now considering non-corporate career paths and see entrepreneurship as the self-development opportunity.

Women are increasingly taking the route to informal sector entrepreneurship in South Africa (DTI, 2005), indicating the failure of the anticipated impact of the existing policy intervention programmes. Self-owned small businesses in South Africa are run by women from a range of social and cultural groups. However, white women are involved less in micro-level businesses compared with their non-white counterparts. Women entrepreneurs are mostly absorbed in the areas of craft, as street vendors and hawkers, in personal services and in the retail sector (DTI, 2006), which essentially refers to black women, hence self-owned micro-level businesses are primarily run by black women who predominantly work in rural, informal settings. Moreover, it is difficult to trace and illustrate small businesses, as usually they do not pay taxes and are hence non-VAT registered. For example, a large number of women who have never worked for an employer have always had their own informal businesses run from homes and vending in the streets. These women start from a smaller base and most often from an 'out of need' situation. However, women executives employed in public or private sector jobs, who cannot cope with the demanding corporate jobs, often choose a self-owned business (Mathur-Helm, 2006). This allows them freedom to attend to their professional and personal lives and helps them strike a balance between the two worlds. Another interesting prevailing trend is found in a very small number of women from the Asian communities. These women have inherited their family businesses earlier run by their fathers, brothers or husbands. Following the death of the patriarch, women have carried on and eventually become the sole proprietors.

Most often it is extremely difficult for women entrepreneurs to break through the micro- and small levels of business to a medium and large business, despite existing support from financial institutions, banks, micro-lenders and the government. Possibly with extra qualifications, skills training, ambition and social and economic empowerment, women may progressively find ways of overcoming this hurdle. Additionally, a shift in the effective voice of women in business, from the survivalist sector to small business ventures and medium to large-scale enterprises (DTI, 2001) might also help. The South African government encourages and provides support to assist women at large to start their own businesses (Mathur-Helm, 2006) through benefits such as management and entrepreneurship training, in addition to affirmative action (equal opportunity for women in jobs and businesses) and financial support. Currently nearly half of all the privately held businesses in South Africa are owned by women and are growing nearly twice as fast as other companies (ibid.). Mathur-Helm's study (ibid.) further found that women in South Africa also create economic opportunities for others through entrepreneurship by building alliances and networks within the small business sector.

Similarly, to encourage entrepreneurial development and to address the most established needs in the small business sector, which may well by implication be suitable for all genders as well as racial groups, the government has introduced a strategic intervention approach. According to O'Neill and Viljoen (2001), this approach aims to encourage small business development through favourable tax concessions, deregulations and educational training for entrepreneurs. They assert that the strategic intervention approach provides a basic economic infrastructure and intends to stimulate further aids that comprise financial aid packages, counselling programmes, procurement policies and programmes, besides the effective business advocacy programmes that alert bureaucrats to the economic benefits of small business development.

Although there is clearly scope for the introduction of more promotional programmes, the government of South Africa has implemented some general initiatives to support women small business owners through encouragement. Their participation is enhanced, through addressing the imbalances in business ownership such as easier access to finance and credit for female entrepreneurs, government recognition for the role that women play in the economy and business skills training (as less educated women may face financial and human capital constraints that may limit their business pursuits) (Dolinsky et al., 1993). The government is also addressing problems such as collateral and credit history given the trends identified in the White Paper (DTI, 1995), such as collateral requirements being higher for female entrepreneurs than for men (O'Neill and Viljoen, 2001), and the problems posed by the absence of a business track record, the poor legal status of women, the family commitments of married women and entry into the male-dominated business sectors.

The DTI was commended in 1995 for coordinating the implementation of the government's strategy to support the SMMEs mapped out in the White Paper. Subsequently in 1996 a National Small Business Act (Act 102 of 1996) was implemented to promote and represent the interests of the SMMEs by establishing the National Small Business Council (NSBC). Together with NSBC, two other development bodies, namely Khula Enterprise Finance and Ntsika Enterprise Promotion Agency, formed the three pillars of the government's strategy to promote a strong SMME sector in South Africa. However, while Khula Enterprise Finance and Ntsika Enterprise Promotion Agency still exist, NSBC was liquidated by the DTI in 1998 (Ndwandwe, 1998). With a special focus on rural women, Khula Enterprise Finance facilitates access to development finance for small and medium enterprises through a network of partnerships with banks, retail and financial institutions. Subsequently Khula Enterprise Finance launched the Khula Star and Micro Start programmes. In addition, Ntsika Enterprise Promotion Agency supports women's enterprise initiatives by providing entrepreneurial and business training to women entrepreneurs (O'Neill and Viljoen, 2001). Despite socio-political changes in the country, present day South African women are still facing socioeconomic struggles (Mathur-Helm, 2004). Some of the structural and contextual barriers encountered by women are illustrated in the following-section.

EXPLORING THE STRUCTURAL AND CONTEXTUAL BARRIERS ENCOUNTERED BY WOMEN IN THE ESTABLISHMENT AND DEVELOPMENT OF SMALL BUSINESSES

Poverty is a major structural constraint to sustainable growth in South Africa, besides the country's economic structure and the overall policy framework (DTI, 2006). Historically, the collateral requirements of financial institutions and perceptions of risk as well as political factors promoted the totally uneven distribution of loans to black people and women at large (O'Neill and Viljoen, 2001). Therefore, due to limited opportunities and resources in the formal employment sector, many women, especially black women, were and are still forced to work in the poorly paid and largely unregulated informal sectors. Moreover, access and control over resources are still based on race, gender and class.

In 1998, Robertson identified some major constraints to the expansion of African women entrepreneurs, which included lack of capital, landlessness, labour, education, family responsibilities, discrimination and lack of training (cited in DTI, 2006). He concluded that the key challenges facing African women entrepreneurs were inadequate access to formal credit, vulnerability of women to adverse effects of trade reforms, restraints with regard to assets (primarily land), a lack of information to exploit opportunities and poor mobilization of women entrepreneurs (DTI, 2006).

Today in South Africa, some of the chief barriers to promotion of women in business include cultural and societal problems, the psychological impact of cultural norms, employment legislation and policy, lack of information, lack of training, difficulties obtaining finance, problems accessing markets, access to technology and business infrastructure (ibid.). Additionally, absence of infrastructure for skills development and capacity-building, fragmented approach to identifying issues and developing strategies to influence policy affecting business and government interventions (ibid.) are further barriers to women's growth as small business owners.

The uneven distribution of business ownership between women and men is also a contributing factor to the entry barriers experienced by women entrepreneurs in particular. This is compounded by insufficient access to finance and credit facilities, insufficient recognition by government for the role that women play in the economies of developing countries, no collateral and no or poor credit history, no business track record, lack of legal status and female entrepreneurs avoiding the male-dominated business sectors (O'Neill and Viljoen, 2001).

CASE STUDIES: SUCCESS STORIES AND HOW THE BARRIERS WERE OVERCOME

There are women in South Africa who have, despite the above-mentioned barriers, achieved exceptional success and gained respect for their entrepreneurial spirit and achievements. Given below are three case studies illustrating their success stories and the ways in which they minimized the effect of the barriers.

BOX 14.1   DR ANNA MOKGOKONG: CEO OF COMMUNITY INVESTMENT HOLDINGS

Dr Anna Mokgokong is a former chairperson of the University of South Africa's (UNISA) Council, a former member of the University of Pretoria's Council and was recently appointed as chairperson of the Small Enterprise Development Agency (SEDA).

Born in Soweto, South Africa, Anna's parents wanted her to become a doctor, and she started her career in private practice. She has subsequently been very successful in applying her medical training and experience to business ends. Anna holds a BSc from the University of Botswana and an MBChB from Medunsa, where she won the Best Family Medicine Student award. She was medical officer at GaRankuwa Hospital, South Africa from 1984 until 1987, when she left to found Hebron Medical Centre, from scratch, developing it into a primary health care and baby clinic with some 40 000 patients. She started her first business while studying, that is, if one omits her trading sandwiches in grade one. While her parents paid her study fees, she had little pocket money. Realizing that the nurses and students around her had money, she saw a captive market. She had the idea of selling exotic handbags, made from ostrich and alligator skin, and so negotiated a deal with a manufacturer to give her a range of bags on consignment. She sold whatever she could, paying for what she had sold, taking back the rest and made a tidy sum. Then in her fifth year, she opened her first formal store, Macmed.

Tenacious Anna is considered a true entrepreneur for having weathered the downs as well as the ups as a self-made businesswoman. She was South Africa's Businesswoman of the Year in 1999, after which her company Macmed was liquidated. It was a tough time for her as she suffered undue negative perceptions due to scandals in the company, which also led her to feel victimized at that stage. She told herself not to let go, to forge ahead and move on. And she did. For Anna, South Africa's 1994 elections heralded fantastic opportunities in the health care sector. In 1995, the partners of what is now Community Investment Holdings (formerly named Malesela Investment Holdings) came together and founded the company out of nothing. Through their negotiating skills they were able to raise funding from financial institutions such as Sanlam and Old Mutual. As a group of black entrepreneurs, they wanted to enter South Africa's mainstream economy and were confident that their proposal had merit and some funders concurred.

As at the end of 2005, it was turning over around R4 billion a year. Anna's primary present focus is the medical field. It's all business, though her business involves her in a number of community activities. She says she has learnt many business lessons on the job and at the helm. 'It's been a steep learning curve, a case of sink or swim, so I had to learn very fast'. She believes that some international exposure, through work, study or travel, broadens one's outlook. According to Anna one only needs to look at the amount of street vendors to comprehend women's tendency to be being 'natural' entrepreneurs. She wants to tell women: 'This is our time . . . There are so many incentives and opportunities for women. Government policy is driving that, and many companies are looking for women providers of services. I believe that if you have that edge to step out into business, this is the time, and I wouldn't give it another two years. I'd say just step out now, actually go out and find that service you can offer that people are looking for right now'. Anna believes many women cannot rely on their partners for income or support: 'They think of ideas, about what to sell, how to trade and make money. So I think that's how it begins. It's the stimulus of need. They go out and say: We're not going to sit and stay hungry! We want our children to be educated. I have to send my child to school, so I have to make the means'. She maintains that many women are multi-skilled as a result.

BOX 14.2   ANGELA DICK: CEO TRANSMAN

In 1983, Angela Dick co-founded Transman, a small placement and recruitment business, which has grown into a phenomenal success. While in its first year of operations, the company achieved sales revenues of R85 000 and set the target of R400 million for 2006. Based in Johannesburg, the business employs more than 300 people directly and has 19 branches in South Africa, as well as one in Namibia.

Angela, who was brought up in KwaZulu-Natal, is the daughter of the well-known South African portrait photographer Norman Partington. She trained as a teacher because there were few career options that women were encouraged to follow at the time, and becoming a nurse or sales assistant did not appeal to her. She taught for seven years before being promoted to a lecturer. As a woman she was treated and paid very differently from her male colleagues. According to her 'there was a huge discrimination'. When she and her family transferred to Johannesburg, they started talking about starting their own business. Angela went into sales for two years. She did very well, earning three times what she did as a lecturer, and has never looked back. There was a dire need for driver training in South Africa: in her words 'There were no qualified drivers at the time and that's how we started the business; I canvassed to train drivers and my former husband conducted the training'.

Canvassing in the industrial areas brought home the harshness of the realities of employment systems of the time. She remembers watching hundreds of desperately poor people waiting outside factory gates every day, waiting to be employed. 'Who would get work on a particular day was left up to a security guard or an unknown supervisor who would randomly select candidates and pay them a pitiful wage with no overtime pay. There were no benefits for temporary workers whatsoever. The arrangement was highly abusive', remarks Angela. She was adamant that there had to be a way to approach management, to negotiate better wages and proper benefits, to identify and select the correct people for particular positions, albeit at a cost. This would provide clients with flexible and reliable staffing services, and it would help protect people from exploitation in the marketplace. Initially, she was met with incredible resistance: 'It took me about five years to gain acceptance from clients. Initially I was accused of spoiling the market. But the companies that understood what we were trying to achieve were extremely supportive. That is how the whole business of Transman actually started'.

In terms of achievement Angela Dick has surpassed her wildest dreams. She says she has achieved these milestones through passion, drive, integrity and the support of a dedicated team. She is determined to ensure a positive legacy for the company and all those connected to it.

Transman is about wealth creation for as many as possible, as well as providing opportunities and protection in the workplace for disadvantaged people. Employment equity has been part of the company from the start and a black female manager was appointed within the first decade. While initially the company's workforce predominantly involved black males, now it has a large female workforce working in a number of roles and sectors, including administration, food production, cosmetics, warehousing and manufacturing. The formation of Transman Empowerment Holdings has opened opportunities for black staff to participate in the share ownership; it has accelerated the up-skilling of staff and has created opportunities in terms of growth, management and leadership. Transman's most recent innovation is a unique franchise opportunity designed to create wealth for entrepreneurs from previously disadvantaged backgrounds.

For Angela, family and work have never been polar opposites. Angela is a mother to five children, and Transman was founded four days after the birth of her fourth child. All in one working life.

BOX 14.3   SHIREEN PILLAY, FOUNDER OF CITY PLASTICS

Born in Durban, South Africa, Shireen Pillay was a straight-A learner but had to drop out in standard nine as a result of family problems. She went on to become a secretary at a plastics company before taking the plunge by single-handedly starting her own company, City Plastics, in early 1995, armed with her experience, the support of one driver, and a light delivery vehicle. A 100 per cent Black Economic Enterprise (BEE) initiative, the company is a distributor of thermoplastic pipes and fittings.

From humble beginnings, she focused on service and quality, and has developed a highly successful distribution network. Now a medium-sized enterprise, City Plastics is celebrating its 10th anniversary with clients, equity partners, management, staff and other stakeholders. Through sound financial management, doors to overseas suppliers have opened. City Plastics has secured the brand of Tecno Plastics, widely used for portable water and in the chemical and food industries. In early 2005, Shireen entered into a joint venture with an international company, Petzetakis Africa and NRB Piping, currently trading as Sekunjalo Zululand. Shireen has managed strong growth figures. Before entering the R20 million plus annual turnover league (one of the criteria for the Ernst and Young SA Entrepreneur of the Year award), the company's turnover was around R7.9 million.

'I had to be a fast learner', said Shireen. She has a mentor, and is a mentor to Jodie Govender, a disabled woman starting a safety equipment distribution business. Shireen stays ahead by attending seminars, reading and networking; she holds a diploma in business management and a certificate in salesmanship and presentation dynamics. She has also commenced studying for an MBA.

Shireen maintains that she has always been a very positive person, even as a child, and that she has aspired to, and is driven by, success. When she left her previous work to start City Plastics, she was just an ordinary employee. She stated: 'So, like all entrepreneurs, we work very hard, we are very dedicated and we really persevere'. Now City Plastics has a staff development programme and it provides financial assistance to the Aids Hospice in Phoenix near Johannesburg, and other organizations.

According to Shireen, 'I come from a traditional Hindu culture where the woman's place is managing the home and the man is the breadwinner, so I had to make sacrifices and compromises in order to pursue my passion for running my own business. Raising capital was a major problem as we had only a council home to our name. After careful consideration of the risks, my husband and I decided we could cede it to the bank for working capital for City Plastics. I was confident that I would not disappoint my family and would turn this opportunity into a thriving and profitable business. During the very first week of business we purchased a brand new Nissan truck. It was stolen and the insurance company did not compensate, but this did not deter me. Initially I had no credit facility with most of our suppliers and we had to buy goods on a COD basis. The competition in the plastic industry is huge, which held risks for my new business and posed major obstacles in securing contracts'.

Business success has been accompanied by recognition from peer groups – mainly business and women's organizations – in the form of awards, guest speaking opportunities and social exposure. Shireen was one of the five finalists of the 2005 Ernest and Young SA Entrepreneur of the Year award in the newly introduced emerging entrepreneur category. Shireen is proud to have broken the mould in a male-dominated industry. 'Imagine a petite Indian woman wearing a hard hat in the company of men, discussing complex issues such as industrial and reticulation piping', she laughs. That, in a nutshell, is Shireen Pillay.

Source: Grobler (2007).

SUMMARY

This chapter addresses the context of gender empowerment through entrepreneurship for women within South Africa. For a sustainable development of women entrepreneurs in South Africa, the participation of women in the economy needs to be promoted by reducing poverty amongst females, increasing their access to educational opportunities and enhancing their approach to decision-making and empowerment. Such initiatives may motivate women to consider and participate in entrepreneurial ventures. However, women generally lack the necessary resources for starting and developing their own businesses, and hence in a developing country such as South Africa, the strategic intervention approach could possibly be the most appropriate, provided assistance and expenditure are closely monitored in the light of relatively limited capital resources.

While research findings (DTI, 2006) indicate that women entrepreneurs have become an important part of the growth of diverse economic trends, in South Africa, women entrepreneurs apply their creativity and innovation to establish an enterprise against difficult odds and multitudinous barriers. With determination and drive they will be able to inch their way forward to make gains that will essentially advance women entrepreneurs in the global competitive economies. However, the challenge is to work at innovations that are particularly South African and of an indigenous nature with universal application, to enable women entrepreneurs to enter the world market as a responsible business community and an economic force. Individually and as a group, South African businesswomen will have to take the initiative of exploiting the points allocated to them in the Codes of Good Practices (women's economic empowerment targets, for example, women hold ownership rights of 10 per cent or more, according to the legislative charters) as part of South Africa's legislation. It can be done by holding government, financial institutions and organizations to broad-based principles, and presenting women's added value to the businesses in terms of proposing their inclusion in business initiatives.

In conclusion, a full fledged study must be carried out to clearly understand the entrepreneurial activities of indigenous women in not only South Africa but the whole of Africa, from small-scale trade in the informal sector to large-scale enterprises. This will place women entrepreneurs, as an important constituent to the economic growth of the African region, on the agenda of the international development agencies, as well as the African governments.

REFERENCES

Balshaw, T. and Goldberg, T. (2005), *Cracking Broad-based Black Economic Empowerment*, Cape Town: Human and Rousseau.

Casale, D. and Posel, D. (2002), 'Feminization of the labour force in South Africa. An analysis of recent data and trends', *The South African Journal of Economics*, **70**(1), 156–84.

Dolinsky, A.L., Caputo, R.K., Pasumarty, K. and Quasi, H. (1993), 'The effects of education on business ownership', *A Longitudinal Study of Women Entrepreneurship Theory and Practice*, **18**(1), 3–53.

DTI – Department of Trade and Industry (1995), *National Strategy for the Development and Promotion of Small Business*, Pretoria, Government Printer.

DTI – Department of Trade and Industry (2001), *South Africa: Economic Policy Analysis*, Republic of South Africa, Pretoria, Government Printer.

DTI – Department of Trade and Industry (2005), *South African Women Entrepreneurs, A Burgeoning Force in our Economy*, Special Report, Department of Trade and Industry, Republic of South Africa.
DTI – Department of Trade and Industry (2006), *Department of Trade and Industry Report*, Republic of South Africa.
Erwee, R. (1994), 'South African women: changing career patterns', in N.J. Adler and D.N. Izraeli (eds), *Competitive Frontiers*, Cambridge, MA: Blackwell.
Grobler, J. (2007), *Top Women in Business and Government*, 3rd edition, Cape Town: Top Companies Publishing.
Klasen, S. and Woolard, I. (2000), *Surviving Unemployment Without State Support: Unemployment and Household Formation in South Africa*, Sonderforschungsbereich 386, Paper 213, Institute for Statistics publication.
Mathur-Helm, B. (2004), 'Women in management in South Africa', in M.J. Davidson and R. Burke (eds), *Women in Management Worldwide: Progress and Prospects*, London: Ashgate.
Mathur-Helm, B. (2006), 'Women and the glass ceiling in South African banks: an illusion or reality?', *Women in Management Review*, **1**(4), 311–26.
Mattis, M.C. (2004), 'Women entrepreneurs: out from under the glass ceiling', *Women in Management Review*, **19**(3), 154–63.
National Small Business Act (Act 102 of 1996) (1996), Pretoria: Government Printers.
Ndwandwe, M. (1998), 'Letdown for SMMEs', *Enterprise*, **127**, 60–61.
O'Neill, R.C. and Viljoen, L. (2001), 'Support for female entrepreneurs in South Africa: improvement or decline', *Journal of Family Ecology and Consumer Sciences*, **29**, 37–44.
Scarborough, N.M. and Zimmerer, T.W. (2000), *Effective Small Business Management* (6th edition), Upper Saddle River: Prentice Hall.
Statistics South Africa (2006), *South African Population Census*.

15 Turkey

Mine Karataş-Özkan, Gözde İnal and Mustafa F. Özbilgin

INTRODUCTION

Entrepreneurship has long been hailed as a significant means to fuel economic development in both developed and developing countries. In line with this, enterprise development initiatives have been frequently presented as remedies for economic and political instability in markets. However, entrepreneurship has remained a largely male-dominated field of economic activity, although women can play an integral role as entrepreneurs in contributing to economic prosperity (OECD, 2001). In the globalizing world economy, in which competition for sources of economic growth are stretched to levels of exhaustion, women entrepreneurs emerge as a relatively untapped resource that can be deployed in order to foster business and employment creation. Although these developments account for the exponential growth of research in female entrepreneurship, our knowledge in this field has remained relatively limited to the English-speaking regions of the world.

In this chapter, we aim to explore women's entrepreneurship in Turkey, a country that has remained relatively under-explored in the English language entrepreneurship literature. We have reviewed the English and Turkish language literatures in order to reveal the complex and multi-dimensional nature of female entrepreneurship in Turkey and to address the following questions: (1) What are the triggers and impediments to Turkish women's entrepreneurial activity? (2) Do Turkish women's businesses, as an outcome of the entrepreneurial process, exhibit similar patterns to those of men, and to those of women in other developing economies? (3) What are the policy and research implications of these factors?

OECD statistics show that only about 25 per cent of all entrepreneurs in the European member countries are women (OECD, 2005), while this percentage is merely 12.5 per cent in Turkey (KAGIDER, 2007). There are a complex set of cultural, socio-political and economic reasons for the low representation of women in entrepreneurship. For instance, Ufuk and Ozgen (2001a), point to the late start of women in entrepreneurial activity as the main reason for their poor representation in the field. Whereas Cindoglu (2003) concludes that women's over-representation in unpaid family work is a key barrier to entrepreneurship.

The scope of studies featuring the demographic, economic, social and cultural aspects of women entrepreneurship in Turkey is limited (Hisrich and Oztürk, 1999; Ufuk and Ozgen, 2001a and 2001b; Kutanis and Bayraktaroğlu, 2003; Cetindamar, 2005). Although a range of explanations is offered to account for the antecedents, correlates and consequences of female entrepreneurship in Turkey, we aim to provide a comprehensive and critical review of the literature in this chapter.

THE POSITION OF WOMEN IN EMPLOYMENT IN TURKEY

Owing to feminist activism, which has its roots in the late nineteenth-century Ottoman Empire, women in modern day Turkey have been enjoying an active role in political and social life since the early 1920s. Turkish women gained the right to vote earlier than their counterparts in many other European countries (Özbilgin and Woodward, 2003). However, their active participation in the labour market, business and commerce has a longer history. Although Shariah (Islamic governance) in the Ottoman Empire enforced sex segregation of public spaces, it has not disallowed women to engage in entrepreneurial activities. Indeed, one of the earlier examples of a female entrepreneur in the Islamic history is Hatice, the first wife of the Muslim prophet Muhammed, who continued trading after her conversion to Islam. Therefore, Islam per se has not been responsible for under-representation of women in business, commerce and enterprise development, but patriarchal interpretations of Islam and Islamic regimes have not been supportive of women's economic activity and independence from men.

In understanding the connections between religion, governance and gender relations at work, Turkey presents a very interesting example. Successfully evacuating religious stricture from processes of public administration in the 1930s, Turkey has maintained a strong secular tradition in government and society. Contrary to most other Muslim majority countries, where it is deemed 'inappropriate' for women to work in the 'public sphere' (Tucker, 2007), Turkey has exhibited a secular and 'legally' egalitarian approach to women's participation in employment. Many scholars (e.g., Kabasakal and Bodur, 2002; Cetindamar et al., 2007) note that Turkey has a unique gender egalitarian culture dating to the pre-Islamic and pre-Ottoman periods and Turkish women seem to have a stronger position compared with women in other Arabic countries, as well as in many Western and Eastern countries.

In 2006 the working population of Turkey was 24776000, of whom 6480000 were women, with 670000 women not working (Turkish Statistical Institute, 2008). The majority of economically active women worked in agriculture (48.5 per cent of women compared with 19.8 per cent of men), while fewer women worked in industry (15 per cent of women compared with 29.1 per cent of men) and services (26.5 per cent of women compared with 51.1 per cent of men) (ibid.). There is also a large informal sector in Turkey in which a sizeable number of women work (e.g., waged domestic household helpers). This group of women are not included in the statistics and they remain outside the social security system, with no provision of subsidized healthcare or pension rights. While the number of women employers was 11786 in 1970, it decreased to 7218 in 1980. During the period from 1985 to 1990 Turkey went through extensive market liberalization and privatization. As a result, entrepreneurial activity was supported and the number of female and male employers increased considerably, with an 80 per cent increase in the number of women employers (Hisrich and Oztürk, 1999). For comparative purposes, data on the status of employed women both in 1993 and 2006 is presented in Table 15.1, which reflects the consequences of continued liberalization and urbanization with migration from rural to urban areas. The figures suggest that there was considerable shift from unpaid family work to regular and casual employment, employer and self-employed status for women. It should be noted that women categorized under the employer and self-employed groups were mainly involved in scientific, technical, professional-related

Table 15.1   Status of employed women

Status of Employment	Total (1993)	Total (2006)
Regular employee	1 102 116	2 388 000
Casual employee	174 198	326 000
Employer	26 967	69 000
Self-employed	408 629	761 000
Unpaid family workers	4 156 241	2 266 000
Total	5 868 151	5 810 000

Source: Compiled using data from the Turkish Statistical Institute (1995, 2008).

tasks, and administrative, executive and managerial tasks, in addition to production and related work, and transport equipment operating tasks.

Compared with 1993, the proportion of employer and self-employed women in the total workforce in 2006 had increased, that is, from 7.42 per cent to 14.28 per cent. The employer and self-employed categories indicate that entrepreneurial women are a small proportion of the total women's workforce. By 2006, the major occupational categories that women (i.e., employer and self-employed women) were engaged with were agriculture, industry (e.g., mining and quarrying, manufacturing, electricity, gas and water construction), and services (e.g., wholesale and retail trade, restaurants and hotels, transportation, communication and storage, financial institutions, insurance business services related to real estates, community, social and personal services) (Turkish Statistical Institute, 2008). Despite changes in the last four decades in labour market activity of women, various authors still argue that women are employed in the labour-intensive sectors of the economy, and are still concentrated in low-pay jobs (Esim, 2001; Ozar, 2002).

THE CURRENT POSITION OF WOMEN AND SMALL BUSINESS OWNERSHIP

The entrepreneurship literature is littered with conceptual frameworks that view the world from polarized and dichotomous lenses. One such framework is that of the distinction made between necessity and opportunity entrepreneurship, which is offered by Van Stel et al. (2007). Opportunity entrepreneurs are defined as those who identify a business opportunity in the market and choose entrepreneurship as their career route due to an opportunity-based motive, whereas necessity entrepreneurs are the individuals who resort to entrepreneurship as their last option to earn money. This framework has the fundamental assumption that entrepreneurs will be pulled and pushed by external drivers and internal motivations. Such framing provides a shallow understanding of entrepreneurial dispositions, failing to reveal deeper structures, resources and relations of power that account for entrepreneurial choices and opportunities.

Looking at Turkey from these descriptive lenses, Hisrich and Oztürk (1999) explain that Turkey is a developing country where women seek new venture creation and self-employment primarily as a means to overcome occupational segregation and to participate in economic development. The GEM framework (GEM, 2007, p.8), which suffers from positivist framing of entrepreneurship through dichotomous dimensions, follows the same conceptualization and labels those individuals who start businesses to exploit a perceived business opportunity as opportunity entrepreneurs, and those who are pushed to start a business because all other options for work are either absent or unsatisfactory as necessity entrepreneurs. Policy-makers around the world are also taken by this polarized view of entrepreneurship as they try to motivate opportunity-based entrepreneurship, as they believe that this group of entrepreneurs can enhance the innovativeness of a country and, therefore, lead to better economic performance when compared with individuals who are labelled as necessity entrepreneurs. One of the important caveats that we would like to make here is that viewing the world through such polarized lenses serves merely to view entrepreneurship in sectors such as services and manufacturing as more valuable, whilst rendering entrepreneurship in sectors like agriculture less valuable. Therefore, this categorization implicitly promotes Western styles of entrepreneurship (due to the domination of service and manufacturing in the Western countries) as opportunity entrepreneurship, while devaluing entrepreneurial activity in the developing and less developed world. We therefore recommend that international comparative works should check for possible biases such as this in formulating value-based labels when exploring entrepreneurial activity and motivations.

Regardless of the type of entrepreneurship that exists in a developing country, entrepreneurial activity contributes to economic growth not necessarily through employment generation, particularly in the case of necessity entrepreneurship. Cetindamar (2005) notes the importance of the productivity gains experienced as a result of entrepreneurs taking the lead in shifting resources from low productivity to high productivity areas, from a Schumpeterian view (Schumpeter, 1934; Acs et al., 1999). Another view is related to the recognition of entrepreneurs in society. Entrepreneurship is considered not only the source of improving economic performance for one country but can also contribute to the fulfilment of one's individual needs for self-expression and improve the social status and respect of entrepreneurs in a society (Mueller and Thomas, 2000). The results of an empirical study in the Aegean part of Turkey, which was conducted with 27 women and 115 men entrepreneurs (Ertübey, 1993), revealed that women entrepreneurs consider themselves about 'average' in terms of their entrepreneurial activities, that is, concerning risk taking. However, they cared more about their status rather than making profits and did not want to lose their positive image within society.

Another study was conducted by Ufuk and Ozgen (2001a) with 220 business owners in the capital of Turkey, Ankara, most of whom worked in trade, manufacturing and service sectors. The authors examined the working status, reasons for being in business and the types of businesses the respondents were involved in. This study identified the three main reasons for becoming entrepreneurs as meeting the family needs, initiating positive social relations and achieving self-realization. Funding was also a salient issue in undertaking entrepreneurial activity and one that will be discussed in more detail in ensuing sections of the chapter. In terms of financing the businesses at start-up, 70.4 per cent of women entrepreneurs stated that they utilized their own savings, 18.2 per cent borrowed from their relatives, 8.2 per cent received financial support from friends and relatives and 69 per cent obtained bank loans (ibid.).

Focusing on the characteristics, performance and problems of 54 women entrepreneurs in Turkey, Hisrich and Oztürk (1999) revealed that Turkish women entrepreneurs displayed many similarities with women entrepreneurs in other countries, although the motivations for business venturing were different for Turkish women. The most repeatedly stated reason for business start-up was that they were interested in the area, followed by the boredom that they felt about being a housewife; relocation; and frustration with their previous jobs or occupations. The authors maintained that these differences reflected the specific cultural and structural context of Turkey, particularly the impact of occupational sex segregation, gender wage disparity and women's high participation in informal and non-supported sector work. The main difference in motivation for Turkish women entrepreneurs, compared with their counterparts in other countries, was that a high percentage of Turkish women indicated that their dissatisfaction and boredom with their status as housewives was a primary reason for starting their businesses (ibid.). Independence and achievement were the other strong influences cited by women, whereas job satisfaction, economic necessity and security were among the least cited reasons for the take-up of entrepreneurship. In another study conducted by Cetindamar (2005) among 137 men and 25 women entrepreneurs in different cities, Turkish women entrepreneurs, similar to their male counterparts, mentioned gaining work independence and creation of employment opportunities as the most important motives for business set-up. The third important motive for women entrepreneurs was personal satisfaction, with 40 per cent of women entrepreneurs valuing this as a trigger for entrepreneurship compared with only 21 per cent of male entrepreneurs.

Given this analysis of entrepreneurial motivation for Turkish women, it is worth examining the scope of their entrepreneurial activity by looking into the nature of businesses they set up and the type of industry sector. The GEM survey (GEM, 2007, p. 22) showed that globally, women entrepreneurs create and run businesses across all of the broad industrial sectors of extraction, transformation, business services and consumer-oriented products, as do men. However, women and men set up businesses in different industrial sectors, as a significantly higher percentage of women's ventures are in the consumer-oriented sectors compared with men's, 60.3 and 37 per cent respectively. Further, 41 per cent of female entrepreneurs operated in the service sector compared with only 18 per cent of men's enterprises. Enterprises established and owned by Turkish women span the whole spectrum in terms of industry, geographical location (urban and rural) and size and assets. They have founded and managed companies in almost all industries ranging from international trade to finance, from IT to advertising, from manufacturing to management consulting (Cindoglu, 2003), although the ratio of male entrepreneurs involved in the production of technology was higher than that of female entrepreneurs (Cetindamar, 2005).

Entrepreneurship is embedded in socio-cultural, economic and political environments and both internal and external environments influence the scope of entrepreneurial activity (Karataş-Özkan, 2006; İnal and Karataş-Özkan, 2007; Altinay and Altinay, 2008; İnal, 2008). Early research in Turkey has shown that in the mid-1990s the government started supporting women entrepreneurs by offering business set-up financing at preferential rates to women who desired to start a small business or home-base working (Hisrich and Oztürk, 1999). In 1995, a state-owned bank called Halk Bankasi offered a credit line of 20 trillion Turkish lira for housewives, equating to approximately 445 000 US dollars at that time, and also established an information centre that guided women who wanted to start up businesses. Furthermore, youth credit was also offered to women under 35 who wanted to set up businesses (Onal, 1995). Indeed, Hisrich and Oztürk's (1999) study on 54 women entrepreneurs demonstrated that the source of capital and other support reflected the infrastructure of the country. The authors found that a high percentage of participants in Turkey, 70.4 per cent, received capital support from the government (state bank), 25.9 per cent used their own capital, 22.2 per cent received capital from their husbands and 22.2 per cent used their parents' capital at the start-up. The most recent example of funding support included a private high street bank's initiative targeted specifically at women entrepreneurs. GarantiBank's 'Women Entrepreneurs Support Package' offers general purpose SME loans, and SME project finance loans. In collaboration with the Women Entrepreneurs Association of Turkey (KAGIDER), GarantiBank also offers training opportunities and has been instrumental in organizing a competition for 'Turkey's Women Entrepreneur Awards' since 2006 (*Turkish Daily News*, 2008).

Several governmental and non-governmental support mechanisms exist in Turkey. KSSGM (Kadının Statüsü ve Sorunları Genel Müdürlüğü), The Directorate General on the Status and the Problems of Women, is an example of a governmental unit that was founded as a result of Turkey's ratification of CEDAW (Convention on the Elimination of all Forms of Discrimination against Women), to ensure the implementation of CEDAW on the social level, through publications and projects. KOSGEB (Small and Medium Industry Development Organization) is an organization under the Ministry of Trade and Industry providing technical, managerial and marketing support to SMEs and it has international links and benefits from the information network of the EU. Another organization is GAP-GIDEM (Entrepreneur Support and Guidance Centers), which offers business support services, is supported by the EU and UNDP (United Nations Development Programme) and is active in encouraging and supporting entrepreneurial activity by women in South East Turkey. Other organizations such as TUSIAD (Turkish Industrialists' and Businessmen's Association) and TOBB (The Turkish Union of Chambers and Commodities Exchanges) endorse the increasing role of women entrepreneurs for the Turkish economy through various platforms, such as forming networking groups (e.g., TOBB Women Entrepreneurs Club) and organizing seminars and conferences on women entrepreneurship to raise public awareness and foster women's entrepreneurship (e.g., the first TOBB conference on women entrepreneurship was held in Istanbul on the 26 August 2008).

One important non-governmental organization that is worth highlighting is KAGIDER (Women Entrepreneurs' Association of Turkey). KAGIDER was chartered in September 2002 as a non-profit and non-governmental organization by 37 prominent Turkish female entrepreneurs, in order to support female entrepreneurship in Turkey. It has grown steadily over the past three years as other successful businesswomen have joined its ranks. In 2007 KAGIDER had 200 members from various sectors, including textiles, communications, human resources, tourism, chemicals, mining and health. Maintaining strong links with the EU, KAGIDER's activities include the development of training and mentoring programmes for women entrepreneurs, incubation support to women and the development of internships and funding opportunities. As one of the most influential non-government organizations that is related to women, KAGIDER puts great emphasis on lobbying activities, publishes statements, provides policy recommendations to the state and public and private institutions in order to make women's voices heard, as well as fostering gender equality in order to enhance women entrepreneurs' status (Kurtsan, 2007).

STRUCTURAL AND CONTEXTUAL BARRIERS

Institutional arrangements of social, economic, political and technological nature affect entrepreneurship, presenting a set of opportunities and constraints to individual entrepreneurs. As is evident in this book, these arrangements vary across cultures and countries. Therefore, the country context has explanatory power over opportunity and constraint structures of entrepreneurship. Developing countries present an interesting context for examining the influence of the resources available for men and women interested in entrepreneurship because findings from data collected around the world revealed that, despite a general resource-scarce environment in these countries, the rate of entrepreneurship among women is usually higher than that in developed countries (Bosma and Harding, 2007).

Institutional and legal contexts are also important for female entrepreneurship, influencing its nature and extent as well as its potential economic contribution (Aidis et al., 2006). Whilst gender equality is formally inscribed in most constitutions, its application throughout the economy and society is often insufficient to overcome discrimination against women. Whilst overt gender discrimination is evident (e.g., wage gaps), covert constraints that are manifest in social structures and institutional environments (including family) also negate female entrepreneurship (Welter and Kolb, 2006). A woman's perceived identity in society and gender role expectations play a significant role in most cultures and the value that society attaches to female employment and entrepreneurship is an important factor in determining women's entrepreneurship. In this regard, Turkish women entrepreneurs suffer from both overt and covert discrimination.

A study of 220 women entrepreneurs in Ankara, Turkey (Ufuk and Ozgen, 2001b) examined the interaction between business and family life, and the respondents reported that being entrepreneurs affected their roles within their families as wives, mothers and housewives negatively. In fact, this was attributed to stress, excessive expectations of family members and a perceived lack of balance between business and family life. However, these women reported that being entrepreneurs positively influenced their roles in social and economic life. Another research study conducted by Celebi et al. (1993) examined the anxiety that women entrepreneurs suffer due to conflict between their domestic and business lives. Large numbers of respondents reported anxiety about failing as mothers, human beings, friends, relatives and housewives. Furthermore, Ozgen and Ufuk's (1998) study on Turkish home-based entrepreneurs found that 70.7 per cent of respondents were faced with role over-loading and 27.8 per cent were faced with role conflicts in accomplishing their roles as wife, mother, housewife and business owner. Role conflict refers to the extent to which a person experiences pressures within one role that are incompatible with the pressures within another role (Coverman, 1989). The multiple roles of women entrepreneurs usually results in women trying to achieve a solution that best fits the needs of all individuals involved (Ufuk and Ozgen, 2001b), and this puts an additional pressure on them. However, there is a danger in assessing these studies at face value, which may lead to victimization of women as unfit for entrepreneurship. From a critical perspective, it is possible to recognize that social construction of domestic, family and work lives privileges men, while disadvantaging women who transgress the fault lines of gender roles.

Women's perceived social identity in Turkey presents a challenge to their entrepreneurial activities. Certainly in Turkey women encounter many challenges in setting up and maintaining a business. They face such gendered problems as obtaining funds (Hisrich and Oztürk, 1999; Esim, 2000; Cetindamar, 2005), business premises, raw materials, lack of customer respect (Ufuk and Ozgen, 2001a), lack of role models and mentors, lack of support networks and limited access to entrepreneurship education and training. In Ufuk and Ozgen's study (ibid.) women entrepreneurs raised the issues of lack of access to funding, bureaucratic procedures and having no experience as the most significant barriers. It is interesting to note that women entrepreneurs would benefit from some improvements to provisions of support that may be afforded to both women and men entrepreneurs. For example, the main expectation of women entrepreneurs from the government was a lower burden of tax. Similarly, a majority of the participant women entrepreneurs also showed their willingness to join entrepreneurial-related training programmes in order to gain knowledge about the business field, communications methods and market economy.

STORIES OF SUCCESS

In this section we present two case studies of successful Turkish women. The first case study is of a young female entrepreneur who has revolutionized her family business and grown the company very successfully by identifying new business opportunities in the cargo industry. The second case exemplifies a successful woman entrepreneur who has relentlessly pursued a business opportunity in the coffee-shop sector with a strong determination to contribute to the economy and society as a role model.

BOX 15.1   EVRIM ARAS SAGIROGLU, THE OWNER-MANAGER OF ARAS KARGO

Aras Kargo is one of the two most competitive and professional cargo companies in Turkey. The leader of this company is a successful young female entrepreneur, Evrim Aras Sağıroğlu. Born in 1978, she is married with one child. After successfully completing her Bachelor's degree in Media and Communications Systems at Istanbul Bilgi University she started work at Aras Kargo (founded in 1979 by her father), and worked in various departments of the company (Uras, 2009).

Although Evrim comes from an entrepreneurial family, the previous successful owners of the Aras Kargo, after obtaining her university education her initial reaction was not to join the established family business and to prove that she could be successful by her own efforts and not by the support of her family

(Annealed, 2007). She studied for a degree in Media and Communications Systems with the intention of becoming an advertiser (*Bağımsız Siyasi Kadın Gazetesi*, 2003). However, after trying hard for several months, she had not been successful in finding a good job due to poor economic conditions in Turkey. In 2001, she even started up a partnership business with a friend but did not find what she expected, and eventually had no choice but to join the family business, Aras Kargo, when she was 23 years old, with the hope of being personally satisfied. At the beginning of her career, she remarked 'I understood that this job was much more difficult than it seemed after I actually started working there. I liked the point that it was a difficult job. At the end of the day it was a new and emerging sector that had the potential to be developed. So, I liked this sector by time better' (obtained from the interview conducted by *Bağımsız Siyasi Kadın Gazetesi*, 2003).

In the beginning, she had an orientation period at Aras Kargo for about nine months and, after working as an intern at one of the branches in 2001, she became an assistant manager at another branch, followed by working in the Customer Services Department for four months in a different branch. She continued to increase her working experience in the cargo business by completing short-term monthly internship trainings throughout each and every department of Aras Kargo Headquarters (Turkish Businesswomen, 2008).

After having worked at Aras Kargo for a short period of time, she became the General Manager and founded the first Public Relations Department in 2003. This corporate identity project was the first step towards the re-engineering of organizational processes. In the following 18 months, she became the Assistant General Manager of Marketing and Sales Department and has been the Chief Executive since early 2008, after her father passed away (ibid.). Evrim stated that she owes her courage to the programmatic and leadership qualities she gained from her father and she has an innovative nature that has contributed to the success of the business (Oztop, 2009). In addition, she stated that she had good relations with her father and had received his support. She learned a lot from him and had looked up to her father as a role model, especially his easy nature (Annealed, 2007).

Evrim stated in her resumé that she gradually advanced in her job. She remarked: 'I was not sure whether I wanted to work in a business sector I did not know in the beginning. My father supported me and initially I started working in the company as a trainee, afterwards I became the manager of a branch, and following this I became a geographical manager of the company. Then I acted as a trainee in every department of the head office' (ibid.).

After taking over the business from her father in 2008, the company has achieved growth and profitability. She regularly travels all around Anatolia to meet up with employees and motivate them (*Gazete Hayat*, 2008). In addition, she supports the Turkish community by preferring to recruit young Turkish university graduates for positions in the company. The company's growth rate and profitability were reported as 16 per cent during last year (Uras, 2009).

She believes that the sector her business is in is very much dependent on human relations, and comments that women tend to be successful in this field as their work involves properly serving customers with empathy and women pay more attention to detail. She added that: 'In all branches of Aras Holding 42 per cent of managers are women and they are much better in accomplishing their tasks/duties. Women's passion and determination have an influence on their job achievement'.

Evrim reckons the secret of her success in business is her employee focus: 'I do not keep myself away from the employees; I treat them all equally and fairly. I do my own work. I progress in work by taking my employees' opinions and respecting them. I would also prefer each employee to recognize their mistakes without myself pointing it out to them' (Annealed, 2007). Evrim's husband, who encourages and motivates her toward work, and her parents, who take care of her son when she is busy with work, are a great support in her being successful in the business (ibid.).

Currently, the company has 23 regional administration centres, 27 transfer/transportation centres, 780 branches and 3000 transportation/carriage vehicles. It has around 10 000 employees, serving 2500 locations (Uras, 2009). Evrim Aras Sağıroğlu has plans to contribute to more corporate social responsibility projects and grow further, even becoming a competitor to DHL worldwide. She has been selected as one of the five most successful Turkish entrepreneurs in Turkey (ibid.).

BOX 15.2   ALEV ALTINKILIC, THE FOUNDING ENTREPRENEUR OF KAHVE DUNYASI (COFFEE WORLD)

Alev Altinkilic is the founder of a chain of coffee shops called Kahve Dunyasi (Coffee World) in Turkey. She is 49 years old and a mother of two children. She is married to a businessman who leads his family business, which is in the area of cacao, coffee and chocolate production. The family firm that her husband runs and owns has large production facilities and they export their products to 21 countries (Milliyet, 2009).

With a synergistic approach, in 2005 Alev Altinkilic decided to set up a coffee shop business that is unique in terms of its product and service, and to develop the business concept for Kahve Dunyasi. The main aspects of the business concept include offering top-quality, fresh-roasted Turkish coffee and other types of whole-bean coffee in a relaxed and pleasant atmosphere, with an emphasis on ambience. In the founding entrepreneur's words, 'the aim was to create a coffee-bar culture in Turkey by offering traditional coffee and related products in a pleasant and modern environment and by so doing to promote Turkish coffee nationally and internationally' (ibid.). Similar to the business idea behind Starbucks, Kahve Dunyasi has become the first Turkish venture that has capitalized on creating a coffee-bar culture by focusing on the overall experience of coffee drinkers. Alev Altinkilic has introduced innovative ideas in her stores to differentiate the business from others. For example, they offer chocolates to the customers that are produced by small prototype chocolate machines in the stores.

Alev Altinkilic has grown the business to 47 stores in the last four years. She employs 625 people (ibid.) and the revenue rose by 67 per cent in the period of 2007–08 (*Gözlem*, 2009). She is determined to internationalize the business in 2010 once the recovery begins to be made from the global economic slow-down. In a recent competition called 'The Entrepreneur of the Year', which is organized by Ernst and Young in Turkey, Alev Altinkilic was chosen as one of the five finalists. She exemplifies a successful women entrepreneur who has relentlessly pursued a business opportunity with a strong determination to contribute to the economy and society as a role model.

SUMMARY AND RECOMMENDATIONS

Women's entrepreneurship is an increasingly salient part of the economic and social make-up of many countries, considering its role in economic and social transformation, particularly in the case of developing economies. Institutional structures and cultural norms provide a varying array of incentives to women's entrepreneurial activity, while at the same time constraining women's success in entrepreneurship. Cultural norms and values shape women's propensity for entrepreneurship and their subsequent actions for entrepreneurship. The triggers include an increasing acknowledgement of women entrepreneurs in society and related policies and support programmes.

In the case of Turkey, patriarchal norms and the rise of religious conservatism has meant that social norms have changed in the last three decades to demarcate women's roles to motherhood and home-making. These changes in social norms present women entrepreneurs with challenges in reconciling competing expectations of work and domestic life. Factors that deter women from entrepreneurship in Turkey include persistent patriarchal social values and associated traditional sex roles, as well as limited access to education and training opportunities, lack of experience in employment and business, a dearth of role models and limited financial and social capital (i.e., limited access to informal and formal support networks).

Traditional gender roles still form a hurdle facing women who are pursuing an entrepreneurial career route: childcare in particular takes up women's time and energy and limits their mobility (Cindoglu, 2003). A gender egalitarian culture and effective mechanisms for work–life balance, including supported provision of parental leave and childcare, could clearly encourage more women to participate in employment and engage in entrepreneurial activity. Bureaucracy, complexities in tax procedures, insufficient official incentives and unstable market conditions and political environment are other obstacles that face both Turkish women and men in their pursuit of entrepreneurship. However, further empirical research that examines these opportunities and constraints that women entrepreneurs face at different stages of their entrepreneurial experience is needed. Demographic, social, economic and political factors are usually interwoven and further research should take into account the complexity and multifaceted nature of the social phenomenon under study. We also call for further research and policy that focus on ways to support female entrepreneurship through changes to the social institutions and economic environment by affording women better access to social, financial and cultural forms of capital and other opportunity structures.

Women find themselves in very different situations compared with men, and these different situations result in different perceptions about the world (Adler, 2004; Brush et al., 2006; GEM, 2007). The implications for policy-making that emerge from this diversity of circumstances and perspectives point to the need for customized or targeted policies for women entrepreneurship. Policy recommendations, therefore, include a firmer and more targeted government support and reforming the existing governmental institutions, in the case of Turkey. Their scope and outreach should be expanded to include the promotion of women into entrepreneurship. Higher education institutions have an important role to play in raising the awareness of young women and supporting their entrepreneurial ideas through entrepreneurship education, training and incubation support programmes. Despite these extensive wish lists, there should be political will and drive to promote female entrepreneurship in Turkey. In the current political climate, the recommendations of this chapter remain marginal to the efforts of the current government, which fails to see the relevance of female entrepreneurship to the success and competitiveness of Turkish economy. Such short-sightedness is not likely to change in the immediate future and real change requires women to get more active in Turkish politics in the long term.

REFERENCES

Acs, Z.J., B. Carlsson and C. Karlsson (1999), *Entrepreneurship, SMEs and the Macroeconomy*, Cambridge, MA: Cambridge University Press.

Adler, N.J. (2004), 'Women in international entrepreneurship', in L.P. Dana (ed.), *Handbook of Research on International Entrepreneurship*, Cheltenham, UK and Northampton, MA, USA: Edward Elgar, pp. 30–40.

Aidis, R., F. Welter, D. Smallbone and N. Isakova (2006), 'Female entrepreneurship in transition economies: the case of Lithuania and Ukraine', *Feminist Economics*, **12**(2), 631–46.

Altinay, L. and E. Altinay (2008), 'Factors influencing business growth: the rise of Turkish entrepreneurship in the UK', *International Journal of Entrepreneurial Behaviour and Research*, **14**(1), 24–46.

Annealed, B. (2007), *Evrim Aras Sağıroğlu: Soyadın Aras, demeleri beni kamçılıyor.*

Bağımsız Siyasi Kadın Gazetesi (2003), 'Kargoculuğa güven kazandırdık', available at: http://arsiv.kazete.com.tr/sayilar/2003/34/index.php?sayfa=ekonomi1&bolum=haberler; accessed 20 February 2010.

Bosma, N. and R. Harding (2007), *Global Entrepreneurship Monitor, GEM 2006 Results*, Massachusetts and London: Babson College and London Business School.

Brush, C.G., N.M. Carter, E.J. Gatewood, P.G. Greene and M.M. Hart (2006), 'Introduction: the Diana International Project', in C.G. Brush, N.M. Carter, E.J. Gatewood, P.G. Greene and M.M. Hart (eds), *Growth-oriented Women Entrepreneurs and their Businesses*, Cheltenham, UK and Northampton, MA, USA: Edward Elgar, pp. 3–22.

Celebi, N., B. Tokuroglu and A. Baran (1993), *Bagimsiz Isyeri Sahibi Kadinlarin Aile ve Is Iliskileri Türk Tarih Kurumu Basimevi*, Ankara: Başbakanlık.

Cetindamar, D. (2005), 'Policy issues for Turkish entrepreneurs', *International Journal of Entrepreneurship and Innovation Management*, **5**(3/4), 187–205.

Cetindamar, D., V.K. Gupta, E.E. Karadeniz and N. Egrican (2007), 'What the numbers tell: the impact of human, social, and financial capital on entrepreneurial entry in Turkey', in *GEM 2007 Report on Women and Entrepreneurship*, p. 32.

Cindoglu, D. (2003), 'Women's microenterprise activity', in the report *Bridging the Gender Gap in Turkey: A Milestone Towards Faster Socio-economic Development and Poverty Reduction*, 16 September, Poverty Reduction and Economic Management Unit, Europe and Central Asia Region, OECD.

Coverman, S. (1989), 'Role overload, role conflict and stress: addressing consequences of multiple role demands', *Social Forces*, **67**(4), 965–82.

Ertübey, N.O. (1993), 'Türkiye'de kadın girisimciligi: Mevcut durum, sorunlar ve öneriler', in N. Arat (ed.), *Türkiye'de Kadin Girisimcilik*, Ankara: TES-AR Yayınları, pp. 223–47.

Esim, S. (2000), 'Solidarity in isolation: urban informal sector women's economic organizations in Turkey', *Middle Eastern Studies*, **36**(1), 140–52.

Esim, S. (2001), 'Why women earn less: gender-based factors affecting the earnings of self-employed women in Turkey', in E. Mine Cinar (ed.), *The Economics of Women and Work in the Middle East and North Africa*, Volume 4, pp. 205–23.

Gazete Hayat (2008), 'Aras Holding'in kurucusu ve Yönetim Kurulu Başkanı Celal Aras'ın vefatından sonra bu göreve kızı Evrim Aras Sağıroğlu getirildi', available at: http://www.gazetehayat.com/haber/Aras-Kargo-artik-bir-kadina-emanet/44707; accessed 19 February 2010.

GEM (2007), *Global Entrepreneurship Monitor 2007 Report on Women and Entrepreneurship*, Babson College.

Gözlem (2009), '2008 atilim yiliydi, 2009 toparlanma olacak', 9 January.

Hisrich, R.D. and S.A. Oztürk (1999), 'Women entrepreneurs in a developing economy', *Journal of Management Development*, **18**(2), 114–24.

İnal, G. (2008), 'A comparative study of the reasons for and means of setting up a small business: the case of Turkish Cypriot restaurateurs and lawyers in North Cyprus and Britain', PhD thesis, Queen Mary, University of London.

İnal, G. and M. Karataş-Özkan (2007), 'A comparative study on career choice influences of Turkish Cypriot restaurateurs in North Cyprus and Britain', in M.F. Özbilgin and A. Malach-Pines (eds), *Career Choice in Management and Entrepreneurship*, Cheltenham, UK and Northampton, MA, USA: Edward Elgar, pp. 484–508.

Kabasakal, H. and M. Bodur (2002), 'Arabic cluster: a bridge between East and West', *Journal of World Business*, **37**(1), 40–54.

KAGIDER – Women Entrepreneurs Association of Turkey (2007), Overview of mission, activities and membership profile, available at: www.kagider.org; accessed 17 February 2010.

KAGIDER – Women Entrepreneurs Association of Turkey (2008), Presentation slides, July 2008.

Karataş-Özkan, M. (2006), 'The social construction of nascent entrepreneurship: dynamics of business venturing process from an entrepreneurial learning perspective', unpublished PhD thesis, University of Southampton, UK.

Kurtsan, M. (2007), 'The gender gap in Turkey', paper addressed at the OECD Istanbul World Forum – Measuring and Fostering the Progress of Societies, 28 June.

Kutanis, R.O. and S. Bayraktaroğlu (2003), 'Female entrepreneurs: social feminist insights for overcoming the barriers', available at: http://www.management.ac.nz/ejrot/cmsconference/2003/proceedings/gender/Kutanis.pdf; accessed 17 February 2010.

Milliyet (2009), 'Turk kahve kulturunu dunyaya tanitacak: Kahve Dunyasi, Alev Altinkilic', 12 January.

Mueller, S. and A.S. Thomas (2000), 'Culture and entrepreneurial potential: a nine country study of locus control and innovativeness', *Journal of Business Venturing*, **16**(1), 52–62.

OECD (2001), *Women Entrepreneurs in SMEs: Realizing the Benefits of Globalization and the Knowledge Based Economy*, Paris: OECD.

OECD (2005), *OECD SME and Entrepreneurship Outlook 2005 Edition*, Paris: OECD.

Onal, G. (1995), 'Ev Kadinina 20 Trilyon Kredi', *Sabah Gazetesi*, 9.

Ozar, S. (2002), *Barriers to Women's Micro and Small Enterprise Success in Turkey*, draft research report, Centre for Policy Studies, Central European University and Open Society Institute.

Özbilgin, M.F. and D. Woodward (2003), *Banking and Gender*, London and New York: Palgrave-IB Tauris Publishers.

Ozgen, O. and H. Ufuk (1998), 'Kadinlarin Evde Gerçeklestirdikleri Girisimcilik Faaliyetlerinin Aile Yasamina Etkisi', in O. Citçi (ed.), 20. *Yüzyilin Sonunda Kadinlar ve Gelecek*, TODAIE Yay. No. 285, Ankara: Yorum Matbaas, pp. 285–302.

Oztop, B. (2009) 'Aras'ın entegre büyüme planı', available at: http://www.turkishtime.org/tr/content.asp?PID={9AE813B1-C8BA-43DF-AF08-32AC089EB11C}; accessed 20 February 2010.

Schumpeter, J. (1934), *The Theory of Economic Development*, Cambridge, MA: Harvard University Press.

Tucker, H. (2007), 'Undoing shame: tourism and women's work in Turkey', *Journal of Tourism and Cultural Change*, **5**(1), 87–105.

Turkish Businesswomen (2008) 'Aras Cargo Yurtiçi ve Yurtdışı Taşımacılık A.S.', Turkish Businesswomen Directory, available at: http://www.turkishbizwomen.com/sayfalarhtml/evrim-aras-sagiroglu.html; accessed 20 February 2010.

Turkish Daily News (2008), 'Women entrepreneurs awarded', 19 April, 1.

Turkish Statistical Institute (1995), *Turkey's Statistical Yearbook 1993*, T.C. Başbakanlik Devlet Istatistik Enstitusu, Ankara, pp. 86–7.

Turkish Statistical Institute (2008), *Turkey's Statistical Yearbook 2007*, Başbakanlik Devlet Istatistik Enstitusu Ankara, pp. 154, 159.

Ufuk, H. and O. Ozgen (2001a), 'The profile of women entrepreneurs: a sample from Turkey', *International Journal of Consumer Studies*, **25**(4), 299–309.

Ufuk, H. and O. Ozgen (2001b), 'Interaction between the business and family lives of women entrepreneurs in Turkey', *Journal of Business Ethics*, **31**(2), 95–107.

Uras, G. (2009), 'Kriz döneminde büyümeyi sürdüren girişimciler var', *Milliyet Gazetesi*, available at: http://www.milliyet.com.tr/Ekonomi/HaberDetay.aspx?aType=HaberDetay&ArticleID=1045787&Date=12.01.2009&b=; accessed 20 February 2010.

Van Stel, A., D. Storey and R. Thurik (2007), 'The effect of business regulations on nascent and young business entrepreneurship', *Small Business Economics*, **28**(2), 171–86.

Welter, F. and S. Kolb (2006), 'Women and entrepreneurship in Latvia', TeliaSonera Institute Discussion Paper No. 4, Riga: TSI and SSE.

16 United Arab Emirates
Nnamdi O. Madichie

INTRODUCTION

This chapter provides a general overview of women's entrepreneurship in the United Arab Emirates (UAE). Based on a review of policy and academic papers the chapter introduces the reader to the socioeconomic development of this emerging economy and more importantly highlights the role of women within it. Following the theoretical analysis a profile of women entrepreneurs in the Northern Emirates of the UAE is illustrated in the form of case studies. Other issues of critical importance include the role of government in fostering women's entrepreneurship development and the challenges of these efforts in a rather underdeveloped (in research terms) context – the UAE.

The UAE government faces two main challenges. First it is confronted with what to do with its increasing number of educated women (77 per cent of the population). Second, it is grappling with the growing levels of unemployment of its nationals. As revealed in a survey by the Ministry of the UAE workforce, the unemployment rate among its nationals was stated to be as high as 12.7 per cent, compared with 2.6 per cent for the majority expatriate population (*UAE Yearbook*, 2009). This chapter highlights these dual challenges from a gender perspective by documenting how entrepreneurship could provide an alternative growth strategy. Evidence shows that the UAE government has not only recognized this option, but has also made remarkable strides in fostering women's entrepreneurship in furtherance of its economic and social development agenda. However, the chapter notes that in spite of these laudable achievements, more can be done not only from the policy point of view, but also in academic research terms. As identified by Erogul and McCrohan (2008, p. 178) 'the literature on female entrepreneurs in the UAE is almost non-existent'. From the scant literature in existence (Baud and Mahgoub, 1999; Haan, 2002 and 2004) studies have primarily focused on UAE women's entrepreneurship with little or no attempt at profiling this population sub-group. Haan (2004, p. 6) confirms this research challenge by pointing out that 'there is a need for a scientifically representative picture of women entrepreneurs in the UAE'.

Consequently, this chapter contributes to the thin discourse in four key areas by (1) updating research on UAE women's entrepreneurship; (2) focusing exclusively on UAE national (i.e., Emirati) women; (3) evaluating the impact of the policy responses of the government to the challenges facing women-owned and managed businesses in the UAE; and (4) extending the discourse beyond the usual suspects, Dubai and Abu Dhabi, by highlighting the experiences of women entrepreneurs in the Northern Emirates (especially Sharjah and Ras Al-Khaimah [RAK]) who have been identified as the most disadvantaged group in the *UAE Human Resources Report 2005* (see *UAE Yearbook*, 2006, p. 242).

THE POSITION OF WOMEN IN THE UAE

The UAE is an independent sovereign state bordered by Saudi Arabia and Oman and sharing maritime borders with Qatar, Iraq and Iran. Its population is 4.5 million, of which only about 20 per cent are Emirati nationals, with the remainder made up largely of nationals of other Arab states, as well as nationals from South and South-East Asia. Established on 2 December 1971, the federation comprises seven autonomous emirates, Abu Dhabi (the capital), Dubai (the commercial nerve centre), Sharjah (the acclaimed cultural capital), Ras Al-Khaimah (popular for its RAK Free Zone), Ajman, Umm Al-Quwain and Fujairah. His Highness (HH) Sheikh Zayed Bin Sultan Al-Nahyan was elected president of the state for a tenure of five years, which was renewed five consecutive times until his death in 2004, whereupon HH Sheikh Khalifa Bin Zayed Bin Sultan Al-Nahyan was elected president and remains in this office to date.

Several reasons have been advanced to explain the skewed ratio of women to men in the UAE labour force. First, the number of men aged 15 to 65 years was 2.12 million in 2005 compared with the women at only 838 941 'mainly because foreign workers are predominantly male'. Second, the UAE society is patriarchal and the changing of traditional views concerning a woman's place in the family remains a rather slow process (*UAE Yearbook*, 2008, p. 249). Nevertheless, times have changed as women now constitute about 22.4 per cent of the UAE's labour force, up from only 9.6 per cent about two decades ago in 1986. This has resulted from a variety of policy initiatives by the government from the federal to the local levels.

The full participation of women in social and economic life is considered to be essential for the future of the country (ibid., p. 245). As outlined in the UAE's address to the 51st session of the UN Commission on the Status of Women, great strides have been made in the empowerment of UAE women since the establishment of the state. From very rudimentary beginnings, when educational opportunities were minimal, the percentage of girls enrolled in primary education has now reached 83 per cent and women account for about 62 per cent of the total number of students in higher education, with a steady growth in the number of women with postgraduate degrees. As a result, 66 per cent of employees in the public sector, including education, medicine, diplomacy and armed forces, are women, of which '30 per cent are in decision-making positions' (ibid., p. 248). The belief that women are entitled to take their place in society and become effective partners in the development process is grounded in the UAE Constitution, which guarantees the principles of social justice for all, in accordance with Islamic principles. In the Constitution, women enjoy the same legal status, claim to titles, access to education, healthcare and social welfare and the same right to practise professions as their men counterparts. For example, the Civil Service Law allows for extensive maternity leave, and in 2005 civil service rules governing additional payments for children and housing were amended to eliminate any gender-based discrimination against employees. New laws have also been issued to allow divorced or widowed UAE women who were married to non-citizens to extend their citizenship to their children. The government has also acceded to a number of international agreements specifically relating to women and children, including the Convention on the Elimination of All Forms of Discrimination Against Women (CEDAW) and the UN Convention on the Rights of the Child (ibid.).

On the political front, women are also making an impact. Since early 2006, two women ministers have sat at the Cabinet table with responsibility for the Ministry of Foreign Trade and the Ministry of Social Affairs and two others were appointed in 2008. However, it was the inclusion of 1189 women among the 6689 people nominated to membership of the electoral colleges in each of the seven Emirates that broke new ground – the empowerment of these women to positions that saw them elect half the seats to the 40-member parliamentary body, the Federal National Council (FNC), the candidacy of 63 women in the subsequent elections and the swearing-in of nine national women to the FNC. These nine women account for about 22.5 per cent of the seats in parliament, a figure that is not only unique in the region but one that makes the UAE 'one of the few countries in the world with such a high percentage of female parliamentarians' (see Dabbagh and Nusseibeh, 2009, p. 15).

The government also continues in its efforts at mainstreaming gender equality and justice in all public institutions and continues to work on removing social and psychological barriers that impede the full integration of women into the labour force, especially in the private sector. However, there is still much ground to cover, 'although great strides have been made, there is a general awareness that the journey has [only] just begun' (*UAE Yearbook*, 2008, p. 246).

WOMEN'S ENTREPRENEURSHIP IN CONTEXT

Entrepreneurship has been defined as the pursuit of an opportunity irrespective of existing resources, and entrepreneurs as those who perceive themselves as pursuing such opportunities (Krueger and Brazeal, 1994). These definitions are gender-neutral and are consistent with Buttner and Moore's (1997) assertion that entrepreneurship is a gender-blind career choice. Although this assertion is theoretically true, in practice gender and environment interact to determine the success or failure of women as entrepreneurs in most emerging markets.

According to four past GEM reports (between 2004 and 2007), high ratios of women to men entrepreneurs in low-income countries have been the result of necessity-based entrepreneurship, rather than of elective decisions to go into business. In low-income economies, entrepreneurship leads to simple business endeavours, which in turn create jobs and new markets. Other studies report that women entrepreneurs differ from men in terms of their motivations, the types of external barriers that they face and the type of help available to women (Buttner and Moore, 1997; Mattis, 2004; Woldie and Adersua 2004). Krueger and Brazeal (1994, p. 101) asserted that favourable environmental conditions such as 'support from political, social, and business leaders and a team spirit in the community' effectively encouraged entrepreneurship among both men and women. Social support from family and friends who provide positive role models, as well as from parents who promote entrepreneurial aspirations during childhood, all contributed to the creation of a positive environment favouring women's entrepreneurship. In contrast, lack of access to seed funds and working capital remain two key environmental factors that particularly discourage women from engaging in entrepreneurial activity. Staub and Amine (2006) argue that many women in sub-Saharan Africa are 'ready to go' as entrepreneurs, if only environmental conditions were more favourable to their efforts. These findings underline the importance and value of the environmental analysis undertaken by these authors. Moreover, their findings suggest that women's entrepreneurship experience in Africa is qualitatively different from that of men, due to the differential impact of environmental factors especially on the former.

Over the years, a number of studies have documented barriers to women's advancement in the corporate world including stereotyping and misperceptions about women's abilities and long-term commitment to business careers; exclusion from informal networks and channels of communication; lack of willingness to 'risk' putting women in key developmental positions especially line positions; and pay inequalities (Kanter, 1977; McCall, 2005; Acker, 1992; *Catalyst*, 1994, 2000; Madichie, 2009; Spring and Rutashobya, 2009). Any one of these risk factors might provide a reason for women to seek alternative employment options. Mattis's (2004) research on women entrepreneurs split women business owners into two groups: international entrepreneurs ('born to be' entrepreneurs) and corporate climbers. International entrepreneurs (driven by pull factors) are women who, though they always wanted to start their own businesses, worked initially for others to gain business experience. In contrast, corporate climbers intended to stay in corporate careers, but ended up leaving because of 'push factors' in the work environment or to take advantage of an unexpected business opportunity (*Catalyst*, 2000; Kephart and Schumacher, 2005; Madichie, 2009). According to Mattis (2004), such 'push' factors played a larger role in the newest generation of women entrepreneurs' decisions to start-up their own businesses.

However, half of the women who had left the private sector to start their own businesses and 44 per cent of women from other employment backgrounds reported that they wanted more flexibility (including child care obligations; participation in community affairs; personal health concerns; and other family obligations), citing this as a primary reason for leaving their companies. Fisher (2004) reported that the new generation of women entrepreneurs have more corporate experience and hold more professional degrees. Moreover, government support and spending programmes have also been at the forefront of the surge of women's entrepreneurship worldwide. According to the National Women's Business Council, the US federal government spent a record-setting US$8.3 billion with women-owned business in 2004 (see Kephart and Schumacher, 2005).

Profiling Women-owned Businesses

Kephart and Schumacher (2005) advanced the concept of 'occupational segregation' by which they meant that certain occupations were predominantly gender-based such as production supervisor for men and elementary school teacher for women. According to them 'the conventional wisdom of the 1980s stated that women were destined to fulfill only supporting roles because of their inherent female weaknesses, i.e. too friendly, too helpful, and an inability to lead or take charge of a situation' (ibid., p. 4), while some believe this support role function is because women are over-represented in lower-paying, non-promotion-type fields such as education and nursing and are under-represented in the higher-paying, and more promotion-based fields such as engineering, information technology and the physical sciences (Hacker, 1997, cited in Kephart and Schumacher, 2005, p. 4). On the one hand, women may choose to leave their careers temporarily and 'stop out' to begin a family and/or care for a family since these duties are still primarily expected of women. When they return, however, they are continuously playing catch-up to their counterparts, never quite reaching it; hence missing out on the promotion track. On the other hand, women who try to balance career and family eventually reach a point where they halt their climb on the ladder to success fearful of not being able to balance all of the pressures or in some cases, just decide that juggling it all is no longer worth the additional stress to them (ibid.).

Taken from the context of sub-Saharan Africa, most women-owned businesses have been reported to operate mainly in the informal sector, are necessity-based, and best described as micro- or small-scale enterprises (McDade and Spring, 2005; Katwalo and Madichie, 2008). They are often run out of the home because women entrepreneurs do not have the funds necessary to acquire or rent business premises (Spring and Rutashobya, 2009). Although a convenient arrangement, the lack of physical space eventually acts as a brake on growth of the business. Other problems facing women who want to start or grow their own businesses have been documented to include lack of accurate market information, lack of operating funds and lack of property to use as collateral. With regard to these results, it should be noted that many people throughout the region, including some governments, regard self-employment as being synonymous with unemployment. For many, only formal employment in the public sector or in large enterprises constitutes real employment, so small-scale entrepreneurs are widely viewed as unemployed, thus prompting the need for the 'promotion of entrepreneurship [as] a positive social initiative' (Amine and Staub, 2009, p. 195).

Amine and Staub (2009) attempted to provide an understanding of how environmental barriers of all kinds can impinge upon the development of women's entrepreneurship. Using institutional theory-driven analysis, with special attention to issues of the social legitimacy of women as entrepreneurs, these authors demonstrate that women entrepreneurs in sub-Saharan Africa faced a daunting array of challenges arising from the socio-cultural, economic, legal, political and technological environments in which they live. Moreover, unfavourable conditions in local regulatory, normative and cognitive systems placed additional burdens on women who desire to become entrepreneurs or to expand their business. In order to address these gender-specific problems, the authors recommended the need for developing social marketing concepts in order to (1) change social beliefs, attitudes and behaviours that negatively affect women entrepreneurs, and (2) improve conditions in institutional systems and market environments. This is consistent with the suggestions of Amine and Staub (2009, p. 195) for the need for 'promotion of entrepreneurship [as] positive social initiatives'.

WOMEN'S ENTREPRENEURSHIP IN THE UAE

This section is discussed under two clear headings, first from the policy environment and second from an academic position. In the latter, it can be seen that there is no clear-cut entrepreneurship policy in the UAE. This is the case even though there are numerous institutions geared towards nurturing such a process especially in terms of developing the national women.

Policy Perspective

At the federal level, the General Women's Union (GWU) has been a key player in the government's strategy to create a supportive and empowering environment for women. Originally conceived as the UAE Women's Federation in 1975, the GWU was established under the leadership of HH Sheikha Fatima bint Mubarak (wife of the first president) with the aim of bringing together under one umbrella all the women's societies in the country. In the intervening years, the government-funded GWU has brought to the fore many inter-related issues of concern for women, children and the family, and it has been instrumental in inspiring much interest in handicraft, health education, religious education and literacy programmes throughout the UAE. It also provides vocational training, job placement services, family mediation services and continues to play a major role in assisting economic independence through the establishment of small businesses (*UAE Yearbook*, 2008).

It was not long ago in 2007 that the GWU launched a programme funded by Women in Technology (WIT), the US State Department-funded programme that offers training to women in information technology, personal skills and professional skills development in the hope of encouraging women entrepreneurs (ibid., p. 251). Moreover, the UAE Businesswomen Council (UAEBC), a nationwide network of business, professional and academic women, was set up in 2002, supported by the Federation of Chambers of Commerce and Industry (FCCI). With over 12000 members, the Council has running investments worth more than Dh25 billion (US$6.81 billion) in various fields, including commerce and industry, construction and real estate development, finance and tourism amongst others (ibid.).

At the local level the Abu Dhabi Businesswomen Group (ADBW) has implemented a number of major training initiatives in cooperation with trading and educational partners to provide valuable work experience for women as well as to encourage women's entrepreneurship. Like its counterpart (ADBW) the Dubai Business Women Council (DBWC) provides women entrepreneurs with assistance for small and medium ventures, from compiling feasibility studies to consultancy in all areas, and setting up business to availability of finance. Although women are high achievers in the educational field and are well-represented in public sector employment, the challenge is to increase women's participation in the private sector. There is a general consensus that indigenous UAE (or Emirati) women 'stand an equal if not greater chance of employment in the private sector, compared with men' (ibid., p. 249).

Academic Perspective

Budd's (2002) study provides a macro-environmental framework for analysing the experiences of UAE women entrepreneurs. By presenting a broad overview of the changing demographic trends of the member states of the Gulf Cooperation Council (GCC) with implications for future policy implications for the labour market in the Arab Gulf region, Budd's paper promises to have the keys to a range of benchmarking efforts.

McElwee and Al-Riyami (2003) highlighted the experience of Omani women entrepreneurs and the meanings they often attached to these experiences. Using in-depth, face-to-face interviews with 25 respondents, they concluded that the majority of women entrepreneurs enjoyed 'what they do and initially ventured into business for personal (social) reasons, to gain autonomy or financial necessity inspired by a role model other than for money (economic reasons)'. These authors also argued that the environment that Omani women entrepreneurs encountered in their daily lives often impacted upon as well as influenced their personalities. Furthermore, Nelson (2004), whose research was based solely on secondary data, drawing upon previous Centre for Labour Market Research and Information (CLMRI) studies, probed into the labour market experiences of Emirati women in the private sector. While her paper provides some insight into the composition of women in the UAE private sector, it however seems to have ignored certain aspects of entrepreneurship that are of more direct relevance here, notably owning and managing a business.

In addition to this, Omair (2008, p. 107) recognized that previous research in women's entrepreneurship had been mostly limited to European and North American settings and that women in different cultural contexts have been given little attention. Focusing on the context of the UAE, therefore, Haan (2002) interviewed ten indigenous women running small businesses with a 'special home business licence' in Dubai. He found that small home-based businesses constituted an effective way of encouraging women entrepreneurial activity in the UAE since these required minimal start-up capital. Two years later, Haan (2004) expanded his sample size by a 'multiple of three' to present the findings of a survey of 30 Emirati (indigenous) women's small businesses based mainly in the emirates of Dubai and Sharjah with the objective of contributing to the formulation of policies and the design of support programmes that will assist them in starting up and expanding their businesses. He identified two main segments, (1) 'traditional activities' undertaken by relatively elderly, modestly educated women entrepreneurs who tended to operate from the confines of their homes; and (2) 'modern activities' mainly managed by young, well-educated and more business-oriented women. One interesting finding is that the support provided to women entrepreneurs engaged in traditional activities often had social and cultural, rather than economic objectives. The preservation of traditional activities being perceived to be part of the country's cultural heritage (ibid., p. 23).

Drawing upon previous studies and using secondary data, Nelson (2004) looked at the labour market experiences of Emirati women in private sector employment. Since entrepreneurship has been identified as an attractive and potentially lucrative possibility for job creation, particularly in developing economies, Nelson (ibid., p. 23) presented it as an 'attractive option for UAE national women given the relatively limited options available to them in the labour market'. More recently, Erogul and McCrohan (2008) explored the motivation of Emirati entrepreneurs for establishing their own business and the support they were receiving from within their personal social networks. Based on interviews with 17 Emirati entrepreneurs, they found that the primary motivating factor for Emirati women for starting their business included the 'desire for independence' and 'to contribute to the development of their country'. They explained this finding by the collectivist dimension existing in the roots of the UAE society and the desire of women to realize their personal talents and capabilities. Erogul and McCrohan (ibid., p. 184) nonetheless acknowledged that more work needed to be done in this area: 'further research is needed to better understand what barriers or inhibitors may be preventing women from becoming [entrepreneurial]'.

CASE STUDIES: EMIRATI WOMEN ENTREPRENEURS

This chapter responds to the 'call to action' by probing deeper into the behavioural profiles of UAE women entrepreneurs and their potential contribution to the national development of the country. As a starting point the chapter presents two case studies (profiled from initial contacts and the promise of a series of snowballing contacts with women entrepreneurs in Sharjah and Ras Al Khaimah) with further links to other emirates like Ajman and Umm Al Quwain (UAQ). In order to identify the prevalence or otherwise of some of the aforementioned challenges impinging on women entrepreneurs in the context of the UAE, two case studies are used for illustrative purposes. The cases highlight how women entrepreneurs from the Northern Emirates of the UAE have been under-researched. The cases were inspired by a newspaper report on how women in Ras Al Khaimah (Zacharias, 2008) seemed to have defied the gender penalties. This prompted the need to initiate contact with the author of the report and thereby resulted in what can be described as a 'snow-ball' sample in reaching the remaining respondents (most of whom are not reported here). In any case, the profiles of the two women discussed in this chapter are used to verify any uniqueness to the dilemmas of women's entrepreneurship in the context of the UAE. In the first case there is a complexity in terms of cataloguing Mozah as a woman entrepreneur, considering that she is also in full-time employment. In the second case also, the complexity arises as a result of the fact that Latifa is still in full-time education.

BOX 16.1   MOZAH

This first case study provides an example of the trends in women's entrepreneurship in general and within the UAE context in particular. The case focuses on Mozah, a 27-year-old female IT graduate of the Higher Colleges of Technology in the Northern Emirate of Ras Al Khaimah (RAK).

Mozah considers herself 'a single lady with an interest in adding value to traditional women's dressmaking – the *abaya*'. This is in order to make the *abaya* more appealing for the modern woman. Her business was established in 2004 and she employs seven people to work on different aspects of dress-making from tailoring to embroidery. Her employees are mostly foreigners from places such as Bangladesh, India and Pakistan. They all also happen to be men.

In addition to owning her business, Mozah is also in full-time employment at the Ministry of Health in Ras Al Khaimah. Mozah was motivated by the fact that she could more or less 'kill two birds with one stone'. In other words she enjoyed the security of having a nine-to-five job to fall back on in the event of business failure. This security buffer makes it rather difficult to appropriately categorize her into the established women entrepreneurial segments identified in the literature.

Unlike some of her peers, Mozah seems to enjoy the full support of her family who are also keen to see something 'new in the *abaya*'. To confirm the level of support enjoyed she is assisted by her sister who is a 'sleeping' partner in the business. Although there are no immediate plans for expansion, Miss Elegant, Mozah's registered company name, has organized and participated in a range of fashion shows across RAK.

Overall, Mozah fits the profile of the 'modern' type of woman entrepreneur identified by Haan (2004) as she is educated, young and unmarried. She also embodies the growth-oriented type by not operating from home.

BOX 16.2 LATIFA

Unlike the first case study, the case of Latifa seems more complicated. Being a marketing major at the College of Business Administration, University of Sharjah, Latifa seems less atypical. However, based on her level of education (she graduates in Fall 2010) she fits the profile of typical modern woman entrepreneurs, that is, young and single. At 21 years old, Latifa, who is also Sharjah (indigenous) born and bred, runs her own business from home. She combines this business with her studies and takes advantage of a free web hosting portal (www.uaewomen.net) to promote her services.

She started her clothing design business about two years ago in June 2007. Working from home and with no business name at the moment, Latifa adds value to ladies' jeans by providing additional designs (e.g., embroidery). Her marketing strategy is arguably the risk-free option where she promotes her services using a range of cost-effective channels such as a free web hosting service, word-of-mouth especially from friends and family and cash before delivery where her customers bear the cost of delivery. Her market development is largely through the use of personal contact networks where trust is of very high importance. She, however, warns that she is more wary of people she knows than she is of complete strangers.

Latifa comes from a military family background and is potentially the first to have a degree in the family on graduation in Fall 2010. She also has a younger sister who is currently on a first year law degree at the University of Sharjah.

Reflecting on her primary motivations for starting her business, Latifa points out that it was purely accidental. Although she was very good in art and design at school it was not till much later that, encouraged by friends, she decided she could actually transform this hobby into a business.

She also highlights that while this is not unique to her, she enjoys support from members of her family. Her father has even given assurance of financial support for not only start-up capital but also procurement of business premises should she decide to formalize her business.

Although Latifa is aware of women business groups such as Hamdan Bin Rashid Al Maktoum Foundation (see www.mbrfoundation.ae), which helps young businesses with good ideas secure seed grants, she does not belong to any of these government groups. Rather she is currently savouring her membership of the Women Business Students Association. As she declared in the course of this interview 1 am a very active member of the WBSA as it provides me with a relaxed environment for free interaction with my peers and lecturers . . . I also enjoy taking responsibility in organizing numerous extra-curricular activities here'. One word she has for aspiring entrepreneurs is 'Be original! Don't go copying my designs!'

CHALLENGES OF WOMEN'S ENTREPRENEURSHIP IN THE UAE

In April 2007 the Mohammed Bin Rashid Establishment for Young Business Leaders announced the findings of the UAE's first Global Entrepreneurship Monitor (GEM) Report entitled *GEM-UAE 2006*, which aimed at mapping out the country's entrepreneurial landscape (Middle East Events, 2007). Compiled by Professors Kenneth Preiss of Zayed University (Abu Dhabi) and Declan McCrohan of Zayed University (Dubai), the report was based on a national survey of 2000 respondents from across the seven emirates and reported to be the most comprehensive exercise ever conducted on business in the Arab world. Some key findings from the expert interviews are quite revealing. Thoughts and opinions expressed have been categorized into five dominant themes: (1) legal; (2) cultural; (3) financial; (4) government policies; and (5) education and training.

Legal

UAE laws and regulations are not supportive of SME entrepreneurship. In particular, much concern was expressed about the system of generic rules, procedures and documentation, which are common to nearly all forms of business structures (both the larger corporations and their SME counterparts – Preiss and McCrohan, 2006). The most dominant legal theme was the issue of foreign ownership of companies operating within the UAE. The existing system does not allow for 100 per cent foreign ownership, except in a small number of enterprises located in designated Free Zones. Hence, non-nationals are forced to purchase trade licences from Emirati nationals. There is a belief that the Emirati use this type of business venture as a source of relatively risk-free additional income. New ventures are often driven by the individual entrepreneur as the risk-taker, with a strong vision for the venture, yet this energy is constrained by the demands of the national partner who is risk averse with a limited entrepreneurial mindset. This situation also seriously impedes the extent of knowledge transfer flowing from an injection of foreign business activity to the host nation. Interestingly, but rather worryingly (ibid., p. 34): 'Many of the local partners, known as "silent partners", often play no role in the day-to-day management of the business but simply provide their signature on company documentation allowing the business to operate legally – but for a "fee"!'

Cultural Barriers

Many UAE families tend to prefer their children to gain employment in the public as opposed to the private sector. This is largely because public sector jobs in the UAE are well known for their generous benefits, comfortable working hours and less demanding work regimes, thus, families tend to disapprove of their child looking towards a perceived riskier career in the entrepreneurial domain over a career in the public sector. Furthermore, 'emiratization' may well be working contrary to the initial intent of the programme, that is, finding a job into which a national can be placed seems to transcend the bigger question: is that job necessary in the first place? (Preiss and McCrohan, p. 35). It was also noted that 'sections of the UAE society often frown upon females starting up and running their own business. As a consequence, those that do start up a business do so in a safe haven of "me-too'" type products like a perfume, chocolate, or craft shop – some of which are operated from home' (ibid.). Another issue raised was the high level of 'fear of failure' that exists in the UAE. This phobia has societal ramifications linked to the 'loss of face', something that is enough to discourage many UAE citizens from ever attempting to start up their own business. Indeed, there are indications that owning a business in the UAE is often more about the prestige and image of having one's own business, rather than creating a successful/profitable new venture. Many key informants stated that a number of supposedly 'successful' businesses were in fact, 'being camouflaged behind family funds' subsidizing the unprofitable business venture (ibid.).

Finance

This was one area where there seemed to be differing opinions amongst the surveyed experts. Opinions were split as to whether access to venture finance is a major barrier facing entrepreneurs in the UAE or that there is no shortage of funds. Some respondents believed that the UAE was flush with liquidity and that accessing finance was not difficult at all, given that one had a good business idea. However, others argued that although the UAE was flush with money, much of this liquidity was being channelled into the real estate and equity markets, thus there was a shortage of venture funding for start-ups. Indeed the GEM-UAE report indicated that (ibid., p. 35):

> A common opinion expressed by a number of . . . experts was that generous government support policies for nationals that have been introduced over the past three decades, that is, since the larger inflow of oil wealth, has created a culture of dependence and, thus, removed the need or desire for business risk-taking through entrepreneurship . . . Nationals have become accustomed to relying on their Government for financial support when things get difficult, thus, removing the need to a large extent for necessity entrepreneurship to flourish.

There was also a consensus amongst the key informants that a formal and efficient channel for funds to be injected into new venture initiatives was non-existent, thereby making it not only more difficult, but also more costly for entrepreneurs to secure finance from resident commercial banks.

Government Policies

There is perceived to be a lot of government goodwill toward, and support for, entrepreneurship, particularly at the federal level. However, it is believed that effort at the government level needs to be 'more efficiently coordinated' so as to more effectively encourage and nurture entrepreneurial activity. Although numerous support and training programmes currently exist in the UAE, their coordination and coherence is cause for concern. For example, there exist the business women's councils across the Emirates: Tanmia, GWU, Forsa and the Mohammed Bin Rashid Establishment for Young Business Leaders.

Education

Most experts hold strong opinions about the state of education in the UAE. The popular belief being that the system needs a major overhaul and that the education system needs to 'encourage more creative and lateral thinking' in students, as opposed to 'rewarding rote learning'. A number of experts also stated that the education system in the UAE prepares students to be employees rather than risk-taking venture creators. The experts also highlighted the need for some practical business skills to be taught at high school level, skills such as financial literacy, including the ability to read and comprehend profit and loss, as well as balance sheet statements. Furthermore, there is a perceived need for skills in preparing business plans and feasibility studies as part of tertiary business education. It was noted that many new/potential entrepreneurs in the UAE were lacking these basic small business skills. It is also a commonly held view that colleges and universities in the UAE were not doing enough in terms of such skills development. Furthermore, it is believed that the opportunity exists for these educational institutions to offer more training and personal development workshops to teach entrepreneurs the basics, that is, the knowledge, procedures and skills on how to become more entrepreneurial.

SUMMARY

This chapter highlights the dynamics of women's entrepreneurship in the context of the UAE, drawing upon a rigorous review of government policy documents on the one hand, and research projects and/or initiatives such as the Emirates Businesswomen Council, UAE General Women's Union, Forsa (an exclusive investment fund for women investors and entrepreneurs), on the other hand. To provide further impetus on the need for this research, we recognize that in many parts of the Middle East, and indeed in most other parts of the world, the women-friendly policy initiatives, as well as discourse, have opened doors for women to contribute to the economy (Henry, 2002). At the same time, they have created a dynamic in which gender space has been bridged and institutions established with the sole aim of furthering the interests of women. There are three clear implications from this chapter.

First, while entrepreneurship in general has been widely reported as a viable alternative to underemployment or unemployment, most is heavily characterized by informality, that is, home-based businesses (see Katwalo and Madichie, 2008; Madichie, 2009; Thompson et al., 2009). Concentration here stifles any plans of future expansion and thus development. The way forward, therefore, would be to transit from the 'informal' to the 'formal' sector of self-employment. However, this also presents its own difficulties (Spring and Rutashobya, 2009, p. 8). In the particular case of Latifa and many others like her there are concerns over what the next steps would be as she graduates.

Second, there is a need to alter the cultural barriers to women's entrepreneurship. As identified by Woldie and Adersua (2004), aspiring women entrepreneurs face additional barriers to success arising from negative social attitudes. Prejudice against women entrepreneurs is experienced much more severely in emerging economies mainly as a result of deeply rooted, discriminatory cultural values, attitudes, practices and the traditions of patriarchal cultures. The UAE seems to fit this profile, but then again these two case studies present a clear illustration on how social acceptance can go a long way in enabling women entrepreneurs to make their mark. While social attitudes are not the only factors hindering women's entrepreneurship, they have been recognized by Gartner (1985) as critical factors. Moreover, such negative attitudes have been identified in the case of emerging economies such as Nigeria (Woldie and Adersua, 2004) as one of the greatest challenges confronting women entrepreneurs.

Third, prescriptions should be appropriate for the malaise. In this case two papers are worthy of comparison. On the one hand, the World Bank (2007) called for reforms and implementation of gender-sensitive indicators. Amine and Staub (2009) on the other hand prescribed the institution of social marketing efforts as the way forward. In the former report, a set of priority policy action areas were identified and characterized into four broad planks urging the need for:

- education reform;
- an alignment of legal reform with economic objectives;
- an institutional framework that values skills to mainstream a gender perspective in policy-making and implementation; and
- a results-oriented approach to policy and decision-making that relies on gender-sensitive indicators.

While all of these needs are recognized, the latter two seem to be of more particular relevance in this context, notably the need for (1) an institutional framework, and (2) a results-oriented approach. The former framework has been recently used by Amine and Staub (2009) to profile women's entrepreneurship in the context of sub-Saharan Africa.

ACKNOWLEDGEMENT

Funding support from the University of Sharjah, Seed Grant No. 090311, is gratefully acknowledged.

BIBLIOGRAPHY

Acker, J. (1992), 'Gendering organizational theory', in Albert J. Mills and Peta Tancred (eds), *Gendering Organizational Analysis*, Newbury Park: Sage.

Allen, E., Langowitz, N. and Minniti, M. (2007), *GEM 2006 Report on Women and Entrepreneurship*, 28 February.

Allen, E., Elam, A., Langowitz, N., Dean, M. and GERA (2008), *2007 Report on Women and Entrepreneurship*, Global Entrepreneurship Monitor.

Amine, S. and Staub, K. (2009), 'Women entrepreneurs in sub-Saharan Africa: an institutional theory analysis from a social marketing point of view', *Entrepreneurship & Regional Development*, **21**(2), 183–211.

Babson College (2008), 'GEM Report 2007 ranks UAE higher for promoting enabling environment for start-up businesses', press release. 23 June; available at: http://www3.babson.edu/Newsroom/Releases/GEM-UAE.cfm; accessed 20 February 2010.

Baud, I. and Mahgoub, H. (1999), 'Towards increasing national female participation in the labour force', (Tanmia) Research Report No. 2, Centre for Labour Market Research and Information, June, Dubai, UAE.

Benzing, C. and Chu, H. (2009), 'A comparison of the motivations of small business owners in Africa', *Journal of Small Business and Enterprise Development*, **16**(1), 60–77.

Budd, B. (2002), 'An overview of demographic and labour trends of the member nations of the Cooperation Council for the Arab States of the Gulf', *Labour Market Research and Information*, **4**(10), 3–21.

Buttner, E.H. and Moore, D.P. (1997), 'Women's organizational exodus to entrepreneurship: self-reported motivations and correlates with success', *Journal of Small Business Management*, **35**(1), 34–46.

Catalyst (1994), *On the Line: Women's Careers Advancement*, New York: Catalyst.

Catalyst (2000), *Cracking the Glass Ceiling*, New York: Catalyst.

Dabbagh, M. and Nusseibeh, L. (2009), *Women in Parliament and Politics in the UAE: A Study of the First Federal National Council Elections*, February, Dubai: Dubai School of Government.

Dzisi, S. (2008), 'Entrepreneurial activities of indigenous African women: a case of Ghana', *Journal of Enterprising Communities: People and Places in the Global Economy*, **2**(3), 254–64.

Erogul, M. and McCrohan, D. (2008), 'Preliminary investigation on Emirati women entrepreneurs in the UAE', *African Journal of Business Management*, **2**(10), 177–85.

Fisher, A. (2004), 'Why women rule', *Fortune Small Business*, July/August, 14.

Gartner, W.B. (1989), 'Who is an entrepreneur? is the wrong question', *Entrepreneurship Theory and Practice*, **13**(4), 47–68.

Haan, H. (2002), 'Report on a survey of UAE nationals in micro, small and medium enterprises', Policy Research Paper No. 6, March, Centre for Labour Market Research and Information, Dubai, UAE, Tanmia/CLMRI.

Haan, H. (2004), *Small Enterprises: Women Entrepreneurs in the UAE*, Labour Market Study No. 19, Centre for Labour Market Research and Information, Dubai, UAE, Tanmia/CLMRI.

Hall, P. and Taylor, R. (1996), 'Political science and the three new institutionalisms', *Political Studies*, **44**(5), 952–73.

Henry, C. (2002), 'Closing remarks at Research Forum: Promoting Female Entrepreneurship – Implications for Education, Training and Policy', Centre for Entrepreneurship Research, Dundalk Institute of Technology, Dundalk, 19 November.

Horn, M. (1995), *The Political Economy of Public Administration*, Cambridge, UK: Cambridge University Press.

International Finance Corporation (2004), *Women Entrepreneurs in the Middle East and North Africa: Characteristics, Contributions and Challenges*, World Bank Group.

Kanter, R.M. (1977), *Men and Women of the Corporation*, New York: Basic Books.

Katwalo, A. and Madichie, N. (2008), 'Entrepreneurial and cultural dynamics: a gender kaleidoscope of Ugandan microenterprise', *International Journal of Entrepreneurship and Small Business*, **5**(3/4), 337–48.

Kephart, P. and Schumacher, L. (2005), 'Has the "glass ceiling" cracked? An exploration of women's entrepreneurship', *Journal of Leadership and Organizational Studies*, **12**(1), 2–15.

Krueger, N. Jr and Brazeal, D.V. (1994), 'Entrepreneurship potential and potential entrepreneurs', *Entrepreneurship Theory and Practice*, **19**(3), 91–104.

Madichie, N. (2009), 'Breaking the glass ceiling in Nigeria: a review of women's entrepreneurship', *Journal of African Business*, **10**(1), 51–66, Special Issue.

Marlow, S. (2006), 'Enterprising futures or dead-end jobs? Women, self-employment and social exclusion', *International Journal of Manpower*, **27**(6), 588–600.

Mattis, M (2004), 'Women entrepreneurs: out from under the glass ceiling', *Women in Management Review*, **19**(3), 154–63.

McCall, L. (2005), 'The complexity of intersectionality', *SIGNS: Journal of Women in Culture and Society*, **30**(3), 1771–880.

McClelland, E., Swail, J., Bell, J. and Ibbotson, P. (2005), 'Following the pathway of female entrepreneurs', *International Journal of Entrepreneurial Behaviour and Research*, **11**(2), 84–107.

McDade, B. and Spring, A. (2005), 'The "new generation of African entrepreneurs": networking to change the climate for business and private sector-led development', *Entrepreneurship & Regional Development*, **17**(1) January, 17–42.

McElwee, G. and Al-Riyami, R (2003), 'Women entrepreneurs in Oman: some barriers to success', *Career Development International*, **8**(7), 339–46.

Middle East Events (2007), 'Mohammed Bin Rashid Est. For Young Business Leaders announces results of UAE's First Entrepreneurship Study. UAE is first Arab Country to Have GEM Report', press release 18 April, available at: http://www.middleeastevents.com/site/pres_dtls.asp?pid=1317; accessed 20 February 2010.

Morris, M. (2007), 'Entrepreneurship as social policy: a case study of the United Arab Emirates', paper submitted at Regional Frontiers of Entrepreneurship conference, Queensland University of Technology, Brisbane, February.

Nelson, C. (2004), *UAE National Women at Work in the Private Sector: Conditions and Constraints*, Centre for Labour Market Research and Information, Tanmia, Dubai.

OECD (2004), 'Women's entrepreneurship: issues and policies', Second OECD Conference of Ministers Responsible for Small and Medium-sized Enterprises (SMEs), Istanbul, Turkey 3–5 June.

Omair, K. (2008), 'Women in management in the Arab context', *Education, Business and Society: Contemporary Middle Eastern Issues*, **1**(2), 107–23.

Preiss, Kenneth J. and McCrohan, Declan (2006), Mohammed Bin Rashid Establishment for Young Business Leaders – *GEM United Arab Emirates: Entrepreneurship in the United Arab Emirates in 2006*, College of Business Sciences, Zayed University, Vol. 1, No. 1, Abu Dhabi: Zayed University.

Spring, A. and Rutashobya, L. (2009), 'Gender-related themes in African entrepreneurship: introduction to the articles', *Journal of African Business*, **10**(1), 1–10, Special Issue Guest Editorial.

Staub, K.M. and Amine, L.S. (2006), 'Women entrepreneurs in Africa: ready to go!', paper presented at the 3rd International Entrepreneurship Conference at the United States International University of Nairobi, 31 May–2 June, in Kenya.

Thompson, P., Jones-Evans, D. and Kwong, C. (2009), 'Women and home-based entrepreneurship: evidence from the United Kingdom', *International Small Business Journal*, **27**(2), 227–39.

UAE Yearbook (2006), 'Social development', UAEInteract, p. 242, available at: http://uaeinteract.com/uaeint_misc/pdf_2006/English_2006/eyb8.pdf; accessed 19 February 2010.

UAE Yearbook (2008), 'Social development', available at: www.uaeinteract.com/women; accessed 20 February 2010.

UAE Yearbook (2009), 'Social development', available at: http://www.uaeinteract.com/uaeubt_misc/pdf_2009; accessed 22 February 2010.

Welter, F. (2008), 'Reflections on women's entrepreneurship', Keynote 15th Nordic Conference on Small Business Research, Tallinn, 22–23 May.

Woldie, A. and Adersua, A. (2004), 'Female entrepreneurs in a transitional economy: businesswomen in Nigeria', *International Journal of Social Economics*, **31**(1/2), 78–93.

World Bank (2007), *The Environment for Women's Entrepreneurship in the Middle East and North Africa Region*, Washington, DC: The World Bank.

Zacharias, A. (2008), 'Women entrepreneurs are making their mark in Ras al Khaimah', *The National Newspaper*, 29 December.

17 United Kingdom
Susan Marlow and Maura McAdam

INTRODUCTION

This chapter explores the socioeconomic context for female entrepreneurship within the United Kingdom. It commences with an overview of the UK labour market as it has been well documented that those entering self-employment usually do so from prior employment where they accumulate many of the resources necessary to begin a new venture (Storey, 1994; Brooksbank, 2006). Consequently, access to and experiences of waged work are critical in shaping the success of self-employment. Analysis of labour market positioning is particularly salient in the case of women given the evidence regarding occupational segregation (Hakim, 2004; EOC, 2006), which in turn constrains access to entrepreneurial resource acquisition.

Having described women's positioning within the UK labour market, the focus then narrows to consider women as small business owners. Within the UK, significant government attention has recently been afforded to policies that encourage and support the entrepreneurial potential of women (SBS, 2003). Yet, whilst more women have begun new ventures since the early 1990s, their share of self-employment, at around 26 per cent, and business ownership, at around 12 per cent, has remained constant (Labour Force Survey, 2005/06). This means that as a sub-sector of the self-employed population, whilst more women are beginning new firms, more of these are then closing or failing. Moreover, drawing from a wide range of literatures (Fraser, 2005; Carter and Shaw, 2006; Marlow et al., 2008) it is evident that women-owned firms are likely to be small in terms of employment, turnover and profit; they demonstrate low growth trajectories and are over-represented amongst part-time and home-based businesses (Carter and Marlow, 2007; Thompson et al., 2007). To analyse these relatively high and persistent levels of churning plus the so-called 'under-performance' thesis, the chapter then explores the manner in which gender, specifically the ascription of femininity as a concept, influences how women 'fit' into the contemporary entrepreneurial field.

However, it is noted that within the discourse on entrepreneurship and gender, there has been a propensity to adopt a universal view of 'women' that denies diversity and ignores agency (Earle and Letherby, 2003). Such universalism has then encouraged a tendency within the literature to focus upon comparisons between the performance of male- and female-owned firms (Ahl, 2006). This has been helpful in establishing broad themes and trends that relate to the influence of gender upon entrepreneurial behaviour but within contemporary debate, greater attention is now being afforded to heterogeneity within gender categories. So for instance, the dynamic manner in which femininity interacts with race, age and class to mould entrepreneurship ensures that there are greater differences within the category of 'the female entrepreneur' per se than there are between male and female business owners (Doyle and Paludi, 1998; Ahl, 2007). A useful example of such heterogeneity lies within the notion of 'success'. As has been noted above, broad trends indicate that women-owned businesses are likely to remain small and are often described as 'under-performing' (H.M. Treasury/BERR, 2008), however, this is not an accurate reflection of all such firms. Indeed, it is essential to draw attention to those women whose businesses do achieve success in both normative and personal terms. Therefore, to illustrate this, two case studies of women whose firms have achieved success within their fields are described. Finally, the chapter concludes with a summary of the arguments raised and further recommendations for policy action and support.

THE POSITION OF WOMEN IN EMPLOYMENT IN THE UK

Within the UK, approximately 70 per cent of the female population of working age (16–65) are in formal employment or self-employment (ONS, 2007). Economic activity is greatest for both men and women between the ages of 25 and 44 where employment rates are 90 per cent and 75 per cent respectively. Within the realms of developed economies, it is evident that the UK has a large and complex labour market with relatively full employment (Dundon and Rollinson, 2007). In terms of educational attainment, girls now achieve more formal qualifications at school than boys and are equally successful in higher education (Hurrell, 2006). For example, veterinary science and accountancy studies are dominated by women but it is noted that their presence in traditional masculine areas such as engineering remains weak (EOC, 2006).

When analysing the position of women within the UK labour market, a number of general trends emerge relating to occupational segregation, part-time employment and home working (EOC, 2006). Hakim (2004) refers to 'horizontal segregation', where men and women are concentrated in different occupations and 'vertical segregation', where men and women are both present within an occupation but the former occupy high positions of status and power and the latter pool at the lower end of the hierarchy. Whilst the notion of individuals choosing different occupations and achieving at different rates is not problematic given the need for economic diversity, occupational segregation is strongly associated with gendered subordination. As such, reflecting arguments by Oakley (1973), that which is associated with the feminine commands a lower value than that associated with the masculine. Accordingly, it is not the intrinsic worth of a task that denotes its value but the gender of the person undertaking it. Gender also works in more subtle ways to create so-called 'glass ceilings' (Patterson, 2007) that constrain women's career progression within higher-status occupations, hence, vertical segregation. Consequently, whilst the UK labour market is regulated by legislation such that overt discrimination is illegal, gender subordination ensures that a woman's occupational choices and career progression opportunities remain constrained by stereotypical assumptions related to femininity (Cranny-Francis et al., 2003).

Accompanying gendered occupational segregation are persistent pay differentials between men and women that span across and within occupations (Pudney and Shields, 2000). In terms of horizontal segregation, this reflects the relationship between value and gender ascription as feminized occupations command lower status and returns. Regarding vertical segregation, women situated at the bottom end of career hierarchies axiomatically command poorer terms and conditions than their male counterparts. In the case of the UK, although the Sex Discrimination Act has been on the statute book for over 30 years, in 2005 full-time female employees earned around 83 per cent of the male wage whilst this gap widened notably for part-time workers to 62 per cent of the male wage (Labour Force Survey, 2005/06). The situation deteriorates further for those of retirement age where we find that women command just 53 per cent of the average male income (Women and Equality Unit, 2008). Persistent income differentials over time, despite regulation, confirm the influence of occupational segregation in determining the recognition and reward attached to feminized work.

From this very brief overview of gender and the UK labour market, it emerges that whilst young women are now outperforming their male counterparts in educational attainment, they are still experiencing disadvantageous occupational segregation. Negative gendered ascriptions and stereotypical assumptions combine to constrain women's opportunities to progress freely within their chosen employment. Accordingly, it has been argued (Mallon and Cohen, 2001; Patterson, 2007) that more women are considering entrepreneurial careers to gain recognition, autonomy and flexibility and so address the constraints of waged employment. To assess the efficacy of this choice, the UK context for female entrepreneurship is described.

As in most western countries, the percentage of UK women in management (34 per cent of all managers) and the profession has increased over the past few decades (National Management Salary Survey, Chartered Management Institute/Remuneration Economics, 2007). However, as in the workforce as a whole, there is still gender segregation in management jobs, with the most popular jobs for women managers being personnel (68 per cent) and marketing (50 per cent) (National Management Salary Survey, Chartered Management Institute/Remuneration Economics, 2004). Furthermore, women are still concentrated in the middle and lower levels of management even in function groups they dominate. According to the EHRC (2008) at the current rate of progress in the UK, it will take another 27 years to achieve equality in civil service top management (up from 20 years in 2007) and 73 years to achieve an equal number of female directors of FTSE 100 companies (up from 65 years in 2007).

THE CURRENT POSITION OF WOMEN AND SMALL BUSINESS OWNERSHIP

UK self-employment and business ownership data demonstrate the relatively low levels of women in enterprise. Currently, 7.6 per cent of all British women in employment are in self-employment, compared with 17.4 per cent of all men (Labour Force Survey, 2005/06). Historical analysis of the Labour Force Survey reveals that, while there has been a substantial growth in the overall self-employed population, the female share has remained stable over the past 15 years (Lindsay and Macaulay, 2004). Since 1992, the number of self-employed women has increased by 12.6 per cent, a faster growth rate than that of male self-employment, while the female share of self-employment (26 per cent in 1992 and 26.6 per cent in 2006) has hardly changed (Labour Force Survey, 1992, 2005/06). Accordingly, whilst more women are entering self-employment, more of their businesses are closing or failing.

That the establishment, sustainability and growth of firms are dependent upon the business owner's possession of, and access to, a range of resources is well established within the entrepreneurship literature (Firkin, 2003). Building on the resource-based view of the firm (Rangone, 1999) and borrowing from theories of capital (Bourdieu, 1977), the concept of 'entrepreneurial capital' has emerged in recognition of the need for entrepreneurs to accrue financial, human, social and symbolic capital in order to succeed (Davidsson and Honig, 2003; Firkin, 2003). The *variety* and *amount* of capital possessed by entrepreneurs has been found to impact on both experiences of business ownership and firm performance (Jurik, 1998; Kepler and Shane, 2007). It is agreed that the acquisition and development of entrepreneurial capital is initiated largely during experiences of the labour market prior to entering business ownership and the proximity of appropriate role models (Storey, 1994; Hundley, 2001). Acknowledging this, women's accrual of entrepreneurial capital has to be contextualized within their wider labour market positioning and experiences (Marlow, 2002; Carter et al., 2007).

In respect to the acquisition of entrepreneurial capital, as noted above, a number of enduring labour market trends restrict the variety and amount of such capital possessed by, and available to women. Consequently, the persistence of a gender pay gap constrains women's opportunities to amass personal funds for investment purposes (Marlow et al., 2008; Women and Equality Unit, 2008). Added to this, occupational segregation constrains the accrual of human (education and experience), social (contacts and networks) and symbolic (reputation and credibility) capital necessary to support sustainable businesses (Brindley, 2005; Jeynes, 2005; Rouse, 2005; Rouse and Kitching, 2006). Finally, the lack of female entrepreneurial role models is much lamented as the entrepreneurial image reflects a strongly masculine tone effectively excluding the feminine (Ahl, 2007).

So it emerges that not only are women less likely to become self-employed, their experiences of business ownership are shaped by their gender. Most women-owned businesses are found in traditionally feminized occupational sectors, including catering, caring, personal and business services; women are largely absent from high-growth, entrepreneurial sectors or as owners of high-grossing professional firms (Boden and Nucci, 2000; Hundley, 2001; Bosma and Harding, 2007). In general, women tend to enter crowded, competitive segments of the service sector that have lower entry costs, and so experience poorer returns (Meager et al., 2003; Roper and Scott, 2007). As such, the disadvantages of occupational segregation experienced by women in waged work are reflected by those within self-employment (Marlow, 2002; Hakim, 2004). The operating profiles of female-owned firms also exhibit feminized working patterns; the available data indicate that around half of self-employed women work part-time (less than 30 hours per week) and around a third base their businesses within the home. Men however, reflect their stereotypical employment profile with much lower rates of part-time and home working, 18 per cent and 24 per cent respectively (Bosma and Harding, 2007; Thompson et al., 2007). Women adopt such operating profiles in an effort to combine economic activity, domestic labour and child care (Belle and La Valle, 2003; Rouse and Kitching, 2006). This is despite evidence suggesting that self-employment provides a poor solution to such competing demands (Greer and Greene, 2003; Williams, 2004; Rouse and Kitching, 2006). Drawing from an econometric analysis of returns from self-employment, Hundley (2001, p. 825) notes unequivocally, 'the presence of small children and greater hours of housework have a negative effect on female earnings'.

While such fragmented approaches to business operation may be a rational response to the positioning of self-employed women in a particular socioeconomic context, they have a negative effect on the normative credibility of the business and the business owner. Further, such feminized operating profiles, which divert from normative models, constrain the performance and so, future prospects of the firm (Boden and Nucci, 2000; Marlow and Patton, 2005). From this brief discussion of the extant literature (see Marlow, 1997; Mirchandani, 1999; Carter et al., 2001; Hundley, 2001; Collins-Dodd et al., 2004; Brush et al., 2006; Carter and Shaw, 2006 for further comment) it is evident that a gendered socioeconomic positioning ensures that women's businesses struggle to perform in a manner that echoes the standards associated with 'successful' enterprises and accordingly, they are represented as lacking. To focus the discussion more specifically, we now turn to an exploration of conceptual and contextual barriers women encounter when engaging with self-employment.

EXPLORATION OF CONCEPTUAL AND CONTEXTUAL BARRIERS TO FEMALE ENTREPRENEURSHIP

Whilst gender identities shift and take differing articulations reflecting context, what remains constant is the subordination of the feminine such that there is a hierarchical valuation of traits and characteristics. As Charles (2003) argues, economically, socially and ideologically, men are able to prioritize their interests over and above those of women. Such inequalities in power and status are absorbed into the fabric of society, ordering relationships and in effect 'normalizing' differences so they appear natural and inevitable and become embedded in perception, thought and action (Wilson et al., 2007). The assumption of masculinity as the norm is well illustrated within the field of entrepreneurship where the notion of an entrepreneurial discourse has been analysed by Smith and Anderson (2004) and Ahl (2007). Drawing upon the work of Foucault (1972), the notion of discourse is perceived as a categorization of meaning that empowers particular world views. As Prasad (2005, p. 250) notes, dominant discourses establish, 'what can be spoken about and what cannot: whose speech or writing may be considered legitimate, what sequence of arguments is to be followed'.

The defining masculinity of the entrepreneurial discourse has been recognized for some time; as Holmquist and Sundin (1989, p. 1) argued nearly 20 years ago, 'entrepreneurial theories are made by men, for men and about men'. It might be assumed that this dominance has been exposed and challenged by the growing body of research and policy interest regarding the experiences of female entrepreneurs. For example, some shift might be expected in the portrayal of the 'typical' entrepreneur as essentially masculine, embodying stereotypically male characteristics and behaviours including aggression, competitiveness and ruthlessness that effectively bar women from the field (Ahl, 2006). However, Smith's (2003) iconographic analysis of the semiotic interpretation of the entrepreneurial image identifies a persistent stereotype of a white male. Smith and Anderson (2004, p. 137), drawing upon analyses of the entrepreneurial discourse, support this stance, arguing that, 'the accepted notion of morality in entrepreneurial narratives is patently a "masculine" gendered form'. Ahl (2007, p. 687) presents convincing evidence for this claim; drawing upon an extensive analysis of published work within the entrepreneurial domain she concludes that, 'the entrepreneur was consistently described in exactly the same words as those used to describe manhood. The result of the construction of the entrepreneur as male, is that women as entrepreneurs are rendered invisible'. As such, the female entrepreneur becomes the 'other' (De Beauvoir [1949] 1988) and so is seen as an interloper in the field. The message embedded within the entrepreneurial discourse being, 'think entrepreneur, think male'.

Evidently, women do not easily 'fit' into the accepted model of entrepreneurship as that which is associated with the feminine is in opposition to normative entrepreneurial action and characterization. So, for example, women-owned ventures are more likely to be described as 'under-performing' in that they 'fail' to achieve similar rates of growth and profit generation as those owned by men (Bosma and Harding, 2007). Female business owners are more likely to have their firms described as 'hobby' businesses so not an outcome of expertise but of a leisure interest (Ahl, 2006). Regardless of the context for the debate however, the defining feature of these descriptions of female enterprise is their failure to meet the normative standards of a credible business, that of full-time activity with the aim of maximizing economic returns, owned by a man.

From this discussion, it emerges that women face a range of conceptual and structural barriers when seeking to adopt an entrepreneurial identity. This impacts upon their propensity to begin and to grow new ventures, where evidence indicates that fewer women engage with entrepreneurship and for those that do, their ventures are less likely to be defined as 'successful' in normative terms. Yet, as was noted in the introduction to this chapter, individuals can use differing degrees of agentic power according to their socio-economic environment and positioning. As such, a middle-class, female accountant in the UK entering sole practice is more likely to build a profitable sustainable business than a self-employed cleaner. In effect, gendered subordination is dynamic, subtle and sensitive to context; equally, individuals draw upon their resources to negotiate around and through their particular experiences of discrimination. For some, this means adopting an 'honorary man' persona, whilst for others it means emphasizing their femininity to gain visibility.

CASE STUDIES: ENGAGING WITH ENTERPRISE

To explore the manner in which women have used their agency to build successful and sustainable businesses, two case study examples of successful female entrepreneurs who have built their business within male-dominated sectors are now described.

BOX 17.1   LOUISE

The first case study example is that of female entrepreneur Louise, founder of a successful IT company located in the South East of England. Louise's business has been operation for eight years and currently has a staff of 12 employees. It is anticipated that the company will achieve a growth trajectory of 20 per cent over the next five years as a result of a product diversification strategy. Although Louise comes from a family of entrepreneurs (both her father and uncle have successful businesses), after obtaining a First Class Honours degree in Information

Technology, her initial reaction was not to start her own business but to pursue a graduate position with a large multinational IT company as business owner- ship, 'was too risky, I just didn't have the experience, I thought if I worked for someone else it wouldn't be as risky later on'.

After working for this company for 15 years in a variety of roles based on data collection and solutions, the identification of a niche market drove her to 'spin out'. Not only had Louise acquired considerable knowledge and expertise during this time but she had also developed a strong network incorporating sup- pliers and potential customers, 'at least when I phoned a customer, they could put a face to a name. I was not a complete unknown'. Independence, being her own boss and flexibility were all cited by Louise as the key advantages of busi- ness ownership. Louise has two daughters (aged seven and nine respectively), and 'being my own boss definitely give me flexibility and means I can take the girls off to school and pick them up again'. However, Louise does acknowledge the challenges of balancing a growing business with family business, 'having a family has restricted the amount of time that I can dedicate to the business and probably keeps my growth plans modest'. It is also interesting to note that Louise's role as both a mother and business woman has resulted in the imple- mentation of child-friendly policies, 'I like to think that my employees know that they work for a company that is child friendly; it is not unusual for one of the male engineers to say "I have to leave early today, I'm doing the school run"'.

Reflecting on the masculine nature of the IT sector, Louise referred to the isola- tion of being within a male-dominated environment and often found that 'lads' talk' exacerbated this isolation. 'That's the main thing that I miss about working for the larger company, there were more women there, a lot more socialization so I do miss female company'. As a result Louise has found female company and support in her local Women in Business Network. Louise cites her former boss as her role model and mentor and feels that this continued support is invaluable in terms of advice and also giving a female perspective. 'She has been great; she knows the industry and knows what it's like to be surrounded by men'. Louise is also actively involved in her local Women in Business Network and plans to become more involved in coaching other female entrepreneurs when she retires. Imparting advice to other female entrepreneurs, Louise remarked 'if I had my time again and wanted to combine a career and family; I would go for self-employment in my 20s if I had the resources; or wait until my 40s when the children are older. But all that is in an ideal world where you meet the ideal life partner at the right time!'

BOX 17.2   JENNIFER

Our second case study example focuses on Jennifer, founder of a biotechnol- ogy company that tests anti-cancer drugs. The company was founded in 1999 and employs 35 people, with an expected growth trajectory of 30 per cent over the next five years. Jennifer enjoyed science subjects at school so a primary degree in biology followed by a PhD seemed like the natural progression for her. After completing the PhD Jennifer took up a post-doctoral position with a cancer research institute. It was during this time that Jennifer acquired in-depth knowledge of the area but also saw the opportunity of subcontracting and collaborating with biotechnology and pharmaceutical companies. However, it was redundancy that actually pushed Jennifer into enterprise, 'My research post had come to an end and I was effectively redundant, so I was at a crossroads, I could have gone for another research post but I probably would have been in the same position two years down the line'.

After sounding out her idea with key contacts in pharmaceutical companies, Jennifer set about formulating a business plan for her company. She refers to the advice and support she got from her local business support agency as invaluable, 'I knew nothing about setting up a business as you have to remember that I had spent my entire life in academia'. In particular, Jennifer found the advice provided regarding approaching potential investors and presenting her business as a viable business option particularly beneficial. The company was initially funded with a mixture of personal funds and venture capital and has recently secured second-round venture capital (VC) funding worth £1 million. When asked about the reasons for going down the VC route Jennifer remarked, 'basically to support our growth ambitions and as a biotech company we could get zero bank backing'.

Like the other case study Jennifer operates within a male-dominated industry and when asked to reflect on this, she remarked, 'I guess you have to be a particular type of person and to not be hurt emotionally. I have had to change a lot'. However, adjusting to this environment has had an impact on her personal life, 'I've had to become quite abrupt and quite square-edged on things and my partner often says to me you can take your corporate hat off now you are at home'. Although Jennifer has no children she feels that as a woman she still is expected to take care of household chores, 'so you have to deal with all the work stress and then you have to come home and do all your domestic stuff – you have to try and hold a lot of things together; deep down men believe that it's a woman's job to look after the home and them!'

Jennifer reckons the secret to her success is her 'employee focus' – 'we are very open; everyone comes to the same meetings, no secrets. Obviously some negotiations are confidential, although they know the gist of what is going on, they do not know the details'. As a result the company is currently committed to an extensive training and development programme for all its employees, and as Jennifer remarked 'I believe that having a motivated workforce is essential, therefore all the employees get a stake in the company'.

Regarding the challenges of business ownership, Jennifer identifies growth transitions and the implementation of structures and systems as particularly challenging, 'in the past there was only four of us, you could write on a piece of a paper and put it on a Excel spreadsheet but now it is all scientific projects or jobs'. The company's future growth strategy is based on the entry of global markets facilitated by strategic alliances with key partners, 'partnerships will form the basis of strategy over the next five years'. As for Jennifer's plans, 'I don't want to run this company forever, I want to sell it and retire'. To sum up then, Jennifer imparts the following words of wisdom to aspiring female entrepreneurs, 'Firstly you need to be passionate about what you do, then you need to get tough and think like a man'.

SUMMARY

This chapter explores the socioeconomic context for female entrepreneurship within the UK. Successive UK governments have introduced a range of initiatives to encourage more women to start new firms but to date there has been limited expansion of female entrepreneurship and few high-profile 'successful' women emerging into the market. Such programmes may encourage females to consider enterprise, however, this may not necessarily remove the barriers women face when attempting to enter sectors where traditionally growth opportunities are more prevalent. This is well illustrated within male-dominated industries such as IT and biotechnology, which the case studies presented attest to.

A number of key threads can be drawn from these case studies. First, to achieve business success, women need support and information about managing financing and overcoming reservations regarding debt, especially equity finance.

Second, the importance of networking and the differences in the networking behaviour of men and women emerged. Women and men develop networks that reflect their own sex thus, given their poorer levels of entrepreneurial capital and knowledge, this can be detrimental for women (Aldrich, 1989). Although empathy and companionship were found from networking, benefits such as critical information sharing and collaborative problem solving were limited. It is clearly difficult to construct supportive and productive business networks when the potential membership is so scarce, as is the case for high-technology female entrepreneurs.

Third is the importance of appropriate role models and mentors; this is particularly evident in non-traditional sectors such as information technology and biotechnology where 'success stories' continue to be overwhelmingly male. Finally, the importance of training and support was noted as women who have undergone some form of enterprise training are twice as likely to be engaged in entrepreneurial activity (GEM, 2005). In fact, the choice of targeted female-focused business support is important, so, for instance, the National Council for Graduate Entrepreneurship (NCGE) reports that 98 per cent of women chose to participate in their Women's Flying Start Programme because it was exclusively for them.

To conclude, it is evident from the case studies presented that for women to be 'successful' business owners in normative terms they need to adopt some features of an 'honorary man', in order to make their qualifications and human capital fit into the contemporary entrepreneurial field. Indeed, current programmes and initiatives to encourage women to engage with business ownership may eventually increase female entrepreneurial activity; this may not necessarily spill over into high-growth, successful enterprises unless greater attention is afforded to the tensions between the demands of starting and growing new ventures and the reality of women's lives. Finally, for many women and indeed men, their definition of a successful business may not necessarily reflect the normative model of economic attainment if the enterprise satisfies their own ambitions. Yet, in broader terms these ventures are not afforded the status and reverence of those that demonstrate normative success so, for women to be recognized as participants in the contemporary entrepreneurial project, they must achieve upon such terms.

REFERENCES

Ahl, H. (2006), 'Why research on women entrepreneurs needs new directions', *Entrepreneurship Theory and Practice*, **30**(5), 595–621.

Ahl, H. (2007), 'Sex business in the toy store: a narrative analysis of a teaching case', *Journal of Business Venturing*, **22**(5), 673–93.

Aldrich, H.E. (1989), 'I heard it through the grapevine: Networking among women entrepreneurs', in O. Hagen, C. Rivchun and D. Sexton (eds), *Women Owned Businesses*, New York: Praeger.

Belle, A. and I. La Valle (2003), *Combining Self-employment and Family Life*, Cambridge, UK: Polity Press and Joseph Rowntree Foundation.

Boden, R. and A. Nucci (2000), 'On the survival prospects of men's and women's new ventures', *Journal of Business Venturing*, **15**(4), 347–62.

Bosma, N. and R. Harding (2006), *GEM 2005 Summary Results*, Babson College, MA; London Business School, available at: http://www.gemconsortium.org/about.aspx?page=global_reports_2006; accessed 23 February 2010.

Bosma, N. and R. Harding (2007), *GEM 2006 Summary Results*, Babson College, MA; London Business School, available at: http://www.gemconsortium.org/about.aspx?page=global_reports_2006; accessed 20 February 2010.

Bourdieu, P. (1977), *Outline of a Theory of Practice*, translation R. Nice, Cambridge, MA: Cambridge University Press.

Brindley, C. (2005), 'Barriers to women achieving their entrepreneurial potential', *International Journal of Entrepreneurial Behaviour and Research*, **11**(2), 144–61.

Brooksbank, D. (2006), 'Self-employment and the small business', in S. Carter and D. Jones-Evans (eds), *Enterprise and the Small Business*, London: Prentice Hall.

Brush, C., N. Carter, E. Gatewood, P. Greene and M. Hart (2006), 'The use of bootstrapping by women entrepreneurs in positioning for growth', *Venture Capital: An International Journal of Entrepreneurial Finance*, **8**(1), 15–31.

Carter, S. and S. Marlow (2007), 'Female entrepreneurship: theoretical perspectives and empirical evidence', in N. Carter, C. Henry and B. O'Cinneide (eds), *Promoting Female Entrepreneurs: Implications for Education, Training and Policy*, London: Routledge.

Carter, S. and E. Shaw (2006), *Women's Business Ownership: Recent Research and Policy Developments*, Department of Trade and Industry Small Business Service Research Report, London, HMSO.

Carter, S., S. Anderson and E. Shaw (2001), *Women's Business Ownership: A Review of the Academic, Popular and Internet Literature*, Report to the Small Business Service, RR002/01.

Carter, S., E. Shaw, W. Lam and F. Wilson (2007), 'Gender entrepreneurship and bank lending: the criteria and processes used by bank loan officers in assessing applications', *Entrepreneurship, Theory and Practice*, **31**(3), 427–45.

Charles, N. (2003), *Gender in Modern Britain*, Oxford: OUP.

Collins-Dodd, C., I. Gordon and C. Smart (2004), 'Further evidence on the role of gender in financial performance', *Journal of Small Business Management*, **42**(4), 395–417.

Cranny-Francis, A., W. Waring, P. Stavropoulos and J. Kirkby (2003), *Gender Studies: Terms and Debates*, Basingstoke, Palgrave Macmillan.

Davidsson, P. and B. Honig (2003), 'The role of social and human capital among nascent entrepreneurs', *Journal of Business Venturing*, **8**(3), 301–31.

De Beauvoir, S. [1949] (1988), *The Second Sex*, London: Pan.

Doyle, J. and M. Paludi (1998), *Sex and Gender: The Human Experience*, San Francisco, McGraw Hill.

Dundon, T. and R. Rollinson (2007), *Understanding Employment Relations*, London: Prentice Hall.

Earle, S. and G. Letherby (eds) (2003), *Gender, Identity and Reproduction*, New York: Palgrave Macmillan.

EHRC – Equality and Human Rights Commission (2008), *Sex and Power*, available at: http://www.equalityhu manrights.com/uploaded_files/sex_and_power_2008_word.doc; accessed 20 February 2010.

EOC – Equal Opportunities Commission (2006), *Sex and Power: who runs Britain?*, available at: http://www.unece.org/stats/gender/publications/UK/Sex_and_Power_GB_2006.pdf; accessed 20 February 2010.

Firkin, P. (2003), 'Entrepreneurial capital', in A. de Bruin and A. Dupuis (eds), *Entrepreneurship: New Perspectives in a Global Age*, Aldershot: Ashgate, pp. 57–75.

Foucault, P. (1972), *The Archaeology of Knowledge and the Discourse on Language*, New York: Pantheon Books.

Fraser, S. (2005), *Finance for Small and Medium Sized Enterprises: A Report on the 2004 UK Survey of SME Finances*, Coventry: SME Centre, University of Warwick.

Greer, M. and P. Greene (2003), 'Feminist theory and the study of entrepreneurship', in J. Butler (ed.), *New Perspectives on Women Entrepreneurs*, Greenwich, CT: Information Age Publishing, pp. 1–24.

Hakim, K. (2004), *Key Issues in Women's Work: Female Diversity and the Polarisation of Women's Employment – Contemporary Issues in Public Policy*, London: Cavendish Press.

H.M. Treasury and Dept. for Business, Enterprise and Regulatory Reform (BERR) (2008), *Enterprise: Unlocking the UK's Talent*, March, London: HMSO.

Holmquist, E. and C. Sundin (1989), 'The growth of women's entrepreneurship – push or pull factors?', paper presented to the EIASM Conference on Small Business, University of Durham Business School.

Hundley, G. (2001), 'Why women earn less than men in self-employment', *Journal of Labor Research*, **12**(4), 817–29.

Hurrell, K. (2006), *Facts about Men and Women in Great Britain 2006*, available at: http://www.unece.org/stats/gender/publications/UK/Facts_about_W&M_GB_2006.pdf; accessed 20 February 2010.

Jeynes, J. (2005), 'Women and the economy: a decade of entrepreneurship', paper presented at the 28th Institute for Small Business Entrepreneurship National Conference, Blackpool, November.

Jurik, N. (1998), 'Getting away and getting by: the experience of self-employed homemakers', *Work and Occupations*, **25**(11), 7–35.

Kepler, E. and S. Shane (2007), *Are Male and Female Entrepreneurs Really that Different?*, Small Business Research Summary Report No. 36 to the US Small Business Administration Office, September; available at: http://www.sba.gov/advo/research/rs309.pdf; accessed 20 February 2010.

Labour Force Survey (1992), *Labour Force Survey Quarterly Survey*, London: Office for National Statistics, April.

Labour Force Survey (2005/06), *Labour Force Survey Quarterly Survey*, London: Office for National Statistics.

Lindsay, C. and C. Macaulay (2004), 'Growth in self-employment in the UK', *Labour Market Trends*, October, London: Office for National Statistics, pp. 399–404.

Mallon, M. and L. Cohen (2001), 'Time for a change? Women's accounts of the move from organizational careers to self-employment', *British Journal of Management*, **12**(3), 217–30.

Marlow, S. (1997), 'Self-employed women – do they mean business?', *Entrepreneurship and Regional Development*, **9**(3), 199–210.

Marlow, S. (2002), 'Self-employed women: a part of or apart from feminist theory?', *Entrepreneurship and Innovation*, **2**(2), 23–37.

Marlow, S. and D. Patton (2005), 'All credit to men? Entrepreneurship, finance and gender', *Entrepreneurship, Theory and Practice*, **29**(3), 526–41.

Marlow, S., S. Carter and E. Shaw (2008), 'Constructing female entrepreneurship policy in the UK: is the US a relevant benchmark?', *Environment and Planning C: Government and Policy*, **26**(2), 335–51.

Meager, N., P. Bates and M. Cowling (2003), *Business Start-up Support for Young People Delivered by The Prince's Trust*, Report to the Department of Work and Pensions, London: HMSO.

Mirchandani, K. (1999), 'Feminist insight on gendered work: new directions in research on women and entrepreneurship', *Gender, Work and Organization*, **6**(4), 224–35.

Chartered Management Institute/Remuneration Economics (2004, 2007), National Management Salary Survey.

Oakley, A. (1973), *Sex, Gender and Society*, London: Temple Smith.

ONS – Office of National Statistics (2007) 'Labour market statistics – time series data', available at: http://www.statistics.gov.uk/; accessed 20 February 2010.

Patterson, N. (2007), 'Women entrepreneurs: jumping corporate ship or gaining new wings?', paper to the 30th ISBE Conference, Glasgow, November.

Prasad, P. (2005), *Crafting Qualitative Research*, New York: M.E. Sharpe.

Pudney, S. and M. Shields (2000), 'Gender and racial discrimination in pay and promotion for NHS nurses', *Oxford Bulletin of Economics and Statistics*, **60**(0), 801–36.

Rangone, A. (1999), 'A resource-based approach to strategy analysis in SMEs', *Small Business Economics*, **12**(2), 233–48.

Roper, S. and J. Scott (2007), 'Gender differences in start-up finance – an econometric analysis of GE data', paper to the 27th Institute of Small Business and Entrepreneurship Conference, Glasgow, November.

Rouse, J. (2005), 'Pregnancy and maternity in self-employment: individualised social reproduction?', paper presented at the 28th Institute for Small Business Entrepreneurship National Conference, Blackpool, November.

Rouse, J. and J. Kitching (2006), 'Do enterprise programmes leave women holding the baby?', *Environmental Planning C: Government and Policy*, **24**(1), 5–19.

SBS – Small Business Service (2003), *A Strategic Framework for Women's Enterprise*, London: DTI Small Business Service.

Smith, R. (2003), 'Constructing the heroic/fabled entrepreneur: a biographical analysis', paper presented to the Babson Kauffman Entrepreneurship Conference.

Smith, R. and A.R. Anderson (2004), 'The Devil is in the e-tail: forms and structures in the entrepreneurial narratives', in D. Hjorth and C. Steyaert (eds), *Narrative and Discursive Approaches in Entrepreneurship*, Cheltenham, UK and Northampton, MA, USA: Edward Elgar, pp. 125–43.

Storey, D. (1994), *Understanding the Small Firm Sector*, London: Routledge.

Thompson, P., D. Brooksbank and D. Jones-Evans (2007), 'Who are the home based entrepreneurs?', paper to the 30th Institute for Small Business and Entrepreneurship Conference, Glasgow, November.

Williams, C. (2004), 'The glass escalator: men who do women's work', in N. Sacks and C. Marrone (eds), *Gender and Work in Today's World*, Cambridge, MA: Westview Press, pp. 105–22.

Wilson, F., S. Carter and E. Shaw (2007), 'Bank loan officers' perceptions of business owners: the role of gender', *British Journal of Management*, **18**(2), 154–72.

Women and Equality Unit (2008), *Working and Living*, available at: www.womenandequalityunit.gov.uk/work_life/index.htm; accessed 24 February 2010.

18 United States of America
Mary C. Mattis and Leslie Levin

INTRODUCTION

Over two decades, women-owned businesses in the United States of America have shown tremendous growth. Although this trend was interrupted by the recent economic down-turn – 10.1 million firms were 50 percent or more owned by women in 2010, compared to 10.4 million in 2007 – growth of this sector of the US economy is projected to continue to outpace the rate of growth of all firms (42 percent versus 24 percent in 2008). Women-owned businesses are employing 13 million people, up from 12.8 million in 2007, and are generating $1.9 trillion in sales as of 2008[1] (Gunelius, 2010).

The first notable report on women's entrepreneurship was Eleanor Brantley Schwartz's 1976 pioneering article, 'Entrepreneurship: a new female frontier', an exploratory and descriptive analysis based on interviews with 20 women entrepreneurs. Schwartz concluded that the primary motivators for the women who were interviewed were the need to achieve, job satisfaction, economic payoffs and independence, the same motivators found for male entrepreneurs by Collins and Moore in 1964. Most research, however, has recognized that socio-historical and cultural factors in the workplace and in society more generally, have influenced women's motivations to start their own businesses.

In contrast to Schwartz's conclusions, Still's 2006 review of research on women entrepreneurs points to changing social and cultural factors as reasons for the growing number of women entrepreneurs in the US: in the 1970s, 1980s and early 1990s women entered self-employment to gain autonomy and independence, to escape the glass ceiling of the corporate world and to gain more flexibility and balance in their lives (Borooah et al., 1997; Moore and Buttner, 1997; Catalyst and the National Foundation of Women Business Owners, 1998; Daily et al., 1999; Still and Timms, 2000; Mattis, 2005; Levin and Mattis, 2006). In the late 1990s and early 2000 researchers found that in addition to other reasons for becoming business owners, women wanted to 'make a difference' by pursuing social goals, such as providing good client service, making a contribution to the community, being a 'good' corporate citizen and pursuing quality, in addition to economic goals (Cliff, 1998; Still and Timms, 2000).

More recent research has found that these differences in women's motivations for pursuing entrepreneurship are related to age: women over 40 were seeking to escape the corporate 'glass ceiling', whereas those under 40 were motivated by the opportunity business ownership offers for wealth creation and for impacting strategy (Center for Women's Business Research, 2001; Korn/Ferry International, 2001).

A 1998 study undertaken by Catalyst and The National Foundation for Women Business Owners (NFWBO) of women who had left corporate careers to become entrepreneurs found that some of the women's decisions to become business owners were situational, related to downsizing or closing of their corporate employer's business, or family events, while other women's motivations were opportunistic, characterized by a desire to be their own boss, to pursue a winning idea, to be in control of their own destiny, to gain independence and decision-making responsibility and to fulfill a lifelong dream (Catalyst and National Foundation of Women Business Owners, 1998). Several of the women who left for opportunistic reasons reported that a customer/client with whom they had worked in their former position had encouraged them to strike out on their own. As a result, some women went from being corporate employees to competitors of their former employer. In their research, Moore and Buttner (1997) characterize these two groups of women who left companies to start their own businesses as intentional entrepreneurs and corporate climbers.

In examining data for the three generations of women business owners represented in the Catalyst-NFWBO study (women who had owned their businesses for less than ten years, for 10 to 19 years and for 20 or more years), researchers found that the share of women who reported that they had left salaried positions in the private sector because of a glass ceiling had more than doubled over the past two generations of women in the study. Twenty-two percent of women who had owned their own business less than ten years cited the glass ceiling, as opposed to 15 percent of women with 10 to 19 years' tenure running their own business and only 9 percent of women who had owned their businesses for 20+ years. This response pattern may also have been influenced by the fact that the glass ceiling had not been named or widely discussed when the earliest generation of women business owners left their jobs. Furthermore, women of their generation did not have the same expectations about fairness in the workplace that later generations of women now have.

THE CURRENT POSITION OF WOMEN AND SMALL BUSINESS OWNERSHIP

In 2008, women were 46 percent of the US labor force. Women accounted for 51 percent of all workers in high-paying management, professional and related occupations. They outnumbered men in such occupations as financial managers; human resource managers; education administrators; medical and health services managers; accountants and auditors; budget analysts; property, real estate and social and community association managers; preschool, kindergarten, elementary, middle and secondary school teachers; and physical therapists and registered nurses. Women are projected to account for 49 percent of the increase in the total labor force growth between 2006 and 2016 (US Department of Labor, 2008).

Women's participation in various industry sectors varies by race and ethnicity: the largest percentage of employed Asian and white women (47 percent and 39 percent, respectively) worked in management, professional and related occupations. For both black and Hispanic women, it was sales and office occupations, accounting for 33 percent (ibid.).

Of persons aged 25 and older, 28 percent of women and 30 percent of men had attained a bachelor's degree or higher; 32 percent of women and 31 percent of men had completed high school, but not college. The median weekly earnings of women who were full-time wage and salary workers was $614, or 80 percent of men's $766 (ibid.).

In 2008, women held 15.1 percent of directorships at *Fortune* 500 companies; this number was 14.8 percent in 2007. The number of companies with no women board directors increased from 59 in 2007 to 68 in 2008. The number of companies with three or more women board directors increased from 83 in 2007 to 92 in 2008. Women of color held just 3.2 percent of all *Fortune* 500 directorships while making up slightly more than one-fifth of women directors (Catalyst, 2008).

THE CHANGING FACE OF WOMEN'S ENTREPRENEURSHIP IN THE US

National data show that women business owners are ethnically diverse; indeed, the growth rate of women's business ownership appears to be higher among minorities in the US than among non-Hispanic whites. Between 1997 and 2006, the number of privately held firms 50 percent or more owned by women of color grew five times faster than all privately held firms (120 percent versus 24 percent) (Center for Women's Business Research, 2007). As of 2010, twenty-six percent of all women-owned businesses are owned by a woman of color – African American, Asian, Latina, or other races. There are currently 2.3 million firms that are 50 percent or more owned by women of color. These firms employ 1.7 million and generate $235 billion in revenues, and were also the fastest growing firms between 2002 and 2008 (Gunelius, 2010). Minority groups in the US also have larger shares of women business owners than non-Hispanic whites, ranging from 31 percent of Asian American to 46 percent of African American business owners (Lowrey, 2006).

Women business owners are somewhat older than women in the US generally; 49 percent of women business owners in the US in 1992 were between the ages of 35 and 54, compared with 34 percent of the population aged 15 or older. Just 18 percent of women business owners were 34 or younger, compared with 38 percent of the US female population aged 15 or older (Catalyst and The National Foundation for Women Business Owners, 1998).

While census data show that women business owners are more highly educated than women in the US generally, data from the Catalyst/NFWBO study suggests that overall the education attainment of the group of women they studied was lower than for a group of high-level corporate businesswomen studied by Catalyst (1998). This unexpected finding may suggest another reason that women leave companies to start their own businesses: one that was not explored in the study, namely, women with considerable business experience, but lacking advanced degrees, in particular the MBA degree, may have left when their companies began to give preference to MBAs in entry-level manager hiring, training and promotions. This was a common phenomenon in the US in the 1990s and may still occur in US companies.

Some longstanding characteristics of women-owned enterprises that could present obstacles to their success appear to be changing. Between 1997 and 2004, privately held, women-owned firms diversified into all industries, with the fastest growth in wholesale trade (283.4 per percent growth); healthcare and social assistance services (130.0 percent growth); arts, entertainment and recreation services (116.8 percent growth) and professional, scientific and technical services (82.7 percent growth) (Center for Women's Business Research, 2007).

The number of women-owned firms with employees expanded by an estimated 28 percent in the period from 1997 to 2004, three times the growth rate of all firms with employees. Seventy-five percent of all firms in the US do not have employees compared with 81 percent of women-owned businesses. The fastest growth rate is in the number of women-owned firms with 100+ employees and, regardless of race or ethnic background, the vast majority of women entrepreneurs have growth as a primary goal (Lowrey, 2006). Further, research conducted by the Center for Women's Business Research in 2005 dispels many commonly held perceptions about women-owned businesses, finding that such firms are just as financially strong and credit worthy as the average US firm, have similar performance on bill payment, similar levels of credit risk and are just as likely to remain in business.

STRUCTURAL AND CONTEXTUAL BARRIERS

Differences between women- and male-owned businesses still remain, largely in the area of how they are financed and in revenue generation. Although women are moving into the equity capital markets, they receive only 9 percent of the institutional investment deals and 2 percent of the dollars. They are far less likely to receive capital from venture capital firms than male-owned firms and are less likely to use commercial credit or equity. While it is the case that women business owners' satisfaction with banking relationships has more than doubled since 1992 (35 percent versus 82 percent), women still have more difficulty financing their business than do male business owners. A study conducted by the Center for Women's Business Research found that women business owners who obtained capital had to persevere, making an average of four attempts to obtain bank loans or lines of credit and 22 attempts to obtain equity capital. Additionally, although 60 percent of *Fortune* 1000 companies spend $1 billion or more with outside suppliers, as of 2003 only about 4 percent of these outside suppliers were women-owned businesses (Center for Women's Business Research, 2007).

Research suggests that female entrepreneurs do employ different business strategies and tactics than male entrepreneurs. Women are less likely than men to purchase their business and to prefer low-risk/return businesses while male entrepreneurs were more likely to start technologically intensive businesses, businesses that lose their competitive advantage more quickly and businesses that have a less geographically localized customer base (Kepler and Shane, 2007).

Interviews with male and female business students and faculty show that stereotypical attitudes toward women in business develop long before they enter the workforce and include the beliefs that women lack career commitment; women are not tough enough; women don't want to work long or unusual hours; women are too emotional; women won't relocate; and women have trouble making decisions (University of Michigan and Catalyst, 2000). Such stereotypes, which people may think are no longer operant, surfaced recently when a spate of articles appeared in newspapers and magazines suggesting a growing number of highly educated women from elite schools in the US were choosing to raise families over pursuing careers in their field, though there was no data that supported this claim (Boushey, 2006).

Stereotypical attitudes about women in business may be reinforced by factors external to the business school environment (e.g., representation of women in the media), as well as by the business school environment itself, for instance, the under-representation of female faculty, the sometimes aggressive, or even hostile tone of male faculty and students, the paucity of top management women in business cases, and by the portrayal of women in stereotypical roles in cases where they do appear (Catalyst and the National Foundation for Women Business Owners, 1998; University of Michigan and Catalyst, 2000; Levin and Mattis, 2006).

Previous research by the authors that examined how women employed in corporations are portrayed in business cases found that women typically don't appear in business school case studies in leadership roles; rather, cases focus on women in stereotypical female roles, sometimes referred to as 'feminized' professions, and on the 'staff' side of the organization (e.g., as human resources professionals), rather than senior 'line' management roles typically dominated by male employees (Levin and Mattis, 2006).

Case studies that were analyzed for that research also featured women employees confronting issues typically viewed as 'women's issues', such as difficulties in balancing work and family commitments, dealing with pay inequities and delayed promotions, and/or a hostile work environment. For a comparative analysis of women and male entrepreneurs, currently underway, we similarly hypothesize that case study portrayals of women entrepreneurs will reinforce stereotypical attitudes of women business-owners. However, for this analysis, we chose to focus on the success factors of highly successful women entrepreneurs.

STORIES OF SUCCESS

Such businesses spend an estimated $546 billion annually on salaries and benefits, employ 7.1 million people and generate $1.9 trillion in sales (Center for Women's Business Research, 2007). Every effort should be made to ensure that women considering careers in business are presented with positive role models of women entrepreneurs. Two key strategies that would advance this goal are increasing the number of women with entrepreneurial experience on business school faculties and using cases in classes on entrepreneurship that provide positive role models of women entrepreneurs.

The aim of this current research is to identify the factors, both external and internal, and the personal and professional strategies employed by women entrepreneurs that contributed to their success in launching and sustaining highly successful businesses. Specifically, it examines the women entrepreneurs' motivations for pursuing business ownership; prior business experience; educational background; industry sector; financing strategies and annual revenues; and management style.

The authors chose to focus on Harvard Business School (HBS) cases because HBS is the largest producer of cases studies used in business schools. With over 6 million copies of its case studies sold annually to business schools worldwide, Harvard's portrayal of the corporate environment is very influential.

Using random selection, thirty-four case studies of women entrepreneurs from the years January 1981–June 2008 were identified out of 193 total cases for entrepreneurs contained in the HBS website inventory for the same period. For the years 1981–90, the products and services offered by the women entrepreneurs featured in these cases were those that would largely appeal to a female consumer base, for example, cosmetics, mail order gardening products, apparel and magazines on health and parenting. By

1991–2000s, the industries represented by women-owned firms profiled in the HBS cases had expanded to include software and online networks, entertainment, food services and transportation.

The corporate women in our previous research (Levin and Mattis, 2006) appeared in largely stereotypical staff roles rather than in line positions or leadership roles, whereas the successful female entrepreneurs in our current research had created large ongoing businesses. While a number of the HBS cases we reviewed discussed younger women just out of business school who were evaluating business opportunities, the successful female entrepreneurs in the cases discussed here tend to be older and have no formal business education. The three cases and the women we will examine represent different time periods in the expansion of women's entrepreneurship, different industries, different business strategies and different personalities, all of which comprise the success factors for the following entrepreneurs:

- Mary Kay Ash, Mary Kay Cosmetics, Inc., 1963;
- Judy Wicks, The White Dog Café, 1982;
- Suzanne de Passe, De Passe Entertainment; Creative Partners, 1992.

The largest company in terms of revenue, and the earliest started, is Mary Kay Cosmetics (MKC). The other two companies have achieved varying degrees of success (Table 18.1).

Each of the women in the following cases possesses a number of personal characteristics that played an important part in her entrepreneurial success, including the ability to:

- learn and move up quickly in previous jobs;
- work well with and respect colleagues and clients;
- embrace risk and seek new ways of problem solving;
- spot opportunities in the marketplace;
- create a vision that satisfied personal and business goals.

Table 18.1 Characteristics of women entrepreneurs and their companies: Mary Kay Cosmetics, The White Dog Café, Suzanne de Passe Entertainment and Creative Partners

	Mary Kay Cosmetics	White Dog Café	Suzanne de Passe Entertainment	Creative Partners
Founder	Mary Kay Ash	Judy Wicks	Suzanne de Passe	
Year Started	1963	1982	1992	
Age at start-up	43	35	45	
Location	Dallas, TX	Philadelphia, PA	Hollywood, CA	
Initial financing	$5000	$75 000	Cash settlement from break-up of Gordy/de Passe Productions	
Funding source	Family	Friend	See above	
Organizational structure	Corporation	Sole proprietor		Partnership
Year 1 sales	$198 000	N/A	N/A	

These early entrepreneurs exemplify both the 'situational' and the 'opportunistic' models. They left jobs for different reasons and they had different levels of education, but whichever path they followed, each one was guided by a strong vision and personal values.

BOX 18.1   MARY KAY ASH, MARY KAY COSMETICS, INC.

Mary Kay Ash (Rogers at the time), a 43-year-old high school graduate, had been an aggressive and successful salesperson in several corporations. In her last position before starting her own business she was National Training Director for 25 years, and when a younger man she had trained was promoted over her, she resigned. In the early 1960s, it was common in corporations for women to be passed over for promotion; from this experience, Mary Kay's vision for her company was formed. Most women at this time worked only inside the home, and those who worked outside needed a part-time schedule to accommodate family responsibilities. Seeing an opportunity, Mary Kay was determined to give women recognition, motivation, support, income opportunities and flexibility. Her moral principles – passed down to Mary Kay by her mother, a strong-willed and positive mentor who was the family's breadwinner – provided the vision for her company, 'to give women the opportunity to do anything they were smart enough to do'. These principles guided every aspect of her company and drove all strategic decisions.

Mary Kay's ability to see new uses for old products led her to initially sell a skin care system developed by a hide tanner; if he could soften leather with his formulas, these formulas, which Mary Kay purchased, could soften skin. Her previous experience taught her that people needed to sell a product that would be used up and enable them to establish ongoing relationships with the customers. Skin care products met these criteria, and Mary Kay decided to sell direct to consumers through 'house parties'; it was more efficient and lucrative to sell to several women at once than to one at a time, as Avon did.

BOX 18.2   JUDY WICKS, THE WHITE DOG CAFE

Judy Wicks, like Mary Kay, had strong values and principles that guided her entrepreneurial spirit. After graduating from college, she served in Volunteers in Service to America. Upon her return to Philadelphia, she and her husband started an alternative clothing store near the university where she saw an opportunity for a market targeted toward students; the business flourished. After she and her husband divorced, she went to work as a waitress at a French restaurant. She was quickly promoted to vice-president and general manager and promised an equity position; within five years she increased gross revenues from $300 000 to $1.5 million. When the restaurant closed, she had no equity and at 35 years old had to find another job.

Wicks' sense of activism and social justice led to the founding of The White Dog Café. She wanted the café to be a special community institution where diverse people would get together to break down racial and cultural barriers and where important issues of the day would be discussed. Wicks realized that in addition to its social value, the community-minded spirit of the restaurant would give her business a distinctive position in a crowded marketplace.

BOX 18.3   SUZANNE DE PASSE, DE PASSE ENTERTAINMENT; CREATIVE PARTNERS

Suzanne de Passe, 45 years old and the only African-American among the women discussed here, worked for 24 years with Berry Gordy*, her mentor and later her partner in Gordy/De Passe Productions. When Gordy reassessed his role in their company, de Passe decided to go out on her own and start not one but two companies: De Passe Entertainment (SdePE), an independent production company, and Creative Partners (CP), an artist management company. The synergy between the two companies is what made them work. The achievement of her vision was as gratifying as the growth of her businesses. Suzanne de Passe is that rare combination of savvy businesswoman and creative talent. She realized that from both a business and a creative standpoint, two companies would work better than one. She needed talent to create television and film productions, and she needed strong management to run the day-to-day operations of a production company. Furthermore, this arrangement allowed her to pursue her passions: hands-on production, writing and directing.

Note: * Berry Gordy was the founder of the Motown record label, initially a major national and then international success, along with its many subsidiaries.

Similar in age and experience to Mary Kay, de Passe had a long and successful career prior to starting her company. Both women had a clear vision of what they wanted to sell and how they wanted to manage their companies, and they had tremendous respect for the people they worked with. In addition to their fast-track experiences, people skills, risk-taking and opportunistic personalities, the most important characteristic of these entrepreneurs was a strong vision that guided the start-up and growth of their companies. The following analysis of business characteristics also looks at management – organizational structure, hiring/training, employee motivation and marketing – salesforce and consumer programs.

Start-up and Growth

Financing a new business venture is difficult for most entrepreneurs, because banks usually do not loan money for first-time, unproven ventures; women usually have even fewer personal or financial resources than do men. The entrepreneurs in these cases relied on friends and business contacts for financing.

'Beauty by Mary Kay', the company's original name, was started using family resources: Mary Kay contributed her life savings of $5000; her son, Ben, gave his savings; and her son, Richard, offered to leave his job and work for his mother at half his current salary. Just as Mary Kay was about to start her company, her husband and business partner died; she became chairman of the board and Richard, the president.

The company started in 1963 with nine sales representatives, referred to as beauty consultants. Sales in the first year reached $198 000 and jumped to $800 000 in year two; Mary Kay was initially concerned with managing rapid growth rather than worrying about profitability. In 1968 the company went public. In 1977, Mary Kay opened a facility in Toronto and began selling in Australia and Argentina by 1981. From the early 1970s to the early 1980s Mary Kay Cosmetics, Inc. traded on the New York Stock Exchange, and its share price increased 670 percent. However, from April to October of 1983 the stock price dropped 65 percent. Demographic and social changes roiled the direct selling market; many women were now working full-time and Mary Kay's target market was aging. In 1985, Mary Kay management led a successful leveraged buyout, and the company has been privately held ever since.

Judy Wicks' restaurant grew gradually. In 1983, Wicks borrowed $75 000 from a friend, built a small kitchen and expanded the restaurant, The White Dog Café, into the adjacent brownstone. In the mid-1980s, she refinanced her brownstone, built a full kitchen, obtained a liquor license and began offering more sophisticated food. Later, she took over a third brownstone and expanded seating capacity to 200. Wicks' restaurant quickly became popular due to excellent food and service and a welcoming atmosphere. During the first five years, revenues doubled each year, and in 1987, she added an international component to the business. By 1995, The White Dog Café and an adjacent gift shop, The Black Cat, had sales of $4 million, net income, $300 000, and profit margin of 8 percent in an industry with a 3 percent average. Through constant hard work and creativity, Wicks combined a successful business with her social values.

For Suzanne de Passe, financing her businesses was easier than for Judy Wicks. When Gordy and de Passe split up, they agreed to a cash settlement, and Suzanne also acquired projects already in development. She knew from the beginning that she would start two complementary businesses; the management company would provide the production company with access to new talent, while the production company would operate as a magnet for potential clients.

While initial financing was not a problem, nine months into the business she experienced a cash flow problem and began to look for a project that would generate weekly income. Film production was out of the question because it was much more expensive than television; they decided to go after a half-hour TV series. De Passe's start-up of 'two sister companies' proved successful, and within a year the business began to stabilize.

Management

Mary Kay Cosmetics (MKC) has two organizational arrangements – one for headquarters, which has a formal reporting structure, and one for the sales force with no formal reporting relationships. As of 1979, Mary Kay Ash was still chairman of the board, and Richard Rogers, her son, was president. Seven vice-presidents reported to Rogers. For a large company that manufactured skincare and cosmetics and required a constant flow of new products, staffed numerous locations, and required a host of administrative, financial and marketing personnel, Mary Kay developed a conventional hierarchical structure.

Management of the sales force was consistent with Mary Kay's vision to create an environment in which each woman was given the opportunity to earn as much as she was able. The beauty consultants' promotion and compensation, among the most generous in the direct-selling industry, are tied to a strict formula that consisted of selling skincare/cosmetic products and recruiting of new beauty consultants. Mary Kay's motivational plan, known as STORM (self-worth, teamwork, opportunity to succeed, recognition and money), was so successful that MKC had one of the lowest turnover rates in the direct-selling industry. Other factors that contributed to the beauty consultants' success included an extensive training program and involvement in product decisions. MKC had relatively fewer products than its competitors; therefore, the consultants were able to more easily master the specifics of the products they were selling, and sales force involvement resulted in less resistance to product line changes and more enthusiasm for new product introductions.

The White Dog Café was run by a sole proprietor. Judy Wicks made all decisions for her company, was responsible for all funding, shouldered all risks and earned all rewards. Although she ran the business by herself, she partnered with a number of domestic and international restaurants to strengthen her company vision as well as visibility for her restaurant.

One of the most important aspects of management for an entrepreneur is to work with people (partners or employees) whose skills complement theirs. As these cases illustrate, each entrepreneur looked for strong managers or partners to help run their businesses.

Suzanne de Passe is a good example of someone who recognized not only the best people to work with but also the best business arrangement for each of her companies. For SdePE, the production company, she wanted people with whom she had worked at Motown. Her new company was similar to the one she had with Berry Gordy; therefore, who better to join her than those people who worked with her at Motown, who knew the business and whom she trusted. She chose Suzanne Coston, her former secretary, assistant and then vice-president for music-related projects, as president of SdePE. Their styles complemented each other; Coston got the deal done while Suzanne made the creative decisions.

For CP, the artist management company, de Passe needed a different kind of arrangement and a different kind of person. Shelley Browning, an entertainment lawyer with whom Suzanne had worked over the years, had a practice that included all areas of entertainment law. Again, Suzanne and Shelley realized their skills were complementary: Shelley got the talent to sign on; Suzanne got the talent to perform. Despite the difference in management styles between the two companies, de Passe wanted to create team spirit and pride among those who worked with her.

Marketing

MKC aggressively markets to both its sales force and its consumers, but, interestingly, the company did not emphasize marketing to consumers until the 1980s. The original mission envisioned the company as a 'teaching-oriented' organization that focused on women's opportunities for personal, professional and economic success.

Five elements were the basis for MKC's marketing plans: high-quality skin care products, an independent sales force, a high level of individualized attention for each consumer, an educational system designed to upgrade the skills of each beauty consultant and a reward system that provided highly competitive compensation for beauty consultants. The beauty consultant and the consumer, in the vast majority of cases, were the same. Beauty consultants were trained to provide a high level of personalized care to each consumer; thus, repeat purchase was common, and, since a significant part of the consultants' compensation was based on their recruitment of other beauty consultants, these repeat purchasers often became the newest sales force members.

MKC created an elaborate marketing plan targeted at the sales force. In order to motivate them, beauty consultants received rewards ranging from a $50 checkbook cover to a pink Cadillac. Among many other rewards, they received personal letters from Mary Kay for positive reinforcement, training manuals to strengthen their skills and 'ladder' pins with gems as recognition for their sales accomplishments. MKC developed an equally elaborate system of performance criteria for beauty consultants to climb the sales force ladder.

The consumer marketing plan was closely tied to the sales force plan. Communications were extremely important to the company, both within the organization and to the end customer. The latter were the beauty consultant's responsibility and all communications programs were designed to help her sell. MKC made little effort to communicate directly with consumers, and if money is any indication, it is clear where company priorities lay. In 1981, MKC spent ten times the money on the marketing communications budget for the sales force as for consumer advertising.

In the early 1990s, recognizing that the majority of both its customers and consultants were women of color, MKC introduced colors that were more suitable for that market. In 1993, MKC's mission remained essentially the same as at the company's inception, but by 1994 MKC had a new set of challenges: stagnating sales, changing consumer trends and increasing importance of the Internet. From a marketing perspective, the Internet presents an interesting challenge for the company. MKC's competitors were investigating the Internet's marketing and selling possibilities including online stores, kiosks, and e-commerce sites. MKC, however, would never use a distribution channel that competed with its sales force: the company's 'Guiding Principles', which influenced every strategic and tactical decision of the firm, prohibited it. Any solution that handicapped the women who bought and sold Mary Kay products would not be considered. Mary Kay's solution, the Internet Personal Page Program, allowed each beauty consultant to create her own personal website, which was informational only. The site offered product information and contact information for a consumer's personal beauty consultant. As always, the company's solution was consistent with its vision and values: the 'high touch approach', in which a beauty consultant reached consumers through frequent, personal interactions, trumped the 'high-tech approach', in which consumers are reached through technology.

Judy Wicks, like Mary Kay, developed all of her marketing strategies and tactics around her personal vision for the company. After several years of financial success, Wicks felt the business had not reached its full potential. Guided by her activist, community-minded spirit, she formulated a new business goal that would integrate her personal, political and social beliefs with her business, in a way that would stimulate growth for her restaurant, and spark a sense of community.

Among the many marketing programs designed to build awareness for her restaurant was a series of lectures by noted authors, academics, artists and political figures who addressed current topics of interest. As a savvy entrepreneur, Wicks realized that the lectures would not only further her mission but give the business a boost; speakers always appeared on Monday nights, traditionally a slow night in the restaurant business. To promote the programs, Wicks wrote a quarterly newsletter that marketed the business and fostered a community of people with shared values. Many of Wicks' marketing programs were aimed at creating a strong sense of community spirit. The White Dog Café partnered with several ethnic inner-city restaurants to showcase Philadelphia's diversity and build a night life for the city whose affluent white population traditionally headed for the suburbs by 5 p.m. She also developed programs for teenagers such as a mentoring program to assist with their school-to-work transition. A non-profit arm of the restaurant, Urban Retrievers, helped teens become involved in community problems and expanded the Café's other non-profit projects.

Wicks' most ambitious programs were those with international sister restaurants in which she led customers on tours of countries with which the US government had foreign policy disputes. One of Wicks' goals in developing this program was to show how capitalism could serve the common good. Wicks, perhaps more than any of the entrepreneurs, put her stamp on the business. For her, The White Dog Café was the outer symbol of her inner values.

Suzanne de Passe's marketing efforts were somewhat unconventional. Rather than making a formal announcement about her new business, accompanied by the typical Hollywood fanfare and extravagant parties, Suzanne wanted to wait until she could announce not just that they existed but that they were developing new projects. The two companies themselves would serve as marketing vehicles for each other; while searching for talent, people would hear about the production company and vice versa. The synergy between the two companies paid off, and one year after start-up, word was already on the street that de Passe was running a 'hot shop'. Suzanne's positive attitude, solid experience and long history with Berry Gordy made her as effective a promotional tool as any marketing program. Although De Passe Entertainment and Creative Partners still had not made any formal announcement, both companies were growing by word of mouth. SdePE pitched two television pilots and produced two mini-series, and CP had a client list of 38 artists.

SUMMARY

The goal for this chapter was to discuss the personal and business factors necessary for the creation of successful entrepreneurial ventures by three American women. Each company was started in a different decade, industry and stage in the development of female entrepreneurship. Each woman faced her own financial, management and marketing challenges. Although there is no single formula for success, there are common characteristics of successful entrepreneurs. Two of the most important factors are creation of a business vision in conformity with personal values, and implementation of business strategies suitable to the company.

Mary Kay Ash wanted above all to create opportunities for women to develop self-respect, become independent and earn as much money as they were able. In the 1960s, when she started her company, women had few options for satisfying work or making money. She built a business where promotion and compensation were based on selling products and recruiting new sales representatives. MKC's management structure created latitude for women to move as far and as fast as they could, and it created products and marketing programs women need to advance.

For Judy Wicks, community and social justice were all-important. She held onto those values she developed in college during the mid- to late 1960s and incorporated them into her professional life. As a sole proprietor, she decided when and how her business would grow, who to hire and how to market the restaurant. Wicks created programs within the community to foster tolerance among diverse groups, and she created international partnerships to show how free enterprise could meet everyone's needs. Every program she developed and every marketing strategy she implemented supported her vision: integration of her business with her personal, political and social beliefs.

Suzanne de Passe had a less obvious 'social' goal than the other two entrepreneurs, but she was just as driven by her personal values. Although she organized and staffed her two companies differently, she had the same goals for both: to create a working environment where each person was part of the team and each had a sense of pride in his or her accomplishments. De Passe felt that as an entrepreneur, she set the tone for the company. Perhaps another implicit goal for de Passe was to pave the way or provide a role model for other women of color to succeed as entrepreneurs. Her greatest satisfaction was not the number of shows in production or the number of artists under contract but the ability to make people around her feel they were contributing to a worthwhile endeavor.

Success for these entrepreneurs consisted of an inextricable link between their personal and business values. Each woman's values were distinct; thus each woman's business decisions were distinct, but for all of them, the values were a guiding force, and the business decisions matched their company's needs.

NOTE

1. Data from the Center for Women's Business Research. The mission of the Center for Women's Business Research (formerly The National Foundation for Women Business Owners) is to provide data-driven knowledge to advance the economic, social and political impact of women business owners and their enterprises worldwide by: setting the national agenda; creating insight on the status and achievements of

women business owners; altering perceptions about the economic viability and progress of women-owned enterprises; and driving awareness of the economic and social impact of this vital business sector.

REFERENCES

Borooah, V., Collins, G., Hart, M. and MacNabb, A. (1997), 'Women and self-employment: an analysis of constraints and opportunities in Northern Ireland', in D. Deakins, P. Jennings and C. Mason (eds), *US Small Firms: Entrepreneurship in the 90s*, National Small Firm's Policy and Research Conferences, London: Paul Chapman Publishing, pp. 72–88.

Boushey, H. (2006), *Are Mothers Really Leaving the Workplace?*, Council on Contemporary Families, available at: http://www.contemporaryfamilies.org/work-family/leaving.html?q=mothers+really+leaving; accessed 21 February 2010.

Catalyst (1998), *Women in Corporate Management: Model Programs for Development and Mobility*, New York, NY: Catalyst.

Catalyst (2008), *2008 Catalyst Census of Women Board Directors of the Fortune 500*, available at: http://www.catalyst.org/publication/282/2008-catalyst-census-of-women-board-directors-of-the-fortune500; accessed 21 February 2010.

Catalyst and the National Foundation for Women Business Owners (1998), *Women Entrepreneurs: Why Companies Lose Female Talent and What They Can Do About It*, New York, NY: Catalyst.

Center for Women's Business Research (2001), *The New Generation of Women Business Owners: An Executive Report*, The Center, August, available at: http://www.womensbusinessresearchcenter.org/search?search=The+New+Generation+of+Women+Business+Owners; accessed 21 February 2010.

Center for Women's Business Research (2007), *Key Facts About Women-owned Businesses*, Washington, DC: CWBR, available at: http://www.womenonbusiness.com/facts-about-women-owned-businesses/; accessed 20 February 2010.

Cliff, J. (1998), 'Does one size fit all? Exploring the relationship between attitudes towards business proprietorship', *Journal of Business Venturing*, **13**(6), 523–42.

Collins, O. and Moore, D. (1964), *The Enterprising Man*, East Lansing, MI: Bureau of Business and Economic Research, Graduate School of Business Administration, Michigan State University.

Daily, C., Certo, S. and Dalton, D. (1999), 'Entrepreneurial ventures as an avenue to the top? Assessing the advantage of female CEOs and directors in the Inc.100', *Journal of Developmental Entrepreneurship*, **4**(1), 19–32.

Gunelius, S. (2010), *Statistics about Women Business Owners from Center for Women's Business Research*, 5 June, available at: http://www.womenonbusiness.com/statistics-about-women-business-ownders-from-center-for-womens-business-research/; accessed 1 July 2010.

Kepler, E. and Shane, S. (2007), *Are Male and Female Entrepreneurs Really That Different?*, Shaker Heights, OH: SBA Office of Advocacy, available at: http://www.sba.gov/advo/research/rs309.pdf; accessed 21 February 2010.

Korn/Ferry International (2001), *What Women Want in Business*, Korn/Ferry International in collaboration with Columbia Business School and the Duran Group, available at: http://www.kornferryinstitute.com/about_us/thought_leadership_library/publication/458/What_Women_Want_in_Business_A_Survey_of_Executives_and_Entrepreneurs; accessed 21 February 2010.

Levin, L. and Mattis, M. (2006), 'Corporate and academic responses to gender diversity', *Equal Opportunities International*, **25**(1), 60–70.

Lowrey, Y. (2006), *Women in Business: A Demographic Review of Women's Business Ownership*, Shaker Heights, OH: SBA Office of Advocacy, available at: http://www.sba.gov/advo/research/rs280tot.pdf; accessed 21 February 2010.

Mattis, M. (2005), '"I'm out of here": Women leaving companies in the USA to start their own businesses', in S. Fielden and M. Davidson (eds), *International Handbook of Women and Small Business Entrepreneurship*, Cheltenham, UK and Northampton, MA, USA: Edward Elgar, pp. 221–35.

Moore, D. and Buttner, E. (1997), *Women Entrepreneurs: Moving Beyond the Glass Ceiling*, Thousand Oaks, CA: Sage.

Schwartz, E. Brantley (1976), 'Entrepreneurship: a new female frontier', *Journal of Contemporary Business*, **5**(1), 37–44.

Still, L. (2006), 'The constraints facing women entering small business ownership', in S. Fielden and M. Davidson (eds), *International Handbook of Women and Small Business Entrepreneurship*, Cheltenham, UK and Northampton, MA, USA: Edward Elgar, pp. 55–65.

Still, L. and Timms, W. (2000), 'Making a difference: the values, motivations and satisfactions, measures of success, operating principles and contributions of women and business owners', Discussion Paper No. 1, Centre for Women and Business, Graduate School of Management, University of Western Australia.

University of Michigan and Catalyst (2000), *Women and the MBA: Gateway to Opportunity*, Ann Arbor, MI: Center for the Education of Women at the University of Michigan.

US Department of Labor, Women's Bureau (2008), Quick Stats, 2007, available at: http://www.dol.gov/wb/ stats/main.htm; accessed 21 February 2010.

Index

Aaltio, I. 49
Abdallah, H. 100, 101
Abhayaratna, J. 11, 12
Aborigines 10
Acker, J. 139–40, 192
Acs, Z.J. 178
ADB 73
Adersua, A. 191, 201
Adler, N.J. 186
Afonso, G. 137
Aga Khan Development Network 124, 125
Ageev, A.I. 147
Ahl, H. 4, 50, 56–7, 132, 139, 204, 207, 208, 209
Ahmad, H. 122
Aidis, R. 104, 147, 153, 154, 155, 181
Aivazova, S.G. 148, 149
Ajzen, I. 69
Al Lamky, A. 101
Aldrich, H. 30, 122, 212
Allen, I.E. 2, 14, 23, 27, 29, 31, 39, 51, 52, 56,
    62, 65
Allen, S. 138
Al-Riyami, R. 194
Altinay, E. 179
Altinay, L. 179
Alvarez, S. 27, 30
Alves De Siqueira, A. 28, 29, 30
Amâncio, L. 139
Amine, L.S. 191
Amine, S. 193, 201
Amjad, A. 118
Anan, S. 51, 56
Anderson, A.R. 208
Andrews, G. 27
Anna, A. 98
Annealed, B. 183, 184
Apter, T. 139
Arif, G.M. 118
Asia Money 122
Aspinwall, L.G. 5
Audretsch, D.B. 73
Australia(n) 10–25
    Bureau of Statistics 11, 12, 14, 15
    decrease in childbirth in 12
    'high growth' entrepreneurs 14
    home-based businesses (HBBs) in 12–13, 14,
        15–16
    indigenous and non-indigenous self-
        employed 14

issues inhibiting women from business
        expansion in 17–18
    lack of entrepreneurial culture in 17, 21
    small business enterprises 14–16
    structural and contextual barriers 16–18
    success stories 18–21
        Boost Juice/Janine Allis 20, 21
        instrumental factors for 21–2
        Second Skin/Jenni Ballantyne 19–20, 21
    trends for rises in female workforce
        participation in 11–12
    women in employment in 11–12
    women as small business owners in 12–16
    women as sole-owners in franchises 14
    see also case studies; research *and* studies

Babaeva, L.V. 90, 151, 152, 153, 159
Bak, J. 27, 30
Baker, T. 98
Baldacchino, G. 75
Baldez, L. 26, 28
Balshaw, T. 163
banks 110–12, 123, 124, 125–7
    see also World Bank
Bannock, G. 139
Bari, F. 118
Baron, R.A. 5, 76, 159
barriers 6–7, 21–2, 30–31, 41–3, 53, 66, 90–92,
    138–9, 153–6, 191
    to access to training 17, 42, 75
    capital-related 52–3
    conceptual/contextual 30–31, 64–6, 154,
        181–2, 208–9, 219–20
    cultural and social 64–6, 154
    to dealing with banks 110–12
    faced and overcome 92–4, 112–15, 168–72
    socio-cultural 90, 94–5
    structural/contextual 64–6, 154, 168, 181–2,
        219–20
    and work–family conflict 37, 42, 50, 53
    see also Guanxi
Barsukova, S. Yu 156
Basargekar, P. 84, 87, 91
Baud, I. 189
Baughn, C. 52, 56, 98, 104
Baukloh, A.C. 133
Bayraktaroğlu, S. 175
Beaver, G. 4
Belcourt, M. 42, 43

Belle, A. 207
Belwal, R. 73, 77
Benschop, Y. 5, 7
Berik, G. 50, 56
Billing, Y.D. 132
Blackman, J.A. 73
Blanchflower, D. 52
Blau, F. 134
Bliss, R.T. 94
Boden, R. 101, 207, 208
Bodur, M. 176
Bonnell, S. 38
Borchorst, A. 60, 61
Borooah, V. 216
Bosma, N. 51, 52, 56, 181, 207, 209
Bourdieu, P. 50, 52, 53
Boushey, H. 219
Bracker, J.S. 4
Brainerd, E. 149, 150
Braunstein, E. 50, 56
Brazeal, D.V. 191
Brazil (and) 6, 7, 26–36
    and case studies: what determines success?
        31–3
        Isabel 33; Leila 32
    competitors to women 29–30
    conceptual and contextual barriers 30–31
    necessity and opportunity entrepreneurs 29
    support for women entrepreneurs 31
    women in employment and as small business
        owners 27–30, 34
Brenner, M. 50, 56
Brindley, C. 207
Briscoe, R. 76
Brooksbank, D. 204
Brown, A. 3, 5
Bruin, A. 98
Bruni, A. 13, 95
Brush, C. 17, 18, 74, 90, 94, 101, 110, 186, 208
Budd, B. 194
Bureau of Statistics 74
Burke, P.J. 138
business ownership, barriers for women in 6–7,
    30–31, 41–3
business ownership across countries (by
    gender), prevalence rates of 3
Buttner, E.H. 5, 90, 111, 144, 191, 216, 217
Buvinic, M. 28

Cai, H. 50, 56
Cameron, A. 111
Campbell, N. 26
Canada (and) 37–48
    government support for women 137
    older and First Nations women 38

Royal Commission on Status of Women
    (RCSW) 38
structural and contextual barriers 41–3
success stories 43–6
    Southmedic Inc./Lee McDonald 45–6
    Summer Fresh Salads Inc./Susan
        Niczowski 43, 44–5
Task Force on Women Entrepreneurs 39,
    41–2, 43
university-educated women 38–9
Women in Business Initiative (Canada) 41
women in employment 37–9
women and men in self-employment 40
women as small business owners 39–41
Women Entrepreneurs of Canada (WEC)
    41
    see also legislation
Canadian Business 43
Canadian Business and Profit Magazine 43
    and PROFIT W100 43
Cantando, M. 125
Cao, Y. 50, 56
Carroll, J. 76
Carter, N. 94, 101
Carter, N.M. 101, 110
Carter, S. 3, 110, 111, 204, 207, 208
Casale, D. 164, 165
case studies 19–22, 31–3, 44–6, 54–6, 66–8,
    79–80, 92–4, 102–3, 112–15, 126–7,
    140–43, 156–8, 168–72, 182–5, 196–8,
    209–12, 222–8
    see also PROFIT W100
Cash, M. 41, 42, 43
Catalyst 38, 51, 192, 218, 219
Center for Women's Business Research 216,
    218, 219, 220
Centre for Labour Market Research and
    Information (CLMRI) 195
Cetindamar, D. 175, 176, 178, 179, 182
Chandra, D. 74
Chandralekha, K. 84, 89, 91
characteristics of women entrepreneurs and
    their companies 221
Charles, M. 208
Chell, E. 2
Chen, C.C. 49
Chen, X.-P. 49
Chen, Y.P. 51, 56
Chertihina, E.S. 149
Cheyne, J. 110
China (and) 49–59
    the 'bamboo curtain' 53
    economic role/social position of women 50
    foreign direct investment (FDI) 50
    gender equality and *danwei* 49

structural and contextual barriers in 52–4
success stories 54–6
   Chief Executive, Guangzhou 54–5
   restaurateur in Beijing 55–6
women in employment 50–51
women as small business owners 51–2
see also Guanxi
Chirikova, A.E. 90, 151, 152, 153, 154, 159,
   160
Choi, T.Y. 30
Chow, C.K.-W. 53
Chu, P. 53
Chung, L. 30
Cindoglu, D. 175, 179, 185
Cliff, J.E. 76, 216
Cohen, L. 134, 206
Collins, J. 13
Collins, O. 216
Collins-Dodd, C. 208
Cooke, F.L. 49, 50, 51, 52, 53, 56
Cooper, A.C. 76, 122
Corral, T. 30, 33
Coughlin, J. 30
Coverman, S. 181
Cranny-Francis, A. 205
Crompton, R. 2
Croulet, C. 75

Dabbagh, M. 191
Dahlerup, D. 61
Daily, C. 216
Danish Enterprise and Construction Authority
   62–3
Das, M. 91
Davidson, M.J. 1, 117, 138
Davidsson, P. 98, 207
Dawe, A. 138
De Beauvoir, S. 209
de Bruin, A. 111
De Lourdes Villar, M. 26
definitions (of)
   entrepreneurship 13, 191
   Guanxi 49
   necessity entrepreneurs 29
   opportunity entrepreneurs 29
   success (COED) 4
Delaney, L. 73
Denmark (and) 7, 60–71
   cultural and social barriers 64–6
   gender equality 61–2, 65
   Jante Law 6, 65–6, 67, 69
   psychological barriers 66
   recommendations 70–71
   structural and contextual barriers 64–6
   success stories 66–9

Munthe plus Simonsen/Naja Munthe and
   Karen Vedel-Simonsen 66–7
Weltklasse/Jeanett Kaare and Charlotte
   Stougaard Espensen 67–8
welfare system as society barrier 64
women in employment 60–62
women as entrepreneurs/small business
   owners 62–4
see also legislation
Derrida, J. 138
Dhillon, P.K. 90
Di Gregorio, S. 124, 129
Dias, M. 27
Djankov, S. 29, 31
Dolinsky, A.L. 167
Douglas, E.J. 10
Doyle, J. 204
Drucker, P.F. 13
DTF 165
DTI 166, 167, 168, 173
Duff, S. 112
Duffy, J. 26, 29
Dundon, T. 205
Dupuis, A. 111

Earle, S. 204
Easter, G.M. 30
Eckhardt, J. 98
economic classification of countries 2
Edelman, L.F. 22
EHRC 206
Elam, A.B. 50, 52, 53
Engardio, P. 73
entrepreneurs as risk-takers 13
entrepreneurship, gender gap in early-stage 14,
   16
EOC 204, 205
Equal Opportunity for Women in the
   Workplace Agency (EOWA) 11, 12
Ericksen, G.K. 117, 125
Erogul, M. 189, 195
Ertübey, N.O. 178
Erwee, R. 166
Esim, S. 177, 182
Essars, C. 5, 7
Estrin, S. 155, 159
Eurostat 132
Eurostat News Release 133

Fairbairn, I.J. 75, 76
Fan, Z. 53
Fay, M. 112
Federal State Statistics Service (FSSS) Russia
   150, 151, 152
Feng, W. 51, 56

Fenwick, T. 43
Ferreira, A.R. 137
Fielden, S.L. 1, 3, 5, 117, 138
Fiji (and) 6, 7, 73–83
    difficulties faced by women in 75–6
    infrastructural facilities-related problems 78
    government commitment and development
        schemes 77
    Household Survey of Employment/
        Unemployment 74
    National Centre for Small and Micro
        Enterprise Development (NCSMED)
        74–5
    National Micro-Finance Unit (NMFU) 74–5
    recommendations 80–81
    SME registration process in 77
    Strategic Development Plan (2007–11) 75
    success stories: Anasaini Adiqisa; Chandra
        Lekha; Mohini Prakash *and*
        Tulia Veikoso 79–80
    women in SMEs 74–6
Financial Times Stock Exchange 1
Fink, M. 133
Finney, B. 75
Finnie, R. 38
Firkin, P. 207
Fisher, A. 192
Foley, D. 13
Foreman. P.O. 65
Foster, M.K. 110, 111
Foucault, P. 138, 208
Fraser, S. 204
Frazer, L. 14
Frederick, H.H. 13, 14, 16, 17, 19
Fritsch, M. 73
Fung, M.K.Y. 53

Gadenne, D. 4
Ganesan, R. 87, 88, 94, 95
Garcia, Z. 74
Gartner, William B. 74
Geddes, B. 27, 29
gender
    barriers to training 17
    bias 76
    and culture of advantage 18
    differences 42, 100–101, 139, 144
    and entrepreneurial behaviour 204–5
    and environment 191
    equality/inequality 49, 56–7, 61–2, 164
    gap in early-stage entrepreneurship 14, 16
    gap in education 117
    and occupational segregation 192, 205–6
    and perception of success 5
    -related challenges 119–20

    role expectations 181, 185
    stereotypes 18, 119–20
    see also 'glass ceilings'
geographical constraints 7
Gibb, A.A. 139
Gibbons, P. 30
Gilbertson, G. 26
Gillani, W. 96, 122
*Glass Box: Women Business Owners in Canada,
    The* 42
'glass ceilings' 13, 37, 53, 101, 144, 205, 217
Global Entrepreneurship Monitor (GEM) 14,
    52, 64, 134, 135, 139, 178, 191, 198, 199,
    212
global increase in women entering small
    business ownership 1–4
Godoy, R. 26
Goffee, R. 13, 95, 136
Goheer, N.A. 119, 120, 122, 123
Goic, S. 147, 154
Goldberg, T. 163
Gorbachev and perestroika 147
Gorbulina, I. 152
government corruption 7
Greene, P. 207
Greer, M. 207
Gregory, N. 53
Grobler, J. 165
Groom, B. 2
Gruzdeva, E.B. 149
Guanxi 6, 49, 51, 53
Guerreiro, M.D. 132, 133, 135, 138
Gulf Cooperation Council (GCC) 194

Haan, H. 189, 195
Haapaniemi, P. 73
Haas, L. 61
Haddad, N. 100
Hailey, J. 75
Haines Jr., G.H. 110, 111
Hakim, C. 133
Hakim, K. 204, 205, 207
Hampson, J. 134
Handy, F. 94
Haque, N. 121
Harding, R. 3, 51, 52, 56, 181, 207, 209
Harris, C. 110
Harvard Business School (HBS) 220–21
Henry, C. 139, 200
Heriot, K. 26
Hindle, K. 13
Hisrich, R.D. 53, 90, 110, 139, 175, 176, 177,
    179, 180, 182
Hitt, M.A. 5
HM Treasury/BERR 205

Hmieleski, K.M. 5
Hofstede, G. 10, 60
Hofstede, G.J. 10
Hoga, J.M. 30
Holli, A.M. 60
Holmquist, E. 208
Hong, Y. 30
Honig, B. 207
Hoy, F. 37
Hu, C.-Y. 50, 56
Huang, J. 49
Hughes, K.D. 38, 39, 41, 42, 43, 117
Human Rights Commission (New Zealand) 107
Hundley, G. 139, 207, 208
Hurrell, K. 205
Hussain, I. 121
Hussain, J. 49, 53
Husseini, R. 100
Hutn, M. 28
Hyytinen, A. 16

IFC 100, 121
Ilmakunnas, P. 16
imaginative thinking and women 19
İnal, G. 179
India (and) 84–97
   associations for women entrepreneurs 88
   economic, educational and socio-cultural
      barriers 90–91, 92, 93–4
   employment in the organized sector 86
   employment of women 84–6
   enrolment of women in higher technical/
      professional education 85
   female participation in labour force and
      workforce 85
   GOI schemes for women entrepreneurs
      88–9, 93–4, 95–6
   government offices, and development
      programmes 88
   government promotion of women's
      entrepreneurship 88–9
   labour force/workforce participation rates
      for educated females 86
   recommendations 94–6
   Second All India Census (for 1987–88) 87
   special schemes of MSMEs for women
      entrepreneurs 89
   success stories
      Mrs Kamala 92, 93–4
      Ms Sunayana 93, 94
   women as small business owners in 86–9
   see also barriers
Indian Council of Women Entrepreneurs
   (ICWE) 88
individual motivation and goals 124

Industrial Portuguese Association (AIP) 137
Industry Canada 39, 40, 41, 42, 44
INE 132, 133
Instituto Brasileiro de Geografia e Estatistica
   27
international agreements
   Convention on the Elimination of All Forms
      of Discrimination Against Women
      (CEDAW) 180, 190
   UN Convention on the Rights of the Child
      190
*International Handbook of Women and Small
   Business Entrepreneurship* 3
International Labour Organization (ILO) 119
   see also studies
Izyumov, A. 150, 152, 159

Jackson, P.A. 53, 57
Jalbert, S. 29, 33, 87
Jamali, D. 99, 100, 101
Jennings, J.E. 41, 42, 43, 49, 50
Jennings, P. 4
Jeynes, J. 207
Johnsen, G.J. 15
Joyner, B.E. 90
Jurik, N. 207

Kabasakal, H. 176
Kahu, E. 108
Kalleberg, A.L. 15
Kandasaami, T. 74
Kanter, R.M. 192
Kanterian 'tokenism' 51
Kantor, P. 95
Karataş-Özkan, M. 179
Katwalo, A. 193, 200
Kautto, M. 61
Keats, B.W. 4
Keeble, D. 73
Kephart, P. 192
Kepler, E. 207, 219
Khan, L. 134
Khatoon, A. 120
Kinivuwai, Luse 74–5, 76
Kirschoff, B.A. 73, 76
Kirznerian opportunity-seeking entrepreneurs
   51
Kitching, B.M. 53, 57
Kitching, J. 207
Klapper, L. 1, 73
Klasen, S. 165
Kleiman, C. 90
Kolb, S. 181
Kollan, B. 84, 89
Komppula, R. 139

Korn Ferry International 216
Korsgaard, S. 65
Krahn, H.J. 37, 38
Krueger, N. Jr. 191
Kupferberg, F. 13
Kupreshenko, N.P. 155
Kurtsan, M. 181
Kutanis, R.O. 175
Kuznetsov, A. 154, 155, 159
Kuznetsova, O. 154, 155, 159

La Valle, I. 207
Labour Force Survey 206
Labour Market Statistics (New Zealand) 109
Lattimore, R. 11, 12
Lebanon 7, 98–105
    micro/macro factors affecting female
        entrepreneurship in 100–102
    patriarchal culture of 100–101
    success stories
        Aisha 102–3, 104
        Sonia 103, 104
    women in employment in 98–9
    women as small business owners in 99–100
Legge, J. 13
legislation
    Canadian Charter of Rights and Freedoms
        (1985) 38
    Canadian Human Rights Act (1978) 38
    Jante Law (Denmark) 6, 65–6, 67, 69
    Sex Discrimination Act (UK) 205–6
legislation (New Zealand)
    Equal Pay Act (1972) 107
    Government Services Equal Pay Act (1960)
        107
    Human Rights Commissions Act (1977) 107
    Race Relations Act (1971) 107
    State Sector Act (1988) 107, 108
Leibenstein, H. 13
Leicht, K.T. 15
Leira, A. 61
Leonardo, M. di 134
Leone, J. 30
Letherby, G. 204
Levin, L. 216, 220, 221
Lewai, V. 74
Liang, Z. 51, 56
Liff, S. 12
Lindsay, C. 206
Liu, J. 50, 56
Lowrey, Y. 218
Lyonette, C. 2

Macaulay, C. 206
Madichie, N. 192, 193, 200

Madlozzo, R. 27, 28, 33–4
Madsen, T.N. 62
Mahgoub, H. 189
Mallon, M. 134, 206
Mamman, A.75
Markman, G.D. 159
Marlow, S. 3, 4, 139, 204, 207, 208
Marshack, K.J. 109
Martins, S. 27, 28, 34
Massey, C. 111
Mathur-Helm, B. 164, 165, 166–7
Matthews, R. 51
Mattis, M. 163, 191, 192, 216, 220, 221
McCall, L. 192
McClelland, D.C. 13
McClelland, E. 87
McCrohan, D. 189, 195, 198, 199
McDade, B. 193
McDougald, M.S. 49, 50
McElwee, G. 194
McKay, R. 13, 90
McMahon, R.G.P. 15
Meager, N. 207
MEGAFON 66
mentoring 22
Menzies, T.V. 13
Metcalf, A. 28
Mill, J.S. 138
Millennium Development Goals 118
Milliyet 184
Ministry of Economics and Business Affairs,
    Denmark 64, 65
Minniti, M. 13, 14, 39, 40
Mirchandani, K. 208
Mitchell, J. 2
Moore, D.P. 5, 90, 144, 191, 216, 217
Morgan, M. 108
Morris, H.M. 73
Morrison, A.M. 139
motivations for business ownership 3
MTSS 132, 133, 134, 144
MTSS/DGEEP 134
Mueller, S.L. 147, 154, 178
Mulholland, K. 138

Naidu, V.J. 84, 89, 91
Narube, Savena (Governor of Reserve Bank of
    Fiji) 75
National Foundation for Women
    Business Owners (NFWBO) 29, 30,
    33
National Management Salary Survey,
    Chartered Management Institute/
    Remuneration
    Economics (2004, 2007) 206

National Sample Survey Organization (NSSO) 84
National Strategic Reference Framework (QREN) 137
National Women's Business Council 192
Ndwandwe, M. 167
Neal, M. 101
necessity entrepreneurs 29
Nee, V. 51
Neergaard, H. 65
Nelson, C. 195
Nelson, R. 98
Neto, A. 29
New Zealand (and) 2, 7, 106–16
   barriers to female entrepreneurship 110–12
   equal pay, work and opportunities for women 107
   government-funded business assistance initiatives 110
   overcoming barriers, recommendations and success stories for 112–15
      Cathy – organic milk and yoghurt producer 114–15
      Ruth – caterer 113–14
      Wendy – specialist consultant 113
   report of Select Committee on Women's Rights (1975) 107
   women in employment and as small business owners 107–10
   see also legislation (New Zealand)
New Zealand Standard Classification of Occupations 109
Newton, J. 12, 18
Ngai, P. 51, 56
Nicolson, P. 7
Nordic Council of Ministers, The 61
Norway 60
Nucci, A. 101, 207, 208
Nusseibeh, L. 191

Oakley, A. 205
OECD 37, 39, 175
OECD statistics 3
Omair, K. 195
Onal, G. 180
O'Neill, R.C. 163, 164, 167, 168
ONS 205
opportunity entrepreneurs 29
Orhan, M. 74
Orloff, A. 61
Orser, B.J. 41, 42, 43, 110, 111
Oswald, A.J. 52
Ozar, S. 177
Özbilgin, M.F. 176
Ozgen, O. 175, 178, 181, 182

Oztop, B. 183
Oztürk, S.A. 175, 176, 177, 179, 180, 182

Pacific countries, studies in 75–6
Pacific Women's Resource Bureau (PWRB) 76
Pakistan (and) 6, 117–31
   Aga Khan Rural Support Programme (AKRSP) 123
   Association of Women Entrepreneurs 123
   Constitution (1973), Article 25 of 122–3
   female literacy rate 119
   illiteracy 117–18
   Ministry for Women's Development/ National Plan for Action 123
   recommendations for enabling women 128–9
   resources and enablers 122–4
   Rural Support Programmes Network (RSPN) 123
   Sarhad Rural Support Programme (SRSP) 123
   as signatory of Millennium Development Goals 118
   status of enterprise by type and gender 118
   structural and contextual barriers 119–22
      access to finance, markets and networks 121–2
      gender stereotypes 119–20
      neglect of small businesses 121
   success stories
      Lok Virsa Boutique, Lahore 126
      Chitral sewing training institute 126–7
   Thardeep Rural Development Programme (TRDP) 123
   Women Chambers of Commerce and Industry 123
   women in employment 117–18
   women as small business owners 118–19
   women-targeted finance programmes in 123
Pakistan: SMEDA's development cell
   First MicroFinance Bank Limited (FMFB) 124, 125–7
   Women Business Incubation Center (WBIC) 125
   Women Entrepreneurs Information Network (WIN) 125
   see also women's support programmes/ associations
Pakistani Poverty Alleviation Fund (PPAF) 123
Paludi, M. 204
Parasuraman, S.P. 5
Parikh, I.J. 84, 89
Patai, D. 27
patriarchal societies 6
Patterson, N. 205, 206
Patton, D. 208

Peters, M.P. 139
Petersen, S.K. 65
Peterson, M. 26
Phillips, B.D. 73, 76
Pistrui, D. 99
Pletneva, S. 152
Porter, M.E. 74
Portugal (and) 6, 132–46
    barriers for self-employed women 137, 138–9
    enterprise case studies
        Francisca 142–3, 144
        Maria 140–42, 144
    funding for women entrepreneurs 139
    gender differences/tensions 139, 144
    need for Association of Women's
        Entrepreneurs 137–8
    theories on male support for women
        entrepreneurs 139–40, 144
    women in employment 132–4
    women as small business owners 134–7
Posel, D. 164, 165
poverty 7
Prasad, P. 138, 208
Pratt, M.G. 65
Preiss, Kenneth 198, 199
PROFIT W100: Canada's Top Women
    Entrepreneurs 43
Prowess 2
Pudney, S. 205

QREN 132, 144

Radaev, V.V. 154
Ragins, B.R. 139
Rangone, A. 207
Rani, B.S. 88
Rao, D.K. 88
Raza, A. 120, 121, 128
Razumnova, I. 150, 152, 159
Reijonen, H. 139
Reis, C. 133, 138
religious constraints 6
report GEN (2009) report 2
reports
    Future Laboratory for Avon (2009) on self-
        employed women in Britain 2
    Prime Minister's Task Force on Women
        Entrepreneurs (Canada) 42, 43
    Ministry of Women's Affairs on work–life
        balance (New Zealand) 108
research (and/on) 173
    anxiety suffered as result of conflicting
        domestic and business lives 181
    barriers faced by women accessing capital
        and resources in New Zealand 110–11

    barriers faced by women entrepreneurs in
        Brazil 30
    enterprises run by women 13
    gap between experience and teaching 22–3
    gender differences in further ventures after
        initial failure 16
    government support to women
        entrepreneurs in Turkey 179–80
    growth in entrepreneurial activity of women
        in general 13
    link between small business and
        entrepreneurial activity 13
    psychological profile and motives of women
        entrepreneurs 159
    self-employed female business owner and her
        business in contemporary Australia 15
    success of female small business operators
        18–19
    women entrepreneurs in Brazil 31
    women SME owner/managers and finance in
        New Zealand 111–12
    women's access to finance in Pakistan
        (International Finance Corporation)
        124
Rezende, F. 28
Riasanovsky, N.V. 148
Riding, A. 110, 111
Ritterbush, S. 75
Riverin, N. 37
Robben, A. 31
Robertson, H. 43
Robles, B. 26
Rollinson, R. 205
Roomi, M.A. 119, 120, 121, 122, 129
Roper, S. 207
Rosa, P. 15, 110, 111
Rosen, B. 111
Rouse, J. 207
Ruivo, M.P. 133
Russia (and) 6,7, 147–62
    barriers to female entrepreneurship 153–6
        corruption 155
        juridical registration of business 154
        tax legislation 154–5
    characteristics/motives of women
        entrepreneurs 159–60
    education and motives of women
        entrepreneurs in 152–3
    Emancipation Reform (1812) 148
    'illiteracy liquidation policy' 148
    legislation protecting women's work and
        motherhood 148
    recommendations 158–60
    success stories
        Galina 156–7

Ludmila 157
  Marina 157–8
  unemployment 150–51
  women as small business owners in 151–3
Russia Trade and Industry Committee 152
Russian women in
  the modern period 151
  the Soviet period 148–50, 155
  Soviet political and bureaucratic system/the
    Party 149
  the transition period 150–51
  the Tsarist period 148
Rutashobya, L. 192, 193, 201

Sajjad, A. 120, 121, 128
Samaha, N.100
Say, J.B. 139
Scandinavian welfare model/women-friendly
  policies 60–61
Scarborough, N.M. 164
Scase, R. 13, 51, 95, 136
Schaper, M. 75
Schultz, T. 139
Schumacher, L. 192
Schumpeter, J. 139, 178
Schwarz, E. Brantley 216
Scott, C.E. 90
Scott, D. 74
Scott, J. 207
Sebrae 31, 34
Shabbir, A. 119, 120, 124, 128, 129
Shane, S. 13, 64, 98, 207, 219
Sha'rani, A. 99, 100
Shaw, E. 204, 208
Sheikh, K.H. 118
Shein, W.E. 139
Shepherd, D.A. 10
Shields, M. 205
Shu, X. 50, 56
Shuvalova, A.S. 154, 155, 156, 158, 159, 160
Sidani, Y. 99, 100
Silva, Ana 137–8
Simon, M. 66
Sinclair, A. 10
Singh, A. 76
Singh, G. 73, 77
Singh, K.P. 84, 87
Singh, S.B. 73, 75, 76
Singh, T. 73, 75
Singh, V. 129
Sinha, P. 89
Sinha, S. 95
Sio, L. 75
Skidmore, T. 28, 30
skills gap for women in small business 17

Small Business Development Corporation 166
Smallbone, D. 51
SME sector 39
SME survey on Fiji 74
Smith, R. 208
Smith-Hunter, A. 26, 30
Society for Research on Women 109
Sorensen, T.M. 65
South Africa(n) 7, 163–74, 192
  associations focusing on women 167
  and Broad-based Black Economic
    Empowerment (BBBEE) 163
  gender inequality 164
  government support for women 166–7
  Khula Enterprise Finance/Star and Micro
    Start programmes 167
  legislation: National Small Business Act
    (1996) 167
  rise in unemployment among women in 164
  structural and contextual barriers for women
    168
  success stories and barriers overcome
    168–72
    Angela Dick: CEO Transman 170–71
    Dr Anna Mokgokong: CEO Community
      Investment Holdings 169–70
    Shireen Pillay: Founder of City Plastics
      171–2
  White Paper on strategy for small businesses
    163
  women in employment and as small business
    owners in 164–7
Spring, A. 192, 193, 201
Statistics Canada 37–8, 39
Statistics Denmark 61, 62, 63
Statistics New Zealand 108, 109
  and New Zealand Census data 109
Statistics Portugal 135, 136, 137, 139
Statistics South Africa 165
Staub, K.M. 191, 193, 201
Stevenson, L.A. 90
Stiglitz, J. 50
Still, L.V. 10, 12, 13, 15, 17, 18, 21, 110, 216
Stockman, N. 49, 54
Storey, D. 139, 204, 207
Strange, A. 4
Strauss, S. 73
studies on/by
  Australian SMEs (between 1995 and 1998)
    15
  barriers for women entrepreneurs: *The Glass
    Box* 42
  business owners in Ankara 178
  characteristics of entrepreneurs in Pacific
    region 75

characteristics, performance and problems
    of women in Turkey 178–9
education opportunities for women (Pacific
    Women's Resource Bureau, 1999)
    76
Lebanese women entrepreneurs 100
motives of women entrepreneurs in Turkish
    cities 179
MS Foundation (USA) 5
obstacles to business development and
    growth (Canada) 42
obstacles encountered by women
    entrepreneurs in India 94
South Pacific countries on characteristics of
    entrepreneurs 75
women entrepreneurs in Aegean part of
    Turkey 178
women entrepreneurs in Brazil 29
women entrepreneurs and confidence (MS
    Foundation) 5
women entrepreneurs in Denmark 62–3
women entrepreneurs in Pakistan (ILO;
    Goheer; Roomi) 119, 120, 121, 122
women and job mobility prospects in China
    50
women and self-owned businesses in post-
    apartheid South Africa 166
Subohi, A. 118
success 19–22
    barriers to 17, 21–2
    perceptions of 5
    in small business ownership 4–5
    stories 18–21, 31–3, 43–6, 54–6, 66–9, 79–80,
        92–4, 102–4, 112–15, 126–7, 140–44,
        156–8, 168–72, 182–5, 196–8, 209–12,
        220–28
    of women in global context 5–7
Sukovataya, V.A. 148, 154
Sundin, C. 208
Sundin, E. 132
surveys (on/with)
    employers and self-employed in South
        Africa (2005) 165
    female labour force in South Africa 165
    Fiji government development schemes 77
    Household Survey of Employment and
        Unemployment for Fiji (2004–05)
        74
    registered small-scale industries in India (for
        1992–93) 87
    self-employment and entrepreneurship in
        UK (Labour Force Survey) 204, 206
    self-employment and women entrepreneurs
        in India (NSSO) 87
    women entrepreneurs in Fiji 76–7

women entrepreneurs (GEM) 179
World Bank Group Entrepreneurship
    Survey (2007) 73
Sussman, D. 38
Sutherland, J. 115
Sweden 60
Swift, C. 110, 111
Syed, J. 117, 120, 128
Symons, G.L. 13

Tam, M. 51, 56
Tan, J. 53
Task Force on Women Entrepreneurs
    (Canada) 39, 41, 46
Tata, Sir J.R.D. 90
Telles, E. 28
Tenev, S. 53
Thomas, A. 30
Thomas, A.S. 178
Thompson, P. 200, 204
Thurik, R. 90, 110, 111
Tibbits, G.E. 74
Tillmar, M. 3
Timms, W. 17, 18, 21, 110, 216
Timothy, D. 73
Tonchu, E. 148, 150, 159
Total Entrepreneurial Activity (TEA) 134
training programmes for women 22
Trofimova, Zh. 151
Troyat, H. 148
Truman, C. 138
Tucker, H. 176
Turkey (and) 7, 175–88
    perceived social identity of women 182
    ratification of CEDAW 180
    recommendations 185–6
    status of employed women 177
    structural and contextual barriers 181–2
    success stories
        Alev Altinkilic 184–5
        Evrim Aras Sagiroglu 182–4
    support mechanisms for women
        entrepreneurs 180
    women in employment and as small business
        owners 176–7
    Women Entrepreneurs Association of
        Turkey (KAGIDER) 175, 180–81
    see also international agreements
Turkey's Women Entrepreneur Awards 180
Turkish Statistical Institute 177

UAE Human Resources report 2005 189
UAE Yearbook 189, 190, 191, 194
Ufuk, H. 175, 178, 181, 182
undervaluing of female work areas 37

UNDP 121, 123
UNICEF 121
United Arab Emirates 2, 6, 189–203
  case studies
    Latifa 197–8
    Mozah 196–7
  Civil Service Law of 190
  education in 200
  empowerment of women in 190–91
  Federal National Council (FNC) of 191
  GEM Report 198
  and international agreements 190
  programmes and organisations for women
      194, 197, 200
  women entrepreneurs in 190–200
    cultural barriers for 199
    education of 200
    finance for 199
    and government policies 200
    legal challenges for 198
    policy and academic perspectives for
        194–5
    and women-owned businesses 192–3
United Kingdom 6, 204–15
  barriers to female entrepreneurship in
      208–9
  case studies
    Louise 209–10
    Jennifer 210–12
  National Council for Graduate
      Entrepreneurship (NCGE) 212
  and Women's Flying Start Programme
      212
  networking/networking behaviour in 212
  women in employment and as small business
      owners in 205–8
  see also legislation
United Nations
  Commission on the Status of Women 190
  Convention on the Rights of the Child
      190
  Development Programme (UNDP) 119
  Human Development Report 117
United States of America 216–29
  federal government spending on women-
      owned business 192
  structural and contextual barriers in
      219–20
  success stories 220–28
    Judy Wicks, The White Dog Cafe
        222–8
    management and marketing 225–6
    Mary Kay Ash/Mary Kay Cosmetics, Inc.
        222–8
    start-up and growth 224

Suzanne de Passe: De Passe
    Entertainment; Creative Partners
    223–8
  women as small business owners and
      entrepreneurs in 217–19
University of Michigan 219
Uras, G. 183

Van Gelder, J.L. 73
Van Stel, A. 177
Venkataraman, S. 13
Verheul, I. 90, 98, 110, 111
Viljoen, L. 163, 164, 167, 168
Vinnicombe, S. 129
Vorobyeva, D. 152

Wajcman, J. 11
Walker, A. 3, 5
Walker, D. 90
Walker, E.A. 12, 13, 15, 18, 21
Wang, Y. 53
Ward, K. 12
Watson, J. 4, 12, 18
Weaven, S. 14
web technology 19
Weeks, J.R. 73
Weller, P. 2
Wells, B.L. 147, 149, 150, 151
Welter, F. 51, 181
White Paper (DTI) and South Africa 167
Wiklund, J. 98
Williams, C. 207
Williams, L.E. 112
Williams, M.L. 101
Wilson, F. 138, 208
Woldie, A. 191, 201
Women in Business Network 210
Women Business Owners, National Foundation
    of (NFWBO) 216–17, 218, 220
Women and Equality Unit 206, 207
women as primary breadwinners 38
women, potential for 23
Women's Electoral Lobby 109
Women's Enterprise Centres 46
Women's Rights Committee (New Zealand)
    107
women's support programmes/associations
    123–4
  Agricultural Development Bank 123
  Canadian International Development
      Agency (CIDA) 123–4
  First Women Bank Limited (FWBL) 123,
      124, 127
  United States Agency for International
      Development (USAID) 123

Wood, G.J. 10, 12
Woodhams, C. 49
Woodward, D. 176
Woolard, I. 165
work–family conflict/obligations 37, 42, 50, 53,
    61, 165–6, 181, 185, 193
World Bank 1, 99, 100, 101, 123, 201
World Fact Book 34
WP100 businesses (Canada) 44
Wu, X. 50, 56

Xian, H. 49

Yuch, L. 49
Yusuf, A. 75

Zacharias, A. 196
Zaidi, A. 121
Zhang, Y. 50
Zheng, W. 49
Zimmerer, T.W. 164
Ziryanov, P.N. 148